Real Encouragement
for Every Day
of the Year

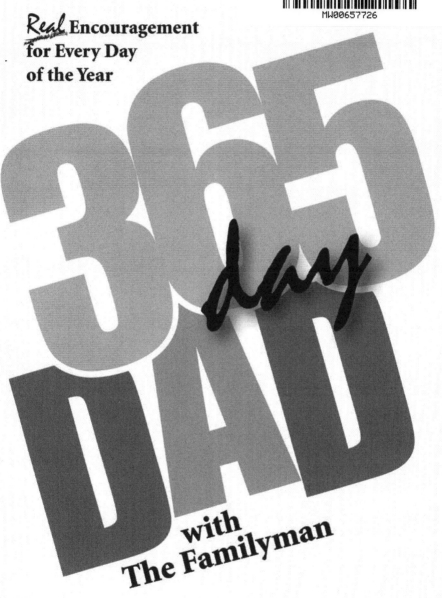

365 day DAD

with
The Familyman

Todd Wilson

365 Day Dad © 2011 by Todd Wilson

ISBN-10: 0-9821941-8-8
ISBN-13: 978-0-9821941-8-8

All inquiries should be addressed to: Familyman Ministries, 611 S. Main St., Milford, IN 46542

Printed in the United States of America

To My Sons

This book is dedicated to you. May these stories about you...help you be the fathers God designed you to be someday. I'm so proud to be your dad.

You 'da future dads,
Dad

Introduction

Hey Dad,

If you're anything like me…you probably don't like reading books. Not many men do. So try not to think of this as a book but as a daily email or text from a fellow dad who is just trying to do his best in the job in which God has placed him.

The purpose of this non-book is to keep you focused on what's most important. Really, it's all about relationships: your relationship with God and your relationship with those around you…mainly your wife and children.

Each of the 365 entries begins with a short Bible reading. You've probably attempted to read through devotionals before, but like me, gotten to about week three before falling by the wayside. Usually, you end up reading Genesis or the book of John a half-dozen times but never get any farther. So I thought we'd start towards the end of the Bible and progress backwards.

After reading the Bible passage, you'll spend a few minutes walking the dad-trail with me. Don't get your hopes up because I'm no super-dad. I'm just a normal garden-variety kind of dad, but I never give up (except when I do).

In fact, I'll give you an up-close and REAL look at what I face on a daily basis. Now just so you don't get confused, let me explain that all these entries were written over the course of about 6 years. That means these are in random order so you might get the impression that my wife is pregnant or delivering a kid every other week or celebrating a birthday…everyday. Sorry about that, but there was no way to keep them in sequential order.

Now, let me briefly describe myself and all of the players you're going to be reading about. I'm 46 years old and have been married to my lovely wife Debbie for twenty years. We have 8 children (six boys and two girls) ranging in age from 18 down to 3.

We live in northern Indiana, run Familyman Ministries, and travel around the country in a big RV (known as the Familyman Mobile) encouraging dads and moms.

Other than that, we're just like your family. We struggle, laugh, holler, and desire to raise children that walk with God, love each other, grow up to be good dads and moms, and who won't burn the house down accidently in the meantime.

I don't know about you, but I'm excited to see what the year holds, and I'm pleased as punch to travel the father-road with you.

So from one dad to another…

You 'da dad,

Todd

Kissing in the New Year

Hey Dad,

Happy New Year! Hope you had a great time with your family over the holiday and are ready to start the New Year. I don't know about you, but I'm not always real thrilled to start a new year…I was just getting used to the old one.

Plus, I'm not the kind of guy who likes to make New Year's resolutions and goals. Like Mary Poppins said so nicely, "Those are pie crust 'resolutions,' easily made and easily broken."

However, I do have two minor…uh…let's call them pseudo-resolutions. Here they are:

1) Empty the trash can under the kitchen sink.
2) Kiss my wife more.

I told you they were minor. Actually, they both came about because of conversations with my wife. For one, she told me that she doesn't like constantly emptying the trash can under the sink. She even hinted that somewhere in the Bible it must say it's the husband's responsibility. I'll have to check on that one. But I decided I'd like to do that for my wife…and at least it's something small.

The kissing one is something I'm doing for my children. I was shocked the other day when my wife relayed a conversation she had with the kids in which they agreed that they hardly ever see us kiss.

I was tempted to argue the fact and point out that I hug and kiss my wife all the time…okay, some of the time. Then I decided that if that's their perception, then I'm going to change it.

I know how important it is for my kids to see us kiss and hug. It proves that what I say about loving their mom is true. When they see me kissing their mom, they feel secure in our love for each other. Even if we argue and get mad sometimes, kissing shows that our love for each other is strong and lasting.

It's that powerful.

Now my wife gets a little skittish about public smooching in front of the kids. She may put up a struggle…but it won't work, because I'm 'da dad and that's part of my training strategy for fathering. And that's what I'm going to do. Plus, it's a lot of fun.

How about you dad? Got any minor pseudo-resolutions? You might think about joining me in my quest for public wife-smooching. It's certainly more fun than emptying the trash can under the kitchen sink.

You 'da dad!

7

To Change or Not to Change

Hey Dad,

With Christmas behind us, it's time to head off down the trail of another year of fathering. The thing we want to avoid is regrets. So today we're going to take a good long look at ourselves in the mirror and be painfully honest (which is hard for us guys because we look in the mirror, suck in our gut, flex our flabby muscles, and think…"I've still got it.")

There are times in a dad's life when he has to make changes if necessary—because he's 'da dad.

That's why I'm planning to make a significant change this year. I even hate to mention it because you guys are gonna hold me to it, and if my wife sees this she's going to be skeptical of my good intentions.

Okay, here it is (drum roll please)—I'm going to TRY to go to bed at the same time as my wife. Ha! There I said it.

See the problem is that my wife likes to go to bed early. I, on the other hand, love that magical time when all the kids are in bed, and I can do anything I want without distraction…BUT…the trade-off is that I miss out on the best part of being married.

In bed, we talk. We talk about kids, school, dreams, and annoyances. Sometimes we don't talk at all, but even then, we're still together. I know my wife likes it when we go to bed at the same time—she's mentioned it on more than one occasion.

So the last several nights, without explanation, I've volunteered to go to bed when she does.

Now I know what some of you are thinking, "Yeah, but what does it matter if you go to bed at different times?"

My answer—it just does. I know some of you can't because of different work shifts. Besides, I'm not asking you to do my goal. I'm just doing what I know I need to do. No excuses, no reasons…I'm just doing it.

But I will ask you, Dad, what do you need to do?

You 'da dad!

8

I've Seen Worse

Hey Dad,

I love being a man! It's so much easier than being a woman, especially at the start of a new year. Womenfolk scrutinize their lives, relationships, and families, see areas that need improvement, and make New Year's resolutions. We men tend to take a quick look around and proclaim, "Looks good to me. What's for lunch?"

It's not that we avoid reality; we just prefer to emphasize the positive side of life, while our female counterparts tend to focus on the negative. Know what I mean? Of course you do.

For example, when I take a quick inventory, I see it like this:

*Communication skills with my wife—I've seen worse.

*Our children's behavior—I've seen worse.

*Physical shape—I've seen worse.

*Spiritual condition of our family—I've seen worse.

There, you see? Everything's fine. I love being a man!

Then my wife has to go and ruin all that. You see, she reads books—the kinds that tell you how to be…"better."

Anyway, a few nights ago I was sitting on the edge of our bed talking happily with my wife when she pleasantly said, "I've noticed this in our children, and it's not good." The smile slid from my face as I listened.

"Hmm," I said thoughtfully, "You've got a good point." Inside, I was thinking, I've seen worse.

A while later, I was soaking my sore back in the tub. In the quiet, God whispered into my heart, "She's right." If I had to be honest, there were some bad habits that our children (and maybe even I) had picked up, and I needed to deal with them. I don't like to deal with problems. I'm a man, and I like to pretend that everything is just fine.

But everything is not just fine. In fact, as I soaked, I thought of several areas that aren't fine…areas that I need to address and spend time mending. So I made a little New Year's resolution list in my head and began to make plans to handle them.

How about you, Dad? Maybe it's time you take a hot bath and take a good long look at your life, your family, your relationship with your wife, and your priorities. And maybe, just maybe, there's something you need to handle. It won't be as bad as you think. Believe me, I've seen worse.

You 'da dad!

Your Annual Father Review

Hey Dad,

Pull up a chair. It's time for your "Annual Father Review." Yep, this manila file folder that I hold in my hand has your name on the little tag at the top. Inside is a complete record of your fathering for the last year. Boy, it's thick...365 pages to be exact. Give me a few minutes to scan the pages, and then we'll talk.

"Hmm...wow."

"Heh, heh...happened to me too."

"Oh."

"Ooooo...that's not good."

Well, that gives me a good place to start. Before we talk through your review though, let me tell you how I got started thinking about "Annual Father Reviews."

Actually, I heard about someone who put in tons of hours at work, traveled, and was hardly ever home for his family. I got to thinking that if that guy were measured at home by the same standard he was measured by at work...he would be fired.

I mean, no employer would allow him to miss days at a time, not show up until all the other employees were asleep, and be absent for most of the important meetings.

That's what got me thinking about an "Annual Father Review." Not for you...but for me. I wondered how I would fare if someone sat across from me with a big file folder containing a well-documented record of my fathering for the last year.

Would he notice that I seem distracted when one of the kids is talking to me because I'm thinking about a project I'm working on? Would he mention the fact that I rush through bedtime so I can enjoy some time to myself? How about all the teachable moments I blow because I'm so angry with my kids? Or, what about my harshness when I need to be gentle?

Maybe if the father-world were the same as the work-world, I would be demoted (father third-class) or have my pay cut in half because I was only doing my job half-heartedly...hmm.

Enough about me, let's open your folder again and talk about your review. You know on second thought, how about if I just hand you the folder and let you conduct your own review? But let me ask you this key question as you thumb through the pages: "If you were measured as a father by the same standards you are measured by as an employee, would you be fired?"

Think about that dad...and choose the best answer—not the easiest—but the best. I know you can do it because...

You 'da dad!

Keep Bob from Ruining the Magic

Hey Dad,

I've had a little trouble getting back into the swing of things. It doesn't help that my wife and I haven't been 'right' for a little while. Nothing major…but sometimes the non-major things seem major.

But after some heavy duty talking…and more talking…and even more talking, things are looking brighter. I'm sure I still have a long way to go in the caring department, but its feel sooooo good when your wife is smiling at you again.

Right now, the snow is falling and my son just finished sharing with me the latest news on the cell phone wars. He loves it…the technology, the apps, the possibilities. To be honest (for the second time in the last three paragraphs), I get a little sick of the whole thing. Not that I'm against the technology. I mean who isn't amazed by a phone that can play music and video games, take pictures, become a map or even a fish tank with seemingly live fish, and about a million other cool things?

It just seems like someone needs to come up with some 'rules' to keep the technology beast in its place.

Wherever I go, whether it's the grocery store, church, or family gatherings, I see kids and adults reach into their pockets as though they have been summoned by some invisible master, slide a sleek cell phone out, and almost imperceptibly glance down at the glowing screen. Sometimes just as stealthily, they slide the phone back in their pocket, but usually only after they've sent a quick reply.

If you ask the cell phone owner who was calling or texting, the owner answers casually, "Just Bob. He just wanted to know what I was doing."

I can't help but feel invaded when that happens. It's like Bob stuck his head into our family time and interrupted…the magic.

As I speak across the country and talk to parents, they tell me how that same Bob has invaded their family…magic.

"We started a family video," one mom explained, "and my two teenage daughters spent the first fifteen minutes texting their friends until I finally turned off the video."

So I've been thinking…if cowboys had to check their guns at the door when they walked into a saloon and since my dad wouldn't let me talk on the phone past 9pm, why can't we as Familymen write a set of 'technology' guidelines and rules, for us as well as our families. Civilization is counting on us.

So dad, check out this familyman list* of technology guidelines.

You 'da dad!

* http://www.familymanweb.com/article/rules-and-guidelines-for-technology-use

A Championship Pillow Fight

Hey Dad,

I can't think of a better job than being a dad. It's times like last night that remind me just how good I have it. We had what you might call a championship pillow fight match. It had been a while since the last one, and I've got to confess that the last several times someone asked, "Dad, can we have a pillow fight tonight?" I put it off with the standard answer, "Not tonight, but we'll do it sometime soon."

But not last night. Last night, I said, "Sure." Minutes after the announcement, we had cleared a space in the family room and faced each other armed with pillows (foam not feather), ready to do battle.

Ike (6) and Abe (5) were pretty new at this game and "took" better than they "gave," but Sam (11) and Ben (12) thumped the daylights out of me.

I knew I was in trouble when Sam smiled and said, "Prepare to feel the sting of my pillow."

Ben, whom I used to topple with a few well-aimed thumps, swung his pillow like a pro and at one point called out to Sam, "You take care of the others, but the BEAST is mine!" Obviously he was under the delusion that he could whip his dad. But I quickly dispelled that myth.

By the time it was over, we all lay panting in a laughing heap of flesh and pillows. Man it felt good.

Then for some reason I thought of my dad, who was working late at the print shop he's owned since I was a kid. He was working late because he was working on a project for his son: me.

I wondered if he felt as glad to be a dad as I do. Although his son has grown up, he was still doing something FOR him, which isn't all that different from having a pillow fight WITH them.

That's when I knew that although he was probably tired, he was glad to be doing it, because he's still a dad, and dads love doing stuff WITH and FOR their children.

So Dad, if your kids are still at home, clear a room and have a good, old-fashioned pillow fight tonight. If your children are grown up, pick up the phone and tell them you were thinking about them today.

Be ye young or old, enjoy being a dad today.

You 'da dad!

Daddy Daughter Date

Hey Dad,

I asked the Familyman Team for ideas for a Daddy/Daughter Date, and here are a few of their suggestions.

"I totally remember my absolutely favorite Father Daughter Day was when my dad took me to a play downtown. It was actually by default because he and mom had season tickets, but she couldn't go because she was ill. I got to go in her place. We had the very best time and I will ALWAYS remember it as my favorite time spent with my dad and I am 47 yrs. old now." ~ Lisa

"My daughter turned 15 a few weeks ago and all she wanted for her birthday was to climb Pikes Peak (yes, the mountain.). So we flew to Colorado on a Thursday night, hiked half way on Friday and hit the summit at noon on Saturday (her birthday!!!). It was hard, I still ache, but my daughter is 15 and still wants to spend time with her dad. I will climb a mountain for that." ~ PD

"For several years, I have taken all my kids on a birthday date. I take the day off work and spend it with them doing what they want to do. They usually plan months in advance. My son likes Frisbee golf or a trip to a BMX track. My daughters usually like to go shopping. I hold doors for them and show them how their future husband should treat them. The day usually includes lunch at a nice restaurant and ends up at home with a meal of their choice on special dishes followed by cake and ice cream." ~ David

A Child Upgrade

1 John 4:7-21

Hey Dad,

My son Ike (almost 7) just paid me a visit in my office. He needed me to fix a broken toy.

Actually, I felt a little bothered by his interruption because I was on a creative roll and knew that if I stopped, I might lose the momentum.

But a dad's got to do what a dad's got to do. So I worked on the toy, while he looked around my cluttered office, picking up stuff and firing questions.

The toy was an easy fix, and I handed it back to him, but he wasn't ready to leave. He wanted to know why I had a Buzz Lightyear sock fastened to the wall, a dead locust lying near my desk, and a happy meal toy proudly displayed.

I was just about to tell him that all those things remind me about how much I love my children when he pointed to one of his drawings taped to the wall. It was a blue rocket with fire spewing from the engines.

"I know rockets don't really look like that," he said, obviously proud that I had displayed it for the whole world to see.

As he looked at the drawing, I couldn't help but think how the little boy who had drawn the rocket had been replaced by this bigger version of Ike.

That's the way it is with kids...new versions replace old versions, and the "cute," innocent things they say and do today are outgrown before we realize it.

Ike has gotten into the habit lately of telling his mom and me his "secrets." He has opened his heart and shared important things that up 'til now he has kept to himself...things like his favorite hiding spots, best forts, and favorite travel memories.

He had his mom write them down and asks me almost every night, "Do you remember all my secrets, Dad?"

"Oh, yeah," I answer, "I remember."

But inside, I'm afraid that one day I will forget. My son is going to grow up and be replaced by a bigger version and will quit telling me what he keeps in his treasure box.

If I'm not careful, I could be too busy to notice this current version, and he'll be upgraded before I'm ready. And it will happen to you too, if you're not careful, Dad.

So, pay special attention to your children tonight...the things they say, the thoughts they share, the way they look...because tomorrow they'll be replaced by a bigger version.

You 'da dad!

14

A Good Dad Is a Thief

Hey Dad,

Show me a good dad, and I'll show you a good thief. I'm telling you, I've stolen most of my great fathering moments from other dads. I got another one a few days ago.

For the last week, we've had four extra kids at our home while their parents checked out a ministry opportunity way out west (the dad owes me big time...like if I ever need a kidney...or two).

Anyway, about the second day, letters trickled in through the mail addressed to his children. I assumed they were from their mother because moms do that sort of thing. But they weren't. Each card was written and signed by their dad.

I assumed he was trying to impress me with his fathering skills. And you know what? He did. He had "pre-thunk," pre-written, and pre-mailed all four cards before he left on their trip. You should have seen their faces when they opened the cards. No doubt about it in their minds, they were loved by Dad.

So I stole his great idea. It was nothing short of cold, calculated thievery. I haven't used the idea yet, but I will. I won't footnote it, give him the credit, or give any hint that it wasn't 100 percent my idea. That's the great thing about pilfering another dad's idea. Once you do, the idea becomes yours—totally.

Actually most of my best ideas were stolen...like sleeping under the Christmas tree...stole it from Steve. Whisking my wife away for an overnight...pilfered it from Rick. Flowers delivered to the house for my wife...nabbed it from my father-in-law. Little love notes hidden on pillows...heisted from Tim.

The important thing is not to miss the idea. My ears perk up when I hear a beaming wife tell another woman what her husband did for her, or when some kid says, "Yeah, my dad got this for me."

So, Dad, be on the lookout for good husband/father ideas and take 'em and use 'em. (If you have time, jot me a note and tell me some of your stellar ideas, and I'll share them with fellow dads.)

You 'da thief!

A Tinkerbell-oscopy

Hey Dad,

I've noticed something disturbing lately about my daughter Katherine, my princess. She's not acting very princess like—especially to the king (that's me). She used to be sweeter, more affectionate, and Tinkerbell-ish.

Now she seems cooler, less feminine, and distant. It saddens me because I know it's my fault.

You see, I haven't treated her very well lately. Instead of snuggling and telling her how lucky I am to be her dad, I find myself speaking harshly to her and pushing her out of the way because I'm busy. Now she has become what I've trained her to be.

But I'm about to undue the damage I've done...dads can do that, you know? Matter of fact, she was just in my office a few minutes ago, and I gave her a big dose of "dad's love."

Seizing the opportunity, I pulled her onto my lap. She giggled and relaxed in my arms. I told her how much I love her and how nice she looked. It embarrassed her, but she was pleased.

That was all fine and dandy, but if I'm to undo the mess I've created, I'm going to have to do a lot more. Here's my plan. I'm going to spend time tucking her in each night. I'll ask about her day and give her butterfly kisses. I'll brush her hair (which females like) and complement her, not only on how sweet I think she is but on what a big helper she's been with little Maggie and her younger brothers.

And when I have to discipline her (which will be soon), I'll remember that she is my girl and needs to be treated gently and lovingly...even as I spank her.

It's just what the doctor ordered for a Tinkerbell-oscopy. I know it will work. Hey, I'd even be more loving if I was treated that way.

How about you, Dad? Do you have a "little girl" that you've been a little harsh with? Work a little bit of father magic this week. Tuck her into bed tonight no matter how big she is, tell her that she's beautiful, compliment her on her behavior, her decisions, and what a lovely young lady she's becoming. Then, keep doing it every day...for the rest of her life. I guarantee you'll get your princess back.

You 'da dad!

Absence Myth Busted

Hey Dad,

It's been a busy week around the Wilson house. My son Sam (12) and I went to New York to speak over the weekend, and while we were gone, my daughter Maggie Rose (3) broke her leg and all my kids decided to get sick. Little Caleb (11 mos.) still can't seem to shake it, and just a few minutes ago I changed what just might be the world's record for the messiest diaper ever!!

The "stuff" was everywhere…all over his feet, his back, his stomach, his hands, the floor…and me. Actually, I got some satisfaction from the quote, "The dad who changes diapers, changes the WORLD." Talk about empowering, although you can't always trust quotes like that. Sometimes we take them at face value…but they just aren't always true.

For example, everyone has heard and believed the quote that absence makes the heart grow fonder. But, I recently discovered that's not necessarily true. Actually, I believe the opposite is true, that absence makes the heart grow colder.

I found this out while I was away from home in New York. For three days, I only had two people to worry about—Sam and myself. Sure I checked in occasionally with my wife and I missed my family a bunch, but something about being separated 400 miles also distanced my thoughts, and possibly my heart, from the people I love most.

If I had been busier or gone longer, the logical assumption is that my thoughts would have dwelt less on them and my heart could have become even cooler.

During all those hours of waiting in airport terminals, I couldn't help but notice all the dads who were traveling on business. I eavesdropped on their conversations and although they talked about sports, business, and politics, not once did I hear any of them mention their families. You know why?

Because absence makes the heart grow colder.

That's scary, and why I've decided to say "no" to most of the traveling without my family. I know what being away from them could do to my heart…and yours, and I don't trust us.

So, Dad, let me ask you a question: does your job require you to travel or be away from home a lot? Let me encourage you to do a little talking with your wife or accountability partner and make some tough decisions to protect your heart.

Here's a new wall plaque: "Presence makes the heart grow fonder."

You 'da dad!

Before They Leave

3 John 1:1-14

Hey Dad,

A while back I asked the guys to help compile a list of things dads should teach their sons before they leave home*. Here's what one dad suggested:

Thumb wrestling

Arm Wrestling

Holding the door for females

Leaving a really long skid mark with your bike

Blowing Bubbles with gum

Shooting rubberbands

Effective negotiating

Secrets of selling (we're always selling)

Boxing basics

Knowing when to walk away from a fight

Laughing at yourself

Camping basics

A firm handshake

The power of an apology

Saving money and compound interest

Real value and opportunity cost

Staying afloat in the deep end for 30 minutes or more

The perfect "cannonball"

Stick up for your little brother

Knowing when enough is enough.

~ Chris Humphrey, Owasso, OK

* http://www.familymanweb.com/article/what-every-son-should-know-how-to-do-before-he-leaves-home

Bad Memories or Best Memories

Jude 1:1-16

Hey Dad,

Well, global warming has finally checked its progress here in northern Indiana, and we have some honest to goodness sledding snow. Actually, one of the great things about working out of your home is that when you get a good snow—you can drop everything and go sledding.

Of course, the bad part of working at home is that when you get a good snow, your kids WANT you to drop everything and go sledding.

"You promised when it snowed you'd take us sledding."

"Hey, Dad, aren't you glad it's snowing so we can go sledding?"

"Dad, all the sleds are in the van."

I knew hiding was no good. They'd track me down and remind me of my promise to go—so off we went.

Now I must add that before we left, my wife warned the kids to be extra careful and not to break any bones—you know how wives can be.

A couple hours later, we were having Sam's (11) nose x-rayed at the hospital.

Let the record show—it wasn't my fault. In fact, we were having a great time. We had the hill all to ourselves; the snow was packed down and fast. The wind was bitterly cold, and the kids' cheeks were cherry red—just the way I like it.

Any misgiving about having to give up half my day to go sledding had vanished, and I was basking in the glory of fatherhood as I watched my kids race down and trudge up the hill, calling out to each other and me in pure sledding delight.

That's when it happened. My sons Ben and Abe zipped down the hill right toward Sam. In a pendulum like motion, Sam's legs were cut right out from under him, and his face was driven into the permafrost.

"Auggggggg!" he screamed as blood gushed from his mouth and nose. What a day!

You know the kids will never forget the time Dad took them sledding and Sam broke his nose. That's the way it is with memories—some of the worst memories make the best memories. I would have missed them all if I had insisted that I was too busy to go sledding—and so will you if you insist you're too busy for whatever they're asking you to do with them.

So, go make some memories—but be careful out there.

You 'da dad!

Beware of THE TRIANGLE!

Hey Dad,

Maybe it was traveling in the Cleveland Triangle a few nights ago that threw off my what-really-matters equilibrium, but for a little while, it was touch and go.

You see, a couple of years ago while RVing through the fair city of Cleveland, our RV caught fire. It didn't burn to the ground…but it could have. After some clever ingenuity, we were able to get back on the road. Then, the next year we were traveling down the same stretch of the Ohio turnpike (within a mile or two of the fire incident location) when the infamous wild turkey appeared out of nowhere and crashed THROUGH our windshield.

So you can see why I get a little spooked traveling anywhere near…THE TRIANGLE. In fact, right before we pulled out of the driveway the other day, my son Ben (13), who rode shotgun with me asked, "So where we going?"

"Cleveland," I answered as calmly as I could.

A second of silence preceded his eerie response, "That's a bad omen."

Nothing bad happened this time, but right when I was inside the triangle, I struggled with remembering what's most important. Tooling down the road, I noticed all the nice, shiny cars that were zipping past my increasingly rusty '89 Ford Taurus. I envisioned the Familyman logo emblazoned on the side of several white, sparkling beauties, and more than once mumbled to myself, "That one would be perfect."

That's when I realized THE TRIANGLE had clouded my rational thinking. I really started to believe that shiny cars matter. It was only after I calculated how many times I would have to speak, how many books I would have to sell, and how many hours of my limited life I would have to spend to pay for one of those shiny cars that I returned to my senses.

You won't win this time, TRIANGLE, I thought. Shiny cars don't matter. Rusty is just fine with me.

The more I thought about it, the more I realized that there must be a lot of "triangles" out there whispering to dads of every age and income, "Shiny cars matter, nice houses matter, big salaries matter, golf scores matter, successful ministries matter, 'stuff' matters."

The truth is…they don't.

It's your relationships with your wife, children, family, and friends that matter.

So Dad, you might be in a "triangle" right now. Take a few minutes and remind yourself of what matters…and what doesn't.

You 'da dad!

Dealing with Bad-Attitude Fallout

Hey Dad,

The sun is shining, and it looks like it's going to be a great day.

Whew, not like yesterday though. By noon, I was ready to stick my kids out by the road with a big FOR SALE sign pounded into the ground beside them.

A bad-attitude storm was brewing during our morning family devotions. I tried to curb its spread but it didn't work.

Five minutes later, I could hardly pray because I was so mad at them. The day only got worse as I was called up to our homeschool to deal with a situation. I sent two to their rooms, hollered at others, and was forced to deal with more B.A.

I'm telling you, by lunch I was sick and tired of their bad attitudes—so much so that I decided to join them with my own B.A. If you can't SELL them, join them, I always say. I became mean, snappy, and critical—not only to my children but to my wife as well.

Everything she said made me defensive, and I reacted harshly. We made it through the day…barely.

That was yesterday. Today, the sun is shining, and I'm feeling GOOD. Fortunately, the kids are resilient, and they've forgotten all about yesterday.

UNFORTUNATELY, my wife doesn't get over things as easily, especially if I go to bed without resolving it. Now she's less than happy, and I passed my B.A. on to her. (Did I mention she's also eight months pregnant?)

It's my fault, too, and now I've got to deal with the fallout of a B.A.

Man, I hate dealing with it. I wish my wife could just get over it without my involvement. But it doesn't look like that's going to happen. So like it or not, I've got to deal with it.

I'll apologize…she'll feel the need to talk first.

I'll have to talk about it…she'll want to point out what hurt her.

I'll say I'm sorry…she won't feel that it's resolved.

I'll let her take some well-deserved punches.

I'll say I'm really sorry for acting like a jerk…and she just might smile and forgive me.

How about you, Dad? Have you been suffering from a B.A. by any chance? If so, make it right. Apologize, talk it through, and then have a family night watching the Olympics.

You 'da dad!

Riding Facebook Canyon

1 Peter 1:13-25

Hey Dad,

I got a letter last week from a fellow dad. He shared how he made a Facebook mistake. It seems an old flame contacted him after the death of his father. He responded innocently a couple of times and then his wife stumbled upon 'her' Facebook message and was devastated.

His initial letter confirmed what I have been feeling for a while now. Ever since being introduced to Facebook, I've had a growing concern about the dangers lurking in the Facebook waters. From the moment I was persuaded to become a member, I saw the dangers of reconnecting with old friends from a simpler, happier time. I noticed pictures of innocent, Facebook teens that I knew posting alluring photos of themselves. I think they meant it in fun...but I thought then as I do now...they're wading into dangerous waters.

Then I started hearing reports of teens that ran off with older teens and husbands and wives who left their spouses and families for people whom they met or re-connected with on Facebook.

The dad who wrote me may not have realized it at the time, but he was headed towards the rocks. Praise God that his wife interrupted the 'innocent' emails.

How many more innocent stories of shipwrecked marriages and families do we need to hear before we say, "Maybe all this fun stuff isn't worth the price of admission?" Here's the clincher. I'm not just talking about our children and wives on Facebook; I'm talking about YOU, Dad. I would just about bet if you 'do Facebook' that you've had a contact with someone that you felt a bit awkward about, yet also felt a little rush like rafting down the canyon. That awkwardness was God warning you that you were wading into deep, dangerous waters.

I know that there are some reading this who by next year will have done something that will alter their lives forever in this 'fun' place to meet people. I don't want that to be you, Dad.

So if you need to pull your raft out of Facebook Canyon, DO IT! If you need to gather your wife and children and say, "Things are going to change", Do IT! Dad, if you value your marriage and family, then you may need to take the raft by the horns and DO IT!!!!!

After all...
You 'da dad!

A Holy Wedgie

1 Peter 2:1-3

Hey Dad,

As I type this, President Obama is beginning his first full work day as the President of the United States. I don't know about you, but my heart swelled with pride and gratefulness as we watched the inauguration on TV.

I may not agree with most of what President Obama believes or stands for, BUT God HAS blessed America, and He HAS blessed my family for allowing us to live in this great land. But underneath all that gratefulness, I felt something I didn't like and couldn't identify until later when my wife and I were able to go on a date and spend some alone time together.

"I feel small," I said turning to my wife in the seat beside me, "maybe because President Obama is not much older than me, because he has a young family, or because the whole world is applauding the achievements of this young dad."

My wife smiled understandingly.

We ate our dinner, laughed, and sat together watching more inauguration coverage on the TV at Applebee's, but I continued to feel...small. A while later, we picked up the kids, went home, and everyone got ready for bed. It was while I was doing my nightly routine of locking up doors and turning out lights that God reached down and gave me a holy wedgie!!!

"Ouch!! That hurts," I said to myself. Then in the quiet of my heart, God reminded me that the most important thing President Obama would do on inauguration day was tuck his girls into bed and tell his wife how much he loved her AND that what I do every day as a dad impacts my family's life way more than anything that will take place in Washington on 1600 Pennsylvania Ave.

It is TRUE, Dad.

I impact the world by tucking my children into bed every night. I impact the world by writing a little love note to my daughter who is going through "the Change." I don't need an important platform to impact the world...I HAVE an important platform because I'm a DAD. And so are you.

Don't forget that...EVER or God might reach down and give you a holy wedgie as a reminder.

So Dad, go impact the world today. Tell your daughter that you're proud of her, wrestle on the floor with your sons, and tell your wife that you're the luckiest man in the world to be living in your house...not the White House.

You 'da dad!

I Love My Calendar Girl

1 Peter 2:4-12

Hey Dad,

Things are pretty busy around here at the moment. We're all scurrying about to get ready for a few days at family snow camp in Wisconsin where I'll be speaking. Should be a lot of fun...unless I ruin it.

Just three minutes ago, I was able to flex a little FatherPower muscle and slay a mini-dragon for my daughter Maggie (almost 5). Yesterday, she burst in the door after running some errands with my wife holding a very girly-looking kitty calendar.

"Oh, Daddy, isn't this beautiful?" she asked dramatically. "This is my faaaavorite calendar."

The rest of the evening she talked about it and how she was going to hang it in her room. Then this morning, she asked me if I could hang it in her room.

To be honest, I was a little busy at the time and don't even remember answering her. She was undaunted and asked me at least two other times. To be doubly honest, I'm not sure I answered her even then.

About five minutes ago, I heard the faint tapping of a hammer against a nail upstairs, and I knew it was my little daughter trying to hang her kitty calendar. So being a good, knight-in-shining-armor dad...I ignored it.

The tapping stopped, and I could hear Maggie talking with her hammering-challenged sister, Katherine, for some advice. It was obvious a few minutes later that they were in over their heads because I heard them consult their hammering-challenged mother next.

"Get a picture hanger out of Abe's (7) blue tool kit," I heard her say.

That's when God pulled me out of my chair and said, "Get in there and help that girl."

The whole operation took about 45 seconds, including the time it took for me to find a small nail.

"Thank you, Daddy," my beaming little daughter said. From the look on her face, I could tell a dragon had been slayed. And it only took 45 seconds.

That's the thing about love. It doesn't take 'much' to show those we love...that we love them. BUT it does take 'something.' We have to get off our duff, and spend a few minutes of our time, thinking, planning, and doing.

Take a few minutes to show your wife and children how much you love them. It might be a small gift, the gift of time, the slaying of a dragon, or...hanging a kitty calendar.

You 'da dad!

Flashlight Dad

1 Peter 2:13-20

"When I was a kid we moved into a really cool house in the woods. Near the river in Jacksonville, Florida. My folks borrowed everything they could to get into this house. So when hurricane David brewed up in summer of '79, they had no money for plywood or anything like hurricane supplies.

Well, being ten years old, and very much feeling like the little man of the house, I wanted to be part of the "hurricane readiness" that I was hearing about on the news. So I thought I needed a flashlight. When the lights go out, I'll be ready. So I commandeered one of those old Eveready brand flashlights.

David came and went and all was well.

Fast forward to my own young adulthood. I coveted a reliable flashlight which at the time was a Maglite. Standard police issue. Guaranteed to be a good backup if an officer dropped his nightstick.

Since then, the LED technology has improved in power and in price. For the average guy, there is a great light at Target. One AA battery, LED light output rivals the 2-3 D cell Maglite, just under $20.

As for Ben (my one and only son,) he was probably about six when a storm popped up on the radar. I dutifully drove out to Home Depot for "hurricane supplies" and Ben wanted to come. As we strolled the aisles, he asked me about this and that. How would we respond to this crisis or that, and I realized that he was doing what I did at 10.

And so, on the spur of the moment, Ben got his flashlight.

Some people talk about "knighting" ceremonies for sons. There is ritual and expectation. Preparation and anticipation. Yeah. No, this wasn't like that. For better or worse, this went down like making deputies. The sheriff knows sumpin' bad's about to happen. "Not sure I kin' handle this on muh own. It could be dangerous. But I'm gonna need... a deputy." The badge gets handed over, now the two good guys triumph where one would be overwhelmed. You've seen the movie, I'm sure.

I got him one with an LED and an internal generator. In a hurricane, there's a lot of hurry up and wait moments. I wanted to have something for him to do. Additionally, I wanted never to have to say: "Turn that light off. Save the battery." So now it's up to him. He slept with that light in arm's reach for the whole hurricane season.

Like so many things, the more prepared I am, the less likely they are to happen. I bought a generator after 2004. We didn't have another significant blackout for three or four more seasons. Sigh. I don't know if Ben can find his flashlight anymore, but as father/son moments go, it was priceless."

~ Submitted by John Trainer

Grandma Taught Me That

1 Peter 2:21-25

Hey Dad,

Man, I feel old. It might be because I'm still suffering from a little bit of a 13th birthday hangover from this weekend.

After spending the night on a WWII submarine for my son Ben's 13th birthday, we had to do something special for my son Sam's 13th birthday. So we surprised our kids with a night at the closest indoor waterpark. The kids had a blast, and we did it up right by ordering pizza, eating junk food, opening presents, and watching a special video. Like Ben's 13th, we had a special ceremony where Sam was prayed over and given a sword (actually a gift certificate for a Prince Caspian Sword when it is available) to serve as a reminder of the great responsibility laid upon him of becoming a man.

It was a great time and one that will be etched in their minds forever.

My grandma taught me that. She lives in a nursing home near my folks. She's getting up there in years and doesn't remember much. She's foggy about her children, can't remember her grandchildren, and doesn't seem to recall being married to the man of her dreams for 60 years. But she does remember her dad.

The really awesome part of that thought is that one day my children might be in a nursing home. Like my grandma, they may not remember much, but could remember their dad (me), who has already been dead for 40 years. They may not remember their own wedding day, but they just might remember pizza in a hotel room, zipping down a big waterslide, and being held in their dad's arms.

I won't kid you; it was a pricey weekend...but worth every cent.

You 'da dad!

Icing on the Daddy Cake

1 Peter 3:1-7

Hey Dad,

Seems like most of the time, fathering is an ugly, thankless job. The kids are demanding and ungrateful...they don't mean to be, it's just the nature of being a kid...they're dependent on their parents.

I'm not trying to say fathering isn't a good thing because it is...it's just that it's so HARD.

Fortunately, when you least expect it, God lets you experience the "icing" of being called "dad." I tasted that a couple of days ago.

I was scheduled to speak to a group a few hours away, and Katherine (8) volunteered to make the trip with me. I usually take one of her older brothers, but she seemed willing to go, so the decision was made.

We prayed in the driveway before we left that we would be an encouragement to many...and I never dreamed that I would be the one who would receive the most. For three hours, Katherine and I held hands, sang, talked, and laughed.

Her face radiated with love and delight.

The cherry on the cake happened within twenty minutes of arriving at the place. I was telling her how much I love being her dad and that she would always be my little girl...even when I was an old man.

"Come up here, Katherine, and sit on my lap," I said playfully in an old man's voice. "You're still my little princess."

Emotion welled up inside her heart, and she said, "Oh, Dad." At the same moment, she lifted my hand and kissed it so tenderly that I wanted her to do it again...and she did. We were in love.

On the way home, she curled up on the seat next to me, pulled a coat over her, and stared at me in the dark.

"I used to love watching my dad drive in the dark when I was a kid," I said.

"Yeah, I know," she answered quietly, "it makes you feel safe."

Yes, I thought, that's what dads do—make their kids feel safe.

Let me tell you, Dad, those kinds of moments only happen when you're alone with your child...and the "alone" moments only happen when you, 'da dad, make them happen. It's not always easy to take a child along with you, but I guarantee that it'll be worth the effort.

So, make it happen.

You 'da dad!

It All Fits on a Sealy

1 Peter 3:8-15

Hey Dad,

Hope things are good at your house. Things are busy here as we prepare for a new baby, speaking engagements, and RV travels in the spring. But I've got to tell you, I had one of those Familyman moments this past week, where for a few minutes, I was in dad heaven.

It was a lazy, winter morning; the kids were sleeping late, and my wife and I were enjoying some quiet time, talking. In fact, she had that look like maybe she wanted to do more than just…talk, when a little voice called out, "M-o-m-m-y."

"Shh," I advised my wife, "Maybe she'll fall back asleep."

No such luck, and a minute later, Maggie Rose was lying between us sucking her two middle fingers with vigor.

Maybe she'll fall asleep and then I can slip her back into her bed, I thought, hoping to get back where we left off. But even as I was concocting my plan, Katherine walked in and slipped her arm around her mother.

How cozy, I thought, just the four of us…scratch that, five of us, I added as Sam trounced in, bounced on the bed, and squirmed into place. A minute later, Ike stumbled in and staked out his portion of the bed. We had just begun to quiz Maggie on who was still missing when Ben flopped on the foot of the bed with a big grin.

That's when it hit me: all that I will ever care about in this whole world fits on a queen-sized Sealy Posturepedic Mattress. It also reminded me of an inevitable time in my life that I have yet to experience but have witnessed a few times in other dads' lives.

I've seen grown-up kids gather around the bed of an old man who is about to depart for heaven. The children's eyes are puffy, and they touch their father lovingly. Again, in that moment, 80 years of living is reduced to the few special people around his mattress who matter most.

In day-to-day living, we forget that, Dad. We get duped into thinking that all that we do at work, at church, or on Wall Street is most important.

But let me remind you as I was reminded on that recent winter morning…all that matters most fits on your Sealy.

You 'da dad!

It's A Familyman Economy!

1 Peter 3:16-22

Hey Dad,

Life is good at the Wilson home. What looked like the makings of an upchuck pandemic has been checked after only two days of my son Cal (almost 2) throwing up every 30 minutes like clockwork. I assumed it would sweep the ranks, but I think it has run its course, sparing the rest of the flock. Since I'm the one assigned to bodily fluid cleanup, I'm relieved.

So on to the topic at hand: the economy. Yes, you heard me right. Everywhere I go the headlines are dominated by the struggling economy and I thought it was time that the Familyman weighed in on the present economy.

After careful examination of the turbulent stock market, the slumping housing market, the rising energy costs, and the general uneasiness of the global economy, I've determined that…there has never been a better time to be a dad.

My advice? Now is the time to plan that family vacation, have another child, or do that thing you've been talking about for years. I know that this advice flies in the faces of most economists, who advise us to hunker down and weather the storm.

But as I always say, when life gives you a storm…find a puddle and splash in it. This is not the time for dads to put off that summer camping trip you've been planning, scrap the adoption plans you've been putting together, or postpone the weekend trip to that special place that you've been promising the kids. Matter of fact, this is the perfect time and could be the only time you've got to do "it."

Forget the cost of fuel and the unstable economy, and stick to your plan. Financial guru Larry Burkett used to say, "Don't sacrifice the present to save for the future…that may never come." I'm not saying go into debt or put yourself in financial jeopardy, but if it's a just a matter of making sure you'll have enough to retire someday—spend it now on the family you have today.

The future has always been uncertain, but the present is certain. I constantly meet dads who put off the present, hoping that things will get better in the future. But what ends up happening is that they miss out on both.

So, Dad, listen to this economist: Take advantage of what you have today. Make the plans, fill up the gas tank, make your reservations, have another child…and then let God worry about the future.

You 'da dad!

Just Another Day of Dad-dom

1 Peter 4:1-11

Hey Dad,

Today's just another day of being a dad. Sure, people will be listening to "The Familyman" on Focus on the Family today and tomorrow, but do you think my kids care? I don't think so.

I even heard my wife trying to build me up in front of some of the younger kids a few minutes ago by saying, "Now, Daddy's going to be on the radio today…"

Ike's (6) answer can be boiled down to, "So."

He's more concerned that I go to Dollar General today to buy him some long balloons so he can tie them into knotted animals or that we have a family night soon where we eat pizza and watch a video.

My older kids are a little kinder to their old dad, but they don't really care either. They try to say nice things like, "That's neat, Dad," but they'd rather spend their time telling me about something that's important to them.

Why do I kid myself? The truth is…they just don't care about what I do as "The Familyman."

They're not impressed by emails that show appreciation for their dad, the number of listeners, or the ruggedly handsome picture of their dad standing next to a Christian legend.

They don't care. They DON'T CARE!!!

What they care about is my involvement in their lives. They want me to listen to them describe the books they're reading, care about building a sword for their friend, and give my input as they set up a miniature plastic house, home to some miniature cats.

Want a real shocker? That's what your children care about too.

They don't care squat about the title you hold, how many employees report to you, the importance of what you do at work, impressive people you might rub shoulders with, or big meetings that you attend. They only care about you and the time you spend with them.

I'm OK with that. And you should be too.

After all, we're dads, and that's what dads do (that rhymes).

So, I think I'll go upstairs and enjoy a bowl of cereal with my kids as the rest of the world listens to "The Familyman." I'll take care of the important stuff and let the other stuff take care of itself.

As for you, Dad, enjoy being a dad today.

You 'da dad!

We Are the Need-Meeters

1 Peter 4:12-19

Hey Dad,

Just got back from a weekend in Asheville, NC (voted by Rolling Stone Magazine as the freak capitol of the country) with my son Sam (13+). We visited the mammoth Grove Park Inn and stopped off at the birthplace of KFC…but didn't see a single freak.

It's always fun when I get to spend extended time with one of my children. It's amazing how different each one is, including his individual needs.

That's why I'm writing…because one of my child's needs is driving me nuts. He has an insatiable need to tell my wife and me how much he loves us each night at bedtime. He's always had a gentle heart, but it's getting borderline ridiculous.

Parenting experts like to describe how special bedtime rituals are…but those experts obviously don't have kids. Our bedtime ritual consists of my yelling and their dawdling. "Come on guys, let's move it. Have you brushed your teeth? Why didn't you think of that before now? No, you can't wear your cowboy boots to bed!!"

It's usually after the yelling has run its course that I make the rounds to each room. I pray, give big hugs, receive slobbery kisses, and then tell them how much I love them.

That's when the problem begins.

"I love you, Dad," he says.

"I love you too, Bud," I answer.

"Love you zillions."

"Yeah, I love you zillions, too."

"You're the best dad in the world."

"And you're the best kids in the world," I repeat back with a sigh. "Good night."

"Good night…Hey, Dad," he adds, "look."

I turn back to see him holding up four fingers, which is Wilson code for "I Love You More." I flash back four fingers with not even the slightest hint of a smile. And then I slip out of his room and down the hallway.

"Tell mom I love her more too," he hollers into the darkness. "Try to come in again soon," he adds. I don't even answer for fear of getting sucked back in.

Tough-guy dads would tell me to say it once and then nip it. But I know that my son needs to say and hear how much we love each other. And so I will give him what he needs, and starting tonight I will like doing it.

You know, Dad, I'm betting you have a child who needs something that only you can give. I'm even guessing that his "need" drives you nuts sometimes. Can I encourage you to try to meet that need today and like doing it?

You 'da need-meeter!

The Abominable Snow Dad

1 Peter 5:1-14

Hey Dad,

How are things going in the dad department? It's a tough, thankless job, isn't it?

The kids demand, whine, and wear you down like coarse, 60-grit sandpaper. But, God has placed in the heart of every girl and boy (no matter what age) the desire to be close to their dads.

It's annoying at times, especially when you're trying to get something done. Like yesterday…I was working in my basement office when I looked up to see my seven-year-old son dressed in winter gear and covered in snow.

"Hi, Sam," I said, glancing up from my computer screen. "Whatcha doing? Playing out in the snow?" I asked as if it wasn't obvious.

"Yeah," he answered, "we're trying to build a snow fort, but it's not working."

I tried to talk him through snow fort basics while avoiding going outside to help him.

He smiled, thanked me, and left.

Five minutes later, Ben, our oldest, stepped through the door and said, "Can you come out and show us how to make a snow fort?"

"Sure, Ben, but not right now."

"When can you come out?" he persisted.

"Later," I answered, but I meant "never."

A few minutes later, God poked me in the chest and said, "Go."

"Go into all the nations and preach the gospel?" I asked, trying to sidestep the issue.

"No. Go play in the snow with your kids."

I knew that's what He meant. I trudged upstairs and grumbled to my wife that I was going out to play in the snow. She smiled understandingly.

I went outside, and we all had a great time throwing snow, building a snow fort, and laughing together.

And to think I came within a hair's breadth of missing that. Not only would I have gypped them out of having fun with their dad, but I would have missed out on the best that God has to offer.

I know that spending time playing in the snow is more valuable than spending time pounding away on my computer, but it comes with a price. I may not make as much money and achieve all that I want, but my kids don't care. They'd pick spending time together with their dad any day over those other things.

So would your kids.

Dad, it's time do the things that they've been begging you to do, because your children need you.

You 'da dad!

Definition for Dad

2 Peter 1:1-11

I recently asked for a good definition of a dad. Here's what they said:

~ A dad is a watchman with an ever-vigilant eye.

~ A dad is a steady rock in the storm with the warmth of a hug waiting inside.

~ A mom and dad are the ones who can just smile at the dirt on the nose (with boys) and the changing of the clothes (with girls) a minimum of 3 times a day.

~ A dad is a rock that that melts with a tear.

~ A dad is a boy with 20+ years of experience at getting dirty.

~ D.A.D. – Delivering A Destiny

~ A dad is a hug after the bad game.

~ One son when asked what is a dad answered "A dad is that annoying little neighbor boy who will never leave you alone."

~ Mom is a queen that cooks and cleans, dad is a king with a silly gene.

~ A dad is the mat at the door for the kids to wipe their feet on.

~ A dad is a funnybone, with rules and wrestling, and a Mom is a heart, with hands and hugs.

~ A mom and a dad are the clean up team.

~ A dad is a workbench with a soft lap and a warm heart.

~ A dad is a hug covered in whiskers.

~ A dad is the picture of my Heavenly Father.

~ A dad is a daddy forever.

~ A dad is a gentle friend wrapped up in a protective tiger.

~ A dad is a grin with sawdust on one arm and a burp cloth on the other.

~ A dad is a snicker with poop all over his hands.

~ A dad is a full-out belly-laugh, tickled by the best entertainment that God ever provided...a family.

~ A dad is an overgrown boy who still makes the same noises but has learned to use soap.

~ A dad is a man with pictures in his wallet where his money used to be.

~ A dad is a kick in the pants wrapped inside a hug.

~ Distributes-Alotta-Dollars

The 2x4 Song

2 Peter 1:12-21

Hey Dad,

I was talking to my mom yesterday about normal stuff when she asked me, "Do you know the Smith's*?"

I confess that I don't know them well, but I have known them for years. They went to the same high school I attended, were very involved in my home church, had a bunch of kids (8 to be exact), and were just a good, solid, Christian family.

"Yeah, I know who they are," I said.

"Well, I just read in the paper that they've filed for a divorce."

"Wow," I said quietly.

"It's devastating," she said. I knew she felt it deeply because my mom cares and has invested her life in women, couples, and family.

Today, I find myself feeling heavy about it too. I won't pretend to blame, guilt, or imagine what they felt; all I know is that unless God intervenes they won't be married anymore...and that feels...heavy.

I wonder what they would have thought if someone told them five years ago that in a few years they would file for a divorce. I just know they would have said, "No way!...You're wrong...not a snowball's chance in Miami."

But it happened.

Actually, it reminds me of a small 2x4 that sits near my desk. On it is the name of a song and a singer. I first heard the song ten years ago on the radio as I was sitting in my car. The song played and I was pierced to the heart by the words. Afterwards, I scrambled to find something to write down the information that the DJ gave me on and managed to scribble it all down on a 12-inch scrap 2x4.

I hadn't thought about the song in a while but have been ever since my conversation with my mom. The song's refrain is this: "Fifty years from now, what will we remember...if we walk away from this, what will we have missed, fifty years, fifty years from now?"

Sure, being married is hard and sometimes you might even want out. But if you walk out, you miss fifty years of great memories...of Christmas mornings with giggling children, and children who graduate, get married, have children, and then laugh around the table in your golden years. You will miss all those great memories if you give up.

Yes, family and marriage is hard...BUT it is worth everything. It may take a few years to work out some of the hardships, but in comparison to 50 years of memories, it's nothing.

So my fellow dad, I don't know what's going through your mind right now, but if you're entertaining the thought of 'getting out', DON'T...and go listen to that 2x4 song that I posted on our site.*

Fifty years from now you'll still be 'da dad.

* http://www.familymanweb.com/video/fifty-years-from-now-andy-denton

Can You Hear ME?!!!

2 Peter 2:1-22

Hey Dad,

Can you hear me? Can you HEAR ME NOW!!!!! I feel like I'm communicating in an unintelligible form of communication because somehow my family can't seem to understand me. I try all different tones and approaches, and I feel like I'm broadcasting, but my kids just aren't picking up the channel.

To be honest, it's not all of them, just a couple of them. But it seems as though every one of my communications with them ends up with them freaking out and me walking away nodding my head and thinking, "What just happened? They just don't understand what I'm trying to say."

And it's not just my children. Even my wife doesn't seem to be receiving my signal. "What's HER deal?" I wonder as I walk away nodding my head. "Can't she UNDERSTAND that I didn't mean it that way?" Until recently, I assumed that they're antennas were just not pointed in the right direction...MY direction.

Then last week I was driving to Wisconsin and had a few hours to listen to an audio CD on communicating with your children. One phrase the man said shot from the speakers and burned into my heart like a red hot poker. "Our job as parents," he said, "is not to be UNDERSTOOD by our kids but to seek to UNDERSTAND them."

As I drove pondering that revelation from God, I realized that I spend most of my time trying to get my children and wife to understand me...when I should be spending my time trying to understand what they feel, where they're coming from, and how what I just said or did felt TO THEM. Talk about having your antenna adjusted.

Maybe I need to make that into a plaque and post it on the door: The chief purpose of a dad and husband is to understand (hear) not to be understood (heard).

So maybe you need to stop trying to get them or her to understand you and spend a little more time trying to understand why they're frustrated with you, not walking around cheerfully, or giving you the cold shoulder.

Believe me, I understand...you 'da dad.

PS—I still need your help. If you have a few seconds, will you pray that I would do what I just wrote? Thanks.

A Bladder from Heaven

2 Peter 3:1-9

Hey Dad,

For decades, theologians have debated about the nature of the Apostle Paul's thorn in the flesh. Although I haven't a clue what Paul's thorn was, mine is a five-year-old boy with a bladder the size of a dime, who can't seem to "hold it." The kid's as cute as a button, with dark eyes and a comical smile, but I forget that when we're driving down the road and he announces, "Dad, I have to go to the bathroom."

It wouldn't be so bad if we'd been traveling all day, but the announcement generally comes five minutes after we pull out of a parking lot. "Why didn't you go five minutes ago?" I ask, as though he's dumb or something. You know the answer.

"I didn't have to go then," he answers, like I'm dumb or something.

Fuming, I pull into yet another gas station, yank him out of the van, and take him to the typically disgusting bathroom where he sits down and piddles a dropperful of "stuff" into the toilet. "I'm done," he says with a smile.

Thirty minutes later, we're tooling down the road, and the "thorn" pricks me again. "Daaaadddyy??"

"You're kidding me!?" I holler.

He cocks his head and grins. He's not kidding. We pull over again, and this time I make sure he knows I'm mad at his bladder and him for inconveniencing me. Then, I hear "the voice" again. It's God.

"You know, , you tell all those dads to love their kids unconditionally, yet you get all bent out of shape over a tiny bladder—that I gave him. Why don't you practice what you preach and love your son…the way I love you?"

That was last week. In a few hours, we're going to make the two-and-a-half hour drive to be with my wife's family. He'll have to stop at least twice—maybe three times. But, I'm ready. When he says, "Dad I have to go the bathroom," I'll look back, smile, and respond, Okay, Ike, we'll stop as soon as we see a place."

How about you? Got a bladderless kid? Consider it an opportunity from God to show unconditional love to your child.

You 'da dad!

Bad News

2 Peter 3:10-18

Hey Dad,

Better sit down for this one. Just got a call from your doctor, and uh...uh...I hate to break the bad news to you, but you only have 48 hours to live. Tough break...sniff...sniff. We were just getting to know each other too. I'm going to miss you.

If you don't mind me asking, what are you going to do with the next 48 hours?

Will you spend it tying up loose ends at the office for the next guy since your work will find a replacement for you as soon as they can? Will you leave the office early and play 18 holes of golf?

Will you get the guys together tonight to watch a ball game on TV, cut the lawn so that it looks good when the guests come to pay their last respects, or put one last coat of wax on your car—your baby?

Is there another program down at the church that needs your attention, a project at work that you'd really like to finish, a fence that needs to be mended, a garden that needs weeding, or a documentary on PBS that you've been dying to watch (no pun intended)?

So many choices—but with only 48 hours left, you can't do them all. But you won't have any trouble deciding, because at the end, everything gets crystal clear.

I know if I had only 48 hours left to live, I'd let the grass grow, forget about the project at work, and not even think about touching the TV.

I'd probably have a picnic under a big tree in our yard with my family, wrestle until the kids (not I) want to stop, and lie in bed with each of them and talk until they fall asleep. Afterwards, I'd sit on the couch with my wife and hold her, and we'd talk until the first light of day peeked through the windows.

And then I'd do it all over again the next day, because they're what's most important. But sometimes I forget that...sometimes you forget that too.

So back to my question. What are you going to do with your next 48 hours?

You 'da dad!

37

Happily Ever After

Marriage is hard. If you don't agree with me, it's because you aren't married or you've fallen hard on your head. It was especially hard around my house this past week.

The problem was my wife thinks like a woman. She gets all emotional and wants to talk about 'it'. I, on the other hand, can deal with the fact that I'm a clod. I apologize and then move on.

My wife, on the other hand, thinks our marriage stinks, that we're hopeless, and we need to resolve it.

I, on the other hand, just know it's part of life and that next week she'll feel differently.

My wife, on the other hand, looks at all the other couples in the world and thinks they're so in love, while we only tolerate each other.

I, on the other hand, know that all the other wives think the same thing about us that my wife thinks about them.

She, on the other...oh, never mind.

Anyway, all I know is that I'm faced with two options. A) I can say she is wrong and hope her feelings change or 3) I can work to meet her needs.

I'd be stupid to pick option one, and although I may be a slow learner, I'm not stupid. I've been married long enough to know that problems don't just disappear, so I'll pick option two. It will mean that I'll have to prove once again that she is the desire of my heart. She probably won't believe me right away so I'll have to be loving even if she doesn't respond—but hey, that's what love is all about.

How about you? Are you working to keep the zing in your marriage? Have you shown your wife lately that she is 'numero uno'? If you haven't, you need to. You're responsible, and God is counting on you.

You 'da dad!

Marlboro Man

James 1:19-27

Hey Dad,

Before I go off into lunatic ranting and raving, I thought I'd begin with a friendly reminder that Valentine's Day is just around the corner. So after you finish reading my tirade, spend two minutes thinking about what you can do to make your wife feel loved this Valentine's Day—I mean really loved.

Okay, enough about that—now on to the R&R.

Here's the short of it. Last week I received an e-mail accusing me of feminizing dads. The reader thought I was telling men to give up their God-given macho-ism and asking them to be wimpy, womanish men.

Well, I've chewed on that e-mail for a week and find myself growing hot…not against the dad who sent it, but against the message to dads that says in order to be the kind of dad God designed, we have to be a Hollywood-style "Marlboro Man".

It is true that we need warrior-men who lead their families, love their children, and fight for their wives. In fact, that is our prime directive. But we do not achieve that by watching Monday Night Football, shooting guns, using power tools, refusing to vacuum, and communicating in grunts. That line of thought is based on selfishness, not selflessness. It is a worldly philosophy, not a biblical one.

The world encourages husbands to go for the gusto, don't be pushed around, take time for yourself, and leave the women's work to the women. In contrast, the Bible says, "live with your wife in an understanding way," "do not provoke your children to anger," "give to those who ask," "turn the other cheek," "serve one another"—and a bunch of other stuff that is easier to say than to do.

Can a man turn the other cheek, communicate with his wife, offer to do the dishes, and still be a man? Yes. In fact, that's the kind of man God wants us to be. It's true that some have feminized men, but trying to be a good listener, servant, and communicator isn't feminizing, it's "living with your wife in an understanding way."

That's what a real man is—a biblical, selfless, go-ahead-and-punch-me-in-the-face-'cuz-I-can-take-it kind of man. That's what God has asked of us, that's what I want of myself, and that's what I encourage you to be.

With all that said, I'm a pretty good man—except when I'm not.

You 'da dad!

Make a Not-Tonight a Tonight

James 2:1-13

Hey Dad,

I'm on the run…and heading out the door for Spokane, WA. My son Sam (15) is flying with me. There is something fun about a father/son trip when just the two of you get to order pizza, stuff your faces with junk food, and watch 'Dirtiest Jobs' on hotel television.

Not that it's not fun being with the entire family…but there is something special about having one on one time. I know each of my kids love the times that we escape the Wilson throng for some parent/child time.

It doesn't have to be a business trip though. My son Ike (10) loves it when he gets to spend 10-15 after-bedtime-minutes sitting on our bed talking about stuff. My kids love it when it's their turn to go grocery shopping with my wife. They talk, and she buys them their favorite snack.

I know some dads who take their kids on date nights or have special game nights or video nights with just one child. Somehow our kids need those times, but to be honest it's a hassle to make those times happen. And I find myself saying way too often, "Yes, that sounds like fun, son…but not tonight."

Dad, can I challenge you to make one of those 'not tonights'…a 'tonight?' It won't be long before you're out of 'tonights.'

You 'da dad!

On the Edge of a Knife

James 2:14-26

Hey Dad,

Have you ever felt like you were standing on the edge of a knife? You know, one slight move in the wrong direction and you're toast?

I felt that way the other morning as I was getting ready to start the day. Things have been busy around here, and I could tell that behind my wife's blank stares, the wheels in her head were in constant motion…making lists, crossing off lists, and adding to lists. I, on the other hand, am oblivious to lists and all that pertains to them.

Anyway, I was just enjoying the start of the day when my wife looked at me and sighed, "I wish I could tell you something without you getting upset and lecturing me." Man, I hate it when she starts a sentence like that. I looked down and saw my feet poised on the edge of the knife. I knew this was going to test my husbanding skills.

"Go ahead; tell me…I won't lecture you." I braced myself for what was coming.

Like a rabbit sticking its nose out of hiding, she hesitated, and then started talking, accompanied by an outpouring of emotion and tears. She felt overwhelmed by projects, homeschooling, and all the lists.

I tell you, I felt my manly side kick in, and I fought tooth and nail to keep from saying, "Oh stop it. Don't worry about all that stuff. Just take one day at a time …" I was even searching for some Bible verse to "encourage" her. Then, I looked down at the knife and realized I was about to step off and impale myself on the point.

Instead, I said nothing. That's right…NOTHING. I just rubbed her back and empathized…all the time biting a hole in my tongue to keep from adding my "wisdom." We sat there for less than ten minutes and then started the day.

Later in the day, my wife thanked me for letting her talk.

YES!! I had survived. I had met my wife's need. Sure, I had failed 658 times in a row before, but this time I did it! I am husband; hear me roar. Of course, I didn't say that to her. Instead, I just smiled without a word like a sensitive husband should.

Dad, it is really that simple! Sometimes your wife really just wants you to rub her back, listen, and empathize when she's had a tough day, feels overwhelmed, or is about to lose it.

Okay, Dad; I predict that you'll find yourself standing on the edge of a knife within 72 hours. Here's my advice…keep your mouth shut, listen, empathize, and rub her back.

You 'da dad!

Here's a PPPUUUSSSHHH!!

Hey Dad,

There are few words that elicit loathing in my mind, words like…audit, root canal, vasec…vasecto…I can't even say it. But at the top of the chart is the word 'charades'.

I'm sorry, but I'm just not a game person, and charades seems like a game in which you have to act energetic and goofy. I don't like to do either of those when I'm relaxing. So you can see why I was less than exuberant the other night when my teenage daughter asked if we could play Disney Charades.

I hem-hawed and made excuses but somehow I ended up in the rotation anyway.

"I'll just be a guesser," I said, hoping that would suffice their need for fatherly involvement and was a little perturbed when they said later, "It's your turn, Dad," and handed me a card with a famous Disney cartoon character on it.

Reluctantly, I stood and did my best, and I think I even smiled…a little. But here's the deal. Forty-five minutes later we were still playing, and I was having fun with them and they were having fun with me.

Later, I was thinking…sometimes we dads just need a little push to get us going. If we could just walk through the forbidding veil of the 'idea' of playing a game, going fishing, throwing a ball, building a potato canon, or having a tea party, we'd find a whole new world of family, fathering fun.

So Dad, let me give you a little nudge. Would your kids love for you to take them out for ice cream, have a pillow fight, play a game, or go sledding? If so, then here's a big PPUUUSSSHHH!!!

You're going to have fun…I promise.

You 'da dad!

The Dream

James 3:13-18

Hey Dad,

Last night I had a dream.

It wasn't one of my usual, recurring dreams…like when I show up for algebra class in my underwear, fly like Peter Pan, or my teeth fall out one at a time. But, this lifelike dream has left me shaken and pondering.

It involved my two eldest sons and me. Apparently, we pulled our van behind this rundown building near a clump of scraggly trees.

For some reason, I needed to go get something, so I left the boys at an old picnic table, telling them that I would be right back. Then the dream got weird with me running across the street with a plastic rocket, trying to outwit a potential bad guy, being sniffed by a horse-sized dog, and finally making my way back though a tangle of trees and brush.

Towards the end of the dream, I remember feeling this urgent need to get back to the boys but knew that hours had passed since I had said I would be right back.

In my dream, I exited the tangle of trees and looked around to see if the boys were there. In the dim light, I could see two small forms sitting at the table coloring pictures. Feelings of shame and guilt washed over me as I walked closer to the table.

They never looked up, but I could sense their disappointment. Then I saw my eldest son's face. He was busy coloring, but his eyes were red and tears were streaming down his face. He was scared but was trying to be brave. He felt betrayed but tried not to show it. I was the one they looked to; I was the one they counted on…and I had let them down.

Then I woke up, but even now, I still "feel" the pain I caused them in my dream.

Now, I know it's just a dream, and I'm not into dream interpretation…but I still can't shake the thought that maybe there is some truth in the sad dream. Maybe I have let my children down. Maybe I've been too preoccupied with "my" stuff lately. Even yesterday, Sam (10) asked again, "Dad, when are you going to give me drawing lessons? You said you were going to a long time ago."

We hear that a lot don't we, Dad—"When are you going to…?"

They're counting on us, depending on us…and too many times we say, "I'll be right back"—only we aren't.

So, I'm going to keep thinking about "The Dream" and maybe you should too. Maybe it's God's way of reminding you and me that we need to slow down and be there for our children.

You 'da dad!

The Holy Grail

James 4:1-6

Hey Dad,

I asked about 40,000 women what they'd like for Valentine's from their husband. Here are just a few of their thoughts:

"I don't really care about the gifts (don't get me wrong; they're nice, as well as helping around the house), but I would love it if he would just give my son a bath and put my son to bed on a regular basis without me telling him so that I can sit down in the evening once in a while to watch a movie. Also to carry on a meaningful, interesting, or fun conversation instead of stuff like work, bills, kids, repairs. I guess that's my love language (book: The 5 Languages of Love)" ~ Terry

"I would love for him to plan a surprise for me! He does make me feel cherished in many ways, but that is something he has never done in our 26 years of marriage. Regardless, I am blessed to be his wife." ~ Karen

"Forget the diamonds…forget the flowers…there are only two things I would love for my husband to do for me this Valentine's Day:
    1. scrub the bathrooms (I mean really scrub them)
    2. Hold my hand in public
That's it!" ~ Marcy

"Anything along these lines: Offering a foot rub-or even to exchange them, instead of being asked. Just taking the lead and offering to go for an ice cream or coffee tea break. One single flower just to be sweet. Putting on some lovely music after the kids are in bed, and pulling me into a slow, cuddle dance…and most importantly, all throughout the year." ~ Nan

"Eating out is great. Cards and flowers are good. But what I would really love is for a few of those "things that never get done" to actually get done. The last couple of pieces of trim on those cabinets he built, clean up the car port, finish that project in the office. That would show me that he is listening and cares enough to push through and get it done just for me!" ~ Bonnie

*Read more at http://www.familymanweb.com/article/wives-i-need-your-help

A Dad Hole is a Sad Spot

James 4:7-17

February 8

Hey Dad,

We've been enjoying watching the Winter Olympics. I know my boys are still talking about Shawn White's snowboard performance and my daughter Katherine can hardly wait to watch the figure skating.

For a family that doesn't watch TV, it's been fun sitting around the tube each night rooting for our favorites. It just feels...togetherish.

I missed a night last week because I spoke in Kalamazoo, MI. The next day my wife told me that my son had asked her that night, "Doesn't it just make you so sad when Dad's not here? I mean it just makes me feel like I want to cry." My wife responded, "Yeah, it just feels like something's not right, doesn't it?" He answered, "That is exactly how it feels."

It kind of shocked me that he would say that because I haven't been a very good familyman lately. I'm not sure why (maybe it's cabin fever), but I've felt...snappy. I seem to take good moments and turn them sour. If anything, I would have expected Ike to say, "You know Mom, it sure seems more fun when Dad is...GONE."

But he didn't. I'm a little stymied and wonder if EVEN I underestimate my FatherPower (the power that I wield in my kids' lives) potential. It seems that on the father grading scale we get an 'A' just for being there, just for sitting in the same room, watching the same program, cheering, laughing, and...being. In fact, 'being' seems to counteract the 'snappy' part. Either that or it causes some kind of kid-amnesia.

Whatever the case, the truth is (whether they admit it or not) your kids feel a sadness when you're not there. I know you're thinking, "Yeah, right, ...not in my family."

You've forgotten, Dad...FatherPower.

You 'da dad!

PS – If you would like to know more about this "father power" phenomenon, get a copy of my book called Father Power. Here's the link to order yours: http://www.familymanweb.com/store/father-power. It's powerful and life changing!!!

45

After the Torch Goes Out

Hey Dad,

Hope things are good at your house. We've been in Germville all week, and I'm still groping around in a sick fog. And, my wife recently gave me the task of coming up with a better boy's name for our upcoming baby (due in 4 weeks). Talk about pressure.

Actually, after the last two weeks of Olympic viewing, the name Apollo Anton Wilson keeps bouncing around my head or maybe Bode Wilson or Victor Petrenko Wilson…or maybe not.

It amazes me how hard and long those athletes train for their one shot at the gold. A consuming drive keeps them going year after year. They make sacrifices and push themselves to the limits. If they're lucky, they get the gold, the crowd cheers, and they bask in their brief moment of glory.

Then the torch goes out and nobody cares anymore.

Even as I watched the games, I thought to myself, So much effort…and for what? A chunk of metal that hangs on a wall and collects dust over the years.

I remember reading the story of a journalist who visited boxing legend Mohammed Ali at his home. He interviewed the champ in a large converted barn that held trophies, plaques, and photos of his illustrious 30-year career.

I don't remember his exact words, but I'll never forget the picture he painted of the ailing heavyweight champion of the world surrounded by his "gold medals" while staring vacantly out a window. In the silence, the author realized that little white spots covered all the photos and awards. It was bird poop.

Apparently, the big barn was home to many birds that had left their mark on his efforts. The life of a champion had pretty much been reduced to a bunch of trophies covered in bird poop.

When will we learn? We dads strive after success, a job title, a dream, or a pot of gold at the end of the rainbow. We work for it, think about it, spend most of our time chasing it, and sacrifice time we should be spending with our families, only to realize one day, after the torch goes out, that it all amounts to a bunch of trophies covered in bird poop.

So let me ask you, Dad. What are you chasing after and at whose expense? And, will it really matter when you get to the end of your life?

You 'da dad!

Love Ain't Cheap

Hey Dad,

In a few hours, we will be celebrating the birthday of our little princess, Katherine. Eight years ago, after a relatively smooth delivery, she became part of our family and changed our lives forever.

We left the "all boy" realm and entered the uncharted, and sometimes emotionally turbulent, waters of girldom. There sure have been more tears since she was born, but along with a truckload of girl emotions, came a sweet angel who twinkles when she enters a room and makes me feel all warm inside when she snuggles on my lap.

That's why we're celebrating big-time tomorrow. She has no idea that in the morning we're taking a road trip to downtown Chicago to the American Girl Place. (For those who don't know, it's kind of like Mecca for little girls).

Here's our plan: Once we get to the Windy City, I'll drop Katherine and my wife off at the store, while I take the other five kids to a museum. At the store, the girls will stroll the aisles "oohing and ahhing" at all the dolls Katherine knows by name until they get to a little doll with blonde hair and blue eyes named "Kit."

That's when my wife will smile and say, "Let's get her."

Of course, Katherine will throw her hands over her mouth and squeal in delight. Then, the three of them will dine at the American Girl Cafe like Victorian ladies.

Girl heaven.

The thing about the celebration is…it's going to cost a small fortune!! An American Girl doll costs more than my first car, and the meal is going to cost way more than McDonald's…not to mention all the time I'm giving up to take them to Chicago. I'll tell you—love may be all warm and fuzzy, but it ain't cheap.

Love has a high price tag. It will cost my patience, my kindness, my gentleness, my time, my energy, and a whole bunch of money. Oh, but as I think about my little girl and the chance to let her know how much we love her…it seems like a bargain.

How about you, Dad? Got a birthday coming up to celebrate? Or, how about Valentine's Day? These occasions are opportunities to be extravagant in your love…to give more than a generic, just-because-it's-expected kind of gift. Show those to whom you SAY you love more-than-life-itself…that you mean it.

You 'da dad!

Carpe Grossa

James 5:13-20

Hey Dad,

Florida may have Disney World, Sea World, and Busch Gardens, but Indiana has Indiana Beach. In fact, Indiana Beach has one thing Disney World doesn't have—a teaming swarm of popcorn-gulping carp (that's a fish). You drop a few pieces of popcorn in the water and hundreds of 20-pound carp rise to the surface like a living raft of fish.

It's awesome, in a disgusting sort of way.

Actually, I experience the same sensation when I go to the card aisle at Wal-Mart on Valentine's Day. Thousands, if not millions, of husbands are piled six deep…with arms grabbing and pushing for any card available.

Shameless.

Of course, we've all been guilty of this. We're bombarded by advertisements reminding us about the day…and her expectations. So being men, we run to Wal-Mart, pick out a $7 card, swing by the candy aisle for a cheap box of candy, and then buy a bunch of roses from a van parked alongside the road.

You tell me what wife wouldn't feel cherished after that? Just in case you're thinking, You're right, ! I'm kidding.

I'm not saying you can't get your wife candy and flowers, but as one husband said recently, "Don't do it on one of those regular holidays where every husband gives flowers."

So what's a husband to do in the remaining ten days till Valentine's Day?

First step, think. Take three minutes right now and think what might show your wife how much you love, appreciate, and cherish her. It doesn't have to be expensive. It might be an enlarged photo of the two of you when you were newly married…flowers, if you're not the flower-getting-type… dinner out at her favorite restaurant, or silky romantic pajamas. (Note of caution: sometimes Frederick's of Hollywood smacks of "Yeah Boy!" rather than I love you.)

One last thing: make her a card. It's easy. Take a piece of paper, fold it in half, and then with a red crayon draw a heart on the cover with the words I love you. Then open it up and write some nice "stuff." You have to fill at least one side of the note.

Now, don't tell me you can't write that much. I don't believe you. Sit down and don't get up until it's done. That's an order. You can do it!

You 'da dad!

Calling All Dads

Hebrews 1:1-14

Hey Dad,

I need your help. You know, a little accountability for the ol' familyman. As many of you know, we're expecting Wilson baby #6 in the next week or so, and I've got a little dilemma. Actually, it shouldn't be a dilemma. I know what I need to do because my wife told me.

The other day when we were talking, she casually mentioned how needy she feels after the baby comes. She wants me to hold her, talk to her, and share how we "feel." You know, like I love and care about her more than life itself.

The problem is: I'm a guy, and we guys have been known to blow a sure thing. I do it all the time. I usually know what my wife needs, but somewhere in the inner recesses of my psyche (whatever that means) I get stupid and go off and work on the computer or clean the garage instead of meeting her need.

You're shaking your head either in disgust or agreement.

Here's where you come in. I need you to hold me to it. After the baby comes…and really up until he/she arrives, as well, I want to love my wife. I want to hold her, stroke her back, be helpful, and share "feelings." But my ugly side is pretty strong.

I'm counting on you, so hold me to it. Okay?

Oh, by the way, your wife was talking to my wife the other day, and she told me that your wife feels needy of your love too. Your wife mentioned that she just wants you to hold her (not grope her), talk to her, and share your "feelings" together.

So…I guess now you don't have any excuses either. So let's get loving!

You 'da dad!

The Valentine's Day Kraken

Hebrews 2:1-8

February 13

I'm sorry!!!

I didn't realize what I was doing…it was not my fault…I'm a victim just like you…how was I to know that I was unleashing a MONSTER!!!

(Slap!) "Pull yourself together, man. Now start at the beginning."

Well, I was trying to be a good fellow Familyman, you know (sniff, sniff, whimper). I thought since Valentine's Day is coming up I'd ask the ladies to tell us what they'd like from their husbands to make them feel loved.

I assumed a few ladies would respond with typical ideas like chocolates, jewelry, or maybe even dinner at Applebee's! But then…then…I can't say it. I released THE KRAKEN!!!

Responses came out of the woodwork with all kinds of horribly painful suggestions…and they all seemed to be pointed at ME!!!! I half wondered if my wife used a different name for all of them. AUUUGGGGG!!!

Well, it's taken me a day to recover from the shock, but since then I've reread many of their responses and I can't help but feel like we've let our women down. Truth is they don't want chocolates, roses, or Applebee's. They want to be cherished by us, not squeezed into our schedule or appeased just to silence the nagging, or given some token gift because the day demands it.

They want us to spend time thinking about what would make them feel loved, take the time to write (not type) a love letter, make the effort to plan a date, finish a needed project, sit and snuggle, hold hands, or spend time like we used to before life.

Many of our wives mentioned they'd like a phone call from the road, an extra special good-bye as we head off to work, or some time alone with us without the computer or television.

As painful as it might be, Dad, you need to go look at the responses…and then you need to love YOUR wife.

Now, I just know I'm going to get some responses from dads telling me that our wives need to lighten up, be realistic, and understand our busy, demanding lives. They'll make excuses about how their wife doesn't really need all that, and insist that THEY have needs too. All to which I'll simply respond…

…You 'da dad!

* http://www.familymanweb.com/article/wives-i-need-your-help

Love Is More than a Fig Newton

Hebrews 2:9-18

February 14

Hey Dad,

Well, I counted my non-throwing-up chickens before they hatched. Last week I assumed the tide had turned after only one Wilson up-chucker. Now five or six up-chuckers later, I'm still not sure we're out of the woods yet.

It sure throws a kink into our plans, especially considering today is Valentine's Day—the official day to make sure that each member of your family knows just how much you love them.

It's usually the day when men make a mad dash to Walmart or Walgreen's on their way home from work to fight over the six remaining Valentine's cards and grab a heart-shaped box of whatever is left on the shelf (nothing says, "I'm madly in love with you" like a heart-shaped box of Fig Newtons).

I know it's hard to find the time to pick out something special for the persons we love the most—although we do seem to make time to find the coolest leatherette cell-phone holder on the market.

Maybe during your lunch hour today you could run out and pick up something for your bride that says, "You're still the love of my life."

Or better yet, as soon as you finish this e-mail, grab a piece of paper from your desk, an old French-fries box from the floor of your truck, or a scrap of paper from the trash, and write out all the things you love and appreciate about your wife. Go ahead; be mushy and nostalgic…like you used to be.

Then find a few more scraps of paper and write a note to each of your children.

I'm telling you, Dad, most wives and children will cherish a note from the man in their life forever—and it's a whole bunch better than a heart-shaped box of Fig Newtons.

You 'da dad!

51

Happy Mulligan Day!

Hebrews 3:1-11

Hey Dad,

How 'bout a little Familyman history lesson? Once upon a time in the 1920's, there was a Canadian named Dave—eh. Now Dave was a pretty successful guy who at one time managed the famed Waldorf Astoria Hotel in New York City—eh.

Dave also liked to play golf—a lot. In fact, it's reported that one time when he was playing in Montreal, he stepped to the tee in his colorful knickers and golfer's cap. All was quiet, as his world became—the ball. With a practice swing or two, his wooden driver flicked just a few inches from the ball on the tee. And then in one fluid movement, he drew the club back over his shoulder and swooSSHHH!! Whackk!!

No one knows for sure, but the ball either sliced or pulled, and went only about three inches, to Dave's consternation and the rest of his golfer buddies' amusement.

And then Dave did something that had never been done before in the game of golf. In pompous pride, he excused the shot as a mistake and re-teed a new ball.

Back in the clubhouse, the members discussed Dave Mulligan's unprecedented and highly controversial move. The rest is history. From that point on, whenever a ball is re-shot and non-scored, Dave gets the credit and we call it a Mulligan.

And I was thinking—what a great concept. We dads and husbands could sure use a day like that: a day where if we've blown it big, we can take a mulligan and start over.

And it's not just dads who need a Mulligan Day. Everyone needs permission to take a mulligan. So if your son left your tools out in the rain, instead of chewing him out, give him a mulligan. If your wife overcharged the credit card, instead of blowing your top, give her a mulligan. If your daughter acted disrespectfully and deserves all the punishment you can heap upon her, give her a mulligan.

Say you've avoided family devotions for years, take a mulligan and start again tonight. Been a lousy dad in the past or treated your wife poorly? Take a mulligan.

Celebrate this day of fresh starts for sons, daughters, wives, and dads—a day that that was started 90 years ago by a golfing Canadian—eh.

So let me be the first to say, "Happy Mulligan Day!"

You 'da dad!

One Purple Loop and Counting

Hebrews 3:12-19

Hey Dad,

Tonight is my daughter's Birthday Eve. She's been talking about her birthday for the last month as if we were approaching Christmas. Just last week I was typing away on my computer when I realized she was behind me working on some kind of construction paper project.

Carefully, she cut the purple paper into long strips, looped the first one, and then stapled its ends together.

"What are you making?" I asked.

"A chain," she answered.

"A chain? What for?" I responded.

Her eyes twinkled, and she smiled and said, "I'm making a birthday chain."

Instantly, I remembered making them as a child the month before Christmas and then stringing them in my bedroom. Each day, I would remove a single loop to serve as a visual reminder of the remaining days 'til Christmas.

This morning, a single, purple loop hangs on her doorknob.

For the last three days, she's been all giggles and sparkles. Talk about having your hopes set high! Visions of being treated like a queen for the day have filled her head.

Her plans include going to Chuck E. Cheese's for lunch, but she's most excited about her birthday present scavenger hunt. She doesn't know it, but I'm going to take her out for breakfast...just the two of us. I'll give her a flower and tell her how much I love her at least a dozen times (stole these ideas from another dad).

I know what you're thinking. Come on, . Just because a kid has a birthday doesn't mean the whole world has to revolve around her for the whole day. Besides, once you start that, you have to do it every year. They'll expect it.

All I have to say to that is..."I hope so."

I hope my kids expect nothing less. I hope they know that I love them so much that I'd want to do nothing less.

Sure it's inconvenient. I'll have to take most of the day off work...and have to go to the mouse on steroids pizza place. But my children are worth every ounce of effort, and so are yours. Birthdays are God-given opportunities to show our children how glad we are that they are part of our family.

If it means inconvenience and effort...so be it.

So, Dad, does one of your kids have a birthday coming up? Make it a good one.

You 'da dad!

You Can Learn Lots from a Dummy

Hebrews 4:1-7 | **February 17**

Hey Dad,

How are things at your house? Life is pretty good at the Wilson's. The snow has melted, the kids are healthy, and my wife and I are doing great…but that wasn't the case a couple of weeks ago.

Marriage is like that. One week everything is fine; the next week you are on the downward hill of the roller coaster of life, screaming your lungs out.

Yep, that was two weeks ago. Let me preface (I like that word) that by saying it was my fault. I could have easily disarmed the situation by being understanding, sympathetic, and reassuring. Instead, I dug in my heels and said, "I'm not gonna budge. I'm right, and you're wrong…and that's just the way it is."

Not the recipe for a successful marriage.

The whole thing started because my wife didn't feel like she was number one in my life. She thought I cared more about "the issue" than her. I, of course, told her that was ridiculous and rattled off about a dozen reasons why she was wrong, none of which convinced her.

We couldn't resolve it…actually, I WOULDN'T resolve it.

For several days (read one week), we existed together with no warmth, no gentle words…just cold facts, snide remarks, and behind-the-back whispers. I hated it but was unwilling to resolve it.

Then, the unthinkable happened…she softened, threw her arms around me, and melted me like butter. That night we talked, and it was over. Later, as she slept, I lay awake feeling like a big dummy, ashamed that she had resolved it when it should have been me.

I am 'da dad. That's what I tell you every week and that's what I believe. But this time I blew it. I wasted a whole week (and then some) because I refused to deal with it.

Now you can say what you like about whose responsibility it is to resolve marital disputes…but the truth is: it's yours and mine.

So, let me ask you, Dad, how are things with your wife? Maybe you're plunging down the hill of the roller coaster of life. If you are, learn from my mistake, and be the one to resolve it. Tonight, when everything is quiet, ask your wife what she feels. Let her talk, and don't defend yourself. Apologize if necessary, but do whatever it takes to make her feel like she's number one in your life.

Remember, you can learn a lot from this dummy.

You 'da dad!

Strangely Quiet

Hebrews 4:8-16

Hey Dad,

Things are strangely quiet around here. If all goes according to plan, we should have a baby by next week. We've cleaned the house, packed the suitcase, and stocked up the kitchen for my mother-in-law, who will be helping in the transition.

We even had two birthday celebrations in the last two weeks. We decorated the dining room table, got out the "you are special" plate, did two scavenger hunts, went to Chuck-E-Cheese's, and went bowling.

Have you ever watched five kids under ten bumper-bowl? It looked more like pin-ball than bowling. You could read a small novel in the time it took Abe's (2) ball to travel the length of the alley.

Actually, I made a tactical mistake in birthday celebrating a few years ago. I set the bar too high. Now the kids expect decorations, scavenger hunts, and day-long celebrations. If we had been smart and just thrown a gift in a sack and stuck a candle in a Twinkie, things would be a lot easier around here five days out of the year…what am I saying? We're about to give birth to another birthday party.

Truth is…I like big celebrations. I want the birthday boy or girl to know from sun-up to sun-down that they are special, and that we are thankful that God placed them into our family, making it a day worth celebrating.

But, that's all behind us now, and everything is quiet again. There's nothing between us and baby Maggie…or Jacob. (Except several hours of excruciating pain and horror…it'll be rough on my wife too). I can't help but wonder what this next child will be like. I know he/she will bring more joy and consternation than I can imagine. I will teach him/her about God's love, and he/she will do the same for me.

I guess that's why I do the big birthday thing. These little humans are the best thing that ever happened to my wife and me. And that calls for more trips to Chuck-E-Cheese, the bowling alley, and whatever else I can concoct!

That's all the news from my house. We'll see what God brings our way.

Hey Dad, make sure you celebrate the kids in your life!

You 'da dad!

The Boy in the Box

Hey Dad,

It's been a busy couple of weeks at our house. In fact, I'm swamped. I have writing projects to finish up, a website that is in constant need of updating, and a mile-long list of odds and ends that need to be done before we hit the road in a couple of months.

In the midst of the busyness, I'm almost tempted to think that all the things I just mentioned "matter most." It sure feels like they're really important. I tell myself, "If I don't do these things, no one will...and if I don't, we won't have any income...and if I don't..." You know how the conversation goes.

You see, all the things I'm trying to get done ARE important...but they're not the MOST important. They're not even close.

Last weekend my wife brought home a Super Clearance Chair-in-a-Box. The jury is still out on the chair, but our little kids LOVE the box. Our youngest boys cut holes in it for doors and windows and attached a smaller box on top for a chimney. With the masterpiece complete, they carried it to their bedroom, and that night Ike (5) asked if he could sleep in it.

"Sure," I said, "but don't you think it's a little small?"

"No," he said, "I'll fit."

He gathered his blankets and a travel Lite-Brite toy for a nightlight, and then he slid through the door and pulled it shut. It was early, so I lay beside the box for a while and talked with Abe and Ike. Abe soon drifted off, and I lay there thinking about the boy in the box.

Ike is growing up fast and soon will be too big for boxes, silly faces, and innocent questions. Before I blink, he will be loading up his "stuff" and heading off to start a life of his own.

While I was thinking about that, a noise came from the box and a thin hand slid from the window opening and held up three fingers. It was the Wilson family signal for "I-Love-You." I held up three fingers toward the dark opening and whispered, "I love you, Ike."

Dad, that's what matters MOST; it always has. But if we're not careful, we'll trade it away for things that matter very little.

We need to remind each other that projects will come and go, hard-to-please clients will always be there, and the balance of the world does not depend on what we accomplish at work. What matters...I mean REALLY matters...is that little circle of people that we call our family.

So Dad, spend your time today on those people that matter most, or one day you'll wish you had.

You 'da dad!

The Fifth Dimension of Fathering

Hebrews 6:1-8

Hey Dad,

I just can't help it. I don't plan for it…or try to conjure it up, but for some unexplained reason, every once in a while, I enter some kind of Jules Verne fifth dimension of fathering and actually travel through time. It sounds weird, doesn't it?

Well, it happened again this week.

It was bedtime. I was sitting in the hallway reading about Megan floating away on a mattress in the great Johnstown Flood of 1889…when I got sucked through time and deposited into the future.

As I stood to say my last goodnight, I was an old man, and instead of reading to my children, I'd just finished a favorite book with my grandchildren. My children were all grown up and THEIR children were in their "old beds" listening to me read just like I did to their moms and dads.

My eldest son Ben, who was now a dad himself of several children, lay stretched out in the dim hallway remembering fondly the times he and his brothers and sisters listened to me read. From the look on his face, I knew that the memories he'd experienced as a boy felt comforting and reassuring now as a man.

The time travel didn't last long, and instead of tucking my grandchildren into bed, I kissed my own children goodnight and plopped into bed next to my wife.

Later on, as my bride was snoozing, I lay in the dark thinking about the future. What would MY kids tell THEIR kids about me (Granddad)? Would they recall listening to me read at night from the hallway, the backyard campouts in the cold, the canoe trips, the popcorn-filled video nights, and laughing around OUR table at our favorite restaurant?

Or, would they remember the things that I promised to do but didn't…or the things that I should've done, but for a hundred "legitimate" reasons, never got around to?

Let me ask you, Dad. What will your children tell your grandchildren about you? Will they tell about the family vacations you took, the board games you played at night, and the times you talked with them while sitting on the edge of their beds, or will they tell them that you were always too busy to do things like that?

So, Dad why don't you travel into the fifth fathering dimension for a moment and then do something with your children this week in light of your trip.

To infinity and beyond…you 'da dad!

Bubba Breaks Things

Hebrews 6:9-20

Hey Dad,

My son, Bubba, breaks things (not his real name). He's always broken things. From the moment he could le around, he's busted, dropped, or spilled things. That's just what he does.

I'm pretty sure there's some kind of genetic breaking gene or some other scientific explanation behind his ability.

I've tried to help him by warning him, "Bubba, be careful, you're going to break…(crack/smash/boom)…that."

Oh, he's remorseful and quick to ask forgiveness, but that doesn't change the fact that Bubba breaks things.

Unfortunately, I've labeled him as a "breaker." Just the other day, he dropped his little sister on her head (not as bad as it sounds)…for the second time in as many days, and I asked him, "Bubba, why is it that you always drop Maggie? None of the other kids drop Maggie. You've dropped her twice…why can't you be more careful…bla bla bla bla bla."

I wish I could say that was the first time I'd verbalized the "breaking label" for him. The truth is that the last couple weeks I've heard myself say more than once, "Bubba, you're always breaking things.…Why is it always you?"

I had labeled my son…and kids shouldn't be labeled. Labels are for cans of food, not kids. Labels hurt and are hard to lose. Bubba doesn't have a chance. His brothers or sister break something and they may be disciplined, but when he breaks something, I remind him about his label.

That was last week. I've determined to erase his label. I'm not going to say those mean, hurtful things anymore. In fact, I was doing something just yesterday, and I heard a crash right behind me and knew Bubba had upset something…breakable. You know what I did?

Nothing. I didn't even turn around. Since then, he's knocked over a few other things, and in my most loving voice I've said, "Bubba, clean it up…things like that happen." He'll probably drop his sister on her head again soon, but I won't look at him with my labeling eyes.

I'm not doing it because I think it will help him be more careful and change. He probably will always drop, spill, and break. But the only label he'll wear is one of a loved son.

How about you, dad? Do you have a child you've labeled? Maybe he/she wears the label of lazy, careless, slow, angry, foolish, difficult, trouble, unloving, or a hundred other labels dads have thought up. Well, it's up to you to de-label them.

You 'da dad!

Posi-labeling

Hey Dad,

Yesterday, I shared with you how my son, "Bubba" (name changed to protect the "guilty") breaks things and that I was going to try hard not to label him as a breaker…because labels are bad. Well, several of you wrote and reminded me that labels can also be good…and you're right. Giving a good label is called posi-labeling (short for positive labeling—I just made that up).

Posi-labeling is not a technique that manipulates kids into obeying or performing better; it's a way of conveying to your children that they are loved, liked, and affirmed. When you posi-label your child, you remind him that you have seen something in him that you like and reinforce something you want your children to believe about themselves.

One dad wrote in and shared that he tells his children often, "You are winners." I'm sure he doesn't say that so that they'll get good grades, go to Harvard, and graduate at the top of their class. I think this dad just wants his children to know that in his eyes and heart, they will always be winners.

You can bet that no matter what the son of that dad faces, he'll always remember, Dad thought I was a winner. That's the power of your words, Dad.

I was also reminded about the power of posi-labeling as I watched The Little Princess on DVD with my kids. At one point in the movie, Sarah (the little princess) was talking to Miss Minchin (the evil school mistress) and stated, "All little girls are princesses. Didn't your father ever call you a princess, Miss Minchin?"

The wicked Miss Minchin softened briefly, and the audience knew the answer—no, her father never called her a princess.

As I watched and thought about posi-labeling, I looked at my daughter and wondered if she felt like a princess. That night I made sure she knew she was, and would forever be, my princess.

Dad, It's not a one-time labeling thing. Positive labels must be applied over and over until they stick. So…why not join me in a posi-labeling crusade? Let's posi-label our kids as delightful, precious, winners, curious, wise, creative, or fun…and if you have daughters—princesses.

You 'da dad!

Just Waiting

Hey Dad,

No baby yet, but we're hoping that any minute the process will begin. In fact, I'm trying real hard not to ask my wife every time I pass her in the house, "Anything happening?"

I guess it will come when it comes. In the meantime, we've been getting ready. Most of the little projects to get done are checked off my wife's list, and I spent a good chunk of yesterday helping clean the house so it will be nice and tidy when the baby gets here.

It was spotless when I hit the hay, but I just know the kids will "unspotless" it within 20 minutes of waking up.

While I was vacuuming, I noticed the little bureau in the entry. Not that I hadn't noticed it before, but I had forgotten that I'd have some updating to do to it in a few days. You see, the names of all our children are scratched into its distressed finish.

I'm not sure why I carved the first name into the bureau, but in a few days, there will be another one to add.

As I thought about the bureau, I was also reminded about the glass birds sitting on our bedroom windowsill. Actually, they look more like 2" blobs of glass (red for girls/blue for boys) but they represent each of our children. When the sun shines through the window, they sparkle…and I smile when I see them.

It's funny—the traditions dads have to commemorate the birth of a new child. My friend Bob told me last weekend that he buys a special pocketknife, has the hospital sterilize it, and then uses it to cut the umbilical cord. Then he engraves it with the child's name and birth date and boxes it away until the day they get married. Cool.

That's what becoming a dad does to a guy. He goes from being a non-emotional, practical human being to a man who gets a lump in his throat the first time his child calls him "dad," walks three tottering steps, or announces loudly in a packed restaurant, "Daddy, I went poopy!"

That's why Bob does the pocketknife thing, why my brother-in-law purchases his wife a diamond to commemorate each birth, and why I scratch names in an old bureau.

That's FATHER POWER. And, Dad, you got the POWER.

You 'da dad!.

Eeyore No More

Hebrews 8:1-6

Hey Dad,

It's another blah day here in northern Indiana. It must be all that global warming that's making it so cold. I keep thinking that the sun's gotta shine and it's gotta get warmer one of these days, but it's just rainy and cold every day.

I think it's starting to affect my mood. I feel cold, gloomy, and Eeyorish inside. It doesn't help that every time I turn on the radio some expert is telling me that the economy will get worse, we're running out of fuel, the climate is changing, terrorists WILL get us, and pandemics are around every corner.

I'm telling you, the media is more poisonous to the average father than a truckload of rattlesnakes. The sludge they peddle causes us to doubt and worry and sucks the joy right out of our homes. Instead, we should trust God to meet our needs and enjoy our families today...because that's all we got. Because if anything is running out, it's time.

My prescription for a media-antivenom is...a campfire. We had one the other night. We had some scrap wood to burn so after it burned down we cooked hot-dogs, roasted marshmallows, and made s'mores. It didn't take all that much time, but something about the fire's warmth and smell slows us all down and highlights the joy of family.

A video night will do the same thing. Enjoy a fun family video (a double feature) or boardgame, apple cider, and popcorn. Better yet, make or order pizza, get some vanilla ice cream and toppings, fill the familyroom with pillows and blankets...put on your pjs, start a fire in the fireplace, and bask in the glow of God's goodness.

Because that's what it's all about...enjoying all that God has given you...today.

You are blessed, Dad, and nothing the media can dish out can ever take that away...just don't miss it by worrying about the future.

You 'da dad!
...thanks for noticing

Man's Greatest Fear

Hey Dad,

As I think about it, the most feared mammals on the earth are: 1) a hungry 30-foot great white shark, 2) an injured grizzly bear, 3) an angry bull elephant, and 4) a pregnant woman who is past her due date.

It's not that my pregnant wife, who is five days past her due date, has threatened to maim me if something doesn't happen soon, but I can tell she's a knot of anxiousness and emotion. (It could have something to do with the fact that we're leaving for a two-month RV trip in ten days.)

I feel my husbanding skills being tested and stretched. My manly, glass-half-full side wants to say, "Hey, God's timing is best. Let's just sit back and enjoy the ride. It'll be here when it gets here. Don't sweat it." But that kind of answer can elicit the grizzly bear reaction (if you know what I mean).

Instead of my everything's-going-to-be-all-right approach, my wife needs me to be understanding. I don't need to tell her about all the people I know who were two weeks overdue or how we should just be thankful for a healthy, normal pregnancy.

She really doesn't want me to say or solve anything. She just wants me to love her through the feelings of being overwhelmed and emotional and say, "There, there, I understand…go ahead and cry while I hold you."

Man, that's the kind of husband I want to be for my wife—not just for a few weeks before and after a baby is born, but for as long as we both shall live.

So would you pray for me as we wait for this slowpoke Wilson? My wife has mentioned before that she feels very needy of closeness with me after the baby comes. Pray that I'll be exactly what she needs…even if I don't get it.

You know, even if you're not married to a pregnant woman who is past her due date, your wife still wants (and needs) that kind of understanding from you.

I'll tell you what; I'll stop and pray right now for you, Dad. We need each other, and I appreciate your friendship.

You 'da dad!

The Eagle Has Landed!

Hebrews 9:1-10

Hey Dad,

The Eagle has landed...the bun is out of the oven...Elvis has left the building. Yes, after waiting for what seemed like an eternity, we are now the proud parents of a precious, pink-as-a-rose-bud, daughter.

Maggie Rose Wilson...7 lbs. 13 oz., 19 inches...blah, blah, blah...who am I kidding? You're a guy! You don't care about that stuff. Women, on the other hand, want to know every detail.

I was reminded just how different men and women are right after Debbie gave birth. I stepped outside the room for a minute as they were taking care of the aftermath. The mid-wife called out to me, "You should see this placenta. It's so healthy and beautiful."

"No thanks," I said, "I've seen my share of placentas." She had no idea that guys don't care a lot about placentas, and the word that comes to mind when I think of placenta is...gross.

That's because men and women are different.

Even while my wife was in labor, the midwife caressed Debbie's shoulders and stomach, offering comfort. I tried, but my hands just couldn't do it. I looked like I was waxing a car.

The midwife offered encouragement, and I gave advice about how to work through the pain. I'm just so...guyish.

The next morning as we talked about Maggie's birth, my wife said, "Just hearing the midwife tell me I was doing a great job in the midst of labor felt so good."

"Did you hear that, ?" God asked. "That's what your wife needs. She doesn't always need you to tell her how to cope with the tough situations that come, but she does need you to tell her she's doing a good job."

"You're right, God, but I'm a guy."

He didn't answer. I knew what I needed to do. Fortunately, I've had several opportunities to put into practice what I learned that morning. I've failed some, but if I want to love my wife...like I want to love my wife, I've got to keep trying.

And...so do you.

So start by telling your wife she's a great mom, and that you've got the best. You might even try waxing...I mean rubbing her shoulders tonight.

You 'da dad!

Worth Every Penny

Hebrews 9:11-15

Hey Dad,

God has graciously answered the prayers of so many of you, and little Maggie Rose is home from the hospital and doing well. She's not up to par yet, but she is light years ahead of where she was a week ago.

Thank you for lifting up our family before the Heavenly Father. It really meant a lot to all of us.

Now it's back to life as usual (besides the little mishap of identity theft, but that's another story). I have to admit the thought entered my mind last week—that kids ain't cheap.

On the way home from visiting Maggie at the hospital, the boys and I swung by Menard's to pick up a few supplies to build shelves in the garage. We hadn't been on the road ten minutes, when Abe (4) hollered, "I've got something in my eye." (It had something to do with the plywood above his head.)

Being a dad, I quickly replied, "Oh, you'll be fine."

Well, five hours later, he wasn't fine. His eye was red, swollen, and it hurt. I'd like to say I was the picture of concern and compassion, but all I could think was, "Oh great, I'll probably have to take him to the emergency room tonight…or worse yet, to some expensive eye specialist in the morning."

The good news is that we didn't have to since it was better the next day. The bad news is that this dad sometimes cares more about how much my kids cost than about them.

I looked at other examples of how expensive kids are to have. I looked at my big, ugly, full-sized van that gets 16 m.p.g., my bigger RV that gets 9 m.p.g., the fact that three of my six kids need expensive dental work, the almost empty gallon jug of apple juice that was full a few hours ago, and the empty toilet paper rolls that are piled up in the trash can next to the toilet like cord wood.

For a few brief moments, I was tempted to think that I am throwing my money away left and right…because of them. But then God whispered in my ear, "There's no better investment," and my heart was filled with gratitude.

Yes, it is true that kids cost money, but they're worth every penny. How about you, Dad? Feeling a little envious when a small sports car pulls up beside your dusty suburban? Do you fantasize about all the money you'd have if you didn't have children?

Take it from me—don't let yourself.

You and I have been blessed beyond measure if we have children. Consider it pure joy to be counted worthy to go broke for your children. There's no greater honor.

You 'da dad!

64

You're 1 Min. Thirty-Eight Behind

Hebrews 9:16-28

February 28

Hey Dad,

I want to share a marriage tip I picked up during the Winter Games. To be honest, it's been a tough couple of weeks in the Familyman marriage department. I'd like to say it was all 'her' fault...but I know the blame falls squarely on my shoulders.

I slumped around the house hardly able to motivate myself to do anything, let alone try to woo my wife. Even the Olympics were tarnished because of my mood. Then the light dawned as I watched a nameless Olympic cross country skier pumping hard and drooling like a hound dog on the trail.

The event was Nordic Combined. It 'combined' the odd events of cross country skiing and ski jumping. The Olympians jumped first and the lengths of their jumps decided the start times of the cross country race. So the guy who jumped the farthest got to start first. The second place jump was five meters behind the first so #2 started a few seconds AFTER the first place skier.

Most pathetic was that some of the best skiers started as much as TWO minutes behind the first place guy. One of the favorites botched the ski jump and had his start delayed by about a minute and a half. Amazingly...he caught up and won.

It wasn't a quick sprint to win...he just plugged away and eventually passed the leader. That night as I lay in bed next to my hurting wife, I figured I was about a minute and a half behind...but I was going to catch up.

The next day I woke up determined. I smiled more, snapped less, and let my wife talk. I didn't make up all the time immediately, but I made up a few seconds, and the next day I gained a few more. Over all, it took about five days to pull up by my wife's side...and yesterday...we both won.

Some would say, just don't let yourself get set so far back...but that's unrealistic. Truth is sometimes even Olympic champion husbands find themselves WAAYYYY BAACCK. Maybe that's where you are today.

Can I give you a little advice? Be patient. Don't be surprised by setbacks. Set your sites on the finish line...and start making up time.

There's an Olympian with a gold medal and a husband who is enjoying life with his wife who both know that it works.

I am that husband!

65

Choose Squishy

Hebrews 10:1-18

Hey Dad,

Everyone at the Wilson household is adjusting well to little Maggie Rose. I may be biased, but I think she's just about the cutest baby I've ever seen…believe me, we've had our share of ugly ones.

Maggie and my wife even made it to our first big homeschool convention this past weekend. I met a lot of fellow dads. I'm telling you, there is nothing better than encouraging each other in fathering.

Men slapped me on the back, smiled, and said, "You 'da dad, !" In fact, by the time the conference was over, I was flying high. Who wouldn't be?

Now that I'm home, things are different. My children have not once told me they appreciate me nor have they thanked me for the sacrifices I make for them each day.

Instead, Kat (7) cries and says, "You don't like me." Ike (4) yells for me to wipe his bottom, and last night, I took a squishy walk through Abe's (3) stomach contents.

I was deep in sleep when I heard "the sound" every parent hates.

"Oh crud," I thought, "not tonight."

As I walked down the hall, I felt wet, squishy spots on my bare feet.

Abe was standing outside his bedroom door heaving dinner on the floor when I got to him. Amazingly, the bed was clean (or so I thought), so I tucked him, only to dip my hand in a puddle of toxic ooze. Yum.

Well, I mopped it all up and went back to bed.

The next morning, Abe was up bright and early. There was not a "thank you" spoken or a "why don't you sleep in" encouraged. He wanted food.

I can see why some dads opt out of their fathering responsibilities. Who wouldn't choose being away from home where people appreciate you, pat your back, and give you raises, rather than at home where they throw up on the carpet, ask for everything and then say, "You don't like me"?

But here's the weird thing: only one of the choices matters. Unfortunately, we dads forget which one that is.

So let me remind you. Today, when you're given the choice between power lunches, a challenging task, and overtime…OR hyper kids, bedtime rituals, and squishy vomit on your feet…

…choose squishy.

You 'da dad!

A Bandless Band of Brothers

Hebrews 10:19-25

Hey Dad,

Looks like it's going to rain any minute. Got home in the middle of the night from speaking in Louisville, KY and got up at a normal time to pick up the Familyman Mobile that was in the shop having a clunk looked at so my brain is a little groggy – and rain sounds good.

Found out that the owner of the repair shop, Lee, is on the Familyman Team, and it's always great to meet fellow FM dads. Afterwards, I drove a few miles to dump the storage tanks and headed home. The air was heavy and fallish, making it a great time to 'ponder'.

I was thinking about the day that I walked down the aisle with my wife, specifically the moment I placed a shiny golden band on her finger and she did the same to me. As I reminisced, I said the words she had engraved on the inside of my ring and I felt…warm.

Then, I thought about my dad's wedding band that he cut off with a hacksaw because it was strangling his finger. He still wears it unrepaired just as he has my whole life. As a kid, I can remember looking at his hands and that silver band and feeling safe.

Last night, Chad, a dad in Louisville showed me his wedding band that had 'shrunk' on his finger looking like it might cut it off or turn it blue. "Why would a dad endure such discomfort for a wedding band?"

I guess I've been pondering wedding bands all week. I've noticed a lot of dads who don't wear wedding bands and wrote an email to a bunch of moms asking them what they thought about that and WOW…did they tell me what they thought.

What I thought was a simple question of 'why don't husbands wear their wedding rings' with a simple answer has turned out to be a question on which I still haven't come to a conclusion. I know there are safety reasons, religious reasons, swelling reasons, and some uncategorized reasons. Some make perfect sense to me and others…I don't know.

All I know is I can't imagine my wife, myself…or my dad without one. I'm not sure what it says or means if someone doesn't wear one…but it feels…warm to me and I would guess it feels safe to my children.

You 'da dad!

Big Glob of Poop

Hebrews 10:26-39

Hey Dad,

I just got back from cleaning up a big glob of kid poop off the bathroom floor. (Didn't your speech teacher tell you to start with an attention grabber?) My wife conveniently left for a meeting, leaving me with our two youngest. One slept; the other played, while I worked in my basement office. That's when I got the call.

"I went poopy. I went poopy..." Isaac shouted. He was still new at the bathroom thing and occasionally had...uh...problems.

I raced upstairs muttering angrily to myself, "Oh, Isaac!" I didn't like the tone of my voice, and I knew I had used it a lot lately. It was the tone that said, "Why'd you go and do that? You should know better...I'm disappointed in you."

It's during those times, when they've accidentally broken something, made a mess, or caused a big inconvenience, that they need my help and encouragement, but instead I offer disgust and disapproval.

Then, their eyes show fear and hurt...fear and hurt that I've caused.

Thankfully, I realized all of that as I ran up the stairs, and by the time I got to Ike, I was a changed man.

I stepped into the bathroom and was greeted by a fresh cow chip. Had I not needed to clean it up, I would have been impressed by the sheer size. He must have been storing up for a week.

Ike looked at me as if to say, "You're mad at me, aren't you?

"I'm not mad, Ike. It's OK. I'll get you all cleaned up. You've done great at learning how to go to the bathroom...and sometimes these things happen."

You should have seen the change that came over his face. It was OK that he had failed. I was not going to yell, and he didn't have to feel bad.

You know dad, your children need your acceptance, when they succeed AND when they fail. In fact, they need it even more then. They need you to hug them when they get a low grade on a report card, break one of your tools accidentally, announce that they have to go the bathroom right in the middle of something important...or leave a pile of poop on the floor.

So, surprise the socks off your kids the next time they fail (you shouldn't have to wait too long), smile, and tell them it's OK and that you love them more than anything.

You 'da dad!

Dream BIG!!!

Hebrews 11:1-12

Hey Dad,

If you have a dream quit putting it off and DO IT!! Let me tell you about Marty. Marty talked to me while I was speaking in Florida about five years ago. As we talked, he told me that he travels a lot and is away from his family several days a week.

"Just this past week, "he said, "I found a note tucked into my wallet from my seven-year-old son." He paused as though he was looking at it in his mind. "It said, Dad, please come home."

"I know I'm blowing it, Todd," he said, "but I don't know what to do."

"That's easy," I said. "Quit."

He looked at me like I had worms hanging from my nose. "Quit? But I don't have another plan."

"Well, don't keep doing something you know to be wrong just because you don't have another plan." I didn't say it, but anyone would quit his job if he could step right into another well-paying job.

"Do you know how scary that is?" he asked.

"Oh, I know it's scary, Marty...but you need to do it."

"But what will I do?"

"I don't know...but do it anyway."

That was five years ago. Four years ago Marty came up to me again. He was still working at the job he had the year before but knew he should quit.

"Then do it, Marty. Time's running out."

"Do you know everyone else I ask say I'd be crazy to leave this great job?"

"Everyone else is wrong!!!" I said a little more urgently, "Just do it."

"But it's scary."

"Of course it's scary...but do it!!"

That was four years ago. Three years ago he came up again and things had not changed. He was hesitant and I encouraged him to quit.

That was three years ago. I haven't seen him since but I know he still has the same type of job. And he has lost five more years of his family's life.

Here's the deal...five years turns into a lifetime just like (snap) that. That's why I'm pleading with you to DO IT!!! Don't put off your dream because it probably won't get any easier. Just do it. Quit looking at the size of the giant and remember the size of your God. Do it!!!! Quit worrying about what might happen and find out what WILL happen. Do it!!!!

You 'da dad!

Avoiding a Blue Hawaii

Hebrews 11:13-16

Hey Dad,

Had a great time at winter family camp last week, but now it's time to trade our mukluks for swim fins because we're headed for Hawaii, where I'll be speaking at the state homeschool convention.

I know...rough life. Hey, someone has to encourage those folks out on that lonely island. Might as well be me.

Here's the scary part...we're taking the whole family. That's right all 10 of us. It should be fun, right? Should be a once in a lifetime experience, right? Should be a tropical paradise, right? Then, why do I feel so nervous?

BECAUSE WE'RE TAKING THE WHOLE FAMILY!!!!!!!

We decided that if we were going to go, we were all going to go. Yes, it will be hard, but if we wanted easy, we wouldn't have had kids to begin with.

But all that lofty talk doesn't curb the uneasy feeling that's been growing inside me. I know that we're headed into turbulent waters. After all, we're taking 8 kids on a 6000-mile, 18-hour trip, and I'm afraid the trip will be ruined because of me...and my stinking attitude.

Hey, I'm pumped right now. I've been playing Hawaiian music and even taught my family the Hukilau Song. But I know how it's going to go...

We'll wake up next Tuesday morning and things won't go as planned. Someone will throw up, forget to pack their shoes, or go to the bathroom in their pants. We won't get out on time, will be rushed through breakfast, or the flight will be delayed.

I'll be a rock of patience and understanding...for ONE TIME. But if it continues, I just can see myself getting bothered, short with my family, and ruining our tropical paradise.

It's happened before, and I'm scared to death that it will happen again.

That's why I need you. Can you pray for me and hold me accountable? You don't have to pray that everything will go easy and that my family will skip though the airport singing the Hukilau Song. Instead, pray that I would be a ROCK of patience and understanding. You know why?

Because I'm 'da dad!!!

And so are you. You may not be headed to Hawaii, but maybe things have been a little tense around your house. I'm praying for you right now...that you'll be a rock of patience and understanding.

You know why?

Because you 'da dad!!! Or as they say on the island, 'Oe na Makuakane!'

Aloha!

Beware of Urgent Reef

Hebrews 11:17-31

Hey Dad,

"Hoist the main sail .... swab the deck...lift the yardarm...raise the mizzenmast!"

This is my scurvy, sailor-side talking. I can smell the sea and feel the wind on my face as I man the ship's wheel while the captain, the Captain, calls out orders from above.

You see, we've just entered some choppy fathering waters. They are filled with dads who have run aground on that cursed Urgent REEF...reef...reef (echo into the distance).

The thing about Urgent Reef is that it seems so, well, urgent. I know in my life, we have less than three weeks until we all pile into the new Familyman Mobile for a three-month tour of duty. It was only yesterday that I got the remaining seats bolted in. I haven't checked out all the major systems, and I haven't even started the RV in five months! Did I say we leave in three weeks?!

The weather has been lousy, with snow and cold served up daily. In fact, I should be working on it right now; but here's the kicker: it's my son Abe's birthday today (7). I already took him to McDonald's for a birthday breakfast—and I'm supposed to take him and his brothers to a pizza/laser-tag place for lunch—and then he'll probably want to watch a fun video tonight and I have an RV to get ready!

"Steady as she goes, Mr. Familyman," The Captain calls.

"I know, sir, but I'm running out of time."

"Steady, lad. Keep your course straight. Take care of the important, and leave the urgent to me."

"I know, but I don't have time for birthday stuff!"

"Mr. Familyman, stay your course, or you'll run aground Urgent Reef. Enjoy your son's special day and forget the urgent, or I'll clap you in irons."

"Yes, sir."

So, I guess I gotta go. The RV stuff can wait, but my son's seventh birthday can't.

Before I sign off, let me warn you about Urgent Reef coming up on your port side. Don't let the tax season, a busy time at work, or some consuming project keep you from doing what's most important today.

If you listen to the Captain, I'm sure you'll hear him say, "Steady as she goes, lad."

You 'da dad!

Fill the Hole

Hey Dad,

The weather's been wonderful here in Northern Indiana. Not as nice as Hawaii, but nicer than Maine where my son Sam (14) and I were this last weekend.

When I got home after being gone four days, my wife reminded me that while I was gone I left a dad-shaped hole behind.

I sometimes forget that. In fact, sometimes I wonder if my children even appreciate anything I do for them. I feel that way right now, especially with the warmer weather, because I don't know how it is at your house, but at my house, the warm weather brings out the pigs...my pigs.

The way I calculate it, for every 10 degrees of temperature increase, the amount of junk, toys, and stuff in my yard increases by a factor of 10. Yesterday, it was 70 degrees and there was so much stuff strewn around the yard that it looked like a tornado had gone through a trailer park.

The bean that tipped the beans is when I spent an hour putting stuff away and minutes later they blew in and got it all out again.

So it's not hard to see how a dad like me could wonder if my kids would even miss me if I was buried under an avalanche of junk.

Then my wife saved the day.

"While you were gone," she said, "Ike (9) walked into our room and said, "Doesn't it just feel so sad without Dad? I feel like I could burst into tears any minute."

The words sounded good. My son needs me and feels the dad-shaped hole that I leave when I am gone. Somehow that makes the piles of junk not seem so bad.

The truth is, Dad, that you too leave a dad-shaped hole when you're gone. Your children may not seem to appreciate you, but they miss you when you're not there. But here's the deal. I know that if I had been gone longer, my son would have missed me LESS, not more. That's what happens. Some dads are gone on business so often and for such long periods of time that their families no longer 'feel' the hole.

Now THAT makes me want to burst into tears.

So Dad, fill the hole.

You 'da dad!

Not-So-GREAT Expectations

Hey Dad,

Gotta make this quick. I'm headed to North Carolina tomorrow to speak and then it's a dash to get things finished up on the Familyman Mobile. We hit the road next Saturday. I've finished lots of my to-do list, but each one I knock off reminds me of another I forgot to write down.

For your viewing pleasure, I recorded a little tour of the BEAST so you can get an idea of how tight it will be for ten people over the next month and a half, which leads me to the reason for my writing you today. Will you pray for this Familyman?

I just know that how it all turns out depends on my attitude. The thing is, I have expectations. I'd like to think it's all going to be fun and games...or at least pleasant. Yet, it seems that on the road it rarely is. Conflicts and bickering creep in over seemingly insignificant disputes...like, He's using MY blue Lego shield. In fact, just moments before recording the Familyman Mobile tour, I had one of those...incidents occur.

I try to be patient but it doesn't last, and then I freak and get all bent out of shape, pout, and let them know how disappointed I am that they've ruined EVERYTHING!!! Sound fun?!

Would you pray that I would leave the expectations behind and enjoy the time I get to spend with my family...no matter what happens?

I'll pray right now that you'll do the same, because it doesn't matter if you're in an RV or your home, being a dad ain't easy.

You 'da dad!

Fathering Vertigo

Hebrews 12:4-17

Hey Dad,

The Familyman-mobile is on the launch pad and preparing for lift off. For those of you who are new to this whole Familyman thing, every year for about 3 months, my entire family crams into a 30-foot RV to travel and speak across the country encouraging dads and moms.

There's a lot to get ready. Getting the RV road worthy is an undertaking in itself, but there is also a ton of other details to take care of before leaving. All that to say…we are in super-busy mode around here. My wife and I are running from one task to another as the clock ticks for departure 13 days from now.

One of the dangers of being busy is a natural dad phenomenon known as Fathering Vertigo. Vertigo is the sensation of being unable to distinguish which way is up. Pilots sometimes experience it when surrounded by clouds. Somehow their brain gets disoriented, and they think they're upside down. If they rely on their senses and not their instrument panel, it can cause them to nose-dive right into the earth.

Fathering Vertigo occurs most often in busy conditions. The busy dad loses all sense of what's important and what isn't. And, here's the danger; he might inadvertently pile drive his family right into the ground.

I've got a case of it now. In my mad dash to get ready, I've lost sight of what's really important…especially with my children. I noticed it recently with my son Ben (13). He has the propensity to get extremely focused on whatever it is he's interested in at the time, whether it's details about the Civil War, building something in the garage, or designing a computer game.

The thing is, in all my running, fixing, and gathering, I don't have time to hear yet another lengthy description of…whatever. Usually, he starts talking and I half-heartedly listen until he gets the idea that I don't care and walks away.

Yesterday, he was rattling off a dozen details all at once, and I answered dumbly, "I agree." He laughed knowing that I hadn't listened at all…but I didn't laugh. Later, I rehearsed in my mind how many times I've blown him off lately. I've shown him not that I don't care about "whatever" but that I don't care about him. If I'm not careful, I might crash our relationship.

But that's why we dads have each other. We can help each other know which way…is up. I know what I need to do. I need to listen to my son, even in my busyness today.

How about you, Dad? I know you're busy (we all are). Have you been suffering from a touch of Fathering Vertigo? Don't rely on your feelings. Do what you KNOW to be right!

You 'da dad!

Me and My Purple Ribbon

Hebrews 12:18-24

Hey Dad,

Yesterday, I got another email about a dad who has had his hours at work cut back. Things were already financially tight—this doesn't help. He's not alone.

Dads all across the country and even the world are struggling to make ends meet. They worry about mortgages, car payments, and how to pay the bills. The experts keep shouting doom and that "we haven't seen the worst yet." And to tell you the truth, I've started feeling a little of that doom seep into my normally positive outlook on life.

So what's a Dad to do?

Actually, a few minutes ago—I didn't know, but my daughter Maggie just reminded me about 10 seconds ago. She's in my office because she's being disciplined. Just a minute ago, she pointed to a thin stack of purple award ribbons on my bookshelf.

"What are those?" she asked with teary eyes.

I started to brush her off so I could finish this letter but instead reached up and pulled them down.

On each ribbon in gold letters, it reads FOR THIS I HAVE JESUS.

I was stunned by the instantaneous memory that accompanied the ribbons. Fourteen years ago, I was in a terrible car wreck—crushed face, legs, feet, and a metal halo screwed into my skull. In the days following the wreck, JK (an old time friend of the family) game me one of those purple ribbons. I don't think he explained it or gave me a pep talk—just handed me the ribbon. But it was enough. I posted it on my bedframe to serve as a reminder that Jesus was enough during the hard days. And you know what—He was. Holding the purple ribbons in my hand now, I know that He still is—and He will take care of you and me, Dad, I promise.

So, in light of all the economic turmoil and predictions—I'll just keep being a dad. I'll get a video from the library to watch with my kids, pop popcorn, wrestle on the floor, play games, have pillow fights, and hold my woman in my arms and tell her how much I love her.

Go and do the same.

You 'da dad!

Revenge of the Dad

Hebrews 12:25-29

Hey Dad,

I just had to write while the iron is hot. It's therapeutic for me to blab to 15,000 dads that my children are—how do I say this gently?—PIGS!! Our children do chores, and they have responsibilities. We train them, we dole out consequences when they don't do a job well, we work on specifics; and still, they're PIGS!!

The mess that nine people can create is overwhelming at times. We can work all day cleaning up one area, and then, voila!, like magic, it's trashed again within about 13 minutes.

So I've decided that instead of banging my head against the wall and lamenting this fact, I'm going to—plot my revenge. Yes, sir, I'm not going to get mad, I'm going to get EVEN [add maniacal mad-scientist laugh here]!

Here's what I've planned so far: First, I have to wait about 20 years until they're all grown up and out of the house. Then, I'll go to each of their houses, starting with the oldest, and working my way down from there.

After a few minutes of light conversation, I'll say I have to go to the bathroom. Once there, the revenge will begin as I take a perfectly neat tube of toothpaste and squeeze it all over the edges of the sink and then, of course, leave the cap off for them to find—behind the toilet.

Then, I'll do my business, not even trying to hit the toilet and, for good measure, I'll pull off every towel they own from the towel bars and wad them up on the floor.

Man, this is good!

Later, when I know no one is looking, I'll take an entire package of Ritz crackers from the kitchen cupboard, crush them in my hand, and sprinkle them all over the floor. Then, I'll take a jar of peanut putter and scoop out a big glob with my fingers, smear the entire outside of the jar, put it back in the cupboard and, of course, leave the lid off for them to find—behind the toilet.

For my entire visit, I'll go from room to room making messes just like they used to make.

But…this is the weird part. I'm beginning to realize that the more messes I make in their house, the more saddened I'll be that they're no longer making messes in my house. I'll hate having a spotlessly clean house all the time.

I need to stop and think about that for a while.

Talk about irony. The very things that drive us dads crazy now will be the things we'll miss the most later.

With all that said, my children are still pigs; but somehow just talking to you about my revenge makes me feel better. And, it's reminded me of what really matters.

Dad, if your children do something that really bugs you, plot a little revenge now, and maybe things will look a little different when you're done.

You 'da dad!

Sand 'da Floor

Hebrews 13:1-14

Hey Dad,

Not much happening around the Wilson house this week. There was the lice scare, but I think we're out of the woods on that one. We took the kids to the dentist yesterday—no cavities. And Abe (2) has gone more than 14 hours without getting into serious trouble.

There is one thing that has gnawed away at my insides for the last few months—an item on my wife's to-do list.

Back in September, while Debbie was away at a ladies' retreat, I had the bright idea of pulling up the carpet to expose the beautiful 100-year-old wood floor. Instead, I ripped up the carpet, exposing the 100-year-old, beat up, mis-matched, crud-coated floor.

Since then, my wife has had one thought on her mind...rent a floor sander and tackle the job. Of course, I wouldn't let her do the job herself. She is six months pregnant and is a month or two too far along to be operating a 150-lb. drum sander. That means I have to do it. And I don't want to. It will be messy and involved, and I just know it won't go smoothly.

The last several weeks I've been putting her off with all kinds of excuses, but in the back of my head God keeps whispering, "Sand the floor." At least I think it's God. It could be Mr. Miyagi from "Karate Kid."

I'm fighting it tooth and nail...but I know my wife would love it if I rented the sander and did it...on the other hand, it really isn't all that bad...yeah, but it would make my wife feel loved...but there are other projects on my list that I need to get at before winter sets in...but they're MY projects, not hers.

Really the choice is simple: sand the floor and prove that I care more about my wife's needs than mine or...what was the question again?

Well, dad, I guess my mind's made up. We'll call the rental place and see if they have a sander available (sigh).

How about you? Has your wife been asking you to do something around the house? (Does a one-legged duck swim in a circle?) Prove your love once again. Get out the tools, flex your muscles, and tackle it.

No excuses.

You 'da dad!

A Triple-Ker-ching Bar of Soap

Hey Dad,

I used to watch The Woodwright's Shop on PBS. The guy was amazing. He could take a log and, with a few old tools, turn it into a piece of furniture. I thought it was because of the tools he used, but now I'm convinced that it's because he's good...real good. I know, because I've tried to duplicate his efforts, and so far, I've managed to turn a log into...firewood.

The same principle applies to fathering. It isn't so much the fathering tools that matter; it's learning to use the tools that we have.

Take last night for example. While my wife ran errands, I picked up some of the mess that we had created in the short time she was gone. As I dumped a pile of girls' stuff into the girls' room, the mirror over my daughter Katherine's desk caught my eye. We had recently hung it, and as I pictured my daughter sitting in front of it admiring her beauty (as girls often do), an idea struck me.

With father-like stealth, I went to the bathroom, picked up a bar of soap from the shower stall, and returned to the mirror, where I soaped the letters SHMILY on the upper edge. Thinking I had done good, I went to the bathroom mirror and wrote the same...and then I wrote it on my wife's dresser mirror. I returned the bar of soap and went about my business as usual.

An hour or two later, I was reading the Bible with my little boys when Katherine stuck her head in the bedroom door and said, "What's SHMILY?"

I looked up, smiled, and then explained that it stands for See How Much I Love You. She blushed and left the room. Ker-ching!

Later, as I sat at the computer, my wife came up and put her arm around me and asked what made me put the SHMILY on her mirror.

"Because it's true." I said. Double ker-ching!!

The cool thing is that they'll leave that little message up for a long time...and each time they see it, they'll be reminded that I love them. Triple ker-ching!!!

All from a bar of soap. Now that's a good investment.

So, Dad, let me encourage you to slink into the bathroom, get a bar of soap, and let those people in your life See How Much You Love Them.

You 'da soap totin' dad!

Snap!

Hey Dad,

This is going to be short and maybe not so sweet. It's rainy and kind of dreary today. Kind of matches my mood. I feel sobered. I think it's partially due to the fact that my Uncle Jerry died last week. We were at his funeral on Tuesday, and not only did I feel that lump listening to his grown children talk about their dad, but I also imagined my children up their talking about me some day. Then, I got this email when I got home...

Dear Todd,

My husband has been receiving your newsletters for some time now and has really enjoyed them. Many times he's read them out loud to me. On May 18th he was killed in a violent suicide bombing while in Afghanistan. I just wanted you to know how much your ministry meant to him, and to our family. He was the ultimate "Family Man". He was a wonderful husband, an awesome dad to our 5 children, an honorable military officer, and a man who loved the Lord above all else. I don't understand why God took him, but I know for sure that he is walking those streets of gold and serving our Lord Jesus.

...My oldest son was deployed to Iraq when this happened, and they brought him home, and put him on the rear detachment so he doesn't have to go back.

Thank you for your ministry. You do make a difference!
Many Blessings,
Connie

Here's the deal, Dad. All this Familyman stuff can end, just like that (snap). Even last night as my kids were playing volleyball, a mom told us that she had been watching five kids for another couple whose husband was dying in the hospital. She whispered so their children wouldn't hear, "He probably won't be coming home ever." (SNAP!)

So my fellow dad, if you're in a funk...get over it. If you've been working too many hours...stop. If you've been too busy to go on a bike ride, camp out, or just about anything else...shape up. You know why? (SNAP!!!!!)

You 'da dad!

I Hate Talking That Talk

Hey Dad,

I don't know about you, but sometimes I hate talking to my wife. Now don't get me wrong. I love talking to my wife. I love it when we dream together about future plans, ideas, and possibilities. I love sitting across the table from my bride when she smiles and sparkles with excitement. I'm telling you, that energizes me and makes me feel like an invincible team of ONE.

That's not the kind of talking I hate.

The kind of talking I hate is the kind where she talks about how we're failing as parents, letting our children down, need to work harder, are lazy in our discipline, and are about as spiritual as a lump of dirt.

Hey, I'm a glass half-full kind of guy. I like to think positive, hear good reports, dream, plan, and imagine...not dwell on the negative, failures, and inadequacies.

Some would say I'm an unrealistic, rose-colored glasses-wearing freak who lives in a dream world and thinks that if I ignore the problems they'll just...disappear.

To that nay-sayer (who sometimes is my wife), I just like to say, "You're right."

I am that way. I do hope that it will all go away. I get tired of working harder, having to be more diligent, and admitting that I'm not always doing a very good job. But the truth that hunts me down is...I'm 'da dad.

I must look at the glass the way it is. If it's half-full or half-empty, the truth is...it's not full. There's work to do, and I need to lead the charge. I need to gather the kids and say, "You guys have not been obeying lately...and it's my fault, because I've allowed you to disobey. Today we're going to start again."

I don't like doing that. I'd rather rent a family video and eat buttery popcorn. But, I'm 'da dad and my family needs me to 'work on that important stuff' as much as they need family video and popcorn nights.

So my fellow dad, as much as you may not like talking with your wife (about that kind of stuff), keep talking. Take off your rose-colored glasses, take a good, long, realistic look at your family, and then saddle up and lead the charge. You know why? Because...

...You 'da dad!

PS—One more thought...now have a family video popcorn night (extra butter).

That Lip Thing

Hey Dad,

I wish God had put some kind of indicator light on dads to show others when they're getting mad. It would be so simple and non-threatening.

"Dad, how 'bout I come back later? I can see that your anger indicator is at a level two."

My kids know when I'm mad because I do that "lip thing." I call it "that lip thing" because my wife responded the other day, when I was obviously mad at her, "I don't like when you do that 'lip thing.'"

I guess I have this habit of biting the left side of my lower lip when I am irritated. I don't know when I started doing it, but apparently I'm doing it more and more.

In fact, I was thinking about it last night around 3:30 in the morning when I couldn't sleep. I bit my lip just to make sure I knew what they were talking about. When I did, I heard myself think really loud, I hate when I do that lip thing.

The more I thought about it, I realized that I use the "lip thing" as a weapon.

Here's how it works:

My wife innocently asks me if I mind watching the kids while she runs an errand, right when I'm busy doing...something for me.

"Sure," I answer quietly. But then I flash her the "lip thing," so that she'll know I'm bothered by her request.

Need another example? I'm busily typing away at my computer and my daughter asks me to help her type up another pet store poster. I look at her and do the "Lip thing." She gets the picture and walks away, knowing dad cares more about work than he does about her.

All that went through my head last night. That's why I decided to try to break the "lip thing" habit. Already this morning, I've counted about 38 times that I've bit my lip and then quickly released it.

But I'm going to beat it!

How about you, Dad? Do you do something to let those around you know how annoyed you are? Maybe you run your fingers through your hair, sigh loudly, tap your feet, cross your arms, tighten your fist...or do that "lip thing."

Really, it's an effective non-verbal weapon and, as one woman said, "it isn't very nice."

So here's a challenge—the next time you feel yourself doing that...that...'thing', stop.

You 'da dad!

Big Scary Question

Hey Dad,

Have you ever been faced with a question you needed to ask but were afraid of the answer? I've got one of those questions to ask of my children—but I'm scared.

I'm not sure how the topic came up this past weekend while I was in Jacksonville, FL, but it did. I was minding my own business talking to a large group of men when I suddenly found myself relaying a story that a fellow dad had emailed to me in the last year.

The fellow dad told how he called his kids together and asked them to go on a little scavenger hunt and bring him what they thought was his most valued possession. He relayed how he was sure they would bring him his Bible or a family photo but was blown away when instead one child brought him the TV remote control and the others brought him other items that revealed where he spent most of his time.

I shared the story with the guys to encourage them to take a look at where they spend their time, not really thinking that I was speaking to myself. Jump forward a few hours 'til later when I was talking to a surfer-pastor who said, "Dude" in every sentence. We talked about ministry and how God was using him, complete with all his rough edges and tattoos. That's when he looked down at his little daughter and said to me, "Hey, dude, just ask my daughter right here what she thinks is most important to me." "I'm not going to ask her," I responded, knowing the answer might be a little awkward.

With self-assurance and a smile on his face he said, "OK, then I'll ask her."

And he did.

The little blonde-headed girl listened to the question and then without a second's pause said sweetly, "Work."

Out of the mouths of babes. I'm sure Mr. Surfer-Pastor went home thinking about what his daughter said more than what I had shared in my seminar.

And so have I.

Since then, I've thought about the answers my children might give—and it scares me. I'm afraid they'll say, "The RV, your projects, or—" I can't say it—"Familyman Ministries."

Dad, I know what's most important to me—and those things aren't. But the real test to see if what I know matches up with what I live comes by asking—The Big Scary Question!

I know what I need to do. Dude, do the same.

You 'da dad!

Fatherus Americanus Habitat

Titus 1:5-16

March	18

Hey Dad,

You know if someone did a documentary on the life of the typical American dad (fatherus americanus), his natural habitat would certainly not be a furniture store.

In fact, I can hardly say "furniture store" without a strong gag reflex. Yet that is where I spent the better part of the day last Saturday.

At one point, while my wife looked at every swatch of fabric known to modern man, I slipped away to stretch my legs and observe other fathers out of their natural habitats. Interestingly enough, their conversations were similar to the one my wife and I were having.

"I like this," one man said.

"That's the first one you looked at," his wife countered.

"You mean you want to buy one today?" another dad said, obviously bored to the point of death.

"YES! We're going to get it today," she fired back.

One dad held a pillow in each hand for his wife to examine. I could tell by the look on his face that he just wanted her to pick one…any one.

Just then, a dad carrying an infant car seat caught my attention. He walked in with a smile on his face, set the baby down, and asked for a tape measure.

Wow! Now that's a good husband, I thought. He cares about what's important to his wife. Then I discovered his true motives. With the tape measure in hand, he whirled around and held it up to the cavernous opening of a TV cabinet.

"Oh," he said in disappointment. "It's only 62 inches wide…our TV is 66 inches."

As I walked around, I felt like I was in some kind of bizarre zoo where the camels were housed in the penguin exhibit. This is wrong, I thought. This is not my natural habitat!

Then it hit me like a full-sized sectional couch…this is exactly where I belong—not necessarily in furniture stores, but alongside my wife, protecting her, enjoying her, and involving myself in what's important to her, because she's important to me. That's what all wives want—and most fail to receive.

So…I marched back to the swatch table and involved myself in fabric picking…because I'm 'da husbandus supremus.

Dad, I'm just betting there's something your wife would love for you to be involved in, like re-doing a child's bedroom, putting up shelves in a closet, or talking about parenting issues. Let me encourage you to jump in there and make it your habitat.

The Lesson of the Cucumber Tulip

Titus 2:1-15 (pay attention to vs. 6) | **March** **19**

Hey Dad,

I want to share a story with you that I heard this past Sunday. Actually, it was the "rest of the story," shared after the service by our guest speaker, Bud. During the sermon, he told how he and his wife had stopped at a house while on a walk to check out a somewhat rare Cucumber Tulip tree. The owner of the tree eagerly talked about it and about his life. But it wasn't until after church that I learned the lesson of the Cucumber Tulip. Around the lunch table, Bud shared how the guy they had been talking to suddenly burst into tears and told them that he should be dead right now.

Bud went on to relay the old man's story of how one day, as a child, he neglected to do one of his chores, and how furious his dad became with him. As a punishment, he was not allowed to go with his father and five brothers to town for a soda later that day, and watched as they drove down the road without him.

Minutes later, while still in sight, there was a terrible accident. The old man, who was then a small boy, ran to the gory scene of the accident to find that all five of his brothers had been killed and that his father had a broken neck. When they attempted to move him, he also died. I'll never forget Bud's observation: "That man carried the guilt and grief for 50 years because his dad left mad and hadn't restored his relationship with his son."

I've thought about that since then and wondered how often I get mad, hurt feelings, and then leave without restoring the relationship. I guess I sometimes assume that I'll be able to "make up" later. After hearing Bud's story, I know that isn't always the case.

So, Dad, learn the lessons of the Cucumber Tulip, the little boy who would become an old man, and the power of an unmended relationship. Let me encourage you, if you have some unfinished business with a child—or your wife—to make it right, today! You don't know what might happen just down the road. You need to keep relationships right, because no amount of time can heal a broken father/child relationship.

You 'da dad!

His, Mine, and Ours

Hey Dad,

I've been thinking about girls lately…no, not that kind…but the daughter variety, especially my daughters Katherine and Maggie Rose. I see their sweet smiles and how much they love their dad, but I know how delicate that relationship is and how easily I can blow it.

Boys are different. They need their dad's involvement and love…but they're boys. Girls are like…miniature females complete with a truckload of emotional needs. Emotional needs that we must fill…or someone else will.

It's not a new thought to me. For a while now I've sensed something that's wrong with a lot of dad/daughter relationships. I've heard many teenage girls mention that their relationships with their dads aren't very good.

Then I had a conversation a week ago with a guy at church whose family works with teenage girls. Speaking up front he mentioned that many of the girls are struggling in their relationships with their dads.

My 'this-is-important' sensor sounded and later I asked him about it.

He answered, "Yeah, most of them feel like they can't talk to their fathers or that their relationship isn't good."

"The girls you work with come from Christian families, don't they?" I asked.

He looked me straight in the eyes, and I could tell he was about to say something important. "They're the cream of the crop," he said. "Their families read the Bible, memorize scripture, and do all the right things."

I stood there for a moment and a wave of despair mixed with outrage came over me. "It's the dad's fault, isn't it?" I mused.

Yep was his only response.

Since then, I've thought more about the interaction with my girls. I noticed how curt I sometimes am, brushing them off or harsh with my looks…then I reminded myself that it's this dad's fault.

You know, Dad, all those emotional daughters who jump ship, flip out, or walk away for some unknown reason feel distant from their dads. They want a good relationship…but have given up and moved on.

You know whose fault it is?

Yep.

His, mine, and ours. Our daughters need us. They need to be treated tenderly, spoken to gently, listened to, and loved…really loved. I don't think it's really that hard…we just need to do it.

So why not do some of that dad-kind of loving today? Purpose to tell your daughters they're beautiful, give them a real heartfelt hug, or buy a little 'something' for them. And most of all let them see you enjoying them.

You 'da dad!

Life is Beautiful

1 Timothy 1:1-7

Hey Dad,

I don't know about you, but I'm feeling a little bushed. I got back late after a speaking engagement and head out again today for Flint, MI for another late night of speaking. It doesn't help that my kids came into my room about every 45 seconds last night.

First, it was my daughter Maggie with some kind of leg cramp. I massaged it out and sent her back to her room...only for her to return a half hour later (just when I fell asleep).

"It still hurts," she said...or I think she said that.

I massaged it again and said (not so much out of pity and concern but out of annoyance), "Just get in bed with us."

I remembered her taking up a lot less room the last time she joined us, but this time I felt trapped between her and my wife, unable to roll over. After an hour of feeling like a mummy, I got up, grabbed a pillow, and flopped down on the couch in our bedroom but not before I stumbled around looking for a blanket...which I never found.

So for an hour, dressed only in my skivvies and a t-shirt, I shivered myself to sleep...only to be awakened by 3-year-old Cal who was prancing around like a flamenco dancer in pain, "I've got to go to the bathroom." For a brief moment I considered letting him go in his pajamas but knew that was not a good idea.

He trotted off to bed and I went back to my shivering sleep on the couch, only to find one-year-old Jed standing beside me with his head resting on my back. If I hadn't been so delirious, I would have hollered. Instead I scooped him up, along with my pillow, and thought I'd take him back to his bed and sleep with him in his nice, warm bed.

I tossed him in his bed only to find that my 10-year-old son Ike was sleeping there for who knows why...and I wasn't about to climb up into his toy-filled bunk bed. So finding the only bed available, Jed and I slipped under Maggie's pink-flowered comforter for a final few minutes of slumber.

While I lay there, I admit that I thought about how nice it would be to have kids who didn't need so much attention. And then I thought about how one day not too far out in the future I would have children that didn't need so much attention...and how terrible it would be.

And with that thought I drifted off to sleep...only to be awakened thirty minutes later by children chasing each other, screaming, and running laps through the house.

Life is beautiful, and I'm glad I'm a dad...but man, I'm tired.

You 'da dad...enjoy it today.

To Battle!!!!!

Hey Dad,

There's just something about boys and their need to kill, maime, and pillage. In fact, just three seconds ago as I began this sentence, I heard something wooden fall down the steps.

Thinking it was something pulled off the stairway banister and hard to replace, I called out blindly, "What was that?"

The sweet little voice of my son Cal (3) called out, "My weapon."

"Your what?" I asked again.

"My weapon," he repeated. I knew then that it was either a wooden sword or gun, both of which we have a large supply.

Now some moms reading this might be shocked by the male's God-given interest in 'doing battle,' but you can't fight it. Actually, this is a great lead-in to sharing with you my first paintballing experience from this past weekend.

I was asked to speak to a small, men's paintball retreat in Ohio. So my sons Ben (16), Sam (14), and I packed our greenest clothes and anticipated a weekend of blasting others and each other. On the 5 hour drive there, we wondered out loud how much it would hurt to be hit by a paintball.

That night we found out…IT HURTS A LOT!!!!! But that's what makes it fun. My wife can't understand it, and when I sent her a photo of the humongous welt on the side of my neck, she thought we were nuts. Of course, I dished out as well as I took (I think). And on the drive home we relived all the hard hits and hilarious action.

Man, it was fun. But what was most fun was doing it with my boys, because to the pacifist's chagrin, there's nothing like battling side by side with your sons…unless of course it's shooting AT them instead.

So my fellow Dad, if your sons don't have any (in the words of my son Cal) "weapons", make some. And if you already have them, why not do a little battle with them tonight? Have a sword fight, an air soft or paintball battle, a pillow fight, or get out the old potato cannon and fire off a few rounds.

You 'da battle-loving dad.

87

Tug-Dad and the USS Puberty

1 Timothy 2:1-8

Hey Dad,

For the record, I don't like getting older.

I'm not talking about me. I can handle the gray chest hair and aggressive nose and ear hair, but I don't like my children getting older.

I know it's inevitable, and I even know that it's good—but I don't like it. Growing older brings transitions. Just when you've finally figured out how the current model works, he/she changes and passes through a mysterious land of transitions. It usually involves body odor, mood swings, and acne.

Another of my children, let's call him Zeke, just crossed the border and its thrown him for a loop. He's normally my easygoing child who smiles as much as he breathes. It takes a lot for him to get bent out of shape. Or I guess I should say it took a lot for him to get bent out of shape. But lately, he's been acting "different." The littlest thing throws him and his emotions are running wild. "That's not like Zeke," I mentioned to my wife a week ago. "Something's going on."

We both knew what it was, and I found myself longing for the transition of potty training instead. It was so easy. He either went in the toilet or in his pants, but he pretty much seemed the same both ways. But this is pub-er, pub-ur…I can barely say it, but he's there.

But here's a truth for you, Dad: kids need their dad to get them through Transition Land. Zeke needs me to understand when he falls apart or acts weird. He needs me to talk gently, come alongside him, put my arm around him and say, "It's going to be all right."

In a way, we're like those tugboats that come alongside ships like the USS Puberty and guide them through brackish, unknown waters. After all, we've been there, done that, and know what to expect.

The sad thing is so many dads get frustrated, and back out of the harbor, leaving their pimple-faced child stranded. Not only does that leave the child frustrated but tugboat resentment can also take place.

So, Dad, if your child is going through a transition, give a loud toot and bring the old tug-dad alongside him and help guide him safely through. He may kick and scream, but don't back away. He needs you.

You 'da dad!

More Powerful Than a Locomotive

1 Timothy 2:9-15

Hey Dad,

You are the greatest power the world has ever known. Sure, there is the power of the INTERNET, atomic power, flower power, the power of a hug, and the power of the pen, but all of these pale in comparison to Father Power.

Over the past couple of decades, I've had the privilege of leading and being part of many men's groups. I've sat in circles and talked about your standard guy things like work, sports, lawn care, and carburetors.

Occasionally, the conversation transitions to spiritual issues like our relationship with God, our wife, and our kids. I've noticed that the two most passionate topics discussed are fathers and children.

Guys can talk about struggles in their marriage without batting an eye. They can feel miles away from God and still joke. Their car can be on its last leg...OK they cry on that one, but on most other topics every eye is dry.

But, ask a dad about his father, and the atmosphere in the room changes. Suddenly, men get all wishy washy and start to fidget in their seats. Some share good memories, others talk about wounds that have never healed.

I've seen grown men describe an event involving their dad that happened thirty years ago with clarity, deep emotion, and passion. Their lips quiver and their eyes glisten. Listening to them talk, you would think it had taken place a week ago, not three decades ago.

What's the reason behind such startling emotion?

Father Power.

~ Excerpt from Father Power

Two or More

1 Timothy 3:1-10

Hey Dad,

Well, it's a sad day in "I'm a pretty good dad – Land" when you learn that the thing you 'don't do'…you do.

Actually, my wife has accused me for quite some time (read-our whole married life) of not always listening like I should. She's had the nerve to say on more than a few occasions that I don't let her share what she's feeling, that I barge in and tell her why she shouldn't be feeling what she's feeling, why she's mistaken in her feelings, or why I'm right about the situation and she's wrong.

Up until recently, I thought she was overreacting and wrong in her assessment and that I was actually a very understanding husband (after all – I am the Familyman) and quite the listener.

Then, my daughter Katherine shot me out of the air like a slow duck on the first day of duck hunting season. I was on the porch with my shot gun-toting daughter, frustrated by the fact that her mother didn't think I listened to her.

I was mid-sentence when Katherine pointed the gun towards me and said, "You don't listen to her, Dad. You don't let her tell you what she's feeling."

Shocked, I quickly responded, "But I let her tell me what she's feeling, and I don't understand why she says…"

She intercepted me politely and said, "You're doing it to me, now." KERPOW!!!!!

I dropped to the ground like a rock.

There was nothing I could say. Cause the truth is: if two people tell you the same thing about yourself…it's probably true.

I've got a long longggggg way to go, but I've been working on it. So here's the take away for you. You're not going to like this, but…if your wife and one of your children say you don't listen…you don't.

If more than one of them says you're grumpy all the time…you are.

If more than one of them says you work too much…you do.

If more than one of them accuses you of being gone too much, being selfish, or being a couch potato who watches too much TV or plays too many video games….you are.

Whether we like it or not, if two or more are saying the same thing about us…IT'S TRUE and it's time to face up to it and change.

I know we can do it.

You 'da dad!

90

We Might Be In-laws Someday

Hey Dad,

An incredibly deep thought hit me the other night while I was answering a pre-dawn call from my six-year-old daughter, Katherine. Nothing serious. I stroked her side, brushed the tangled hair from her face, kissed her cheek tenderly, told her I loved her, and tip-toed back to bed.

That's when the thought hit me: Your son might grow up to marry my daughter someday.

Back in bed, I wondered if your son will treat my daughter like a princess when they're married. Will he stroke her side and tell her how precious she is when he finds her crying after a hard day of mothering? Will he listen intently as she describes something that's important to her? Will her sparkling eyes make him smile or will he be more interested in reading the paper, working on the computer, or watching a ball game?

That's why I'm writing this. I want to make sure you're training your sons to treat my daughter like a princess, just in case some day they meet, get married, and have a family of their own.

Hope you don't mind, but I worked up a little list of things I'd like for you to address with my possible future son-in-law.

1. Train him to be involved with his family. He can't do his own thing.
2. Train him to be a good listener. Eye to eye—no distractions.
3. Train him to be gentle. No harsh words or roughness.
4. Train him to be able to say "I'm sorry"—even when he feels wronged.
5. Train him to have a real, growing relationship with God. He can't go it alone.
6. Train him to care more about loving his wife and raising his children than he does about his career.
7. Train him to be able to say "no" to his own desires and "yes" to hers.

I know I'm putting a lot on your shoulders, because your son (or future son) will learn most of these things by the way you treat your wife. Because your son will treat my daughter like you treat your wife. And so will my sons. (They might grow up to marry your daughters.)

You owe it to my princess, and I owe it to yours.

You 'da dad!

Keep Your Yap Shut

1 Timothy 4:1-5

Hey Dad,

I've realized recently that I talk too much. I hate to admit it, but I need to keep my big yap shut more often.

A week ago we were using some free bowling coupons my wife had saved from Tony's Pizza boxes. It was quite the sight and had it not been for the bumpers along the gutters, the score would have been in the single digits for sure.

The kids didn't care though; they were having a blast in spite of my early efforts to ruin their fun by trying to get them to bowl RIGHT.

"No, you're doing it all wrong...hold your hand this way...stand here...no, not like that, like this..." Even I could tell they were going from smiling to frustrated.

"Just let them do it their way and have fun," my wife said nicely. But what I heard was, "Keep your yap shut."

The truth is, it doesn't matter if my son bowls right, colors within the lines, gets all A's, chooses the college I want him to...or does everything else like I think he should.

Sometimes we just pick our children to death over the most unimportant things. Even SOME of the important things aren't THAT important after all. Maybe one of the single greatest things we can do to love our children and wife is to KEEP OUR MOUTHS SHUT. When we feel like adding our two bits, nitpicking, giving unasked for advice, or just pointing out the obvious...maybe we should keep silent as the grave and smile instead. Let them do it wrong, find out for themselves...and love having you for a dad and husband.

Mums the word.

You 'da dad!

Batman in Skivvies

Hey Dad,

I don't know about you, but I feel like I'm up to my eyeballs in busyness. My folks are here, our house is a construction disaster, we leave for Atlanta tomorrow, we have to be in Washington next weekend and then in West Palm Beach, FL the weekend after. So you can imagine my surprise to find my daughter Katherine standing by my bed at 5AM obviously frightened.

"What's wrong, Katherine?" I asked.

"A bat flew over my head?" she answered trembling.

"No, it didn't Katherine. You just imagined it."

"I'm serious, Dad. It touched my hair!"

I sighed a not-glad-to-be-getting-out-of-bed-to go-on-a-wild-goose-chase kind of sigh, but as I peered out into the hallway I knew she was not mistaken. In the darkness, I saw not one but TWO, winged denizens of the night.

Fear gripped me. But like any Dad worth his salt, I felt the fear and faced it anyway.

I stepped into the hallway, and they dive bombed me. First one, then the other…back and forth, I bobbed and weaved. It was like a Bruce Lee movie.

Sensing my rage, the bats escaped downstairs but I was on them. No tennis racket in sight, I picked up a small carpet square and started swinging, unaware that I was standing in a well-lit picture window clothed only in my underwear.

The bats were fast but proved no match for THE FAMILYMAN. Whap! Down went one, and a few minutes later I stood breathless over both of their motionless bodies.

I had vanquished the winged foes and protected my women folk, and it felt good.

The next morning, my wife wrapped her arms around me and said, "Thank you, Bat Slayer."

It was nothing, Mam, I thought, just doing my duty.

If only I had kept the momentum going. The next night my wife woke in the night and said, "I feel like my bladder is going to explode if I don't go to the bathroom…but I'm too afraid to go out in the hallway because there might be a bat."

"Oh, there aren't any bats," I said and rolled over and fell soundly asleep.

I let my queen down. The bat-slayer was de-throned.

That's the thing with being a Familyman. Some days you succeed…other days you fail. BUT you never quit trying. You know why? Because…

You 'da dad!

Captain Dad Sparrow

1 Timothy 4:12-16

Har Dad,

"Lift anchor, hoist the main sail, cue the pirate music! Put your backs into it you bilge rats!! We're headed into black waters and trouble awaits us!!!"

"But Sir," a young, pimple-faced teenager with fear in his eyes hollers above the roar of the sea, "these waters are uncharted and littered with reefs, wrecks, and dead men's bones. One wrong move and we're doomed to a watery grave in Davy Jones' Locker."

"Don't be afeared boy. I've been through these waters before, and together we will get through." With the salt spray in his face, Captain Dad Sparrow laughs and guides the ship through the treacherous waters...And they all live happily ever after and make a few sequels.

That's the way it is with unknown waters, captains, and...teenage sons.

It's hard sailing in the waters between childhood and manhood. The testosterone is flowing, bodies are changing, and emotions are high. Older sons argue over stupid things, challenge our instructions, and want to step out on their own but are scared to death to do so.

It's during the teen waters that I've seen dads toss up their hands in frustration, withdraw, and quit. "Fine...you don't want my help? Good. You're on your own, buddy."

Dad, our sons don't need us to quit, they need us be patient, understanding, and to guide them through the turbulent waters...waters that WE have traveled...but have forgotten just how difficult they were.

Yes, your younger sons need you...but so do your older sons (maybe even more). They need you to come alongside them, talk to them, look them in the eye, and shoot straight with them. And they need you to remember what it was like to do stupid things, want to fit in, and slump around like the bones have been sucked from your body and left sludge in your veins.

Dad, stay at the helm and guide them through. I know it's hard...but never let go of the wheel. When they walk away, go after them. When they say, "You always...or you never..." let them talk. Pray for them, never stop loving them, and show them what it means to be a man. The seas are rough...but you're the captain...

...You 'da Cap'n!

Howler Monkey Dad

Hey Dad,

I'm going to have to make this short because this is the day we've been counting down for two months...it's BIG TRASH DAY, a once-a-year occurrence in our small Midwest town. Unfortunately, you can't just pile it out by the road; you have to haul it to the town lot where they have some enormous dumpsters waiting. Oooo...I can hardly wait.

Actually, it's just what the doctor ordered after a dismal last week. Yep, it all started minutes after I sent out last week's familyman talking about something good and mushy regarding fathering. In fact, I bet I had just hit the send button when I heard some commotion coming from upstairs.

Being a good, godly, involved husband and dad, I ran upstairs to find one of my children and my wife duking it out over...nothing. So I jumped in swinging.

"Don't you ever talk to your mother that way," I said losing control quickly. I think both child and wife were shocked by my ferocity, and apparently 'said child' did not agree with my observations or conclusion...and just kept going.

That's when I reached that rare form that is only witnessed on the animal channel when <u>Howler Monkeys</u> are going berserk. In short, I flipped out, blew my top, FREAKED, and lashed into my child with such ugliness that I would be embarrassed for you to witness.

As it always does, the firestorm subsided and I felt like dirt...lower than dirt. I had failed my child, my family, and my God. Usually, within a few minutes I go and apologize, but I was still steaming and allowed a whole day to go by without resolution, all the time feeling like a loser dad.

I wallowed in the fact that I didn't deserve to be a dad or a family leader, and obviously needed to be stripped of my familyman title. But sometime during my miserable day, God whispered in my heart, "You child needs you to keep on...keep trying...to get back in the ring...to ask forgiveness and to embrace him and be restored."

"But, I'm a loser-dad, God," I cried out.

"I know," He said, "but I still love you...and so does your family."

That's when I made it right. Truth is I do blow it. Sometimes I'm mean and insensitive....but they need me and even love me.

The other truth is: your family needs and loves you, too.

So, my fellow sometimes-loser-dad...you still 'da dad!

The Techno-Beast

1 Timothy 5:8-16

Hey Dad,

A while back I got an email from a dad talking about his little video "problem":

"Video games were one of the reasons why my wife left me. Video games on my days off from work were my drug of choice. I was working every chance I had, ignoring everything else in my life. I loved my job, and actually loathed the times that I was scheduled off, until I found Everquest. Everquest is an online role-playing game from Sony that allows you to live out a fantasy life in a virtual world. Many of the players in this fantasy world refer to the game as "Evercrack" as the addictive properties mimic those of crack cocaine. I received a rush from playing the game and would forgo sleeping and eating for the opportunity to play. There were days that I would play for 20 hours straight, sleep for 4 hours (or less) and then sign on again. In those brief times I did sleep, my dreams were filled of images from the game."

Sadly, this is not an isolated story. As I speak around the country, I've shared his story. It's usually as I leave the platform that a woman approaches me (which always makes me nervous) and whispers, "Oh yeah, my husband does the same. He'll hide in the bathroom to play his little games or sneak out of bed at night and play for hours."

Some of the wives say it with tears in their eyes, but still others say it with disdain and unbelief. I'm telling you Dad, this video technology "thing" is so much bigger than guys who like to play video games. The techno-beast destroys families. It will destroy yours if you let it, AND it will destroy your child's future family if you don't help him tame the beast now.

~Excerpt from Taming the Techno-Beast

My Son Hacked Off a Limb

1 Timothy 5:17-25

Hey Dad,

It's bitterly cold outside, but spring is coming. I can hardly wait because I'm a 'plant guy'. I like flowers, shrubs, ornamental grasses, and trees of all kinds.

This time of year, I eye the plants in my yard and see what their prospects are for the summer. I check the red twig dogwood branch for swelling buds, pull back the old growth from last year's perennials to see tender shoots poking up, and blame the deer for nibbling the tips off my white pines.

With that in mind, you can imagine the battle that ensued within me a couple of hours ago when I saw my oldest son, Ben, tromping across the yard carrying a sharp bow saw.

Twenty minutes earlier, he had asked me how to make a sling shot...not the kind with tubular metal and high-strength surgical hose, but the old-fashioned kind made from two rubber bands and a 'Y' shaped branch from a tree.

Minutes later, something outside the window caught my eye. It was Ben, with saw in hand, walking across the side yard with determination in his face. I knew instantly which tree he was heading for—my flowering crab. It had been rescued from a demolition project, and for the last four years, I had groomed and trained it into a nice shape.

"He has an entire woods to choose from, and he's going to cut a honking big branch off MY flowing crab," I thought. That's when the battle started. Gardener vs. Dad. The gardener had plenty of valid arguments, but the dad inside of me said, "Hey, I'm growing kids, not trees."

Later, Ben walked by the window holding the honking big branch cut from my 'baby' and came inside to show me the beginnings of his sling shot. He smiled and looked to see my response. This was crucial—one moment of weakness, and I would blow it and teach him that trees are more important to me than he is.

I looked at the severed limb and said, "Wow, that's a good stick. That'll make a great sling shot."

Victory.

Dad, is your son or daughter constantly asking to use your _____ (fill in the blank)? Take a deep breath, smile, and let them. You know what? Flowering crabapples, shiny cars, gleaming tools, and the things you're holding on to don't matter squat, but the kids who mess them up—mean everything.

You 'da dad!

Raccoon Warrior

1 Timothy 6:1-9

Hey Dad,

Well, in spite of the worst spring weather imaginable, we're just about ready to hit the road. My wife is out in the "beast" (RV) right now, putting away clothes, food, and a hundred other odds and ends.

All the lists are checked off, except one biggy that looms over my head.

It all started about a week and a half ago when my wife heard some "not normal" scratching, squeaky sounds coming from just above our couch. She called me in as the wildlife expert, and after a few seconds I said, "Sounds like baby raccoons to me."

After a quick sound check on the internet, my hunches were confirmed.

Since then, I've been contemplating my options. 1) Do nothing and let the raccoons destroy my house. 2) Hire a pest expert and get rid of the vermin as well as a wad of cash. 3) Get rid of them myself and spend the money I saved on gas for my RV.

It was clear to me. This was about more than saving money...it was a test of my manhood. The plan: get a live trap, catch mama, then cut a hole in the ceiling of my family room and fetch out the babies. Couldn't be easier.

First night. Set trap...nothing.

Second night. Set trap. An hour later, mama left through the opening under the eaves and I rushed out and sealed off the entrance with a board and chicken wire (as my sons watched mama to make sure she didn't attack me).

Next, I sawed a hole in the ceiling, got some protective gear and a headlamp, located the five baby raccoons, and plopped them in a container to be reunited with their mama the next morning.

But the next morning, the trap was empty and the kids reported hearing some faint scratching sounds in her usual spot. I checked the boarded-up opening to find the chicken wire pulled off and the board pulled out...nails and all. Yow!!

So, now I have the babies who won't last long, a mongo-strong raccoon above my family room (again), and three emotional, Greenpeace-save-the-raccoons kind of women in my house who look at me like I'm some kind of raccoon-killing murderer.

All that to say...it's not easy being a dad. And just when you're ready to coast and enjoy the good life, a family of critters takes over your house.

So, Dad, if things are going good...enjoy it while it lasts. If not...it doesn't really matter, because rain or shine, pestilent-free times or raccoon infestations...YOU 'DA DAD!!

I'll get her tonight...hopefully.

Eureka!

1 Timothy 6:10-21

April **3**

Hey Dad,

I think I've discovered something—something BIG! In fact, I just may go down in history with great discoverers such as Columbus, Einstein, Edison, and Galileo. I mean those dead guys came up with some great ideas, but I've discovered the key to understanding women. Jump back!

It's their hair.

No, I'm serious. I'm pretty sure that a woman's hair is the mystic portal that controls her thinking, emotions, and behavior. I was first alerted to the possibilities of this theory about a month ago. My wife had been complaining about her hair and had been a little on the grumpy side.

"It's driving me nuts…It feels so yucky…I want to do something different with it," I often heard her saying.

I confess that I wasn't the most understanding husband. "It looks great that way!" I always responded. "Why would you want to cut it?"

Eventually, things came to a head (no pun intended). While we were visiting St. Louis, my wife saw a hairstyle that she liked and asked the lady were she'd gotten it done. This was the first tip-off to my theory. I mean a guy never asks another guy where he gets his hair done.

"It's just about 20 miles back that way," my wife told me wearing a big smile, which soon vanished when she heard my very guy-ish response to why we weren't going to drive way out of our way just to get a haircut. But I recovered after seeing her disappointment and begrudgingly took her to get her hair done.

You should've seen the transformation when she stepped out of the hair salon. It wasn't the haircut, but her countenance was completely changed—she was smiling and radiant.

You know, it's not just her though. I've heard my sister-in-law say she gets cranky when her bangs reach a certain point on her forehead. And while we were with my brother and his wife a while back, she too mentioned how her hair was driving her nuts.

I probably wouldn't have made the full-blown discovery had it not been for my daughter Katherine who about a week ago also said, "I wish I could get my hair cut before we go to Florida."

Not her too! I thought. So acting upon my discovery, I said, "Let's get your haircut when we stop at Walmart."

You should've seen her eyes light up. I'd discovered the mystic porthole of love—her hair.

So Dad, if your wife's been a little on the cranky side, then let her go get her hair done. Actually, I don't think it's so much about their hair as it is that we show them we care about what they care about.

Flower Power

2 Timothy 1:1-18

Hey Dad,

Here it is, the week before Easter, and I still haven't taken down our Christmas wreath from the front of the house. That means I have two things to do before Easter: get rid of the wreath and run down to the Milford florist and order two corsages for the Wilson gals.

When my wife was a girl, her dad used to surprise all his women with fresh, spring corsages on Easter Sunday. A few years ago, I added the tradition to our family.

You should see Katherine's eyes light up when I pin it on her. She thinks I'm wonderful. Now to a guy, a flower on a pin seems kind of dumb, but to a female, it is a token of affection from the man in her life for all the world to see.

Last year we were out of town, and I wasn't able to buy corsages. I was amazed how many women at my sister-in-law's church wore them. I watched as they adjusted their corsages, looked at their flowers, and then snuggled into their husband's side.

After the service, a tall guy tapped me on the shoulder and said, "Hey, , I wanted you to know I got a flower for my wife like you said in the Familyman Weekly."

He pointed to the rose pinned to his wife. Then he noticed that my wife wasn't wearing one and his face went pale. "Where's your wife's flower?"

I started backpedaling, "Well, you see...uh, uh...I knew we were going to be out of town...(cough) and um...I just didn't think I'd be able to get one down here easily." I hoped I sounded convincing.

"It's an excuse," he said, "but not a very good one." He walked away, leaving me feeling scolded and embarrassed. Later, as I thought about it, I admired his boldness. It was an excuse...and not a good one. I should have done it anyway. He was right. We need more guys like that; dads, who won't let us clods get away with random acts of stupidness.

That's why I'm going to get the corsages no matter what and why I'm telling you to do the same.

So, get down to the florist and pick up a corsage for the ladies in your house (it doesn't have to be expensive). Let the world see how much you love them.

You 'da dad!

Family Emotions or Devotions?

Hey Dad,

I heard somewhere that if you want to be a spiritual giant, you need to have family devotions. All the great men of the faith did; at least that's what everyone says. Apparently, they got up a couple of hours before dawn, gathered the family around the table, read the Scriptures for two hours, prayed for three, and then sang great hymns of the faith, while the children listened quietly as mice.

Well, this is one spiritual "guppy" whose family devotions look more like a blue light special at K-Mart. One kid is standing on his head on the couch, one is hidden under a blanket, one is "quietly" strumming a pint-sized guitar like the lead guitarist in a heavy metal group, and another woke up grumpy at life while I babble away like a Baptist missionary preaching to a bunch of Papua New Guinea natives who have no idea what I'm saying!!

We try singing, but it's hard to sing, yell at kids, and worship God at the same time. Sometimes I have to stop in order to send one child to the bathroom for me to deal with later. "Sam, why don't you close us in prayer before someone gets hurt." Amen.

Ahhh…wasn't that relaxing and uplifting? NOT!

So, you know what I'm going to do?

Try again tomorrow.

That's all I can do. I know spending time together as a family for "devotions" is best. It must be because it's so hard, and all the good things are hard.

How about you? You up for God's best?

Here are Tips for Semi-Successful Family Devotions:

Take charge—make it happen—You 'da dad!!

Keep it short…think baby steps.

Ease into it. Why not just pray as a family? Take prayer requests, have different people pray, and that's all. Later, move on to step 4.

Make it simple-There is no magic recipe for making family devotions a piece of cake. Just read a few verses out of the Bible, talk about them, and pray.

Throw away all your expectations of heaven on earth.

Keep at it.

You 'da dad!

Greater Love Has No Dad Than...

2 Timothy 2:14-19

Hey Dad,

Spring is here! It's nice to feel the warmth as we tool down the road in the Familyman-mobile. Actually, the RV does well in the cold. All you have to do is make sure you have plenty of propane and everything stays nice and toasty.

So you can imagine how cold we were when we ran out of propane about 2 A.M. one 35-degree night in the middle of a Walmart parking lot.

Actually, if I completely covered myself with all the covers it wasn't too bad—but I knew the kids had fewer blankets than my wife and I did.

They're tough, I thought to myself, and they're kids—they like the cold.

From underneath our makeshift tent, my wife mumbled, "Put our comforter on the girls."

I hesitated, hoping she'd think I was asleep—or frozen to death.

She didn't buy it, and a few minutes later my girls were snug as two bugs.

In the early morning hours, I slipped out before everyone was awake and picked up a little space heater (reason #238 of why it's good to camp at Walmart). As I set up the heater, Katherine looked at the nice, cozy comforter tucked around her chin and said, "Thanks, Dad, for giving us your comforter."

A twang of guilt moved in my heart. "I hope it made you feel warmer," I responded.

Silence followed, and then she looked into my eyes and asked, "Were you cold without it?"

I smiled, hoping she wouldn't know the ugly truth—that I didn't want to give it up. But she asked the question again. Her adoring eyes and the tone in her voice told me that she was really saying, "You gave up your covers for ME? You were cold so I could be warm? I can't believe you love me that much."

She loved me for my sacrifice—although I didn't want to make it.

That's the kind of love my wife and children really want: the sacrificial kind. The kind that misses a business meeting to have lunch with them, turns off the ballgame to play a game, or gives up one of my comforts to bring comfort to them.

Here's the truth: Greater love has no father than this, that a dad gives up his comforter for his kid.

So, I'm going to look for things that I can willingly (or not so willingly) sacrifice for them—because they're worth it. Go and do the same.

You 'da dad!

Family Hashing

April **7**

Hey Dad,

Things are going pretty good. Not at all like a couple of weeks ago when the kids were terrible. They were constantly bickering, fighting, and thinking of numero UNO. I know my wife was frazzled, worn out, and wondering when I was going to officially deal with it. Fortunately (or unfortunately), I have a pretty high terrible-kid-tolerance. But enough was enough. Even I was tired of the turmoil.

"Everyone upstairs to the yellow room," I barked. "We're having a family meeting, and I don't want to hear one complaint." Normally we meet in the familyroom, but I wanted a change in venue to highlight the seriousness of THIS meeting.

"OK," I began, "this has gone on long enough...things need to change." Then for the next thirty minutes I talked, they talked, I threatened, I talked some more...I asked forgiveness...I talked more, they offered suggestions, and then we closed in prayer.

Later, as we were going through the Wilson bedtime ritual, my son Ike smiled warmly and said to me, "It's weird, Dad, but it felt really good during the family meeting."

That is so funny to me. I mean we've done all kinds of fun family things like going to the beach, eating at Chuck E Cheese's, traveling across the country...but Ike never EVER said any of it "felt really good." His comment made me wonder if hashing things through as a family "feels" closer and warmer than doing fun things as a family. There must be something comforting and reassuring to know that no matter what—we're a family. We may blow it often, but we still regroup, ask forgiveness, and work together for the common good.

So I was going to encourage you to do something fun as a family this week, but instead let me encourage you to have a family meeting. Ask how things are going; talk about issues that need to be addressed. And whether they verbalize it or not...it will FEEL good. In fact, maybe 'hashing' is the best part of family. Go figure.

You 'da dad!

Get Back on the Stud Wagon

2 Timothy 3:1-9

Hey, Dad,

I've always considered myself...well, you know, a stud. But I've come to realize that I've been giving my wife second-rate goods.

Here's what I mean. I was talking to her at lunch today. Somewhere in the conversation, I commented on a single guy we knew who had recently shed some pounds and was looking pretty stylish. He hadn't always looked that way. When he was married, he looked more like me...an overweight slob whose idea of style is jeans and an old favorite shirt.

Now that he's unattached again, he cares more. I've seen the pattern before. When men and women are looking, they care about how they're lookin'. That's what bothered me. I looked down at my grubby shorts, sloppy shirt, and ran a hand over my unshaven face. Normally, I like the shabby-chic look, but now I just felt ashamed.

I used to care how I looked—especially when I was courtin' my future wife. I wanted to be fit, trim, and studish for my girl. But after we got married, I exchanged studish for slobbish. My thoughts were confirmed with a simple comment that my wife made yesterday. We were talking about buying me a new shirt, and she said, "I like it when you look good."

The truth is Dad, our wives like it when we look good.

I guess what bothers me most is that I haven't cared much about how I look for my bride. I should. I should care about how I look for my wife as much as I did when she wasn't my wife.

It's not about vanity, it's about loving my wife. It won't be easy for this dyed-in-the-wool slob...but I need to do it...for her.

How about you? Have you let a few things slide? Do you have holes in your T-shirts, a spare tire that would fit a monster truck, or a grizzled face? Come on! Let's get back on the stud wagon for our brides. It's time to shed a few pounds, splash on a little cologne, and look and be our best for them.

Because they deserve the best!

You 'da dad!!

I've Got Your Back

Hey Dad,

Greetings from the Walmart parking lot in Waxahachie, TX. We spent yesterday at the amazing Renaissance Festival of Scarborough Faire. Then, I spent a chunk of the evening "parenting."

It was one of those moments you'd rather skip but afterwards becomes one of those you wish you could live in because it feels so "right." I would have missed the whole thing, only to find later that it had grown to an ugly proportion, if a fellow dad had not been watching my back.

We were shooting the breeze when he said, "I need to talk to you about something." I was blindsided when a few minutes later he informed me about something one of my children had done but knew I was probably unaware of.

I was surprised and felt my parenting world starting to sway and wobble. We talked for a while, and then I thanked him for "watching my back." Although the situation was serious, he had prevented it from becoming a much bigger deal...all because he was watching my back.

Last night, we addressed the whole thing and it went just the way those kinds of things should go. We talked heart to heart about growing up, God's plan for my child, and how we want him/her to know they can always talk to mom and dad. It wouldn't have happened without my dad-friend though.

That's the thing about fathering. You can't see everything, all the time, every time. We need dads who've "got our back" and who aren't afraid to tell us like they see it as soon as they see it. My friend was that dad, and I am forever grateful.

You need to have a friend like that AND be a friend like that. If you don't, then go to one of your friends or stand up at your church or men's group and tell them that since you can't see everything, you need them to watch your back in fathering.

And I promise you, Dad...that I will always shoot straight with you because I've got YOUR back. You've got my permission to do the same with me.

You 'da dad!

Plan Now to Be Old

2 Timothy 4:1-8

Hey Dad,

Today, we're packing up the Familyman Mobile again. I think we're ready. In fact, thanks to the generosity and bravery of a great older couple, my wife and I were even able to go out on a date together.

As we stopped by their house to pick up our kids, we sat and talked for a few minutes. As we did, the conversation turned to favorite gifts they had received.

Mrs. G left and returned with a jar and a wooden box. After a brief explanation, Mrs. G opened the box and pulled out some notes that their daughters had given to them on a special occasion.

On each piece of paper, their family had written a favorite memory about their mom and dad. They quickly read through a short stack of notes, smiling as they read and remembered each one.

As they read, I noticed that almost every memory that Mrs. G read from Mr. G's stack had something to do with a special time one of the girls had with their dad or of something extravagant he did with them or for them (like letting them get an ice cream cone...or spinning on the diner counter stools).

All the good memories had something to do with him making them feel special and loved.

As we were driving home, I imagined myself receiving a similar gift thirty years from now. Then the thought hit me—I should be working now to assure that my stack of memory notes is thick.

I heard the perfect example about a week ago when I was talking to a mom. She said her husband had sent their young daughters some flowers.

The girls saw the man arrive to deliver the flowers and assumed they were for "mom," but were overwhelmed when they saw that they were for them. I'm telling you those girls will record that in their memory list...because they will remember that forever.

I'm going to work at giving my kids memories of how much they are loved by their dad. I'm going to stop the ice cream truck, let them spend the quarter to ride the horse at Walmart, stay up late eating popcorn with the older boys, and send my daughters flowers.

How about you, Dad? Start planning now to be old. How can you show your children a little extra love...today?

You 'da dad!!

Hoist the Mizzenmast

2 Timothy 4:9-22

Hey Dad,

In a week and a half, my family will set sail for a three month RV journey across a chunk of the country to encourage dads and moms. In the meantime, we're trying to get all of the things on our "to do" list done.

On top of all that, my wife mentioned that the house feels really grimy. I knew she had too much on her plate to get it all done by herself so...being the captain of the ship, I called a family meeting and told the sailors (the kids) that we were going to swab the decks and make the mizzenmast shine (whatever that is).

Even this morning, I had to gather the kids to work out a few bad attitudes. That's okay, because that's what captains do. Yes, there is the very real possibility of mutiny...but ARRRRR...I give 'da orders and pull my weight like 'da rest of dem, 'caus I'm 'da cap'n.

Pirate talk aside...we've got a lot to do before we pile into the Familyman Mobile. This will be the longest we've ever been out on the road before. As much as we're looking forward to it, I know the quarters can get mighty tight and tempers can fly.

Well, I'd better run...I just thought of another thing to get done before we pull out of the driveway. Dad, I know you're busy too. You've got projects at work and home...dealings and meetings...but don't forget what's most important.

You 'da captain!

Houston, We Have Liftoff...Almost

1 Thessalonians 1:1-10

| **April** | **12** |

Hey Dad,

After months of preparation, we're ready to roll...except we don't have an RV. After working for hours trying to solve my taillight issue, I made an appointment for this past Monday at the RV-fixing place.

So on Monday, in the pre-dawn hours, I fired up the FM3 (which purred like a panther) and backed down our long driveway with my son Ben (age 14.8) as my guide. I was just about to pull down the road when Ben, with a smile on his face, ran up to the driver's window.

"You knocked down the mailbox," he said with a little too much levity in his voice.

"Thanks, Ben," I said. "I appreciate you letting me know."

Well, anyway, the RV-fixers quickly found the problems but had to send away for the parts...so here I sit, pacing like a caged lion, planning to leave tonight for our first gig.

But besides that, we're ready to leave—unless you count the fact that we still haven't de-winterized the beast or finished packing her and that Maggie threw up all over her bedroom floor last night, possibly signifying future "episodes" with other family members while on the road.

That's the life of a dad, and my calling. And it's your calling, too. Nothing ever goes like it's supposed to; road trips are never easy; unexpected expenses inevitably arise; kids throw up all over the carpet—but you're still 'da dad!

So bring it on.

You 'da dad!

Who Knows

Hey Todd,

Take it from me. I don't care what it is that keeps a dad from taking or making the time to invest himself in his children's lives, it's not worth it. There may come a day, like it did to me recently, that one of them may not be there anymore. I know I will see him again in that great resurrection day, but I would give everything I own, and then some, just to have one more day to spend with my son. Even though we really did spend a lot of time together, it will never be enough. I regret I didn't spend more time. Sadly, most dads will have the opportunity but waste it on themselves, and life will go on just the same. However, you never know what God has in store about what we might be taking for granted.

Respectfully,
Wayne
Mustang, OK

Don't Hurry, Be Happy!?

1 Thessalonians 2:13-20

Hey Dad,

The kids are in bed so I thought I'd jot off a note before we take off in the Familyman Mobile. In the morning, we head to the tropical destination of...Duluth, Minnesota. We're headed to the state homeschooling convention where we'll be speaking and encouraging dads in the land of 10,000 lakes.

I have to admit that I'm a little nervous about driving our 30' gas-guzzling beast, 600 miles across Wisconsin. The kids are pumped about life in a mobile home (which will probably wear off about 20 minutes down the road.)

Even my wife is looking forward to the trip...although she warned me that the success of the weekend depends greatly on me. I hate it when she says that.

She reminded me that I have a tendency to be in a hurry to get wherever we're headed. I can't deny it, because I know I do. It's just that when I get behind the wheel, I like to make good time, and I'm not wild about interruptions. Of course, it's not just me, it's most men.

What is it with dads and being in a hurry, anyway?

We seem to be in such a rush to get...nowhere. We don't like to pull over at quaint spots, rest areas, or tourist traps more than a mile out of our way. Sometimes we get consumed with making the three-hour trip in two hours and fifty minutes.

For example: when women go on a trip, other women ask what they saw. When men go on a trip, the conversation goes something like this: "How many miles did you drive?" (Answer: a lot) "How long did it take you?" Most men don't care about what they see...it's all about how fast they did it.

So here's my plan: I'm going to stop often, slow down, and stop looking at my watch. When they want to take the exit in Bemidji to see the concrete statue of Paul Bunyan and Babe, his big blue ox, I'll do so without out sighing. I'll stop to have our picture taken often, stop thinking about the miles out of our way, and start concentrating on our family adventure. I'll have some pictures when we get back, and, I'm sure, a story or two.

Be a good dad this week. Don't be in such a hurry. Have a family adventure of your own...and enjoy your big, comfy bed.

You 'da dad!

I Am a Hypocrite!

Hey Dad,

It dawned on me last night as my children slept and I sat on the porcelain throne that I'm a hypocrite. That's right. There's no denying it; I'm a hypocrite. I say I trust in God, but my actions prove otherwise. My son Abe pointed it out.

To bring you up to speed, I'm still at home as of today. The Familyman Mobile is still on the launch pad. I've been acting that anxious-grumpy way you get when you feel the weight of the RV on your shoulders and everyone around you seems oblivious to all that needs to be done in order to assure that things will go smoothly.

Actually, I dread hitting the road, and it shows. Last night, Abe passed me in the hallway, hugged and kissed me, and looked into my face questioningly.

"Dad, do you like the old RV better than the new one?"

That seemed like a funny question. "No way!" I said, "I like the new RV a ton better."

"Then why don't you seem happy to drive in it? You were always happy when we drove in the old one."

It wasn't until later that I realized that I was a hypocrite. Abe was right. I was happy when we started out in the old one. I knew that RV. I had worked on it, driven thousands of miles in it, and felt secure in it and me (notice I didn't say in God).

The new RV is untried and untested, more complicated, and it has had some launch pad difficulties. It is harder to trust in—and I don't feel like I know what I'm doing. But, while sitting on the throne, I was reminded that I'm not to put my trust in RVs, myself, or anything else. I am to put my trust in God...and quit my bellyaching.

After all, it was Jesus who said, "Who of you by worrying can add a single mile to your RV?" (RV translation).

Dad, from a recovering hypocrite, let me ask you, "As you face what you're facing, who or what are you trusting in?" You know you're not trusting in God if you've got a knot in your stomach right now. That's a byproduct of misplaced trust.

So maybe you need to do what I'm trying to do. Stop worrying, pray, and put your trust in God, not RVs—you know what I mean.

You 'da dad!

The Grass is Dead

Hey Dad,

"My father taught me that it is important to work hard on your marriage. No matter how hard it gets or how green the grass looks on the other side, you must work hard for your marriage and family. He taught me that a fatherless home is a rough place to be, and that there is nothing more important than a child's need for his father. I also learned that the need for your father's love and involvement in your life doesn't stop at childhood. I learned to ALWAYS nurture my husband's relationship with my children, because next to their relationship with God, it is most important. My father taught me all of this with his absence."

~ a mom

So Dad, don't forget that what you do today outside your office is the most important thing you do!

You 'da dad!

The New Familyman Motto

1 Thessalonians 4:13-18

| **April** | **17** |

Hey Dad,

Well, we're taking it to the wire on the baby front. My wife's due date is Saturday. So far nothing's happening, which is plunging her into pre-partum depression. Oh, don't worry, I'm her knight-in-shining-armor, and I'll come to her rescue. We'll keep you posted.

On a non-pregnancy note, I'd like to announce that Team Familyman finally has a motto. Oh, sure, we have great products, a witty and dashing host, and even a Familyman-mobile with a honkin' big horn, but we've never had a motto—until now.

I'd like to take credit for the phrase, but all I did was steal it. Actually, fellow Familyman Ken Howard called me up out of the blue last week and shared it with me. I was immediately taken by the phrase that he stole from a professor of his, and after several days I decided that it would make a great motto for us dads.

Are you ready?

For effect, picture 10,000 dads in flannel shirts, unshaven, and wearing goofy lumberjack hats facing a podium made from duct-taped tires. In unison every dad stands, removes his lumberjack hat and says, "I'm a pretty good dad—except when I'm not."

I don't know about you, but I think that captures the spirit of fathering perfectly: I'm a pretty good dad—except when I'm not.

The truth is: dads try their best, trust in God, have some successes, fail miserably, and try some more. That's a good dad. That means you're a good dad—except when you're not. And that's okay. There are no super dads, perfect fathers, or flawless parents. Don't think for one moment that there are or that " has it all together." I'm telling you right now, I don't. I don't even know where it all is! But I just keep trying and praying.

So stand with me and repeat the Familyman motto: I'm a pretty good dad—except when I' not.

Again.

One more time.

Meeting adjourned. By the way, next time it's your turn to bring the cookies.

You 'da dad!

Make Lemonade

Hey Dad,

"Reality TV" is all the rage. That's where supposedly real people are placed in supposedly real situations and then filmed. I've never actually seen one of the modern episodes. I quit watching reality TV after Gilligan's Island went off the air.

But I've come up with a great idea for a show. It involves eight dads and their children. Each is given a dirty car which they would have to had wash...you know, with a hose. The last father to go insane wins.

Of course, the more I thought about it, I realized that the world isn't up for that much REALITY in its reality. I know that when we washed the car the other day it got plenty ugly.

Oh, the kids love washing the car. They love to get out the bucket with its multi-colored sponges, mom's dish soap, and fight over who gets to use the hose.

Usually, they spend most of their time making a huge muddy spot in the driveway instead of washing the car. That's why I offered to help this time, forgetting how aggravating it can be to wash a car with five kids helping.

Actually it was everything I expected: the kids were covered with soap bubbles, there was plenty of laughing and miss-aimed hose-squirts, and the car ended up dirtier than when we started.

BUT the kids loved it. They always do. Which means, we'll have to do it again.

So dad, want a great dad/kid activity that won't cost much...except your sanity? Sometime in the next couple of days, announce that you're going to wash the car and you'd like their help. Be prepared to get soaked, see the kids covered in suds, and have a filthy, dirt-streaked car afterwards. But I guarantee it will be worth every moment of mayhem.

If your kids are older and have cars of their own, offer to help them detail their car. You know, clean every nook and cranny until it shines. Talk about quality time.

Your kids will love you for it and will probably say what Sam said to me that night as he lay in bed: "It was fun washing the car today, Dad."

You 'da dad!

Big News!

Hey Dad,

We've had a major breakthrough in parenting at the Wilson household (or RVhold). We've been struggling in this area for years, but I think we've beaten the beast...and stumbled upon a vital parenting principal as well.

I think we've finally taught the kids to screw the lid back on the tube of toothpaste!! You may say, "That's it?" But it's been a source of frustration for a long time. I mean, you'd think it would be simple enough to take the lid off, apply toothpaste, and put the lid back on. But noooooo...my children just can't seem to accomplish the last step.

It's disgusting. I go to the bathroom sink, only to be greeted by an oozing, toothpaste-encased tube of toothpaste. It looks a little like a stalactite sitting on the edge of the sink sporting weeks of accumulated dried and hardened toothpaste. We've tried asking, hollering, and threatening—but nothing has worked. Until now.

We decided to tackle this "problem" head on. Instead of trying to change all their bad habits and behaviors at once, we decided to start with this one simple habit. So, we told the kids what was expected and unveiled a shiny new tube of toothpaste. For the last few weeks, we've been working hard on it. Even last night, I went to brush my teeth and found a gooplessly clean tube. So I stuck my head out and said, "Good job with the toothpaste, kids...keep it up."

Now, the toothpaste beast isn't dead yet, but it's on its last leg. It may not seem like a big deal to you, but it is a big deal. Actually, I think I've even unlocked the key to parenting: baby steps. Tackling one area of change at a time...and starting small.

Usually, we look at our children and see the multitude of glaring areas that need to be changed. We set goals, but then we get frustrated and give up in failure. Instead, maybe we should tackle the smallest area of change and refuse to move on until it's beaten. Sit down with the kids, state the goal (or desired behavior), and then cheer them on as you guide them to obedience and change.

How about you, Dad? Are you feeling overwhelmed by all of the areas that need improvement in your kids' lives? Pick one little area that needs to be addressed, and beat it.

You 'da dad!!

It Doesn't Take Much

Hey Dad,

I just got a photo of a smiling kid in a cardboard box fort along with this email...

"These boxes had been sitting in our basement since last spring, and my husband had been telling our son for a loooong time that they were going to do something special with them. One evening I left for some time alone, and when I returned, our son had to show me the super cool fort that dad had built him. I think they went through 2 full rolls of packaging tape, but our son thought the fort was awesome, and as to his opinion of his dad.... "He is awesomer at everything!!!!" Cardboard boxes, tape and time. Amazing how little it takes."

~ Amy S.

You know, Dad, she's absolutely right. It really doesn't take all that much to become a hero to your child or your wife. It just takes a little time, a little effort, and a little money.

Maybe tonight you can strap on your cape and do that "something" that you have been promising for a while.

You 'da hero!

Birth of a Cliché Dad

2 Thessalonians 2:1-12

Hey Dad,

It's finally happened. I've crossed the line. I've joined the ranks of frustrated dads who have resorted to cliché. In the past, I've piously cast judgment on parents who use lines such as, "Don't make me come in there...I'm going to count to three...Don't come running to me if you cut off your legs with that saw."

Now...I can't say it...I am one of them.

It happened the other day as I was nose-to-nose with about a dozen of my children in the RV. I was barking orders and trying to get them to function as a well-oiled machine. At some point during the drill, the kids were resisting my instructions and I was beginning to get louder.

"Come on you guys," I puffed. "Get moving."

Apparently I overdid it, and one of my children began to cry. That's when I became one of them...or us.

"Son, if you don't stop crying right this instant..." I can't believe I said this, "then I'm going to give you something to cry about." Uggg.

Even as I said it, I could hear a collective chuckle from cliché dads everywhere. The pious scales fell from my eyes, and I saw myself for who I really am: a frustrated dad who had resorted to cliché.

That's what happens when a dad gets to the end of his fuse. Nothing seems to make sense, so he says...stupid things and utters vague, meaningless threats.

And to tell you the truth, I've felt frustrated lately...not so much by them as by me. I know I've been blowing it lately. I've had my little agendas and when things don't go like I'd like them to...I get frustrated, get mad, say and do stupid things, and end up treating the people I love the most...the worst.

I'm sure there is some spiritual answer to all this: be consistent, walk in the Sprit, and throw away my agenda...but somehow I'm not sure it's that easy. Maybe that's why the ranks of dad cliché users are so large.

I think the real answer is to just keep trying, keep praying, keep asking forgiveness, and never stop loving those people who call you dad or honey.

I know it ain't easy...but the good things never are.

You 'da dad!

When Life Gives You a Turkey...

Hey Dad,

Today looks to be a beautiful day for RVing. In a few hours, we should be pulling into the Boston, Massachusetts area for a convention. We've been on the road since Sunday but ran into a little problem on Monday morning (sound familiar?).

You're not going to believe this! Okay, if you've kept up on our travels or ever owned an RV, you will. We were traveling along, making good time, when BAM! out of nowhere, a giant turkey smashed through our windshield. That's right—through...as in no longer outside in the wild...but inside with the whole Wilson family.

Glass and turkey feathers were everywhere. The turkey was flapping around, kids were crying, and my wife was trying to protect sweet Maggie Rose from the insane turkey. We pulled to the side of the road, and I was able to open the RV door and let Mr. Butterball out.

We called 911, calmed everyone down, and assessed the damage. Oh man, it was a mess! My wife was bleeding on her face, Maggie was covered in glass, and my laptop was smashed.

That was then. A day later a new windshield was over-nighted to us, they installed it, and we got back on the road. I've got to admit that we're tired, somewhat discouraged, and a little gun-shy.

My wife commented on the fact that had we pulled out just one minute sooner or later that morning, we would have missed the turkey. Which means: there are no ifs in God's program. So, God had a perfect plan for us in this turkey disaster.

As I think about it, had we pulled out a minute earlier, we also would have missed spending the night in a hotel, swimming for hours, reminiscing about our adventures, and spending time together. I would have missed Katherine holding on to my neck in the pool and planting big, love-filled kisses on my cheeks.

In our travels and mishaps, I've noticed that sometimes God's best is hidden in turkey feathers. I'd be a wise dad to thank Him for the "things" that I consider schedule interrupters. And so would you.

So when God gives you a turkey, make lemonade.

You 'da dad!! If you don't make the lemonade, no one will!

Thanks Barry

2 Thessalonians 3:1-18

Hey Dad,

In some parts of the country the sighting of a Robin heralds the coming of spring. At my house, the bicycles, scooters, and junk scattered across my yard does the same!

Just yesterday, my kids used cement blocks to build ramps for their scooters, and Abe (9) and Ike (10) started construction on a tree house. In fact, in a little while I'm taking them to Lowe's to pick up a few building supplies. I hate the messes, but I know our mess-days are numbered. Barry, as in Manilow, reminded me of that the other night.

I was sitting in my living room enjoying some peace and quiet when it got a little too peaceful and quiet. As though instructed to do so, Katherine (13) and Cal (3), who were the only other ones downstairs at the time, made their exit, leaving me all alone.

Normally I would have enjoyed the quiet moments, but a song on the stereo caught my attention. I can't remember which song it was, but it was an old, melancholy Barry Manilow tune. Barry must have cast some kind of spell on the music because I felt emotionally tired and old...not just 45 years old...but 75 years old. For that brief moment, my kids were NOT upstairs playing a game anymore but were grown up and had families of their own, leaving me keenly aware that all the pillow fights in the family room, conversations and arguments around the dinner table, and gatherings around animated videos were over. I saw a tree house that was weathered and falling apart, Legos that hadn't been used in years, and scribbles on wallpaper that were reminders of the best life had to offer.

As Barry sang, I felt saddened for not enjoying it as I should...and then I was back. Kids ran down the stairs chasing each other and screaming, "Dad, he's going to kill me!!!!!"

Man, I was glad to be back.

Still pondering Barry's lesson as I read my Bible this morning, I scrawled a little note at the top of the page telling them how much I love them and how blessed I am to be their dad. One day, when I'm gone, they'll be thumbing through 'Dad's Bible' and get a lump in their throat when they read the note.

Instead of making them wait all those years...I think I'll tell them tonight as well.

Dad, let me remind you; you got it good...don't miss it.

You 'da dad!

PS – Yes, I'm still a man although I listen to Manilow.

The Bubble Girl

Colossians 1:1-14

Hey Dad,

It's a beautiful, spring morning here in Northern Indiana. The sun is shining, the temperature is well below freezing, and there is a winter storm warning for the next two days. Perfect weather for finishing up the last-minute details before we hit the road next Wednesday—not!

Actually, I feel a little overwhelmed and discouraged. I'm having a tail-light issue on the RV, which I hadn't anticipated, my grandmother will be going to heaven soon, and...did I mention the winter storm thing?

Here's the real kicker: time is passing at lightning speed, and I don't like it. Just yesterday, my wife was talking to an old high school friend who mentioned that her daughter would be going to college in the fall, and she was saddened by the thought that she was leaving.

When my wife relayed their conversation to me, I was taken back in time to a restaurant table filled with a bunch of young couples that were entertained by a little girl in a highchair who could say, "Bubbles."

Now the restaurant is gone, some of the couples are no longer couples, and the little bubble girl will be going to college in the fall...and I've got a lump in my throat.

That's the thing about time. It sneaks up on you and changes things before you notice or can do anything about it. It takes little girls and boys and turns them into men and women. It takes fried-chicken-making grandmothers and confines them to wheelchairs unable to communicate...eventually transforming them into fond memories.

Time's doing "it" right now. My little daughter who begs her very busy father to play Candyland will quit asking one day. And about the time I'm starting to have time...she won't be there.

Drat that dastardly time!!

But my "drats" won't change things. My only recourse is to enjoy my family, the cold weather, and a game of Candyland today...because the bubble girl is going to college in the fall.

So my fellow dad, I know you're busy, but let me encourage you to enjoy your family today—and remember the bubble girl.

You 'da dad!

Blind Sided

Colossians 1:15-23

Hey Dad,

Have you ever felt like you were blind sided by a 9-year-old? You think you're a pretty good dad (except when you're not) when WHAM! You're blind sided.

My experience with this took place not long after I had gotten back from speaking in Spokane, WA. I was exhausted from a twelve hour day of travel and time zone hopping. I had given and received dozens of hugs and I missed yous and put the kids to bed with a bunch more of the same.

A few minutes later, I lay in bed talking over the weekend with my wife. She was sharing a special mom/son time she had with our son Abe (9). Apparently, one of the nights some of the other youngin's were not cooperative at bedtime and it got a little ugly. Abe was stellar though and was rewarded with a little one-on-one time talking to Mom in her bed.

My wife regretted her response to the whole ordeal and asked, "Do you feel like I'm angry at you all the time, Abe?"

"No..." he said.

"Well, that's good," I interjected, feeling relieved on my wife's behalf...because you know how moms can be, but she wasn't finished relaying the conversation.

"But I feel like Dad is," he said softly.

WHAM!!! BLIND SIDED!!!!!!! I was too tired to show much response, but I felt like the air had been knocked out of me. How could I have treated my Aber-Baber like that? Yes, he gets into trouble a lot and has about as much energy as four children combined...but I felt terrible that he thinks I'm always mad at him.

Since then, I've tried to react differently. I've still had to correct (though less than normal), but I've watched my tone and tried to smile and hug him afterwards. I'm going to change, Dad. I'm not going to have any of my children feel that way about me...even if I have to let some things that annoy me slide. My children will know that I love them, like them, and take pleasure in them.

So, Abe, thanks for blind siding me. I needed that!

Maybe you do too, Dad.

You 'da dad!

Caught in the Web

Colossians 1:24-29

Hey Dad,

Just heard about another dad who got caught in the web of Internet pornography (maybe that's why they call it the worldwide web). Man, I hate that! I'm not shocked or appalled...just saddened. I mean, Satan knows what kind of bait to use when he goes fishing for men.

I'm sure that dad didn't anticipate where it would lead. It began with a simple click of the mouse when no one was looking. Afterwards, he begged forgiveness from God and promised himself that it would never happen again. But it did. Over time it became easier. He hated what he was doing...but IT always called him back for one "last look."

Well, it's out in the open now. There are children who are embarrassed and a wife who feels betrayed. God can restore the marriage, but the husband is going to have to work like a dog to save it. Was it worth it? No. But still IT calls.

Satan starts fishing early too. I can remember playing over at Jay Morrison's house when I was in the second or third grade. We were in the basement when he pulled out some magazines, and we thumbed through the pages.

IT's been calling ever since. IT calls in the Walmart checkout line, the lingerie department, hotel televisions, and in places when no one is watching. Every day, we dads hear IT's call and have to make right, inconvenient choices...not only for ourselves but for the families we love. We can't afford to travel alone, let our eyes roam, or surf the Internet without accountability. We can't just fight temptation, we need to run away from it.

Dad, it's up to us to protect our children too, especially our boys. Use Internet filters (see resources below), limit access, or get rid of it altogether. Be careful about sleepovers (remember what you talked about in the dark?), who your children hang around with, and keep those bedroom doors open. Nothing is TOO extreme.

Let me ask you a dad-to-dad question...Are you in over your head? Are you headed out to deep water? It's time to get help. Let another dad know. Don't trust yourself to handle it on your own. It won't work. Ask other dads how they're doing in this area. Don't settle for their first answer. Be persistent and be vulnerable.

Now, pray for your own purity, another dad's that you know, and the dad that I heard about. Seek out help (if needed) and call your wife and tell her that you love her.

You 'da dad!!

Influence...Oh, Yeah

Colossians 2:1-7

April 27

"I'm 48, 4 kids (3girls/1boy), 2 oldest girls out of the house, my 3rd daughter who is 18 and graduating high school this June shared a college prep essay she wrote. The topic was " who in your life has been the biggest influence and why?" her answer is " I immediately think of my dad". she goes on to say I'm the most frustrating person she knows, its rare we are not disagreeing about something, when I'm mad at her, she is quick to snap back, something "no doubt" she learned from me. But here's her last paragraph:

"My Dad has had an influence on me in so many ways and that is apparent when people come up to me and tell me how much like my dad I am. I believe the influence my dad has had on me will benefit me in my future, wherever it might take me and I hope that I can remain as much like my dad as possible because, as mad as he can make me sometimes, I love him a lot and he is someone to look up to."

We aren't perfect, but boy do we influence. I would never have guessed I would be the topic of this essay, but it shows the difference we make in our kids lives. Keep trying!!"

We 'da dad's ~ Chris Hayes

123

Clean His Clock!

Colossians 2:8-15

Hey Dad,

I've never really considered myself the warmongering type. I don't condone physical violence, attend hockey games, or watch championship wrestling.

But I do believe that boys should stand up for girls...especially my girls.

A while back my wife and I were sitting at the kitchen table when Katherine (9) and Sam (11) wandered over and started talking.

"You know the last time we were at so 'n so's house?" she asked. "One of the boys said this to me..."

The words were inappropriate for little boys to say to little girls, and my jaw tightened.

My wife, being the levelheaded one, started to ask a few questions. Before she got very far, I jumped in and said plainly, "Sam, if anyone ever talks to your sister like that again...take him OUT."

My wife turned to me shocked by my harsh instructions.

"Honey," she said, "That isn't..."

I wasn't finished. "If anyone talks like that to your sister...clean his clock!"

"Knock his block off..."

"Punch out his lights..."

"Honey..."

"Sweep the leg...take no prisoners!"

My sweet wife tried to soften my advice, but I wouldn't let her. No one talks to my princess that way, and I wanted my son to know right then and there that he has my blessing to do whatever it takes to protect the honor of his sister.

Since then, I've calmed down and had time to think...but my thinking hasn't changed. I want my boys to grow up knowing that their chief responsibility is to protect the women in their life who need a knight in shining armor that will slay dragons and ruffians alike for them.

Not long after that, my wife and I were talking to another couple about a tense situation where the wife's integrity was challenged. She weathered the situation, but confided, "I just wanted my husband to stand up, draw out his sword, swish it around, and say, 'Stop talking about my wife that way!'"

Your wife wants to know that her mild-mannered husband will get violent if her honor is at stake. She wants you to stand up to your in-laws, siblings, family members, or acquaintances and come to her rescue. In fact, the best way for you to train your boys to stand up for their sister and future wife is for you to stand up for your wife.

So, Dad, if you have some sword swooshing to do...do it!

Fake Diamonds Are REAL

| **April** | **29** |

Hey Dad,

    I'm sitting here at Crater of Diamonds State Park (AR—not Arizona but Arkansas) admiring the diamond that I found. Oh yeah, people come from all over to this big, muddy field to look for diamonds. Here's the kicker: whatever you find you get to keep!

    Why just within the last year, two diamonds over six karats each were found. In fact, they average about three diamond finds a day here. Most are no bigger than the head of a match.

    There's not much to it, actually. Some people dig big holes or sift the soil through wooden screens in hopes of finding the treasure, but others (including some of the big diamond finders) just look along the surface for anything that looks shiny.

    That's how I found my diamond. I just looked over and there it was. It's a big, pretty, reddish-looking one. It must weigh about two pounds and is as large as the palm of my hand—what, you thought I meant a genuine diamond? Of course I didn't. The chances of finding a real diamond are like finding a diamond in a big, muddy field. What I found was just a smooth orange rock, but I'll treasure it like it's a REAL diamond.

    And when I get home, I'll clean it off, write the date we found it on it, and place it by my desk or in another prominent place next to all my other "fake diamonds." You see, I've got a bunch of fake diamonds from all over.

    I've got a leaf from Mount Vernon, dirt from the dam at Johnstown, water from the swimming pool at Fort Wilderness, a palm frond from a condo we stayed at in Florida, Ike's pirate tooth, Abe's pacifier, and even the steel ball bearing that Ike swallowed (it came out the other end).

    They're all fake diamonds—souvenirs of special moments with special people. They don't have any value on their own. But to me they're invaluable, and they help me remember moments with the REAL diamonds I never want to forget.

    So, Dad, keep an eye out for fake diamonds. It might be a Coke can from a picnic, a rock from a special place, or a special shirt that your child outgrows. Hold on to them, and let those "fake diamonds" remind you of the "REAL diamonds."

You 'da dad!

Cool Hand Dad

Hey Dad,

I've been thinking about the old Paul Newman movie "Cool Hand Luke" lately. Actually, I started thinking about it last week after talking to several fellow dads.

As I talked with them about their teenagers who were giving them fits, their wives who didn't seem to think like them, and the deceptively deadly pull of success that beckons to them everyday, I saw tiredness in their eyes and heard emotion in their voices.

I listened to them and nodded in understanding until they finished. Then in a gentle but firm voice I said, "Man, I know exactly how you feel, but...You 'da dad!. You may feel like giving up, but your family is counting on you. You can't give up on them. Get back in there, because although they may say harsh things...they still need you."

They sighed, stiffened their chins in determination, and nodded in agreement. "You're right, ," they said. "Thanks for the reminder." And then they walked away, ready to give it another shot.

That's when I started thinking about Cool Hand Luke. It's about a guy who winds up in a prison chain gang and repeatedly tires to escape.

Early on, cocky Paul Newman arrives at the prison camp and is challenged by a moose of a man to a boxing match. Everyone knows Cool Hand Luke will be knocked out cold in the first round, but to the surprise of everyone, he just won't go down.

He smiles, gets pounded to the ground, and then staggers up to get knocked down again, and again, and again. Everyone tells him to stay down but he just gets back up. It's brutal. Eventually, even the BIG guy feels sorry for him and begs him to stay down...but he won't. You think his dirty and bruised body is incapable of moving at all when he drags himself to a standing position and lifts his hand to defend himself...again.

That's fathering and husbanding!!

That's what God has called you to do, Dad...to keep trying, loving, and standing up when it would be a whole lot easier to lie down and stay down. To everyone's amazement, you stagger back to your feet and keep at it. You know why?

Because YOU 'DA DAD!!!

Ahhhh—This is the Real Life

Hey Dad,

Ahhhh—this is the life. I don't mean the easy life where you sit around a pool in sunny Florida at Disney World's Fort Wilderness enjoying the good life in peace and quiet; I mean the hard, Familyman kind of life where you sit around a pool in sunny Florida at Disney World's Fort Wilderness enjoying the good life while your kids argue and complain, and I yell at them.

This is real life—the place where bad attitudes don't take a vacation and you can't just coast on the fathering bicycle of life. Now don't get me wrong, we've had a great time of R&Ring. We've swum/swam/have swimmed...spent a day at the Magic Kingdom, and are looking forward to a couple more days of playing.

The thing is, I just always assume it will be easy. I picture laughter, smiles, and easy. What I get is hard.

Yesterday, I was pottied on twice, finger-printed with melted ice cream, and had a screaming baby strapped to my chest while pushing a giant tandem stroller filled with two crying kids, snacks, a backpack, a diaper bag, and who knows what.

Kidless old people watched us with our small herd and smiled. I smiled back, but inside I loathed them for the ease with which they ate, strolled, and laughed.

That was yesterday. By the time night fell, God reminded me how blessed I am to have my herd. The air temperature cooled and lights twinkled in the trees, but it was the nighttime parade that softened my heart. Surrounded by my children and magical music and lights, I felt the overwhelmed feeling of a dad who is truly blessed.

The feeling continued as we left the park, rode the boat back to the campground, pulled up to the Familyman-mobile and then proceeded to commence the hard task of getting everyone to bed at midnight.

Already this morning, I've had a "talk" with one of my children, hollered at others, and "sparred" with my wife.

But hey, this is the life—the real, good, Familyman sort of life. Just the way I like it.

So, remember, no matter how hard today is or how hard tomorrow might be, this is—the good life.

You 'da dad!

For Dad Eyes Only

Colossians 4:1-18

Hey Dad,

This is going to be a quickie. We're sitting in a parking lot in Harrisburg, PA, and the kids are anxious to get going. But I do want to give you a heads up on Mother's Day is coming up.

Now if your kids are like most kids, then that thought hasn't even entered their minds yet. So it's your job to "make it happen."

Yes, I know that your wife is not YOUR mother. But, she is the mother of YOUR children and needs to be honored by her children and YOU. Here's the plan: stop by a card shop on the way home from work today and pick out a card telling your wife how much you appreciate her.

Then, run by a florist or Walmart and pick up some flowers or a corsage ($5.96). Next, have the kids make a banner or card telling your wife how much they love and appreciate her.

Finally, plan to eat out on Sunday. Don't even think about letting her go home and cook lunch. Pick her favorite restaurant, do a picnic in the park (you do all the work), or pick up some finger lickin' good chicken on the way home.

Oh, and one more thing—make sure that you hold your wife tight, look her in the eyes, and tell her how you're the most blessed man on earth to have such a great wife—and then don't forget to call YOUR mother and wish her a Happy Mother's Day.

Top it off with a small gift and you will have given your wife a first-rate Mother's Day.

You 'da husband of one GREAT MOM!

A Homosapien Beach

Philippians 1:1-11

Hey Dad,

Greetings from the Bayou! For a family of Midwestern Yankees, there's some mighty spectacular countryside down in the Biloxi/New Orleans/Baton Rouge area. Not only can you still see remnants of the Katrina devastation, but you can also enjoy beautiful white sand beaches here.

But the thing about beaches is...they're not all created equal. In fact, you can go a long way and be really disappointed. Some have shells, surf, and wildlife...some don't. Recently, we stopped off in Pensacola, FL. After crossing a big bridge, we stopped at a toll booth and asked for directions to an RV friendly beach.

The smiling lady gave us a map and the promise that they even had some all night beach parking for RVs. Cool!!! Nothing better than camping on the beach for free and waking to the sound of the surf.

So...we drove to the end of a slim spit of land and found a large public parking lot filled with cars and a few RVs. Now I should have paid more attention to the car with the sign in the window that read, "Honk if you're a homosapien." (But it didn't say sapien). When I pulled into my RV spot, I noticed that my RV neighbors were two men wearing very tight Speedos.

In fact, I noticed that the entire parking lot was filled with a lot of Speedo-wearing men and groups of women (sporting a sign saying they were having a lesbian party) carrying tents down to the beach.

"Get back in the RV...we're leaving...NOW!!!!" I commanded.

We left, feeling bothered by the ruined night on the beach. As I was driving away from the Homosapien beach, I thought about how nice it would be to have a Familyman Beach directory. After all, for a Midwesterner to drive 500-1000 miles only to find a beach filled with homosapiens, jellyfish, or oil sludge, it can be mighty disappointing.

So I started a list of beaches with the best...waves, shells, sand, wildlife, RV parking, and family goodness. Check it out.* You just might avoid the awkwardness of finding two Speedo-wearing guys holding hands.

You 'da dad!

* http://www.familymanweb.com/article/familyman-friendly-beach-directory

I Made Katherine Cry

Philippians 1:12-14

Hey Dad,

Everywhere we travel, I meet guys who are part of this great team we've assembled...and you're part of it too. The thing I like about it is that it's nice to know we're all in the same boat. Every dad struggles with loving his wife and his children, and the pull of the unimportant.

That's comforting to me...especially after making my daughter Katherine cry. That's right I, the Familyman, purveyor of good fathering and the embodiment of sensitivity, made my daughter cry.

It was one of those RV days. You know the kind. I was on edge. Anyway, at one point my wife was in a store doing something so I thought it would be a good time to pick up the mess.

"Katherine, would you pick up the stuff on the floor?" I asked nicely.

A few minutes later, sticking my head out from under the dinette to come up for air, Katherine called to me from the back bedroom.

"Dad, come here. I want to show you something."

I got up looked at the mess that she had not touched and walked back to the back bedroom to see the smile of anticipation in my daughter's face. It quickly vanished after I laid into her for not doing as she was told.

Even as the tears flowed down her cheeks, I continued. Then the dam burst and she wept openly and said, "I was just so excited to show you this."

My heart was broken for making Katherine cry. I was so focused on me and my instructions that I forgot what was most important...my relationship with my daughter. The truth is, if I had been a good dad at the moment, then I would have listened more and talked less (and a whole bunch softer).

Since then, I've been making an extra effort to heal the wound that I caused. I want my princess to know that she's more important to me than everything...including her behavior. I've talked softly, stroked her feminine side, and showed her that I'm glad she's my princess.

So, don't make your daughter cry, and if you have recently...make it right.

You 'da dad!

Vacation-Ruining Were-Dad

Philippians 1:15-20

| May | 5 |

Hey Dad,

Have you ever noticed that traveling often brings out the worst in dads, kind of like a werewolf when a full moon appears? Although we're not on vacation, we have been able to see some cool things while we've been traveling around encouraging dads and moms.

Take the other day. We were zipping along some mighty pretty countryside on our way to the Grand Canyon. In my head, I pictured the Brady Bunch in their station wagon happily singing, "Row, row, row your boat," as we passed the miles away. In reality, my kids were arguing over who got to sit in the front seat last, who had the last licorice whip, and why life is so unfair.

I tried my best to point out how blessed we were to be seeing the Grand Canyon—but it didn't work. Instead I heard things like:

"How much longer?"

"Are we going to stay long?"

"Can we go swimming?"

Then it happened—the transformation. I became a Were-Dad. I hollered, threatened, and guilted the kids with comments like, "Do you know how fortunate you are to be seeing what we're going to see? Do you know how many people would kill to see the Canyon? Why don't you look out the window and see God's incredible creation? Roarrrrrr!!"

Transformation complete.

I was so mad that I gave up and pulled out of the game. That's why if you check out my RV blog, you won't see any pictures of me at the Grand Canyon. That's because I didn't want my picture taken. I didn't want to smile, have fun, or be a good dad.

In fact, I was so bad, I was afraid to get too near the canyon's edge because I thought one of my family members might push me over.

Things might have improved if you had been there. What I needed was another dad to stick his finger in my chest, look me in the eye, and say, "Quit your sniveling. You 'da dad!!"

But there was no other dad, so I missed out. Later, I apologized and things got better. But I'm still convinced that we dads need each other. We need dads praying for other dads every day—even when they travel with their families or go on vacation.

Dad, I don't know how things are at your house, but if things have seemed kind of rough, and you feel like pulling out or hanging on to your bad attitude, let me just say from one Were-Dad to another, "Quit your sniveling, because You 'da dad!!!"

It'll Grow Back

Hey Dad,

You know I've got a lot to learn when it comes to spending generously on my family. I try, but my bent is a little on the stingy side. Fortunately, God brings other dads across my path to remind me of what's important.

Walt, Pete from Long Island, a dad at Fort Wilderness, my father-in-law, and, most recently, my cousin Scott have all helped teach me this lesson.

Now Scott's encouragement came to me through his brother, Brian, whom we had dinner with a couple of weeks ago in Charleston, SC. Actually, I haven't talked to Scott in way too long, but I attribute the source of this fatherly wisdom to him.

I'm not sure what Brian was sharing across the table at CiCi's Pizza. I think we were talking about his upcoming family vacation to Disney World when, with a smile, he shared the cost of the tickets for a couple of days for his family of four.

"Wow," I said. "That's a lot of money."

That's when he zinged me with a nugget of dad wisdom.

"Like my brother Scott says," he responded with a smile, "Yeah, it's a lot of money, but it'll grow back."

That little phrase has been bouncing around in my noggin and has gotten me through an expensive boat ride to Ft. Sumter, dinner at the Rainforest Café, special treats at a gas station, and a half dozen other situations.

'Cause the truth is—it'll grow back, but my kids are growing up. I won't always have the opportunity to spend money on my children and wife, BUT IT'LL GROW BACK.

So let me encourage you with my cousin Scott's bit of advice. Take the vacation you've been talking about now, because it'll grow back. Get ice cream treats for everyone, because it'll grow back. Buy the special, unexpected gift for your wife because IT'LL GROW BACK.

Hey, Dad, and even if it doesn't, you'll have spent it well.

So have a great day—today. Spend it while you can enjoy it, like Walt encouraged me years ago; go for the big pretzel, like Pete taught me; and get flowers just because, like my father-in-law showed by example, because—it'll grow back!

You 'da dad!

One on One

Hey Dad,

I asked dads to share some one on one dad/child ideas. Here's what some of them said:

I will sometimes hide one of the three kids under our bed or in the closet until the other two are in bed then we let them come out for an hour or so and we watch a show, play "I spy," or plan what we would have on our imaginary farm that will probably never happen but is still fun to talk about.
~ Mark B. (OH)

One of our kids fav's is IHOP before church on Sunday morning. (and mine too). ~ Matthew D. (SC)

Sometimes my son (9) will work out with me to the workout video. It's a good way for us to bond and for me to express the importance of exercise.
~ Travis B

1. Camping and Hiking in the Rain Forests of the Rockies. Elevation gain, rain, 6" snow on the tent in the morning, fresh blueberries, Bear scat, Bear sightings says it all for bonding with the eldest boys.
2. Model Railroading with my sons Lionel set for his one-on-one Papa time.
3. Hot Chocolate and playing games at the local Starbucks. My daughter loves being out with Papa on a date. Starbucks host have a nice touch for Papa and daughter time to add to the time.
4. Sharing a Timbit 20 at the local Tim Horton's—Canadian thing, hey.
~ Mark E. (Canada)

One on One (cont.)

For the last 7 years we've been doing 1:1 (one-on-one) nights with our kids. If there was one think I could look back on with my kids and be proud of (besides teaching them about God) this is it. This is a great time, not just for dads, but for moms too. In a larger family that homeschools, it's rare for mom to have any time alone with the kids outside of these 1:1 nights. My kids look forward to it all week. Sometimes we go hiking, sometimes we go to the library and the coffee store, sometimes we go out for ice cream, sometimes we just play a video game (though rarely). We just try and find something that the parent and kid will both enjoy doing together.

~ Chris H. (SC)

My wife and I had five children in five years (youngest are twins), so things could get a little hectic at our house. In order to make each child feel special on their birthday (or closest date available), we decided that my wife would take them out for the day to any places they liked. They did not have to do any schoolwork that day (but their siblings did). We began this practice when my oldest son was two. My mother-in-law usually babysat the others. When they were young, we usually spent hours at one of the local play places and ate lunch at Chuck E Cheese's. As they got older, their lists included a Children's Museum, Toys R Us, Best Buy, Circuit City, American Girl Store, Lego Store, the library, a movie, Cold Stone, Krispy Kreme, and nice lunch restaurants. The child paid for anything other than gas and lunch. I always spent an extended lunch hour with them, gave the child walking-around money (his age worth of dollars to spend that day), and sometimes even took the day off work. We still do this for each of our kids, often having great conversations as we sit through a long lunch. We didn't realize how much those dates meant to our kids until recently when my oldest (18 now) was asked what one of his favorite memories is. He responded by telling all about HIS day each year when everything was devoted to him and everything he liked. , the only things we paid for were gas, lunch and the child's walking-around money! But the memories are priceless. God is good!

~ Tim H.

Just Show Up

Hey Dad,

The sun is shining, my children are great, my marriage is even better, and I feel on top of the world. Life just doesn't get any better than this.

Yeah, right!

Actually, the sun is nowhere to be seen. The air is heavy and gray. My kids are out spray-painting the bottom of a saucer-sled to look like the shell of a turtle, my wife does not like me a whole bunch, and I feel behind in everything.

You know, some super-dad experts would lead us to believe that fathering is easy, marriage is always a joy, and when life gives you a lemon...you get the point.

Being a dad and husband is hard and is not for the faint of heart. Kids are demanding, wives get upset, and life tumbles down on you like junk in an overstuffed closet.

But in all that, God is good to dads—especially this dad. Why? Because today, I get to be with the people I love the most (even when I don't like them much). Who knows what will take place in the next dozen hours? Maybe Maggie will smile sunshine into my heart with a warm kiss and hug, Ben will ambush me with a bear hug, or Ike will ask a deep question that only a dad can answer.

All I have to do is show up at the right address. I don't have to put on a fake face or be Mr. Happy Dad. But I do have to be there, even when the temptation is to pull out and bury myself in all the stuff that needs to be done.

It's times like these when we need other dads cheering, "Hang in there! You 'da dad!! You 'da Husband! You can do it!!"

So, my fellow overworked, under-appreciated, and sometimes ready-to-toss-in-the-towel dad, "Hang in there! You 'da dad!! You 'da Husband! You can do it!!"

You 'da dad!

Wives and Kids Aren't RV Toilets

Philippians 3:1-12

| May | 10 |

Hey Dad,

While working on my perpetual RV toilet problems the other day, I pondered this question. Why can't wives and kids be more like RV toilets? I mean with an RV toilet, you find a stinky mess, tackle the project with gusto, assess the damage, buy the needed parts, reassemble the whole thing, and ba-da-bing, problem solved.

But kids and wives…well, that's a whole different matter. Oh, you find yourself in the same stinky mess alright, but it just isn't as easy to fix as an RV toilet. Instead of assessing, tackling, and fixing, it's more of a 'stumble your way through' kind of thing.

In fact, at my house it feels like I've been battling this 'problem' for an incredibly long time with no signs of success. So what's a fixer to do?

Besides just keeping at it, the 'said fixer' needs to throw away the whole notion of 'FIXIN' because wives and kids ain't like RV toilets. They don't need fixing, they need a man who listens, seeks to understand, loves unconditionally, never gives up, keeps fighting for them, and cares more about them than the 'stink.'

Sound easy? Of course not. But you can do it…and so can I. Thanks, I needed that.

You 'da husband/dad!

From a Daughter

Philippians 3:13-21

Hey Dad,

This letter from a grown daughter says it way better than I ever could.

From a Daughter ~

"I had a wonderful relationship with my Christian father growing up. He was a third-grade teacher and an unusual man—emotional, tender, open and very affectionate without crossing the line. I'm convinced that it's because of him (and the power of the Holy Spirit), that I was able to remain pure until I was 33 (that's how old I was when I married). Because I knew open lines of communication and affection were available to me anytime, I simply did not feel the need to seek other loving arms before God's incredible timing. The father/daughter relationship is a delicate but extremely important one. Don't mess this one up, Christian dads! You model God for your sons and daughters."

~ Aleta

You 'da dad!

Knight in a Shining RV

Philippians 4:1-9

Hey Dad,

Just got back from the windy city of Duluth, Minnesota. In a nutshell...1200 miles, 24 hours of driving, and 170 gallons of gas...but because we have a bathroom in our RV—no bathroom stops!! I know I said I was going to try to enjoy the ride and smell the flowers, but it was easier said than done (especially with one eye on the road and the other on the gas gauge, which moved faster than the speedometer).

While we were there, we had a great time encouraging dads and moms in the things that are most important. I was reminded again how hard marriage and parenting really is. I met a lot of wives who desperately want and need their husbands to be involved in the family.

The thing is...we dads seem to be awfully busy nowadays. We're working or traveling a lot of hours, and when we're home, we have our "projects." Our wives are trying to make up for our absence, but they're struggling. They need us to be there, to encourage them, to hold them if they cry, to protect them, and to be their knights in shining armor.

I know my wife needs me to do those things. I let her down last weekend. I didn't tell you about the hard part of RVing. The shower didn't work, space was cramped, and the kids were exhausted and irritable.

She got upset, and I was bothered.

I was bothered that she was acting so...weak. I wanted her to buck up and enjoy the adventure. It was later that I remembered that that's how she was created: a fragile, exquisite vessel that needs to be cherished.

Your wife is the same. She may act tough and look like she can handle it all, but the truth is, she can't. She needs her man...she wants her man. You can't delegate it, do it over the phone, or catch up on the weekend. You gotta be there.

Dad, maybe you need to leave work a little earlier today, pick up a bunch of flowers from Walmart, and hold her in your arms "just to talk" after the kids go to bed.

That's what I need to do.

You 'da husband!

Life in the Crucible

Philippians 4:10-23

Hey Dad,

"It was the best of times; it was the worst of times." Whoever wrote that was obviously an RVer because that's what RVing does—it brings out the best and the worst in families, and dads.

Let me bring you up to date. We pulled up anchor and set sail in the Familyman Mobile for Minnesota on Monday. Since that time we have traveled about 600 miles without a single mechanical failure (which for an RVer is almost miraculous). We've stayed at some of the finest Walmarts and Sam's Clubs anywhere and were able to go to the Mall of America yesterday, where Abe leaned over and told me, "You're the best dad in the whole world."

That's the best of times.

But we've also had some ugly times in the last couple of days. The kids have been out of sorts, and I have been a mega-grouch at times. I've been harsh with them and my wife (hey, she was telling me how to drive!). Plus, gas is $2.79 a GALLON (multiply that by 75)!!

I've tried to be Mr. Spiritual Leader, explaining to the kids how we are to be salt and light in this world, and how we need to put others before ourselves. But that's when I usually start to clench my teeth and blow my "spiritual giant" persona.

Man, I wish there was some kind of pill I could take to make me what I want to be. Because the truth is, my family's attitude depends on my attitude. They mirror me. And your kids mirror you.

Yow!

But there is no pill. The way I see it, I have two options: I can either stay on the grumpy train or I can try again. In fact, I think as soon as I send this out, I'll gather the family, ask forgiveness (again), talk about what God wants from us as a family, and keep on going.

I once was asked, "What makes a good dad?" As I've thought about that question, I think the answer is this: A good dad keeps trying.

He blows his cool, gets snappy, or says unkind things. BUT he apologizes and keeps trying. He gets back up on the horse, jumps back in the ring, and gets back behind the wheel of the RV.

That, my fellow dad, is what a good dad is. And that's what I'm going to do.

And so can you.

You 'da dad!

The Perfect Time for Dreams

Ephesians 1:1-23

Hey Dad,

In the three weeks since we began our RV travels, I've noticed that RVing brings out the dreamer in fathers. It usually happens as I'm talking to a fellow dad and he finds out that I'm traveling a chunk of the country with my family in the old Familyman Mobile. His eyes sparkle and there is an excitement in his voice.

"You know my wife and I have talked about traveling in an RV. It sounds like a lot of family fun," he says.

"Are you kidding?" I respond, trying to slap some good sense into his brain. "It's cramped; you break down alongside the road; you need to take out a bank loan just to fill the gas tank; and it brings out the BEAST in EVERYONE." But as I talk, my heart softens, and I finish by saying, "Yeah, it is fun. You should do it."

But then, the dreamer standing in front of me vanishes and the sparkle in his eye is replaced with a faint sadness as he rattles off all the reasons why his family can't. "The baby is too young; my wife is pregnant; things are pretty busy this year at work; the kids wouldn't appreciate it."

But I'm not licked yet and have a well-thought-through response.

"Sounds like the perfect time to do it. After all, life will never get any easier. In fact, the real danger as dads is that we'll put off all the good stuff until it's just too late. Then, all we'll have to show for our practical decision-making is a pile of regrets.

So, Dad, if you've been putting off a family vacation, a special project around the house, a trip of a lifetime, or some other family dream...put it off no longer. Now is the time. Gather the family together and say, "We're going to do it."

Then get ready because it will be hard, stressful, and will bring out the BEAST in EVERYONE. And I wouldn't trade it for anything.

You 'da dad!

Lifeguard on Duty

Ephesians 2:1-10

Hey Dad,

Greetings from the oldest city in the USA—St. Augustine, Florida! Actually, we're staying at a state campground on Anastasia Island. Today, we toured the Castillo de San Marcos (an old fort), walked the 219 steps to the top of a big black-and-white striped lighthouse, and even managed to spend a couple of hours at the beach. Oh, and yesterday I managed to rip the taillight off, and put a gash in the fender of, a brand new Mercedes.

The beach was beautiful, although there was a big sign describing how the rip tide might suck you or your children out into the middle of the ocean. No big deal for the average swimmer. But this dad takes the ocean, rip tides, and signs that read, "No lifeguard on duty—swim at your own risk" very seriously.

I've always been a little scared of the ocean, and when my kids are in the water, I'm on them like a tick on a hound dog. They played while I watched, standing in the surf ready to jump into action if I was needed. I didn't care what the signs said—THIS DAD IS ON DUTY! I am my children's lifeguard. Other children may be up to their heads in dangerous surf. But not mine. My kids may beg and plead and say it's not fair. But I don't care, I'm the lifeGUARD.

I was reminded a few days ago that my lifeguarding involves more than just beach duty; it involves most areas of their young lives.

Take the other day. We pulled into a parking lot and stood face-to-face with a trailer plastered with a half-naked young lady selling something. My son noticed. In the past, he wouldn't have, but now he's older. And he NOTICED.

I thought it over for about 800 miles of RVing and know what I need to do. I'm the lifeguard, and I'm on duty. I can't keep him from seeing everything, but I can do a lot to keep him from seeing MOST of it. I can talk to him about looking away. I can keep him away from places that he might be exposed to images, and I'll be an example of purity even when he's not watching me. Why?

Because I know those images are like rip tides, they lead to deep water where men die. But my sons and daughters won't have to worry about the deep water because I'm on duty!

How about you, Dad? Have you let your guard down? Your kids are counting on you to keep them away from the rip tides of life. Do what you have to do. Don't listen to their pleas of "that's not fair." You 'da Lifeguard and you're on duty!

You 'da dad!!

Listen to the Tingle

Ephesians 2:11-22

Hey Dad,

In RV-ing, as in life, God often causes a little tingle to creep up the back of the neck that should NOT be ignored, informing you that what you're about to attempt is NOT a good idea—especially when you're behind the wheel of an RV.

I experienced the tingle from God a couple of days ago as I looked at the steep incline into the Denny's parking lot. The tingle definitely said, "I wouldn't try that if I were you—yep, looks like a mighty steep angle—your hitch is going to drag big time."

I heard every word, but we were hungry and Denny's was looking good, so I went for it!

A few seconds later, I was stuck solid and my wheels spun like I was on ice. I tried backing up—no good. Rocking—nope.

Quickly, I jumped from my seat, pushed open the RV door, and ran to the rear of the RV to see the foot of the trailer buried four inches in the asphalt.

Oh, man, I should have listened to the tingle, I thought.

Just then a police officer walked up to me and said in a very perturbed tone, "You just had to pick the busiest time of day and the busiest street in Pittsburgh to get stuck."

I looked up and saw three lanes of traffic both ways—and I was blocking at least three of them. All the faces I could see had the look of—what an idiot!

Already a couple of Pittsburghians had squeezed by and shouted out a welcome to their fine city—but I can't repeat their kind words.

The policeman wanted to call a tow truck, but I was already hacking at the asphalt with a hammer and screwdriver. Hey, if I could get a mama raccoon and her babies out of my ceiling—I could get this trailer unburied.

It took about 20 minutes, but (by God's mercy) we got the trailer separated from the RV, the pin pulled from the hitch (which was also below grade), and the RV up the ramp and free from the asphalt's evil grip.

That was close. It could have been bad—and expensive.

As it turned out, nothing was damaged, and I learned a valuable lesson: listen to the tingle.

I also feel it when I'm about to lose my cool and say something to my wife or children that I shouldn't, look at things that men shouldn't look at, or go certain places that men shouldn't go.

The tingle is a gift from God to stupid dads to save them a heap of hurt.

So take it from this RV-ing dad—listen to the tingle.

You 'da dad!

Lost in Akron

Ephesians 3:1-21

Hey Dad,

Just got back from speaking in downtown Akron, OH and other than the horrific experience of losing one of my children for a while, we had a great time. Now let the records show that it was NOT my fault…not that I haven't 'misplaced' a kid or two in my day, but I was totally innocent this time.

One of my teenagers was supposed to be watching a video with four of the younger boys in the RV while my wife and I were inside at the convention. After a short time, my wife returned and asked, "Where's Jed (our 2-year-old)?"

After assessing the situation, she wisely called 911, and after a few frantic minutes the 911 operator said, "I think we have your son." I finally showed up on the scene and sprinted down a hill to see a policeman step around the corner carrying my son. Ahhh…

We later learned he had wandered out of the RV, was pulled out of a downtown street, held up at a music concert that was taking place (to see if he belonged to anyone), and then spotted by someone who had seen him on our website and recognized him as belonging to us. The policeman was super nice about the whole thing, but we felt like loser parents.

Later, as I walked around, sobered by the event, I visualized my little boy touring the city of Akron all by himself, alone, and scared. It tore me up thinking that no one was watching him, when in a gentle, reassuring whisper God said, "I never took my eyes off him."

He's right. We can't watch over them every second but God can, and HE does. And He is watching over your children right now, no matter where they are or what they're doing. You know why? Because He's 'DA DAD!!!' And I'm sure glad He is.

PS – After the lost child escapade, I had a bunch of dads tell me their lost kid stories. It was therapeutic for them and encouraging to me. So…if you have a "lost kid/wife" story, I'd love to hear it. As the old saying goes, "Stupid loves company."

The Day My Son Became a Man

Ephesians 4:1-16

Hey Dad,

This week my oldest son passed from the ranks of kiddom into adulthood...or kind-of-adulthood. He cut the grass.

Many cultures have their own test of manhood. Some have to kill a water buffalo with their bare hands or slide headfirst into the burrow of a giant python. In America, it's using a lawnmower. For me, it was a Toro walk-behind—a real beauty.

For my son, it's a gray, industrial-strength, riding mower...eighteen horse-power of muscle and whirling razor-sharp blades. Ben was mesmerized as I instructed him in proper lawnmower safety, adding gory details of what a mower could do to an operator who was not careful.

Finally, he climbed aboard the beast, engaged the blades, and commenced becoming a man. I envisioned listening to the lovely sound of a mower cutting grass in the distance as I sip lemonade while swinging in my newly installed hammock. O.K., so maybe were not there yet.

As I watched him zip up and down the semi-straightish rows, I couldn't help but think about how my boy was growing up. The longer I watched, the more I didn't like it. In my mind, I pictured him driving a car, then going off to college, getting married, having children of his own, and only seeing him every couple of months. If I had thought that stopping the mower and refusing to let him cut the grass would slow the growing-up process, I would have done it right then.

But I knew it wouldn't matter. He will grow up whether I like it or not.

That's why I knew it was time for him to learn to ride the mower. I was training him for the time when he would be grown up.

I'm training our children for the future. That's why I let the boys help me change the oil in the van, work in the garden, and have our daughter help my wife in the kitchen.

Dad, what are you doing to train your children for the future? It's a little scary to think about them growing up, but it's even scarier to think they'd grow up without being prepared. That's your job.

You 'da dad!!

Make It Hap'n, Cap'n

Ephesians 4:17-32

Hey Dad,

Well, we're back home for a little while. Even made it through the Cleveland Triangle without mishap. Just in case you've forgotten or hadn't heard, in the last two years our RV caught fire and a turkey flew through our windshield within a couple miles of each other...in the Triangle.

I have to admit, I was a little nervous when we approached The T. Just to be safe, I checked my speed, cleared a path to the fire extinguisher, and had my cell phone ready to dial 911. But nothing happened. Once again, God graced us with smooth sailing.

Now that we're home, I'd like to think that I can kick it into cruise control...but there is no cruise control setting on the fathering steering column.

In fact, over the last several weeks, I have become painfully aware that I have a lot of work to do at home. I've noticed many bad habits and bad attitudes that have crept into our family...probably picked them up on the road (certainly not from us).

Now I don't mean to be a nag, but I've noticed that maybe your family has picked up some bad habits as well. You see, in the last two months, I've talked to lots of dads and moms all over the country. I've had dads tell me about teenagers with bad attitudes, obnoxious lers, and marriages that have lost their carbonation. Many are discouraged and weary of the battle.

I always give them the advice that I'm giving you and giving to myself: Deal with it.

It's up to you and me, Dad, to turn off the cruise control and deal with the issues facing us. Our kids are counting on us to keep working and training them, never giving up for an instant (well okay, maybe for a few seconds...but not any longer than that).

I know it's exhausting and unrelenting...but that's okay; we're the dads. We can handle it—bring it on.

I'm going to start by having a family meeting. I will apologize for allowing things to get out of hand, set a clear path, and then get behind the driver's wheel, because I'm the captain, and we don't have cruise control on this ship.

So, make it hap'n, Cap'n.

Aye, Aye...You 'da dad!

Father Power!

Hey Dad,

We had a real boomer of a storm the other day. Debbie was gone, leaving me with the kids during naptime. I was busy at the computer when a thunderous CRACK rattled the house, which was followed by a blood-curdling scream.

It was Abe, our 2 year old.

"Oh great!" I thought. "There goes my afternoon."

Abe was at the top of the stairs looking into the dark sky.

"Scarewy," he cried several times.

He sobbed uncontrollably as I carried him to his bedroom and tucked him back into bed.

"It's okay, Abe. I'll lie here on the floor beside you."

As I did, he stuck out his open hand and I grabbed it. Immediately he quieted and closed his eyes.

Half an hour later, he was sound asleep, clutching my finger like a vise-grip. Periodically, he'd open his eyes to make sure I was still there and then drift back to sleep.

Staring into the sleeping face of my son, a deep sense of Father Power covered me. My son was sleeping in the midst of an incredibly violent storm because he knew his dad was beside him. My presence was more powerful to him than a million gigawatts of electricity and destruction. Wow!

As I lay there, I realized I was teaching my son about God. My boy would grow up knowing that God is always with him because I was there.

When he gets stung, I come. When he calls out at night, I come to his side. When he is sick and upchucks all over his bed and himself, I swoop out of the dark and hold him in my arms, clean it up, and then tuck him back into bed.

That's Father POWER with a capital P. It's felt by children from birth to adulthood. My kids need it—and so do yours. If we're not there for them, we handicap them and teach them that God isn't always there when they need Him.

And I guess that makes the only force greater than Father Power—the power of a missing dad.

So...be there!

You 'da dad!!

Mr. Outsider

Ephesians 5:22-33

Hey Dad,

I'm all alone by myself: no wife, no kids (except for Caleb [7 weeks], but he's asleep). NO, THEY DIDN'T LEAVE ME, although I wouldn't blame them at times. This is the first time in seven weeks that I've found myself in such a predicament. Up until right now, it's been wall-to-wall Wilsons.

They left me behind to do some work while they check out the pool at this state park in Virginia. It's been a whirlwind of activity since I wrote last, but we did find a few hours last week to sit and enjoy the pool at Fort Wilderness Campground in Orlando, FL.

Actually, I just wanted to SIT and enjoy doing nothing while the kids played in the pool, but some other "outside" kid ruined that idea.

It was great up until that point. The kids were playing nicely while I watched from a cozy deck chair under a shady canopy.

Then along came Mr. Outsider. One minute he wasn't there and I was enjoying doing nothing; and the next minute, he was there, and I was forced into a father decision-making mode.

My choices were these: 1) I could continue to sit there (which I was really enjoying) and let my kids interact with this other kid that I knew nothing about, or what they might talk about, or what he might expose them to. I could just assume he was an okay kid and that he probably came from a good family who had taught him the same values as I had taught my kids. Or, 2) I could assume nothing and get out of my chair and make sure I was there, guarding, watching, and protecting my kids.

I wish I could say I was out of my easy chair before I had finished considering my options, but it really was a nice, comfortable chair, and the water looked colder than usual. But these were my kids I was talking about.

So I dragged my carcass out of the chair, whipped off my shirt, and waded into the cold water to make sure everything was okay.

Later, I was reminded that I am going to need to be even more involved in their extracurricular activities as they get older. And that can only mean one thing—less time for MY extracurricular activities.

If I'm not around to do the things my kids like to do, well then, they'll find someone else who is around to do those things with. And it might just be someone who doesn't think and believe like I do.

So, Dad, here's a challenge for you and for me. Let's get off our lawn chair, out of the A/C, and off the sidelines and get in there so we can be the greatest influence in our children's lives. If you and I don't, someone else will.

Is that overprotecting? You bet. And that's what dads do.

You 'da dad!

The Extra Mile

Ephesians 6:1-9

Hey Dad,

It's my son's birthday today (Ike): an RV birthday, which isn't nearly as fun as a home birthday. But I'm up for the challenge. I am determined to go the extra mile to make my son's birthday great. Already, Ike and I walked from our convenient Walmart parking lot hotel to a McDonald's that was less than 30 yards away.

It was his idea, along with the request that he get his own cinnamon roll. When we returned, he opened the door to a chorus of "Happy Birthday" and an RV filled with balloons, streamers, and a big birthday banner. We're off to a good start, and it isn't even 8:15 A.M. yet.

The rest of the day is his. We're going to a Bass Pro Shop, a big cave, and hopefully stop at a hotel to see if we can use their swimming pool. Plus he'll open his gifts along the way.

It will be a lot of fun for him, but a lot of work, effort, and money for us. It would be easier to go about our day as normal and then have cake and presents at dinnertime, but I'm committed to going THE EXTRA MILE.

That's what separates dads from normal people.

Take my friend Pete, from Long Island, for example. While on vacation this past fall, he was determined to take his family to collect water from each of the great lakes. Now it wasn't too hard, because they happened to travel near the lakes. But for a bottle of water from the last lake, he had to travel a couple hundred miles out of his way. That's THE EXTRA MILE.

Actually, it was his example that encouraged me to drive the 150 miles out of our way to go to Walnut Grove, Minnesota (home of the Little House on the Prairie). Sure, it was a rinky-dink museum with a rinky-dink campground. But hey, I was going THE EXTRA MILE.

That's the kind of dad I want to be. I want to celebrate birthdays in a big way, drive miles out of the way to experience America, stop the ice cream truck on a busy summer night, take a bike ride TWO nights in a row, and take the time to dump some Mentos in a 2-liter bottle of Diet Coke.

I want to be an EXTRA MILE kind of dad. And I want to encourage you to be that kind of dad, too. After all ...

You 'da dad!

Neither Rain Nor Snow

Ephesians 6:10-24

Hey Dad,

You know, mail carriers have nothing on dads. Sure, it's true that neither rain, nor snow, nor gloom of night will keep them from their appointed duties. But is everyone watching their every move when it's raining, snowing, or glooming? I didn't think so.

Dads aren't so lucky. Not only do we have to do our dad duties in all kinds of weather, but also our kids all always watching—and learning. I mean always!

Take the other day. We had spent the night in a Lowe's parking lot, which put us about 100 yards away from the main entrance to Walmart. Because we needed a few items before we hit the road and because it was pouring down rain, I offered to go inside so my wife could stay nice and dry.

So along with a few kids, I crossed the semi-flooded parking lot, loaded up a cart, and pushed it back to the RV. By the time the cart was unloaded, I was wet to the drawers.

There was only one little thing left to do—battle with myself. You see, the cart corral was a long way away from where we were parked, it was raining bats and hogs, and my kids were watching and waiting to see what I would do.

Sure, Walmart asks that we put the carts back in the corral, but I was in the middle of a gully-washer, and there were other carts that were scattered throughout the waterlogged lot. But my kids were watching and would know that I didn't follow the rules.

Maybe they weren't watching. Who am I kidding? They're always watching—and so is God.

Sooo, I pushed the cart over to the corral in the rain, got soaked to the bone, and taught my children an invaluable lesson—because our children are always watching us, Dad.

They see us when we drive ten miles over the speed limit, make an illegal U-turn, share meals on the all-you-can-eat buffet, or leave the grocery cart in the middle of the parking lot. And it doesn't matter if it's raining, snowing, or glooming. They're always watching.

So, my fellow dad, be on your guard, leave a good example, and don't forget to put your cart back in the corral.

You 'da dad!

No Regrets

Hey Dad,

A while back I wrote, "You never know what tomorrow holds." Little did I know that a few days later, my daughter Katherine would be rolled through a large pair of double doors at midnight to have an emergency appendectomy performed on her ruptured appendix.

Katherine is doing great now, but it was a reminder to me about how quickly the family that we hold dear can be taken away...just like that. That's what happened to my friend Robert Rogers.

I first heard Robert's story on a local radio station and later wrote an article about him for a men's magazine. The memorable thing about Robert was that he loved, I mean really loved his wife and four children. He made sacrifices for them, played with them, and cherished his role as a dad. That's what makes his story so terrible and one that you must hear.

Actually, it all happened one year ago almost to the day. Robert and his family were on their way back from a wedding a couple of hours away from their Kansas home. There were torrential downpours, and they hit a stretch of flooded highway. They tried to inch their way through, but eventually their van swamped and died.

The kids were asleep in their car seats, and Robert assured his wife that everything would be okay. But to their horror, the water rose until it filled their van up to the steering wheel.

The kids awoke and screamed. They were terrified as the water reached their toes. Being a good dad, Robert prayed and led them in singing their favorite praise choruses. Then, the unbelievable happened.

According to eyewitnesses, a 7-foot wave slammed into the van, lifted it up, and pushed it across the highway and into a 30-foot gully. The van was under water. Quickly, Robert kicked out the driver's window to avoid drowning. Instantly, everything and everyone that wasn't buckled in was sucked out of the van and into the raging black river.

Miraculously, Robert survived, but over the next 24 hours, he was called to face the unbearable task of identifying the bodies of his wife and children.

"I miss so much being called Dad," Robert told me, "but I know that had I gone to heaven with my family, the story would be over. It would have been just a blip in the media. Now I have the opportunity to tell of God's faithfulness and encourage fathers to savor every moment...to make every day, every hug, every moment, sacred."

"I don't have any regrets," he says humbly to fellow dads. His desire is to make sure you, as a father, can one day say the same.

Dad, may Robert's story be heavy on your heart and aid you in choosing the best...today, because you may not get tomorrow.

50 Years From Now

Thanks for a good early morning cry!

I have been getting my two oldest daughters up with me before work and doing Bible memorizing with them and so I started the song Slow Fade right as my oldest, Lillian 9, climbed into my lap...yeah, got choked up.

I have been struggling with problems in my marriage for years. And really they are problems with me and they have been eroding my marriage. I think the root has been a lack of contentment. God has given me more than I could ever have hoped to dreamed to have imagined and yet I still hold on to the decaying, wretched, filth of this world....I have cried out to God and He has always faithfully answered, truly His mercy and loving kindness are forever!

I think the hardest part has been feeling comfortable with God again after taking such great advantage of His grace. The arrogance and selfishness in my heart make it hard for me to understand why my wife didn't leave me years ago. But by His grace, she has endured.

God has gotten my attention through a series of events and my wife and I are going to "A Weekend to Remember" this weekend, it's an all weekend marriage seminar. I know this isn't a one time fix all, but we are working and by His grace I am certain Lana and I will be together 50 years from now. I also have been counseling and confessing my sins and struggles with my Pastor and brothers in Christ. Not without God forcing me to though, I must admit.

If there is any way I can encourage other men to stop sinning now, confess your sins, yes it is hard, turn from your sin, be open with your wife, find strong brothers in Christ to lean on, stay close to the Lord, and most of all DON'T GIVE UP!!!! ~ G K

NYC and Understanding Ike

Galatians 1:11-24

Hey Dad,

A lot has happened in two weeks. Most of it took place in or around New York City. We saw it all...or most of it. On the first day, we rode an eternally long train, went to the top of the Empire State Building, walked 100 blocks to

Central Park, saw Times Square and buildings that were in movies, and rode a Ferris wheel inside a giant Toys "R" Us.

The second day we saw the Statue of Liberty, rode a subway (without being mugged), went to Ellis Island, and peered into Ground Zero. I was as sick as a dog but had the time of my life (Debbie was sick the day before).

You know, of all the things that I saw and learned while we were in NY City, the one thing I'll always remember was that I learned that Isaac likes to be called Ike better than he likes to be called Isaac.

When I overheard him tell that to one of the grownups who had asked him what he likes to be called, I was astounded...not so much that he chose one name over the other, but that I didn't even know that about my son—and I should have.

The whole time we were in NY my mind kept asking the questions: Why didn't I know that? And what other things don't I know about my children that I should?

• What do my other kids prefer to be called?
• What makes them feel really loved?
• What do I do that frustrates them?
• If they could change something about themselves, what would it be?

You know, Dad, all the things I've seen and learned in our travels means very little compared to really knowing my children and my wife.

So here's my plan: in the next week I'm going to find out the answers to some of these questions. I'll probe, prod, and ask unassuming questions, all for the sake of knowing my children and wife better than anyone else alive.

Can I challenge you to do the same? Start with this simple question, "What name do you like me to call you best?"

You 'da dad!!

Daddy Is a Girl's Best Friend

Galatians 2:1-10

Hey Dad,

You know, there's just something very pink and tinkerbellish about girls. Sure, there's also a ton of unbridled emotion and changing of clothes that goes hand in hand with having a girl, but there's just something wonderful about daughters. My daughter Katherine has proven that to me more than once in the last two weeks.

The first time happened on a beautiful, fall night when we were still able to eat dinner on our screened-in porch. We were halfway through dinner when Katherine asked a question, and I responded in a fairly normal way—I thought. Katherine was hit with a wave of emotion and burst into tears. I was touched by her brokenness, and in my softest, most fatherly voice I said, "I didn't mean it that way, Katherine. I'm so sorry..." Her tears stopped and later that evening she walked up to me and apologized for her outburst, and we hugged and talked.

A few days later, I walked past her and she gave me a funny look. "Dad," she said, "can you dance with me?"

I have to admit that I was taken back by her question—she's never asked me to dance before. But without hesitation, I put my arms around her and swept her off her feet to giggles of delight.

Then, last Thursday, a tornado touched down just a few miles from our home. The radio blared its emergency test warning—but it wasn't a test. Katherine was a mess, and she's never even seen The Wizard of Oz. The entire night she clung to me and wanted to hear my words of assurance.

And lastly, she proved it to me again when our whole family went to the mall recently. As I walked to the pretzel booth, Katherine walked with me with her arm around my waist—like a teenager with her boyfriend. It felt a little weird, but it grew on me as we walked. In fact, by the time we got to the pretzel place, I was kind of bummed that she removed her arm.

Okay, so here's the point, Dad. Our daughters find comfort, security, and love in us. They need us to sweep them off their feet from time to time, talk gently, and try to understand their emotions. If we're not there for them, some other guy with baggy jeans will be.

So, Dad, be there. Make the time to hold your daughter on your lap, ask her about her day, and put your arm around her waist like you're a teenager and she's your girlfriend—because she is.

You 'da dad!

Dictator Dad

Galatians 2:11-21

Hey Dad,

Things have been hopping at the Wilson's. Last week, my son Ike and I flew to San Diego to speak, and this week we're all at Harvey Cedars Bible Conference in New Jersey, and then we turn the Familyman mobile toward Wisconsin. Throw in a few upchucking children, and you can see how we're feeling a little frazzled.

Along the drive to NJ, we stopped at <u>Gravity Hill</u> (which I had wanted to do for several years) and Valley Forge. Valley Forge was great (and free) and Gravity Hill was not so great and out of the way (and also free).

I guess we were all expecting some mind-bending freak of nature; instead we left with a confused four-year-old. Now Caleb's never sure if we're going up hill or if we just "think" we're going up hill.

But at least my kids can now say, "We've been there, done that...because my dad made us go."

Yep, I've decided it's no more 'Mr. Nice Guy-Let's Vote' kind of dad. I've tried that and found that if I let them have their way, they'd never see or do anything except watch an occasional movie and have ice cream.

So I've changed my tactic. Instead of saying, "Who wants to go see...?" and then spend the next hour convincing them they'll enjoy it and the next 5 hours mad that they're not, I'm just going to say (after consulting with my wife in private), "We're going to do such and such."

Oh, they may hate it...but they're going to SEE IT. Call me Dictator Dad.

That's what dads do...because we're 'da dads.

So if you've been thinking it would be fun to take the family to _____. Don't ask – say, "Get in the car because we're going to_____.

They may not know it...but they're counting on you and will recall great memories because you made them GO!

You 'da dictator dad!!!

Epic Pooportions

Galatians 3:1-14

Hey Dad,

I don't want to count my chickens before they're hatched, but I think we're about out of the poop-woods. For the last week, my son Jed (2) has had a serious case of the runs. I'm talking EPIC proportions.

Just a couple of mornings ago, he walked into our bedroom like usual and stood beside our bed while we tried to ignore him hoping he would go bother one of his brothers or sisters instead.

A minute later, my nose smelled trouble. Pulling myself up to get a better view, I was shocked to see that the entire front of his shirt was soaked...with poop.

"Oh, man," I groaned. "Jed, what happened?"

Not one to shirk my responsibilities, I grabbed a diaper and stripped my son, causing a puddle of brown ooze to pour onto our bedroom floor. I'm not exaggerating when I say I've never seen anything like it in my 17-year career of having kids. My wife and I finished cleaning up and plopped him in the bathtub hoping that it would be a short lived thing.

It wasn't, and a day later he walked into our bedroom for a repeat performance...leaving a second poop stain beside my bed. "Surely, this thing has to be about over," I thought, trying to bring a ray of sunshine into my poopy world. And it looked like it was until my wife called me into our game closet to show me a circle of brown paint that someone spilled on the floor...but it wasn't paint.

As I was cleaning up that mess (my wife's not much help in this department), I began to feel 'small.' Maybe it's because I had just been reading about a guy who ran a large ministry to families. His website was filled with fantastic ideas and big plans, and his picture looked so...so...professional as he smiled at me in a casual jacket and unbuttoned shirt, like he had just stepped out of a board meeting.

I thought about that as I scooped poop off the closet floor. I'll never have a ministry like that, dress like that, or accomplish all those big plans. Actually, the thought was a little sobering, and I felt a tad resentful toward my poopy child.

BUT then God whispered in my heart, "You have something better."

"Thanks God," I prayed with the stench in my nostrils, "I needed that."

So, let me remind you Dad, you may not have nice things, a big nest egg, or a stellar career...but you have something BETTER. And if you do have some of those nice things...don't forget for one moment that you too have something BETTER.

You 'da dad!

One Song and a PowerPoint

Hey Dad,

We've only been on the road for three and a half weeks, but I'm tired—even though things have gone about as well as they could possibly go. We've had no mechanical problems (yet), no one has gotten sick (yet), and my wife Debbie has not left us to fly home (yet).

During all this time though, I've noticed that my children are getting older. My son Ben's face looks more like a teenager's, Sam's foot is almost as big as mine, Katherine looks tall and less little-girl like, and even Caleb, at almost five weeks old, looks more like a real baby and less like a wrinkled prune.

Growing up happens so quickly. In fact, it won't be long before my kids' entire time at home is compressed into one song and a PowerPoint presentation.

I learned that a couple weeks ago when I spoke at a graduation in Missouri. For each of the graduates, they showed a PowerPoint presentation. There were pictures of little boys and girls dressed up as pirates and princesses, pictures of kids with animals and around Christmas trees. There were photos of babies who had fallen asleep on their dad's chest as he snored away.

But the pictures weren't only of kids. In each of the PP shows, there were young dads with lots of hair and moms with outdated hairdos. They all looked so happy and carefree, unaware that time was passing so quickly.

As I watched, I found that a baseball-sized lump had caught in my throat and tears filled my eyes. In each of the shots, my children's faces replaced the photos on the screen. I had lived most of those moments.

Then something happened. The song that had been playing in the background ended, and the show was over.

One song. That's all it lasted. An entire childhood was compressed into one song and a PowerPoint presentation.

It struck me then that I would soon be watching my children's slide shows and that all of "this" will be over. There won't be any more cramped times in the RV, arguments over who will sit where, or complaints because I got the wrong kind of donuts.

Here comes that lump again.

Here's my prayer for you and me, Dad: "Dear God, let me enjoy this day with my family no matter what happens or how hard it gets. Let me remember that it only lasts for one song and a PowerPoint presentation, and then they're grown up. Amen."

You 'da dad!

It Doesn't Matter

Galatians 4:1-20

Hey Dad,

Whenever I speak to a group of dads, I ask the question, "What do our children need from us?" After speaking to thousands of dads, no one has EVER answered, "A lot of money...a nice car...a father with an important job...great vacations on tropical islands...a healthy retirement account...a nicely manicured lawn...fame...a big house...stock options...a membership at the country club.

Why is it that dads never name those things?

It's because they know that none of that stuff matters to children. The only person those things matter to is US. We can say that the reason we work so many hours is so that we can provide these things for our children, but the reality is they don't even need those things. Sadly, we deprive them of the things they do need because we're too busy going after the things they don't need.

Repeat after me.

Cars don't matter—they can be rusty, shiny, cheap, or expensive...but they don't matter.

Houses don't matter.

Furniture doesn't matter.

Big bank accounts don't matter.

European shoes don't matter.

Golf doesn't matter.

Hobbies don't matter.

Big ministries don't matter.

Careers don't matter.

Abs of steel don't matter.

Stuff doesn't matter.

Family matters!!

So the question begs asking, if these things really don't matter, why do we spend most of our time trying to get them?

~Excerpt from Father Power

Roll the Tape

Hey Dad,

I was going to share something brilliant with you this week...but that has just changed in the last three seconds. That's because I just had to discipline my son Cal for something he said to his sister Maggie.

Actually, I seem to be doing a lot of discipline this week. This time it started with his sister saying in a rather whiny voice, "Dad, Cal said, "Dumb Maggie." The tone in her voice made it "clear" that she was totally innocent.

"Tell Cal to come here," I said wishing to not be needed by any of my children for just thirty minutes. I could hear her smile as she went to go get the 'victim.'

A minute later, Cal still dressed in his pjs walked up to me with doom on his face.

I turned to him, administered the appropriate discipline, and then waded into my fatherly instructions.

"Cal, you don't ever talk like that," I said holding his chin to help focus his eyes on mine. "We NEVER talk that way in our family."

As the words left my mouth, in my mind I heard the words, "Roll the tape!"

In a flash, God replayed the tape from yesterday, and I heard the words spew forth form MY mouth, "What are you, a dummy?!"

Oh no, we NEVER talk that way in our family. Who am I kidding? Cal learned to say 'dumb' from me. We may NEVER talk that way...but I talk that way. In fact, it seems unfair and cruel to discipline my children for stuff that I taught them.

As the old saying goes, more is caught than taught. I can "say" all I want, but the truth is my children will follow my example.

So, I still need to discipline them for wrong behavior, BUT I first need to work on me. I need to watch what comes out of my mouth, how I drive, how I interact with family members and others, and where I put my trust.

I hate to bring this up, Dad, but you might need to take a good long look at your children's bad behavior and see if they learned any of it from you. You still need to discipline them for their wrong behavior, BUT first you need to work on you.

Roll the tape!

RV Marriage Book

Hey Dad,

Hope this doesn't offend any of my fellow dads in Texas, but we were all glad to leave the Lone Star State. I'm thinking we had a little too much unplanned time there...or maybe it was the way those Texans drive! Not only do they drive on the shoulder of the road...and are OK with that, but they have some mighty mixed up on and off ramps in their cities.

I'm sure we were almost killed at least a couple of times. Poor Gloria (the voice on our GPS) never talked so fast, "Get in the right lane...bare left, no I mean right...not that right lane, the other right lane...watch out for that oncoming car...Ahgggg!!! Can someone please unplug me?"

Whew! I'm getting worked up just writing about it.

Anyway, the kids and the RV are doing great, but all the time in the RV tends to put a strain on our marriage. In fact, I'm thinking about writing a book entitled "The Familyman's RV Marriage Guide for Men." I'm not sure of all the details, but I've been thinking about at least one chapter entitled, "The longer you wait to fix things, the harder they are to fix."

Not only does it apply to RV problems like leaky toilets, tail light issues, and smoking motors, but it also applies to marriages...especially mine. You see the problem is that I'm a glass half-full kind of guy. I like to assume that things will get better on their own if I ignore them. Problem is...they don't, especially when it applies to marriages...especially mine.

So, when I can tell that my wife is out of sorts, I kind of like to think that all she needs is a good night's sleep. So, I plop into bed and go to sleep instead of dealing with it. Next morning, I wake to find that my wife is not over "it". Instead, she's a little MORE out of sorts. A few 'sleeps' later, and I've got marriage issues.

I'm just so stupid. When will I learn that if I take the time to address the problem when it's first detected, it would make life a whole lot better for all of us? Because the truth is: the longer I wait to fix things, the harder they are to fix.

So, Dad, if you're like me and have some "things" to fix, you better get at it.

You 'da...Mr. Fix-it!

Demon Toilet

Galatians 5:7-15

Hey Dad,

I've been whipped by a toilet…not just any toilet, mind you, but by my Sealand Traveler Model #510 RV toilet. It's not the first time I've battled the dragon commode. Last year, I had some major leaks, replaced the flushing mechanism, and had some more leaks. But I thought I had solved my problems when I de-leaked it last fall.

But the slumbering beast awoke with a spurt of water. I quickly diagnosed the problem as a faulty vacuum breaker, removed the old one, drove 40 miles for a new one, only to find out it was almost the right one. I tried to jerry-rig it with success only to find another leak…and then proceeded to beak the fitting on the supply pipe…and spent the rest of the day and now into the wee hours…skunked again!!!

RV Water-closet Beast: 2…Familyman: ZIP!

While driving to Ace Hardware to get a piece that would not work, I realized I'm not a 'believer.' Oh, don't get me wrong. Yes, I believe that God sent His son to die for my sins and I have placed my trust in Him…but I don't trust Him.

It's obvious by the way I've acted all day long with my toilet from hell. After all, I can say all I want about trusting God, believing that He is in control…but my actions betray what I REALLY believe.

Actually, I've usually prided myself in believing. I've been the picture of calm during the economic crisis and political change…but my leaky toilet is another thing altogether.

But even as I sit here, I know…I mean KNOW that God is in control, that He only does what is good for Him and Me, and that I don't have to pop a gasket when my RV…pops a gasket.

If I truly believe all that, then I can be a dad and husband who doesn't snap at the people around me even when things around me fall apart. So, my fellow dad, I don't know what you're battling today, but let me encourage you to BELIEVE that God has it all under control.

I'm going to bed now…I'm bushed.

I'll wake up and battle the toilet once again. And even if it beats me, I will BELIEVE. Do the same.

You'da dad!

She's My Wife and I Ain't Sharin'

Galatians 5:16-26

Hey Dad,

I feel like I've had a black cloud hovering over me the past couple of days. At first I thought it was due to the RV makeover that I've plunged into. You know how it goes; everything you start leads to two or three other things. To remove the carpet, I had to remove the seats, which means I had to remove the seatbelts and the wires, the lights, and the trim, only to find that the sub-floor needs some attention as well.

But I really don't think that's the cause of the cloud. It blew in with some news about a couple that we've known for years but haven't seen in awhile.

It seems that not all that long ago they took in a college boarder, a young male. Well, apparently, now the wife thinks she's in love with him, and...you know the rest. It makes me ill, angry, and "dark cloudish."

Actually it serves as a wake-up call to me and to you, Dad. The situation happened because the husband let his guard down (I'm not blaming him for her actions). I guess he assumed, "What's the big deal? She would never be attracted to him; she's more than 20 years his senior."

But he forgot just how dangerous this kind of situation can be and let his guard down.

My job as a husband is not only to guard my children and myself, but my wife and marriage, as well. I need to look at every guy who walks into my territory as a possible threat. I trust my wife, but I can't trust "him" for one minute. I've just heard too many ugly stories involving best friends, relatives, and co-workers to let my guard down. The stakes are too high.

So, Dad, take a good, long look at some of the males in your wife's life. Is there anyone you feel a little uncomfortable with? Does some guy seem a little too friendly with YOUR wife? Is she spending some no-big-deal alone time with him? Don't blow it off as "no big deal."

She's your WIFE, and you ain't sharin'.
Be on guard! Grrrrr!!

You 'da husband!

Summer of the Potato Cannon

Galatians 6:1-18

Hey Dad,

This side of Memorial Day, there are three whole months of dad-opportunities stretching before us. Look at all these things just waiting on us to make happen: bike rides, lightning bug safaris, vacations, baseball games, lemonade stands, garage sales, and ice cream trucks.

The things is, you gotta have a plan. Otherwise, the next three months will zip by, leaving you with your mouth hanging open and egg on your face. You know what that's like...remember those promises you made last year to the kids?

You said, "Yeah, we'll do 'that' this summer...it sure is going to be fun." Then, you forgot, but your kids didn't.

We can talk all we want about being a great dad, doing fun family things, training our children to love God, but if we don't do the things we say, we're just blowing smoke. Truth is, wanting don't get nothing done.

This summer is going to be different. We're gonna have a plan. We're going to make a list of activities we'd like to do in the next three months, post it somewhere to serve as a reminder, and then check them off one by one. Ha! No more Mr. Dream-dasher here.

So, Dad, what do you want to do this summer? Remember, it's for them, not you. Don't write down: play more golf...instead, write down: take the kids to play a round of golf...or go putt-putting as a family. Maybe you have a project the kids have been begging you to do, like build a tree house or put up a basketball goal. I know what is at the top of my kids' list: a potato cannon.

My son Ben got a book* that has detailed instructions on building a PVC potato cannon capable of projecting a spud the length of a football field. A great dad, who actually built one, said it shoots out a three-foot flame at night. What boy wouldn't love that?

The only problem is it will take some serious time to build it...but I've been promising to build it for two years, and this summer we're going to build it!! 'Cause I have a plan.

So, go get your wife's ideas too, jot them all down, and do it!!

You know why? Because...

You 'da dad!!

*Backyard Ballastics by William Gurstelle

Take the Gameboy by the Horns

1 Corinthians 1:1-17

Hey Dad,

Hope you're enjoying the summer with your family. My son Sam and I are getting ready to fly down to Florida today for a speaking engagement this weekend. Right now, I'm trying to set the house in order to alleviate some of the extra stress on my brave wife.

Actually, I just checked in on my boys who are busy restoring order and cleanliness to the garage that they destroyed over the last week with all their "projects."

My son Abe was showing off the "table" he built for me to hold some of my tools. His face beamed as he watched my eyes pan across the splendor of the old door he'd nailed three blocks of wood to as legs.

"Do you like it, Dad?" he asked.

"Oh yeah," I answered. "It's awesome. How did you know how to make that all by yourself?"

He smiled, humbly basking in the glory of his father's praise.

I didn't even say anything about the tools, scraps of wood, and nails and screws all over the garage floor.

This is the way things have been ever since we got home from traveling. The kids have been sawing, nailing, building, sword fighting, cap gunning, and "messing." They have to—because we told them they couldn't play on their computers this summer. Gasp!

In fact, they've even been banned from their normal one-hour usage on Monday, Wednesday, and Friday. They balked a little when we announced it, but they haven't complained a bit since.

Instead of blankly staring at their computer screens, they've filled their days with playing, creating, and enjoying the summer. It's been nice...real nice.

Dad, I talk to parents all over the country who are sick of their kids' computer/gaming addiction. So, can I encourage you to "take the Gameboy by the horns" and declare a summer break from computers, video games, Xbox, and Nintendo Wii?*

You may not be real popular at first with your kids, but they can deal with one month of "summer fun." If they can't, then that's exactly why you need to pull the plug for the rest of the summer.

So take the challenge, and help your kids enjoy their summer.

You 'da dad!!

*Check out my book **Taming the Techno-Beast** at www.familymanweb.com

163

Know It All Dad

| June | 7 |

Hey Dad,

The great thing about our children is that they're so easily impressed. They think we (their dads) are the tallest, strongest, richest, and...smartest. This letter from Simon proves it.

"I've been meaning to share this with you for a week! On Thursday, I went home and announced to my family that I was making waffles because it was National Waffle Week (I did not share my source: the You 'da Dad Daily Calendar!) to which my nine-year-old daughter said, "Daddy, you know EVERYTHING!" Man did I feel PUMPED! It also reminded me of the tremendous responsibility we have as dads."

~ Simon

So Dad, want to impress you wife and kids? Today is National Chocolate Ice Cream Day (it's true)...so load up the van and take the fam over to Dairy Queen or pick up a gallon of chocolate ice cream to celebrate the day.

You 'da smartest!

164

Taking Care of Business

1 Corinthians 2:1-16

Hey Dad,

Things are busy here at home. I've probably put on more miles running errands and trying to get RV problems solved in the last four days than I did driving to Minnesota.

Normally, I'd let the problems slide...you know, go to plan B. But I'm trying real hard to love my wife by handling 'things.' It makes her feel loved when I do. I know this because she told me so recently...not in so many words, but it's what she meant.

A couple of weeks ago, she asked me the question, "Do you know what made me feel really loved recently?"

In my head, I was thinking of any notes I had given her, the small gift I had gotten her when I drove somewhere to speak, or the romantic things that I like to surprise her with. Before I could answer, she said, "When you got the van washed for me."

I smiled as though I knew that, but inside I was thinking, "That's it?? Washing the van made you feel loved?" (Okay, I'll admit that the last time I washed our cars was when President Clinton was still in office).

But since then, I've had time to think about what she said. You see, my wife feels loved when I take care of the things that matter to her (like a filthy van). She likes it when I handle those "guy" things on my own. That's why I got on the phone first thing Monday morning and called the shop that worked on the RV brakes, the mower shop that has our mower, the garage that works on our cars, and an Amish guy who repairs RV refrigerators.

It wasn't that I was so diligent about tackling the problems...in fact, I was thinking the whole time about how I could do the plan B's (like turn the fridge into a big ice cooler with blocks of ice). I made the calls because I knew it would show my wife how much I love her...because I was taking care of things...because I was her knight in shining armor.

I'm still taking care of things this morning and my wife may not thank me profusely or lavish me with kisses, but I know she feels loved and cared about because wives feel loved and cared for when their husbands take care of "things."

Let me ask you this question? Is there something that you need to handle for your wife? Maybe you have a light that doesn't work, an unfinished project that needs finishing, or a car that needs to be run through the car wash.

Take care of business.

You 'da husband!

Thank You, Puddle Jumper Girl

1 Corinthians 3:1-9

Hey Dad,

A big Familyman thank you for praying for clear skies and a smooth flight this past week. I'm telling you, it was about the smoothest flight I've ever taken.

I also want to thank you for all of the great nose hair removal advice. I was overwhelmed by the first-hand—or nose—experiences and advice.

I thought I'd share some fatherly wisdom that I gained from eavesdropping on two girls while on a prop-driven puddle-jumper from Denver, CO, to Billings, MT.

Actually, I didn't get the whole conversation, but my ears perked up when two just-out-of-high school girls were talking about past family vacations.

Apparently, they were discussing what they enjoyed most about traveling when they were younger, and I heard one of the girls say, "What I really miss most is falling asleep in the car and having my dad carry me in, and then I'd wake up in my bed. I really miss that."

Maybe it was the way she said it so seriously or the way the other girl nodded in agreement, but I couldn't stop thinking about what she said.

This was a girl who hadn't been carried by her dad from the car in years, and yet that's what she missed most.

I remember that same magical feeling of being carried in from the car by my dad, trying hard not to let him know I was awake. I felt secure being held in his arms. And after being reminded by that girl on the plane, I decided I miss being carried by my dad, too.

Then I thought about how easy it really is to ensure that my children have the same good memory. And you can ensure the same for your children, too, Dad.

I know sometimes it's a pain—especially if you have more than one child, but carrying in your children from the car pays big dividends. And all you have to do is—do it. So thank you puddle-jumper girl, wherever you are, for the reminder.

You 'da dad!

The Big Ugly—ME!

1 Corinthians 3:10-23

Hey Dad,

It's an awesome experience to squeeze a 30-foot RV through a narrow street crammed full of cars. The stress level was high, but nothing like the other night in downtown Boston.

It was a black, stormy night...not unlike a Lord of the Rings kind of blackness. We innocently entered the city limits of Boston thinking we'd find a warm inviting Walmart to overnight at. But noooo there were no Walmarts anywhere.

It was then that my stressed out, chemical thingamajiggers in my body started to rise. It didn't help that every time I stopped to ask directions, I couldn't find anyone who spoke English!! It was like a bad dream.

I wound down narrow streets—I mean really narrow streets, went the wrong way on a one-way street (on purpose), and was ditched by some "nice" person who said, "Follow me."

That's when things got stormy inside the RV too. I was mad and ready to bite off the head of anyone who talked to me. It didn't help that while I was hunched over the steering wheel, soaked to the bone from walking out in the rain, and trying to see out through the pounding rain into the darkness, my kids were calling out, "Dad, you told me I could sit in the turn-around seat and Samuel is sitting there..."

Kaboom!!! Hiroshima and Nagasaki combined.

Wisely, my wife closed her eyes and her mouth. Oh, I know what she was thinking. It's what all wives think when their husbands spend 2½ hours lost.

By the time we found a strip-mall parking lot that we were allowed to park in, I was exhausted. We turned the RV into bedrooms and everyone got to bed. I brushed my teeth and slipped into bed next to my wife who was just as tightly strung as I was. I was still fuming, but God whispered into my ear, "Tell your wife you're sorry for how you acted."

"What, are you kidding?" I argued. "I did the best I could. I did the best anyone could."

"Just do it," He said.

So I did. I rolled towards my wife and apologized for acting like a jerk. She didn't respond right away, but a few seconds later she rolled towards me, hugged me, and said, "Thanks for getting us here. You did the best you could. I'm sorry it was so hard."

That was it. It was over because I softened and apologized.

You know what, Dad? It'll work for you too. The next time you blow your cool and freak out (which will probably be in the next 48 hours), just soften and say, "I'm sorry. Will you forgive me?"

You 'da dad!!

The Breakthrough

Hey Dad,

My wife is in a laundry mat, and I thought I'd type up this week's Familyman. So far, we've had a great time speaking and traveling.

Actually, I'm not being totally honest about the 'so far so good' part. I should have said since early last week things have been good. Because that's when 'the breakthrough' came. In fact, from this point on I'm going to be serious…dead serious because what I'm about to share is private, and I asked my wife if I could share it because it was a big deal and highlighted my insensitivity and the power of a miscarriage and resentment.

For the last four months, my wife has felt…weird, gloomy, and depressed. I've seen a lot of tears, and to be honest I thought my husbanding skills were being put to the test. It had gotten so bad that we were beginning to think it was a hormonal thing…but then the breakthrough came.

We were in Dallas, TX lying in bed. The kids were asleep and my wife started to share how she was talking to another wife about her miscarriage that occurred about four months ago. As she told the wife the story she began to cry…which happened again as she relayed it to me. Not only did she cry, but she wept from the heart and proceeded to tell me how hurt she was by my response to her miscarriage in January.

You see when it happened I was bothered by the timing and the inconvenience. I was unkind and insensitive…in fact, to put it bluntly, I was mean. Later, I asked her to forgive me…but I guess Debbie couldn't forget the let down from my meanness.

Then we talked and she cried and cried, and I held her and told her how sorry I was over and over again. She cried some more, reliving the pain I had caused…and then the stormed passed and in the morning came refreshment and smiles.

It was gone. Four months of resentment and hurt…gone.

My fellow husband, that's the power of resentment, of unresolved conflict…and it's my job and yours to take it to the end. If your wife has been 'cold' unfeeling, and snappy it might be because she's hurt by an unresolved conflict, your insensitivity or 'meanness.' Dad, let me push you to bring it up…to resolve it…to allow her to cry and blame you…and to make it right.

You 'da dad!

The Love Slug

1 Corinthians 4:6-21

Hey Dad,

I'm writing this from a parking lot in beautiful Eden Prairie, MN. Actually, I'm kind of excited because this week's "Familyman Weekly" is being sent out wireless while on the road...ooooh.

I'd like to say it's been smooth sailing for our first road trip of the season...but it's been more like the perfect storm.

Here's an excerpt from my RV Blog:

"April 12—It's raining, and the wind is fierce as I write this from Fagan's Chevy dealer. We spent the night here, after being towed here by a guy named Dwayne...after stalling at the Edgarton Oasis. The boys loved watching the huge wrecker do its thing and getting to ride in it too.

Yesterday, the sun was shining and we were all loaded up and ready to go...but as I went to start the RV, the battery was dead. Not to be easily discouraged, we jump-started the RV, and a few minutes later, we were on the road...but a few minutes later, and less than two miles from home, we heard a terrific crash. Lo and behold, the huge awning had come undone and unfolded as we drove down the road. But wait, there's more...The night before we left, the RV refrigerator tried to kill me...Oh yeah, my wife says to add that Maggie (our 1-year-old) threw up around 4 a.m. this morning, too. But that's beside the point."

What amazed me in all the chaos and my stressed out-ness was that my children love their dad. I don't know why. I sure don't deserve their love most of the time.

I was reminded of that as I stood outside the dead RV waiting for the expensive wrecker to arrive. I paced back and forth and gave orders to the kids that I didn't want to see their little faces come out of the RV door.

So what did they do? They stuck their little faces out all the windows, asking questions a mile a minute. I answered their questions, but it was obvious that I wasn't pleased about it. That's when Ike (almost 6) cold-cocked me with a love slug. "D-a-a-a-d," he said for the twenty-fifth time.

I whirled around ready to let him have it and there he sat holding up three fingers (I love you) and said, "I love you, Dad." He knocked the wind out of my angry sails and melted my heart.

"I love you too, Ike."

He smiled. You know that's one of the greatest things about being a dad. We try, fail, yell, and accuse...and they still love us!

You know what? No matter how much you have let your children down lately, the truth is they love you tons. So, get back in there and keep trying...I know I will.

You 'da dad!

The Passing of a President

Hey Dad,

We just got back from New York. Everything went great...that is, if you don't count the fact that our RV caught on fire. Here's the exhausting story in a nut shell: there was a whoosh, some crackling, and flames. Fortunately, we had a fire extinguisher on board and put it out before the thing burnt to the ground...at least I think it was fortunate.

Twenty-four hours later, we were back on the road, and the rest of the trip went off without a hitch. We even visited Niagara Falls and ate at a Canadian McDonald's.

While we were in Canada, I learned that former President Reagan had died. I felt sad. Of all the presidents...I felt closest to him. He embodied the American spirit and made me proud to be part of this country. But that's not why I felt sad.

He was a great American President, but sadly, he wasn't as great a dad...which is a lot more important.

A few years ago, I saw an interview with one of the President's sons...I think it was Ron Jr. Anyway, they asked him how it was now that his father had Alzheimer's.

I don't remember anything else of the whole program, but I'll never forget his son's answer—and neither should you.

Without hesitation or emotion he said, "Not much has changed. He wasn't really there for us growing up."

I say this very respectfully of a man and president that I greatly admire-but he forgot about what mattered most. And what mattered most was the family he had been given by God to care for.

Now, here's what I want to ask you, Dad. Be honest. If things go on like they are right now, will your kids one day say the same about you? Have you gotten so busy in what seems important to you that you've forgotten what really is?

It's not too late to make some life changes, but one day it will be. Even if you have to sacrifice a chunk of money, a career, or fancy "stuff," It's worth it.

I know it's hard-gut wrenching hard, but I know you can do it.

You 'da dad!!

The Ice Cream Truck

1 Corinthians 6:1-11

Hey Dad,

Greetings from just outside the Daisy Fresh Laundromat in Mt. Vernon, IL. My wife is in doing the laundry while the kids and I watch an exciting episode of the Beverly Hillbillies. Things are going well, if you don't count the fact that we've had more water leaks than a rain barrel hit by a shotgun. I think I'm down to the last one. Ahhh—life on the road.

Oh, I forgot to mention my run in with—bump, bump, bump, bummm—the ice cream truck man. I knew he would find me, but I didn't think it would be this early in the season. I usually don't hear his diabolical call until well after the first of June. So you can imagine my horror yesterday when he arrived.

We were enjoying a local park in southern Indiana. The sun was shining, the birds were singing—and then I heard it: the unmistakable demonic clang of—bump, bump, bump, bummm—the ice cream truck man. A wild light sprang into my children's eyes and they commenced the pleading.

"Can we get something from the ice cream truck?"

"Are we going to stop him?"

"Can we, please?"

"Please! Please!!"

I pretended I had slipped into a coma and was unable to respond. It didn't work. Of course, my wife had long ago fallen under the spell of—bump, bump, bump, bummm—the ice cream truck man, and knew that a few bucks would buy a cone full of memories.

What really irked me about the whole thing is that I knew she was right (she normally is). Hey, I don't mind spending a small fortune on my RV, but spending a few bucks on some overpriced ice cream about kills me.

The truth, though, is that in a month I won't even remember what part I bought for the RV. But my children will never forget the time we ate Tweety Bird-shaped ice cream treats at a beautiful park on a gorgeous spring day.

So, Dad, let me give you a little heads up. It won't be long before your children say, "Dad, can we, please?!"

Before you say no, count to three, think about the memories you'll be making...and remember—bump, bump, bump, bummm—the ice cream truck man.

You 'da dad!!

Body Fluids and Broken Stuff

1 Corinthians 6:12-20

Hey Dad,

Well, we're officially home from our travels, and it's a good thing. After being on the road for a good ten weeks, cramped in the small confines of our RV, it feels good to stretch and spread out. We were especially ready to get home after last weekend in Columbus, OH.

Prior to heading into the long weekend of speaking, sickness had entered the Wilson ranks, and I pictured the worst—kids with fevers and upset stomachs scattered throughout the RV. But somehow I didn't visualize ME in that picture.

Actually, everyone was feeling pretty good the first night (minus our three-year-old, who threw up that morning), and we had a great night in the Columbus convention center parking lot with some friends who hosted a little tailgate party featuring home-smoked pork barbeque.

But things took a turn for the worse in the pre-dawn hours of the last day.

"Someone threw up," my wife said as she poked me with her elbow. One sniff, and I knew she was right.

I didn't argue about who should take care of it. Knowing she's a "gagger" by nature and pregnant, I knew that I'm chiefly responsible for the body fluid detail. So I climbed out of bed to find one of our big kids covered in...regurgitated pork barbeque.

In the dark, hardly able to maneuver, I did the best I could to get it cleaned up, leaving some of it for the morning—and then climbed back into bed. But the stench was incredible, and I slept with the covers over my nose like a filter.

The next morning I felt a little queasy, and, by the time we finally got home that night, I was sicker than a dog and spent a good chunk of the next day in bed. I still feel a little funny, but there's a ton of stuff to do around the house—stuff to clean, put away, and organize. Plus, did I mention that everything we own is BROKEN and that my wife feels weary and overwhelmed?

It sure would be nice to run away about now, but hey, I'm 'da dad. Life is good, but most of the time it isn't very easy. Some dads opt out and take the easy road. Not you and me. We keep fixin', keep working, keep mopping up body fluids, and keep on loving our wives. We never give up—although it sure sounds easier sometimes.

I gotta go; more things to fix.

You 'da dad!!

Anniversaries for Dummies

Hey Dad,

Are you as excited about this Sunday as I am? After all, Father's Day is the single greatest holiday of the year...well, it should be!! Actually, my kids are probably more concerned about the 21st—known around my house as Kid's Day.

We've chosen the first day of summer to celebrate our children. But right now, I can't really concentrate on Father's Day or Kid's Day. I'm still a little woozy from celebrating our anniversary yesterday. The thing about anniversaries is that we dads usually botch them (I've got a few under my belt). If we're lucky, we get our wife a card, but even that sometimes gets lost in the shuffle. The thing is...most men just don't care much about special days.

Know what? We should. Especially marriage anniversaries. If not for our sake, then for our wife's. What wife wouldn't love for her man to make a big fuss over the day that they were united as one?

So here it is: "Anniversaries for Dummies" (you may substitute the word Men for dummies if you'd like):

The card. Get one. Don't just sign your name. Write something...you know, why you love her and how you'd do it all over again if you were given the choice. Think mushy.

The gift. I know what you're thinking, "But my wife and I decided not to do gifts anymore." Get her a gift anyway. Or, better yet, get her a gift for every year that you've been married...like her favorite candy, sunglasses, fun earrings ($4.96 at Walmart), a snazzy pen, pretty stationary...you're on your own for the rest. Pick up some wrapping paper and wrap each gift separately.

The date. Get a babysitter and go out. Tell her to order whatever she wants.

The mood. Look through your wedding album, wedding video, or old love notes.

Check your motives. Make sure all that you do isn't only for what you might get in return...if you know what I mean! So...do it for her, not you.

Now you might be saying, "Yeah, but that'll take a ton of effort and cost money."

My answer, "Duh." That's what love is.

You 'da dad!!

I'm One of THEM (1 year later)

1 Corinthians 7:8-11

Hey Dad,

I can't believe it. After years of shaking my head in disbelief and horror at THEM for their lack of commitment and love, I've entered their ranks. I'm one of THEM. Even as I admit it, I feel shame and defeat.

What am I talking about?!

I thought it was evident. I'm talking about those husbands who forget their wedding anniversary!! Oh the shame!! I should've known better—I did know better. My track record has been stellar up until now. I'm the type who always makes a big deal over it with gifts, notes, and an outpouring of romance and emotion. I plan weeks in advance to let my wife know how much she means to me and how I'm the luckiest man in the world to have her as my wife.

But that's all water under the husband-bridge. Now I'm one of THEM. This year, it snuck up on me in the busyness of life and RV traveling. I was blind-sided with a Hallmark card neatly tucked into my suitcase last weekend when I was in Montana. How sweet, I thought, she got me a card to tell me how much she misses me.

I opened the card, read the note, which wished me a happy anniversary, and it still didn't hit me. How sweet, I thought again, she even remembered that it's the day of the month of our anniversary (we sometimes celebrate that). Then the truth slapped me in the face—IT'S MY ANNIVERSARY AND I MISSED IT!! I'M ONE OF THEM!!

Of course I apologized, and my beloved wife was very loving and understanding, but that doesn't change the truth. It goes on my permanent record (in my mind). I'm doomed to wander the earth like Jacob Marley warning other dads so that they might avoid my fate—so that they won't become one of US!!

So, consider yourself warned, Dad. Stop and check the calendar right now, and then take three minutes to plan something special for the woman you married.

Don't worry about me. There's still hope. I'll have to be extra creative, but I never let a huge blunder keep a good dad down. I can still let the woman of my dreams know that I'm so glad she said, "I do."

Make it a good one, and remember my fate!!

You 'da dad!!

174

Feeling Like God on Father's Day

1 Corinthians 7:12-20

Hey Dad,

You might think by the title of this week's Familyman that I think my kids will treat me like God on Father's Day...yeah, right. They just don't seem to get the magnitude of Father's Day. In fact, yesterday, my daughter, Katherine was talking about doing something special and thoughtful for her grandpa for Father's Day.

"Katherine," I said defensively, "he's not YOUR father...you're supposed to do something neat like that for YOUR father...that's ME."

She looked at me rather startled by the realization and said, "I'm not going to do all that for you."

Little darling.

So, when I titled this week's Familyman "Feeling Like God on Father's Day," I was certainly not talking about how they treat me but about how I FEEL about being their dad.

You see, my friend Rudy sent me a couple of instrumental CDs this week. I was excited to hear them and had them in the CD player a few minutes after receiving them. While they were queuing up, I got Maggie up from her nap, made my way to the family room, slipped into the rocking chair, and held my little girl tightly on my lap.

She sat dazed, recovering from her deep sleep. Her flyaway hair tickled my chin as the music from the new CD played, swelling with emotion.

As I listened, the emotion of being in love with my daughter covered me like a gentle wave. Thoughts of gratitude and thankfulness filled my heart and a lump grew in my throat. Man, I felt so glad to be the dad of my children. I may blow my cool from time to time, and they do get to me every once in a while...but I felt so in love at that moment.

Later as I pondered what happened in that chair with the music, I wondered if God ever feels that way about His children...about me. Does He ever get a lump in His throat and feel overwhelming love for you and me?

The answer most certainly is YES. I know we disappoint him, ignore him, and act ugly sometimes. But I would just about bet that He still gets a lump thinking about you and me. He must love being our Father.

That's what Father's Day is all about—not that our children honor us, but that we remember the great honor of being their dad.

So, Dad, put on some special music, hold one of your children on your lap (if you still can), and REMEMBER how much you love them...and how much HE loves you.

You 'da dad!!

Father's Day!!

1 Corinthians 7:21-28

Hey Dad,

June is the month we celebrate Father's Day. I don't know about you, but I don't feel like I've earned it lately. In fact, I was a little stinker yesterday. It's not that I don't try—I do. But sometimes I just blow it.

What made it worse was that I had a radio interview and the topic was—you guessed it—fathering. Since I'm not very good at faking it, I told the interviewer that I hadn't been a very good dad that day.

And then something happened. The average interview went to a higher level, because as I shared my failures, he also shared how he blew it just the night before.

Man, not only did I enjoy his failure story, but it reminded me how we dads are all in the same boat. We try to care for the needs of our family and love our wives and children, but often blow it.

And that's why we celebrate Father's Day and why my hat is off to you, Dad. You have the most demanding, important job on the planet. After a failure, you pick yourself up, dust yourself off, and start all over again (sounds like a song).

The news is full of stories about presidential candidates, powerful businessmen, and famous movie stars. But what you do every day as a dad is more important than all that stuff combined. Your impact in your children's lives ripples across generations to come.

You 'da dad!!!
You 'da dad!!!
You 'da dad!!!

So, my fellow normal dad who blows it from time to time, you're doing an awesome job. You may or may not get a goofy shirt for Father's Day or get a nap, but know that this dad thinks you're 'da dad!

You 'da dad!!

Kids' Day

Hey Dad,

I know I've mentioned the idea of Kids' Day before, but I want to again so that it doesn't accidentally slip by you this year.

Kids' Day is the perfect time to let your kids know how glad you are that they're yours. You ARE glad about that, right? Kids' Day allows you to demonstrate that truth to your children, who need to be reminded of it as often as you do.

It doesn't take much preparation.

Here's what you do: Call your wife and tell her you'll take care of dinner tonight. Then do something special: grill out, roast hot-dogs over a campfire, go to the Dog-n-Suds drive-in, have a picnic, or go to a favorite family restaurant.

Then, on the way home from work, stop by Walmart and pick up a slip-n-slide, squirt guns, fireworks, or other toys your kids have been talking about. After dinner, get out the new toy or go for a long bike ride, to the beach, or a drive-in.

Oh, one more thing: Write a small note to each of your children telling them how much they mean to you.

That's it! Don't have time today? That's okay. I didn't either. That's why we had our Kids' Day yesterday.

We went to a local mountain-bike trail, did the slip-n-slide thing, went to a favorite breadstick place, and then I presented the older kids with a ticket to go see the Disney movie Cars.

Okay, that's all the time for instructions I have. The rest is up to you.

Make it a good 'un.

You 'da dad!!

177

Lighten Up!

Hey Dad,

I don't mean to complain, but kids sure are inconvenient. Take our newest arrival...who still hasn't arrived. The child is not even born yet, and he/she's causing us grief.

That's right. The newest bun in the oven is still in the oven!! And we're about to go nuts. It's not like this is our first baby and we made the mistake of setting our expectations too high...we're veteran parents and should have known better.

"Don't think you're going to go early just because you always have," the experts say.

Well, we did...and now we're wondering what the problem is with this little kid. I'm even starting to get an attitude about "the straggler." I'd send him to his room if he wasn't already in it.

The thing is, I know things won't get any easier once he/she does arrive. He won't nurse like he should, poop like he should, sleep the way I'd like, or do long division. In fact, as he/she grows older, I'll set my expectations too high, frustrating him and me.

That's what dads do. We get all bent out of shape when little "Johnny" doesn't read like the others, run like the others, or "get it" like the others. Even as Christians, we get bothered that our child isn't showing the spiritual maturity that we'd like him too...not that we did either; but that was different.

So what's a dad to do?

Lighten up and let God handle it.

My son/daughter will get here when God decides it's time. He will have his first bowel movement right on time. He will learn to read when he's supposed to, and he will never be behind or ahead of God's plan. In fact, he will become what God wants him to be when God wants him to be what he's to become.

And it won't help an ounce if I get all anxious and try to rush it.

Know what I mean? I'd just about bet that you have a son or daughter that you've been "pushing." From one pusher to another, it's time to lighten up and let God handle it.

Whew, I feel better already. I think I'll go tell my wife to spend another 20 minutes on the trampoline.

You 'da dad!

The power of THE NOTE

1 Corinthians 9:1-12

Hey Dad,

Just got back from a speaking trip in West Palm Beach, Florida with my lovely bride. It's been a while since we have been able to leave the kids behind and get a little husband and wife time. I love husband and wife time.

There is nothing better than strolling hand in hand, eating a leisurely meal, and holding each other on a plane ride. I'm telling you, Dad, if you haven't spent some alone time with your bride recently, you'd be wise to plan a little for the future. It doesn't have to be on a tropical beach somewhere; an overnight, while the kids stay at Grandma's will do.

It's just what the doctor ordered.

The only drawback is leaving the kids behind (of course that is one of the nice parts too). Our kids start getting a little 'funny' right before we go. They get insecure and emotional, but I have a secret weapon to quell their fears—the note.

The day before our departure while I was scurrying around my son Abe came up to me and said, "Don't forget to write me a note, Dad."

My pattern has been to write a note to my children whenever I do any traveling. But at that moment when Abe asked, it sounded overwhelming.

"I'm super busy, Abe," I responded. "I just don't know if…"

He knew where I was headed and interrupted, "It doesn't have to be a long note."

He was right. It doesn't have to be a long note. Actually, it's not even the actual words that mean the most. It's the NOTE that means something. It conveys that I was thinking of, am thinking of, and will be thinking of the one left behind.

There's something comforting about finding a note tucked into some unexpected place that says, "I was just thinking of you…I'm so glad I'm your dad…and I can't wait to see you when I get back."

So I left little notes for all eight of my children (which took about 6 minutes to write) and scattered them about Grandma's house.

No one ever said, "Thanks for the note, Dad," but they didn't need to because I know the power of The Note.

So, Dad if you have a little trip coming up…do The Note. Even if you aren't going anywhere…do The Note.

It's mighty powerful and like Abe said, "It doesn't have to be a long note."

You 'da dad!!

Thwack!!

1 Corinthians 9:13-18

Hey Dad,

Ever have one of those fathering moments when right out of the blue you get a big "thwack" right across the head with the proverbial 2x4? I had one of those the other evening.

We had just gotten back from another round of traveling, and we were all tired. It was going to be a pizza and video night. Unfortunately, the library was closed which ruled out a free video, but I announced that I'd drive the 45 seconds to the Milford video store to rent a video.

Besides, I could use the five minutes of peace and quiet. Quickly, I made my way to the door.

"I wanna go wiff you," Abe (3 yrs. old) said.

"Not this time Abe," I said. "I'll just be gone a few minutes...and besides, you don't have your shoes on." In one fluid movement, I opened the door, slid out, and closed it behind me.

I could hear Abe crying on the other side, "I wanna go wiff Daddy." My heart was unmoved.

That's when the "thwack" came. It took me back to a dreary day in Duluth, MN, where my friend Bob said that dads should never go anywhere without taking along a child for the ride.

I agreed. It is a good way to avoid temptations. That's not what he meant.

"I mean you should never go anywhere without taking along a kid," he said emphatically. "Never ever. Even if you're just going to the hardware store, you need to take along a kid. Because great things happen in the car."

All that went through my head when the "thwack" came. I did an about-face, walked back in the door, and said to my wet-cheeked son, "Come on Abe, you can go with me."

Now, don't read too much into this. We didn't have any meaningful discussions. In fact, I'm not sure he even talked...except to ask for candy.

But we were together, and that's what mattered.

Truth is, some of my best fatherly memories are car rides with one of my kids, whether it's a deep conversation with Ben, giggles with Sam, or tender hand holding with my little princess. Bob was right—great things happen in the car.

So, Dad, consider this e-mail a "thwack." Whenever you get in the car, try to take one of your kids with you. It'll be inconvenient, but you'll be glad you did.

You 'da dad!!

Tomorrow They May Not Care

1 Corinthians 9:19-27

Hey Dad,

Just in case you didn't know this about me, I'm cheap...although not as bad as Ebenezer Scrooge. Now with that said, let me tell you a recent story about how I overcame my natural cheap tendencies to love my daughter extravagantly.

It all happened while we were enjoying a much-needed rest in Florida from life on the road. Surrounded by thousands of pale, pasty-skinned tourists, we noticed several princessy-looking girls all dolled up with sparkling hair and pixie dust.

My boys hardly took notice, but all the womenfolk in my family oohed and aahed. I could only imagine how much it cost, and later found out that your basic princess hairdo/makeover cost about $50. Fifty bucks!!

As the days ticked by and we continued to see more walking princess-hairdo billboards, a growing prodding began to whisper in my heart: Katherine would love that.

I know, but it costs fifty bucks!, I inwardly argued. And it won't even last two days.

But the feeling wouldn't go away, and it had been working on my wife as well, because on the last night we both looked at each other and said, "What do you think about doing the princess makeover for Katherine?"

Then my wife added, "This could be the last year that she'll want to. Next year she might feel too old."

Sold!

That night we surprised our daughter with the princess treatment. She was overwhelmingly grateful, and as she walked towards me with sparkles in her hair, she beamed.

"Thank you soo much, Dad," she said as she hugged her old man.

"You look beautiful, Katherine," I whispered.

Well, I was wrong. The hairdo lasted four days, and Katherine loved every minute of it—and so did I.

You know, Dad, the makeover cost less than a seventh of a tank of fuel for the RV, which barely lasts two days. But my daughter will always remember the night she got the princess hairdo and how she felt loved by her mom and dad.

I'm telling you, Dad, loving someone extravagantly doesn't have to cost $50. One dad wrote me and told how he brought home candy bars to everyone in his family as a surprise. Same result.

It's not about spending money, though; it's about using your time, money, or energy to show love extravagantly from time to time. It's about sleeping out in the backyard, building a tree fort, or taking a much-promised road trip. It's all about doing it today, because tomorrow may be too late.

Tomorrow? Maybe Not

Hey Dad,

There are few things in life as exhilarating as standing beside your sons as the first shot is fired from your homemade potato cannon (walking down the aisle with your daughter on her wedding day might edge it out).

After talking about making one for the last two years, we finally did it. We bought the parts, put them together, and collected a few spotted apple "bullets" from our ancient apple tree.

I had my doubts. I assumed that the spark from our little gas grill igniter wouldn't work or that we would have a fatal flaw in our design. Anyway, we set it outside the garage and pointed it towards a big tree on the edge of the woods.

Tension was high. Ben shoved the apple down the barrel, I added a three-second burst of hairspray into the firing chamber, and then we screwed the ignition cap over the opening.

"Here we go," I said to the boys as I pushed the igniter button …

KERPLOW!! With an explosive burst, the apple disappeared up over the woods and into the neighboring county. We looked at each other in disbelief.

"Awesome!" Ben and Sam said, as though they had just witnessed a great moment in history.

Now if that isn't cool, I don't know what is.

It was also ETERNAL. No, not the cannon part, but the time we spent together and the feelings they felt. That will last forever.

I almost missed it, because as you've noticed, summer is winding down. And the time to get such ETERNAL things accomplished is almost over.

It's a problem we dads have. We assume that we will always have "tomorrow" or a "later."

I've been reminded several times in the last two weeks that we may not. In fact, next week I'm going to tell you about my friend Robert and how his entire family was taken away in an instant.

Until then, Dad, you are not guaranteed a "tomorrow," nor are your children. Remember those plans you made at the beginning of the summer? You talked about going fishing with the kids, a trip out west, a picnic at the park, or a bike ride to a favorite spot.

So, if you have some summer promise to keep—make it happen.

You 'da dad!!

Welcome to the REAL World

1 Corinthians 10:13

Hey Dad,

Let me introduce the latest Wilson—Caleb Rex Wilson. Now, I know what you're thinking: Caleb Rex? Sounds like a dinosaur. I know it does, but we wanted to use my dad's name (Rex). The problem is, it just doesn't go with a lot of biblical names, and that's probably why it's taken us five boys to use it.

Anyway, from my perspective (the one not actually giving birth), the delivery went great. It was fast, smooth, and easy. My wife is doing great, and Caleb is adjusting to life at the Wilsons'...which is a lot to handle when you're a little guy.

For the last nine months, he's enjoyed the comforts of his own climate-controlled, world-insulating waterbed. But after a short trip through a tight space, he suddenly found himself in the arms of two people he would later know as mom and dad. For the first 24 hours, he enjoyed the warm quiet of the birthing center...but it soon came to an end.

After we were discharged, I carried him to the front door and paused to adjust his blankets before stepping out into the crisp, windy Indiana parking lot. "Well, Caleb," I said anticipating the contrasts, "Welcome to the REAL world."

He didn't respond, but inside I knew he was about to enter a harsh, blustery world where ugly things can and do happen. "Don't worry," I added, "Your dad will teach you everything you need to know."

Since that moment, I've thought about that big promise I made to my son and that I've made to all my children. I can't help but wonder how I'm doing so far.

Have I held up my end of the bargain? Have I been doing what I need to do to train and prepare them or have I been too busy with my stuff? Caleb is less than a week old, and already he's teaching me things.

So Dad, you and I have a lot of important stuff to do in the coming week. We've got kids to get ready for the REAL world. We need to teach them about God and their place in the world.

Your children are lucky to have you...and you're lucky to have them.

You 'da dad!

Boys, There's Work to Be Done

1 Corinthians 10:14-33

Hey Dad,

We're home—not for a stop-off, but for good. I'm telling you, there's nothing like the pure ecstasy of going into a regular bathroom, taking as much time as you want, and using as much toilet paper as you want and never having to see it again.

The only drawback of getting home is the mountain of stuff that needs attention. There are cars to fix (how do they get broken when no one has driven them?), landscapes to tame, and a big RV that needs to be emptied (3½ months' worth of junk, souvenirs, and supplies).

My kids would like to take it easy and kick back (which we've allowed), but I'm often calling up to their rooms and saying, "Boys, there's work to be done."

But that's not the real work. The real work isn't something that can be checked off a list that easily. The real work has to do with my family. You see, the last couple of months in the crucible have brought some ugly stuff to the surface—not only in my children, but also in me.

Along with some pretty spectacular sights, we have also seen some bad attitudes, crummy responses, lack of obedience, and overall yuckiness that need to be dealt with. That's the great thing about living in a crucible: It reveals what was already there to begin with, but needed a little coaxing to see. Life on the road does just that.

The really awful thing about the whole deal is that so much of the "dross" I saw in them is the same "dross" I see in me. I heard stuff coming out of their mouths and said, "Don't talk like that!," only to hear the same things come out of my mouth 15 minutes later.

So after using this week to rest and relax (yeah, right!), we start on all the hard work. We'll meet on the screened-in porch and talk about what we all need to work on, how we plan to do that, and what will be expected of them—and me.

I wish I had some kind of magic formula, special pill, or some incredible method to share with you so you can work on the "dross" in your family too. But there is no more of a magical potion for cleaning up the crud in your life than there is for cleaning up the crud in your yard.

It's just hard work...led by a dad.

And guess what?

You 'da dad!

A Father's Love

1 Corinthians 11:1-12

June **28**

Hey Todd,

"My daughter, Rachel (3) has gotten into the habit of coming into our room in the middle of the night and sleeping with Mom & Dad. In an attempt to help break her of this, I encouraged her that if she could stay in her bed for a week, we would go on our first daddy-daughter date. She was excited and accomplished the task.

A few nights later, as I tucked my son Mitchell (8) into bed, he asked, "Dad, what can I do to get some special time? Not aggravate for a week?" As you might guess, he is the one in our family that stirs the pot. I started to answer him, yes, that would be a great thing, but I realized what he was really asking. I knelt down by his bed and whispered to him, "You don't have to DO anything. If you need some special time, all you need to do is ask. I will always have time for you."

Whew!! I almost told him that my love and attention was conditional. What a terrible thing for a dad to tell his son. With God's grace and through the power of the Spirit, I got this one right. Now, I just have to stay alert and look out for the next close call. My prayer is that I come out on the right side more than I goof up. One day, that will be true."

~ Andrew W.

Embracing the Were-pigs

Hey Dad,

It's bad...real bad. If you were to pull into my long driveway, the first thing that would catch your attention is the vast number of bicycles in the yard. You'd probably assume that there must be pert' near 75 children living in our home. But that's not the only thing dotting the yard.

There are a couple of shovels sitting in the grass, a half-dozen sleds, a hatchet, four super-soaker squirt guns, several winter coats, one flip-flop, a butterfly net, and a rusted pile of...oh I don't know, 10,000 nails and screws.

But that's not all. There are various lengths of rope, a board that has about 50 holes drilled through it, a half-dozen orange Frisbees in various states of 'intactness,' a knitted ski mask, a yellow hula-hoop, four scooters, two rip-sticks, and one skateboard.

Not done...a dinner knife from our best flatware, one of my Craftsman screwdrivers, a small roll of electrical tape, and a saw, along with several swords made from wood, old golf clubs, and sticks.

Looking for that ever-elusive silver bullet that will change the way we live and re-transform my were-pigs into neat and orderly children, I created a list of rules for my children.

Here's the deal. I'm pretty sure it won't work. As my dad likes to say, "You can have things or you can have kids"...which I've translated into "You can have a clean, tidy yard OR you can have kids...but you can't have both."

So dad, from one dad of a were-pig to another...deal with the fact that you won't win!!! In fact, don't just deal with it but ENJOY it...embrace it...because one day your yard, house, garage, and car will be orderly, neat, and tidy...and you'll wish they weren't.

You 'da dad!

When the Going Gets Tough

1 Corinthians 11:23-34

June	30

Hey Dad,

We're having a little attitude problem here at the Wilson house this morning. For the last few weeks, we've been enjoying life "off" the road. We've enjoyed our big beds, big bathrooms, big yard, and big everything else.

Today, we head back out on the road for several days down South. Bye-bye big—hello cramped, tight spaces. To make matters worse, my brothers' and sister's families are vacationing at a lake just a few miles from where we live while we're gone. My kids desperately wish we could be here with their cousins and the rest of their kin.

I wish I could say I'm all pumped up for the trip, but I'm not. But I know that this is when my family needs their dad most. This is one of those moments that, when the going gets tough, the dad gets going. Besides, as their dad, I know that it will be really good once we get there. It's just the leaving and getting there that sounds hard.

My family needs me to hold the team together, keep the family purpose and vision in front of us, and do whatever I can to make the miles enjoyable. That won't be easy.

But I'm 'da dad!!

So, I'm going to lead them all in prayer before we leave, stop for ice cream along the way, work hard at keeping my cool, be conscious of the circumstances, and use my very calmest voice.

The truth is, we all face situations that nobody likes. Sometimes you have to go to family reunions that no one wants to attend, go to weddings of people you hardly know, or do projects that are messy and drawn out.

In order to keep the troops happy, some families let their kids abandon ship—stay with friends, stay behind, or choose not to participate. But when they do, they miss out on the best. Because some of the best times seem like the worst times: times where the family has to come together to accomplish something or to encourage someone else.

So, Dad, got something you're dreading looming before your family? Rally the troops, stand behind the helm—and stop for ice cream along the way.

Gotta go finish loading the RV.

You 'da dad!

You're not a Victim

1 Corinthians 12:1-11

| July | 1 |

Hey Dad,

I'm going to do something I've never done before, and that is address a letter that has been sent to me by more than one well-meaning dad. Of course, I'm going to change the name and details a little so those well-meaning dads won't feel like I'm picking on them.

Hey Todd,

Sure enjoy getting the Familyman Weekly, but I'm getting a little sick of you complaining about how hard it is for you traveling around the country with your family in an RV. Do you know how many of us would love to do what you're doing? But we can't because we have REAL jobs.

Signed, Envious in Minneapolis

Dear Envious,

First of all, you envy MY life? Have you not read about all the mechanical breakdowns, fathering meltdowns, and hardships of having nine people in a 30-foot RV? Take today, for example: The kids are loud and annoying, I'm mad at everyone because I spent at least an hour being lost in New Jersey, and now we're sitting in the back of a crummy parking lot doing laundry. My fellow dad, sometimes I fantasize about working in your REAL job where you leave the chaos behind and wear shiny shoes and non-wrinkled, clean clothes to a quiet office. Oh, yes, I do love my life on the road with my family, BUT it is hard, real hard sometimes.

But what concerns me about your letter is that you write as though we dads cannot choose the life we want. If you truly desire traveling around in an RV with your family, then choose that.

Yes, you may have to make some lifestyle changes, but if that's what you want, then go for it. If you want to have the summer off, then get a job (like a teacher) that gives you the summers off. You may have to live in a smaller house or have only one car, but if that's what you really want, then CHOOSE it. Don't sit around lamenting the fact that you can't. You can. You just have to make some choices.

I did. I chose to take the harder road by taking my family with me when I speak. I know most speakers pack their bags, say good-bye to the family, and then jump on a plane and stay in quiet hotel rooms for several days. That's their choice; not mine.

Dads, we are not trapped by the roll of the Job-Wheel-of-Fortune. We have no one to blame but ourselves for our choices of where we are or what we are. We are free to choose the best or the worst at any time.

So, Dad, I'm going to keep sharing about the choices I make—good or bad. And, I'm going to keep encouraging you to CHOOSE the best.

One Dumb Dad

Hey Dad,

The story is told that a successful businessman was honored at a university graduation for his success and achievement. The crowd applauded as the man took the podium to address the people. Oddly, He looked up towards the ceiling and said, "Is this good enough for you dad?"

It was sad, but apparently the man never got the approval of his father. He built a monstrous corporation and made billions, but it was never good enough.

Later, I heard the same businessman's father tell a reporter that the way to assure your children will be great is to keep them insecure. Don't let them ever think they've done a good job...otherwise they'll quit trying. Instead, withhold (there's that word) praise, and they'll keep seeking to do better."

Well, from one dad to another, let me just say, "THAT'S THE DUMB-EST THING I'VE EVER HEARD!!!!!

Children need our praise and approval as much as they need air and water. A child who feels his father's approval will be forever secure in his love. And not only that, he will feel secure in God's love.

On the other hand, a child who is always trying to win his father's approval will forever be trying to win God's approval.

Maybe you didn't have a father who praised you and so it's hard for you to praise your children. For the sake of your children, it's time to change.

Every kid needs to feel 'liked,' not for what he achieves but for who he is.

~ Excerpt from Father Power

My Knight in Shining Armor?

1 Corinthians 20-26

Hey Dad,

Rread this letter closely. Feel her pain and then ask, "Could my wife have written this letter?

"It is comforting to know I am not alone walking through a difficult marriage. I have withdrawn from my husband because it has become too difficult to continue to engage him. When I attempt to express the difficulties I am having, he tells me what I am doing wrong and then pressures the kids to do better because they are making my life too difficult. So, I just don't tell him or I tell him as little as I can. Unfortunately, I don't tell him about the joy and successes either. He is largely inactive with schooling. He doesn't know what the kids are studying and he doesn't show any interest. I try and update him on their progress and he seizes on the mistakes and shortcomings. So, again, I say as little as possible. The less I say, the easier it is to live in the house but the harder it is to live.

My husband has convinced himself that whatever problem I am having, it's because of something I am failing to do and has nothing to do with him. He is not culpable for the sorry state of our relationship. The blame can be found somewhere in what I have done or neglected to do. How dearly I long to be loved and respected regardless of the mistakes I make. My Father God does love me in that way, and it would be such a wonderful thing if my husband did too.

The advice of studying your wife cannot be overstated. Really take some time to learn who she is and why she is and then pray and ask God to show you how you can LOVE her."

~ Just a mom

You're a Grand Old Dad

1 Corinthians 12:27-31

July	4

Hey Dad,

    I wish I had some incredible tidbit of fatherly wisdom to offer right now, but my brain is tapped out. Let me just wish you a happy Fourth of July. Make it a good one with your family. Take the whole weekend off, grill some hamburgers, wave some good old-fashioned sparklers with your kids, and take the whole family to a fireworks display.

    While I'm thinking about it, I've heard from several Familyman soldiers who are protecting our freedom overseas and could use your prayers...because it's not easy being a dad away from one's family, especially during holidays.

**   So thank God for freedom and the privilege of being a Familyman, and remember to pray for those who are on the line protecting that freedom.**

    And let me personally thank all of you fellow Familymen who are separated from your families so that we're able to be with ours.

You 'da dad!

Brother-in-Law

1 Corinthians 13:1-7

Hey Dad,

Hope you had a great Fourth of July. We went to my in-laws' lake cottage. I ate too much, played out in the sun with my family, and enjoyed the rocket's red glare and the bombs bursting in air. About the only bad part of the weekend was the odd feeling that came over me early on the morning of the fourth.

With the sun shining, the sky as blue as can be, and the water warm, I was basking in the sun when I noticed something…disturbing. One of my nephews ran up to Alan, my brother-in-law, and asked, "Dad, can I go skiing?"

"Sure," he answered cheerfully. A little too cheerfully for my liking. He walked down the long pier, uncovered the boat, gathered the skis and life jackets, untangled the rope, and then took them skiing. I would have said, "Maybe we can tomorrow."

Later that night, one of the older kids asked Alan, "Dad, can we help light some of the fireworks?" Ha! I knew they were way too young for something like that and was flabbergasted when he said, "Sure." I would have responded, "Maybe next year." While watching their fireworks display, a feeling of "dad-envy" crept over me.

The next morning Alan again said, "Sure," to a boat ride, more skiing, AND fishing.

By the last day, I had discovered one of Alan's secrets to fathering—he says "Sure" a lot.

Fifteen minutes later, the chance came to try out my theory. I was on the front porch enjoying the shade when my four year old asked to go on a jet ski ride. "Sure," I said, pleased with my convincing tone.

Later Alan asked, "You want to go 'tubing' with me and the kids?"

"Sure," I said. I was glad I did—and so were my kids.

You know, maybe it's time for us dads to say, "Sure" more often. When your son wants to shoot some hoops, say, "Sure." When your daughter wants to talk about her future, say, "Sure." When your wife asks you to fix the broken screen, answer, "Sure!"

You may not feel like it, but say it anyway. No excuses or "I'll do it later"…just, "Sure."

Try it out for the next two days. Not only will your wife and kids enjoy it, but so will you. Who knows? Maybe with a little practice, Alan's fathering secret will become yours too.

You 'da dad!

Bugged About Lightning Bugs!

1 Corinthians 13:8-13 | **July** | **6**

Hey Dad,

On Sunday evening, after a long, hard weekend, I was enjoying the peace and quiet. A gentle breeze blew through the house refreshing the very bones within me…if only my wife would've brought me a tall, icy glass of freshly-squeezed lemonade, all would've been right with the world.

Enter Isaac (5).

"Hey, Dad…remember, you said we'd catch lightning bugs tonight? Is it time?"

He smiled a sunny smile. The kind of annoying "sunny" that shines through the blinds in the morning and hits you right in the eye.

I held my breath and thought about pretending I was dead. He stood before me with the goofiest (and most adorable) grin on his face, waiting for my answer.

Seconds ticked by, and I could hear the beat of my own heart as my mind scrambled for some…any kind of reasonable excuse. Too wet? Nope, dry as a bone. Maybe tomorrow night? Naw, I said that last night. I don't want to risk getting the West Nile Virus from a mosquito? It would take an hour to explain it to him.

"Sure, we'll catch lightning bugs tonight," I heard myself say before I could stop it.

"Good," he answered cheerfully and was off like a shot.

An hour later, we were outside scooping up lightning bugs and putting them in a jar. The kids laughed and squealed in excitement during the hunt. Later that night, Ike and Abe fell asleep watching the lightning bug zoo that hung on their closet doorknob.

Before I went to bed, I peered in on the sleeping boys and the jar with the glowing bugs and remembered the jars of lightning bugs I took to bed as a kid.

You see, we did something eternal that night. Something that my children will never forget. They may not remember the lightning bug part, but they'll remember the "they did it with dad" part. And to think it all took only ten minutes…and I almost said "No."

How many other things have I missed that would've only taken a few minutes or a few hours? I'd rather not think about it…but I'd better. We play for keeps, us dads.

So, have you gone on a lightning bug safari yet? Tonight would be perfect. Maybe there's something else the kids have been asking you to do. Tonight would be perfect for that as well.

You 'da dad!

193

A Great Adventure

Hey Dad,

Take a look at this letter from a dad who has quit talking about "it" and is going to do "it."

Todd,

"I wanted to say thanks too about encouraging our children. My wife and I are taking your advice. As an encouragement to our three younger children for all of their hard work this year, or should I say they think it was hard work, we are taking them for a one night, two day adventure at the Great Wolf Lodge in PA.

Our children do not know we are going there. It will be a total surprise for them. My wife and I planned this all out and we will be leaving on a Sunday right after church. They will think we are going to take them and their older brother out to eat, which we are, but they will also get two days at the Water Park. I can't wait to see their faces when we drive into the parking lot of GWL.

GWL offers discounts to families who homeschool during their "off" season times. Check it out on the web if you have never been there before. This will be our first time there, but I imagine it will not be our last. I'll let you know how it goes when we get back."

~ Rob, Dalton, PA

You know, Dad, it's time to turn, "We'll do that sometime" into a "We're doing it now."

You 'da dad!

Papa Said Yes

1 Corinthians 14:26-40

Hey Dad,

I've been working like a dog on our house project, every part of my body aches, and we have some serious computer problems. The good news is that the new addition over the garage is buttoned up and ready to battle the weather. The bad news is that I'm still too whipped to write much.

And so, I'm going to share with you something I just came across while spending some quiet time in the "throne room." It's taken from the June/July edition of Country Magazine and is written by Linda Brooks.

"I have very few memories of Papa, my maternal grandfather, as he died when I was six. I remember Papa had a pigpen across the dirt road from the farmhouse. One day while we were visiting, my older brother and I found Papa cleaning out the pigpen. The pigs wallowed out a nice, big hole, and my brother and I asked if we could play in it before the pigs were allowed back in.

He said yes! We had a grand old time in the pigpen…My mother must have been dying at the thought.

(Here's the kicker) I can count my memories of Papa on one hand. What if he had said no? We would have accepted that…and I would have one less memory of him."

Dad, as I read the above article I thought about how Dave, our contractor friend, allowed Ike (10) and Abe (8) to swing and climb on the exposed rafters of the new construction. I would have said "No"—because I 'mostly' say no.

Truth is, I need to say "Yes" more often. And I'm guessing so do you.

I'm going to soak my sore body.

You 'da dad…this weekend say, "YES!"

195

The Messier the Better

Hey Dad,

Every muscle in my body is sore. My arms are stiff, my toes ache, and even the tips of my fingers feel swollen. For the last eight or nine days, my wife and kids and I have been working like dogs trying to turn our junk-infested garage into a productive Familyman Ministries office/warehouse.

It took a whole day just to get all the old stuff out of the garage, and every day since then, we've been dry-walling, painting, and cleaning up. Actually, I should've sold tickets just to watch our little circus of construction performers.

"Hurry, hurry, step right up to see the Amazing Wilsons. They paint, they spill, all while their dad yells at them."

Talk about tense times. My sons, Ben (14) and Sam (12), and I hung drywall on the 10' ceiling perched atop a makeshift scaffold. They held it in place while I pushed against the drywall with my stocking-capped head until I'd sunk several screws deep into the studs. It was scary, but they swayed and giggled as I fumbled for the screws in my tool belt.

We finally got it all hung, and yesterday Ben and I tackled the messiest job in the world. It seemed simple in theory, texturize a ceiling. Besides, I assumed I didn't need to do a super job smoothing out the ceiling since we were going to spray stuff all over it.

Well, we rented the machine and managed to spray plaster and Styrofoam all over us, the floor, and every single item still in the garage…and even got some on the ceiling. By the way, it doesn't cover up uneven drywall.

But hey, we're almost done, and it looks—okay. I could've hired someone who knew what they were doing, and it probably would've been done in half the time and not cost all that much, but my family would've missed out on working as a team.

Years from now, I know Ben and Sam will point to the ceiling and say, "We hung that." Ben will laugh when he recalls the time dad sprayed "ceiling stuff" all over him, and Kat (10) will remember her first real painting job.

That, my fellow dad, is worth sore fingertips and an imperfect ceiling.

So, if you're thinking of a little family construction project, let me encourage you to get the whole family involved. It won't turn out perfect, but the time spent together working on it makes up for it.

You 'da dad!

The Familyman and the Six Pigs

1 Corinthians 15:20-32

Hey Dad,

High-powered, Super Soaker squirt gun left in the yard again—$8 Deranged dad on a 22hp Super-Soaker-shattering riding lawn mower—$2,500 Lesson learned—priceless!

Okay, so I didn't run over the Super Soaker...but I wanted to as the culmination of a week of living with six pigs, whom I affectionately call my children. They make messes faster than my wife and I can keep up. It seems like they get a puzzle out of the cabinet, spend 45 seconds working on it, run off to spread Honey-Nut Cheerios all over the floor of the kitchen, and then rush outside, leaving half of their clothes scattered near the trampoline entrance.

Oh, I've tried different techniques to curb their slob-like behavior like: a Jubilee box, taking away privileges, and the never-effective hollering rampage. Then I got the idea about the lawn mower. As I fired up the mower, I knew this

was going to be the day they LEARNED their lesson. Like my dad says so often, "The best lessons are the ones that cost the most."

I was going to run over, slice, dice, and julienne, anything I found left in the yard. Super Soaker...ZZZUNK! Beloved cowboy boots...KERPLEWY! BB guns, Frisbees, wooden swords, shirts, socks, and bicycles...CHUCHUNAGUNGA!! Yeah, baby!! They were going to learn their lesson.

To my chagrin, Katherine was picking up all the junk around the trampoline...including the Super Soaker. Thwarted again.

I cooled down and called a family meeting together. I decided on a different approach. "Kids, we need to work harder at thinking about others. Every time you leave a banana peel, say, on the arm of the couch, your mom has to come by and throw it away. That means more work for her. So, we're going to think more about others as we play..."

I waxed eloquent for 10 minutes, and they all nodded in agreement. I thought I had connected until Sam ran from the room leaving behind a small game he had been playing with.

"Sam, get back here!" I said, pointing at the game.

"Ooops," he said with a smile.

That's the way it goes, Dad. We have family meetings, discipline children, try new techniques, and wake up the next morning only to start all over again.

As tough as it is, I love being a dad...and I love my six little pigs. But the next time I cut grass...watch out Super Soaker.

You 'da dad!

If You Build It...

Hey Dad,

Whew! Things are busy humming in the Familyman Factory. The fruit flies are back in full bloom, and I spent a chunk of yesterday evening dumping about 50 gallons of over ripe RV dump tank...by hand (or bucket). I had the bright idea of dumping it in a big trash can and then hauling it away...not the smartest thing I ever did...but a half bottle of hand sanitizer undid the damage that the sloshing trash can caused.

In all this chaotic busyness, my son Ike (11) wants to build a boat. That's right, a fully functional, motorboat...and he wants me to help. Not to be prophetic, but Ike is destined to be an inventor...and possibly horribly maimed by one of his inventions. While he hasn't abandoned his plans to build a jet-pack (he bought the plans off the internet), he's 100% gung-ho on building a motorboat.

Like any good father who is trying to get his son off his case, we looked on the INTERNET for simple boat plans hoping that he would be daunted by the supply cost. Instead, we found plans for a reasonably inexpensive boat called the Puddle Duck.

Now, he wants me to take him to Lowe's and get the supplies. I know it won't stop there...then he'll want me to help him cut the pieces and build it. AND I don't want to build a boat right now (read – ever).

BUT, I want to fan the flames of my tow-headed dreamer...

BUT, I'm super busy...

BUT, maybe it wouldn't take as long as I think...we could crank it out in a week's worth of evenings...

BUT, I don't have a week's worth of evenings...

BUT, He's going to grow up, and I won't have these father/son opportunities forever...

BUT...BUT...BU...B...

I know...I know...I'm 'da dad.

Thanks, I needed that.

I'll build the stupid boat.

Don't think you're off the hook. You 'da dad...too. Go build a whatever.

I'm 'da skipper!

Building Homes NOT Houses

1 Corinthians 15:50-58

Hey Dad,

We're in a sprint to finish up the painting on our "over the garage project." The mess is horrendous. We have six of our children crammed into one very crowded bedroom, drywall dust coats everything, and most of our kids are speckled with paint.

Actually, that last statement is due to the fact that my wife is better than I am. She allows the little ones to be involved in the project. Even little Maggie Rose (5) was slapping paint on the wall with a brush.

I'm sure I would have said, "You're too little....go watch a video."

Had I gotten to her first, she'd never have the memory and satisfaction of helping on the "project."

It's not like I don't ever let my kids help. I've worked my older kids like dogs. Ben (16) and Sam (14) have framed, pulled wire, installed insulation, and done just about everything else on the project.

But I do have limits. I like it done well, and...well, when the little kids are involved, not only is it not done well but it also takes about 10 times as LONG. I usually have good motives and give them a try, but then I get frustrated and holler, "Go watch a video."

I had Abe (8) help me with wiring a couple of weeks ago. His job was to pound the small wire staples into the framing to hold the wires in place. Do you know how hard it is to watch a kid turn a two-second job into a two-minute one? Of course you do...you're a dad!

The echo of six persistent children asking to help paint, drywall, sand, and use power tools is maddening.

"When can I paint?"

"Mom said I could."

"Hey, that's my roller!!"

"Oops. I accidentally got it on this."

"GO WATCH A VIDEO!"

That's why my wife is better than me. She doesn't like the mess, chaos, or yammer any more than I do (she may even like it less), but she knows what's important. Paint drips and smears are not important. Dinged drywall doesn't matter. BUT training our children IS important. Having them involved, being part of the team, and working as a family IS important.

That's what parenting is about. Is it easy? Nope. Will our homes be as neat and designer-ish as our kidless counterparts? NO WAY.

But we don't care because we're building HOMES not HOUSES.

So, Dad, let me encourage you to get your children involved. Have them help you finish that project you've been working on. I guarantee they'll make the job harder and it won't turn out as good. But every time you see that look of satisfaction on their faces and every ding, drip, or mark, you will be reminded that it was worth it.

Don't Try This at Home

Hey Dad,

We got a trampoline last week. We'd been promising the kids for at least a year and finally made good on that promise. Kids never forget the promises we make—ever.

The sun was shining as we piled into the van for the 15 minute trip to Walmart, and we looked like the Brady Bunch on some kind of TV adventure. All smiles and sunshine.

I was worried about not having a big enough van to get the trampoline home, but fortunately trampoline makers have figured out how to pack a 14-foot, 215-pound trampoline with sides into two boxes, leaving plenty of room in the back of our van.

Once home, I learned a lot about trampolines, my kids, and myself. First, putting a trampoline together is not a 20-minute project. In fact, you should never attempt to put a trampoline together unless you're well rested, your kids are in another state, and you wife is taking a nap.

I was exhausted that day. It also didn't help that I don't have an engineering degree, that the kids were pulling parts out of the box at incredible speed, and that my wife thinks I'm dumb.

Halfway through the project, I was ready to send them all packing and to stuff the trampoline back into the box in which it came. Four hours later, it was done, and we ate dinner.

After setting down some rules for trampoline use, we watched the kids bound, laugh, and call out, "Watch this!" Sitting next to my wife in the evening shade, I couldn't help but feel like it had turned out to be a good day. Hard, but good.

Most good days are like that. Usually I see the potential hardness and say, "No, thank you"; but when I do, I miss out. And so do you.

So when the kids ask to build a treehouse, a blanket fort, have a tea party, or rebuild a transmission, think through all the pros and cons, take a good nap, and then do it! Of course, it will be hard; but it will be good.

You 'da dad!

Absence Makes the Heart...

Hey Dad,

Here's a letter I received that sends chills down my spine.

Todd,

"You were right when you said the more dad is away, the less we are missed, not more. I think I've noticed that and I want to be missed. My son said to me last summer as I told him I couldn't be home to play, "It's okay, Dad. I'm getting more used to you not being here." That was a hard one! I don't think he was even trying to manipulate me to be home more; he was just stating it the way it was. Nor do I think he was aware of what that sentence would do to me. But it was pretty painful and reigned me back in a little. Thanks for your exhortations to be with family."

You know, Dad, everything that dad wrote is true. It's only a matter of time before his son will hardly notice when his dad is gone. The dad needs to act quickly while the iron is hot...because although the words struck deep, tomorrow they are easily forgotten or dismissed.

Here's the deal: If your child could say something similar, then do something about it ASAP. Don't wait for the feeling to cool. You're both running out of time.

You 'da dad!

My Underwear Drawer

2 Corinthians 1:1-11

Hey Dad,

Hope you're enjoying the summer with your family. I'm always shocked by how quickly it speeds by, especially once you pass the 4th of July mile marker. The goal is to get to the end of the summer with no regrets, no I-wish-we-would-haves, and no unfulfilled good intentions.

That really sums up the goal of a father's life, right? I was reminded of that by a little piece of paper I found in my underwear drawer recently. It was a note that my daughter tucked in my suitcase about a year ago…I think. My son Ben (17) and I had to speak somewhere and my daughter hid the note for me to discover at the hotel.

It was a sweet, "I love you, dad" kind of note, but the line that re-caught my attention was the last line. She signed it, "Your Princess." She wrote that because that's what I call her.

"Good night, Princess," I say with a quick kiss.

"Good morning, Princess," I chime as she stumbles down the stairway.

As I held the note, I was reminded that I haven't been treating my princess very princessly lately. In fact, I've found myself annoyed by her outbursts and outpouring of emotion. At times, I walk from her room with clenched teeth, while muttering just loud enough for her to hear my negative comments.

Then I re-read the underwear note and realized that I need to make my princess feel like a princess again. It begins by changing the tone in my voice but also includes calling her princess. And so I have.

How about you, my fellow dad? Maybe it's been a while since you called your son, "Buddy, Champ, or Big Guy." And maybe it's been a while since you called your daughter…princess. She needs to hear that from you.

You 'da king!

You never know what encouragement you'll find in your underwear drawer…besides underwear.

Feeling the Aftermath of Katrina

2 Corinthians 1:12-24 | **July** **16**

Hey Dad,

Compared to the upheaval and destruction that some of our families are facing down south, I need to shut up about current gas prices and be thankful to even have gas. The aftermath of hurricane Katrina has been felt all the way up here in northern Indiana.

The pictures and stories of people wading through the murky brown waters have affected me. Those folks know firsthand what's important and what isn't now. Their homes have been destroyed, and all their worldly possessions have been washed away or ruined, but when interviewed about the situation, they inevitably say, "I'm just thankful that my family is all right…that's all that matters right now."

On the flip side, those who have lost a family member care about nothing else. You'll never hear them say into the camera, "I lost my cordless drill and golf clubs…and look at my car! What am I going to do?"

A few minutes ago, I was standing in my garage looking at the mounds of bikes, tools, toys, and junk that I've collected and thought, "None of this matters."

The books that I've written, the treasures that I've collected, even the photos and scrapbooks that hold irreplaceable memories…don't matter.

The landscape, the house that we've labored over for eight years, and the Familyman Mobile that we've come to love…don't matter.

My dreams for the future, my plans and aspirations to change the world…don't matter.

What matters is a little boy named Ike who spiked his hair up yesterday and paraded around the house thinking it was pretty funny, little Maggie Rose who adorably wrinkles her nose and shrugs her shoulders, Katherine who puts little sparkles on her cheeks, Ben and Sam who are becoming more like men every day, Abe who has a "fever" and is milking it for all it's worth, and my beloved bride who is in need of a little "together time."

The reminder is part of the aftermath of Katrina. So, Dad, be thankful for your nice, dry home…and cherish the family you have tonight.

You 'da dad!

Stock Tip...Invest in Gatorland

Hey Dad,

My wife is in a laundry mat here in Nashville, TN, and I thought I'd type up this week's Familyman. So far, we've had a great time speaking and traveling. Before stopping to do laundry, we spent the day at President Andrew Jackson's home—the Hermitage. If you're in the area, it makes for a great field trip.

The one drawback to the Hermitage (as well as just about everything else in this country that's worth seeing)...is that it's expensive. I mean what ever happened to America being the land of the free? From my seat in the Familyman Mobile, it looks like anything BUT free.

Now, I know it takes money to run a million dollar museum, and I'm more than willing to chip in...but I am continually amazed by how much everything costs...a whole bunch more than I anticipate.

Whenever you take a reasonably-priced museum or attraction and multiply it by 10 family members, you've got all the makings of a wad of cash. And for this certified cheap-skate, sometimes I'm tempted to make some weak excuse as to why we should pass. But fortunately, I've learned some things from other Familymen that help me do what is right.

So here's some financial advice that would probably make Dave Ramsey...die and then roll over in his grave. Most of it comes from other Familymen.

Spend it while you're young (Walt, an old guy told me that).

It's not a lot to spend on gas; it's a little to spend on your family (Paul H. reminded me).

Don't ask God to make it cheaper; ask Him to supply your needs (Dan P.).

It'll grow back (attributed to my cousin Scott).

The Grand Canyon isn't getting any closer, gas ain't getting any cheaper, and you're not getting any younger (I came up with that on my own).

You know, Dad, life is expensive, but as my dad once told me, "the alternative is...to stay home." So...when given the choice to spend it on your family or save it for retirement...spend it on ice cream or go to Gatorland.

You 'da dad!

Go Home Dad

Hey Dad,

If life is a highway, then we've taken the exit ramp to Bugtussle. Not that I'm complaining, but since leaving Kansas City last week our family has been a coughing, hacking mess. Actually, things were beginning to calm down until my wife threw up this morning as we were tooling down the highway to San Antonio.

That threw a little toxic wrench into the works. We had planned to visit the Alamo and stroll the Riverwalk today. We did check out the Alamo (while my wife took a nap in the RV) but decided to put off the Riverwalk until tomorrow.

Right now, we're camping downtown in an expensive parking spot. I have to admit, it's a little freaky spending the night in the middle of a city surrounded by tall buildings, constant traffic, and people carrying big backpacks or pushing grocery carts.

Actually, it's kind of fun watching the world pass by through our RV windows. It reminds me a little of the Jimmy Stewart movie Rear Window. In fact, I was just thinking about an event that took place outside our RV window last year while we were parked in a Walmart parking lot somewhere in the USA.

My wife and I were lying in bed at night talking when a car (driven by a woman) pulled up within a few spaces of our RV. A few minutes later, another car (driven by a man) pulled up beside the first car.

The guy in the car quickly got out and joined the woman in her car and was very "friendly." I watched with great fascination. I'm not going to go into great detail, but as I watched this take place, I knew someone was cheating on someone else. I was so mad that I had a half a mind to walk out, knock on the window, and say, "Go home, Dad!!"

I didn't. Instead, the man got back into his car about an hour later and returned to his family, leaving me with the feeling that I let him down. I was also struck by the thought that someone is always watching. You may think your "sin" is going unseen, but someone is watching. The "watchee" might be your son or daughter, the guy at work, a guy in an RV at a Walmart parking lot, or God Himself.

So Dad, while I sit here listening to drunken lunatics whoop and holler in the distance, let me warn you that if you're doing stuff you shouldn't be doing and you think what you're doing is in secret—you're wrong. You are being watched.

Let me tell you what I should have told that man in the Walmart parking lot, "Go home, Dad!!"

Grab the Feelings by the Horns

Hey Dad,

You know one of the great things about traveling around in an RV is that it is good for my marriage—eventually. Unfortunately, it takes about three weeks out on the road before it gets to that point. During the first couple of weeks there is a lot of stress, tears, and frustration.

I'm totally focused on the RV, leaving little room for talking, sharing, or close time with my wife. I get snappy and feel exhausted. As the early weeks pass, I get less sensitive—and my wife gets more sensitive.

In fact, at the start of this past week, my wife didn't like me too much. She said I didn't care about how she felt. Truth was, I didn't. I just wanted her to buck up and take it like a trooper, so that's how I was treating her.

After a couple of weeks of insensitivity, I said I was sorry—but that didn't solve anything.

"I need you to resolve this," she said one night in tears.

"I thought I did. I said I was sorry; what more is there to resolve? I was insensitive and so I'm sorry. There, I said it again. So let's move on."

She was unmoved by my logic and began to tell me how she just needed to talk about it.

Oh no, I thought, not the "I just need to talk about it some more" comment.

I just don't get it. I should by now, but I don't. I like the quickly-ask-forgiveness-and-move-on approach. Pretending it's resolved is so much easier than "talking about it." But since my approach wasn't working, I thought I'd give it a try and said, "So what are you feeling?"

You know what? It worked. We talked about how she felt, how I had been an insensitive clod (what's new), and then—we held each other, and all was right with the world—almost. I'd like to say everything is back to normal, but my wife still needs me to keep talking (go figure). Now I know some husbands would ask, "Why does it always have to be us who resolve it?"

I know what they mean, but instead of lamenting the fact that it's hard being married to a woman, I say, "Bring it on!" because I'm 'da husband.

So, Dad, if your wife is acting a little "non-mannish" and needs something resolved, then grab the bull by the horns and ask, "So what are you feeling?"

After all, you 'da husband!

A Swallowed Hook and a Dad

2 Corinthians 4:7-18

Hey Dad,

I love it when I'm traveling along life's highway minding my own business, and God suddenly points out the window and says, "See that's what really matters, Todd."

That's what happened this past Sunday. I have to admit I felt half numb from corralling kids (my wife was home with a couple of sick ones) when something out of the ordinary caught my attention.

Halfway through our church service, during the time when people stand up and share how they saw God work the past week, Paul, a dad about my age, stood up holding his son in his arms—or maybe it was his coat. Anyway, his voice was full of emotion, the kind that comes from the gut, and that's what made my ears perk up. This is going to be a good one, I thought.

And it was.

He began his testimony with one of his all-time favorite memories. In fact, the memory that he shared with our little church took place over 15 years ago. It involved a day off from work, a big catfish that swallowed a hook, and his dad.

Good memories almost always include a dad.

As Paul retold the catfish story, his voice cracked as the emotion caught in his throat. Here was this grown man telling a story about his dad that happened 15 years ago, and he had to work to hold back the tears.

That's when God got my attention and said, "Remember Todd, that's what matters. What you choose to do with your children today will be cherished lovingly for decades to come. Many of their best memories will be with YOU."

Then God added one more little zinger.

"So make sure you're there."

Paul finished his testimony, but I've found myself thinking about the catfish and the dad ever since. You see, my fellow Dad, that is Father Power. And you've got 'da power.

I know you have a lot of important "stuff" to do. But let me remind you as God reminded me, "Make sure you're there."

You 'da dad!

207

Right Around the Corner

2 Corinthians 5:1-10

Hey Dad,

We watched our Hawaii trip photos the other night on our Wii. We discovered that we could put our camera card in the thing, and it made a little slide presentation, complete with music.

As we watched those 4-month-old pictures, it became clear to me that I have issues. Serious ones. While everyone else laughed and giggled, I found that a softball had lodged in my throat making it hard to breathe and tears filled my eyes making it hard to see.

It wasn't that the pictures were sad as much as it was the thought that the past gets here so fast. Just a few days ago, I walked the beach with my daughter Maggie (5). We laughed and sang silly songs, and her little girl giggle made the sun seem all the brighter and the beach all the beachier.

Now it's just a memory, a four-second slide on a Wii slideshow, and...here comes that softball again.

You see, that's the way it is with time. It rushes by, and not just during tropical vacations, special events, or important moments but everyday. Right now, I can hear the muffled thumps of my kids wrestling on the floor above me; one day it will be silent.

Last night, we moved our son Jed (1) out of our room and into the little boys' room. For over a year I listened to his breathing, coughing, and the way he'd thump his foot in a regular rhythm. Last night it was quiet.

Man, I hate time. It ruins everything. See? I told you I have issues. I'm not even sure what to do except enjoy today with my wife and children and to encourage you to do the same.

I'm telling you, Dad, the past is almost here and it ain't waiting for you to finish that important "thing" you're working on and is consuming your time even before it shows up.

You 'da dad...today!

A Great Investment Tip

2 Corinthians 5:11-21 | **July** | **22**

Hey Dad,

On Monday night, I took our four oldest kids to a baseball game between the Ft. Wayne Wizards and the Dayton Dragons.

Not real exciting. For the first four innings, no one hit the ball and no one was seriously injured…even though one guy is probably nursing a goose egg after taking a foul ball on the noggin'.

I'm pretty sure Katherine (6) and Ike (4) didn't have a clue what was going on. They were more excited about the prospects of ice cream after the game than the actual game. In fact, between the half a dozen bathroom breaks, Katherine and Ike did more wrestling than watching. Fortunately, the stands were pretty sparse and they didn't make a nuisance of themselves.

Sam (8) enjoyed the sixty-second circuses between innings. There was the human bowling ball, the T-shirt cannon, musical chairs, and the race between three bags of potato chips.

Ben (10) was the only one who kept his eye on the game, and asked a million questions: "When's half-time?" "Is that the referee?" "Who pays if a foul ball breaks a windshield in the parking lot?"

They all had a great time though. It was obvious because one by one each of them slipped into my lap, kissed my cheeks, and held my hand.

On the way home, we got our ice cream and they quickly fell asleep. All except Ben. He sat next to me up front and asked questions faster than I could track them. We talked about outer space, the ocean, and heaven.

He was eating up his alone time with dad while the others slept…and so was I. I couldn't help but think that our Q & A time would one day end. I didn't want to forget it.

That's why when I got home I tacked the ticket stub above my computer. In fact, the more I look at it, the ticket looks like a deposit slip. Stuck to my wall, it will serve as a reminder of the investment that I made in my children that night. We dads need reminders like that.

How about you? Have you made any good investments lately? Or, have you been investing in "stuff" that doesn't even matter?

You 'da dad!

A Rocky Moment

Hey Dad,

Score one for the Familyman! I feel a little bit like Rocky at the top of the steps with his arms in the air prancing around like the heavyweight champion of the world! I did it! I responded just like a good, godly father is supposed to respond. Sure, there have been the thousand-plus times when I have been the textbook Jerk-o-dad, but yesterday…ho, ho, ho, I DID IT!!

I was working in my basement minding my own business. Outside, my son Sam (11) was cutting grass and the other kids were either busy doing there assigned jobs or playing. I didn't hear Sam coming, but when he opened the door, the look on his face told me that something was bad. Immediately, I assumed he had broken our new riding mower, and in my head I pictured a smoldering heap of yellow metal out in the yard.

"Dad," he said slowly, "I accidentally ran over the hose with the mower…and it stopped." Sam stood there silently awaiting his doom.

BUT it didn't come. I'm sure my face paled for just a second; but in that second something happened, and I quickly gave myself a remember-what's-important talk. I listened to myself; the muscles in my face relaxed, and I said, "Let's go take a look at it, Sam."

Surprised to still be alive, he followed, and I found the mower just as he said, behind the house with the garden hose poking out from its deck like a struggling octopus.

"That's OK, Sam. I've done the very same thing at least a couple of times myself," I assured him. I untangled it, started the mower, and told Sam he did a good job handling the situation.

"Hey," I said to my relieved and smiling son, "Don't run over the picnic table."

He laughed, and we both went back to our tasks, glad to be father and son.

Well, that was yesterday. Who knows what today holds and how I'll respond to the next crisis. I'd like to think I'll react that way every time…but I know me. BUT yesterday…now, that was beautiful.

So, Dad, I'm not going to give you a simple three-step instruction on how to respond correctly every time. I know you; sometimes you succeed and sometimes you fail. We're dads, and we just keep trying. And every once in a while, we mount those steps and raise our arms and prance around like the heavyweight champion dad of the world!

You 'da dad!

A Terrible Good Dream

Hey Dad,

We just rolled in last night after being gone for two weeks to Colorado for a family wedding. While we were there, we saw all kinds of awesome sights and have decided that the mountains of Colorado are almost as beautiful as the cornfields of Indiana.

As we pulled in, I knew that summer was officially over. It's time to buckle down and get the family back into a routine and shore up some of the areas that I have let slide over the past summer months.

There's one area that has weighed heavy on my heart the last couple of weeks. God pointed it out to me through a dream—not that HE appeared to me in a dream, but it was a powerful dream, nonetheless.

I can still remember it very clearly—although if I were to tell you all the details it would sound pretty weird. In my dream it had been announced that Jesus was coming back and that He was taking all of the Christians to heaven. For some reason, I was walking through the crowd of people who were going to be left behind. I'm not sure why I was doing this, but I was laying my hand on their heads and offering words of comfort (not sure what kind of comfort I could give at a time like that).

As I was walking through the crowd of "left-behinds," I came upon my young son. As I saw him, I immediately realized that he wasn't going. I burst into tears at the thought of one of my children not being with me in heaven. We would be apart, and I never want to be apart.

Then I woke up, but the thought wouldn't leave me.

I was reminded that the chief purpose of dads is to prepare their children to meet God. If we have not prepared our children for that moment in time, all the fun memories, Kids' Days, and sleeping under the Christmas tree mean—nothing.

We've got to teach and train our children to love and trust God so that one day when they meet Him, He will say, "Well done my child—your dad did good."

That means—I need to buckle down and get the family back into a routine and shore up some of those areas that I have let slide over the past summer months. I'll tell you next week about what I plan to do—but until then...

...Why don't you spend some time thinking about my dream and how you would feel if your son or daughter was the one left behind?

You 'da dad!

An Algae-Sucker Kiss

Hey Dad,

I like kissing my wife...not those little pecks that couples offer each other as they run out the door, but those soft, sloppy kisses that I gave so profusely when we were dating. However, my wife doesn't always share my sentiments...especially around the children. But now she has to! It's for the sake of our children that she needs to latch onto me like an algae-sucker on aquarium glass. I've got convincing evidence.

Here's what happened. The other day I walked into the kitchen and spied my attractive wife. She didn't know it at the time...but she wanted me...or at least my lips. So I wrapped my arms around her and kissed her...and she kissed back.

As we were kissing, we noticed our daughter Katherine (8) standing on a bench in the dining room watching us through a large opening as though she was staring through a storefront window at an American Girl doll display. She didn't hide her eyes in embarrassment, blush, or giggle...she loved it and was beaming. I think she would have liked us to do it some more...and so would I, for that matter. "Thanks Dad," her eyes seemed to say, "for kissing mom like that. I like it when you do that. It makes me feel safe and secure knowing you love Mom so much, and I hope I find someone who loves me that much one day."

Actually, two months ago we went to a family wedding. At one point, my wife and I took to the dance floor for one song. The music played softly as we waltzed back and forth looking into each other's eyes just like we used to. Again, there was Katherine, standing right near by watching her mom and dad...dancing and in love. Her big eyes sparkled, and she smiled radiantly. When I asked her the next day what her favorite part of the wedding was, she said, "When you danced with Mommy."

So that's why I'm telling my wife that she has to kiss me in public. She owes it to our children. They need to see real love demonstrated by Mom and Dad. And so do your kids.

They need to see you kiss your wife, sweep her off her feet, and smile as you look into her eyes. Don't be embarrassed. Show the kids what real love looks like.

Man, I'm going to find my wife right now!

You 'da dad!

Bounce Back

Hey Dad,

I thought I'd share with you ONE of TWO secrets of successful fathering (the first one was "Just keep trying"). The second one is called "Bounce Back," and I recently discovered it on my way to speak in southern Indiana.

Actually, at the time I learned it, I wasn't much in the mood for traveling or for speaking because it had been "one of those days." More accurately, I had just gone head to head with one of my children.

It was one of those ugly moments in fatherdom when your blood boils, the veins in your neck pop out, and your voice gets mighty loud. What made it worse is that the child I was 'dealing' with showed no signs of softening under my godly correction, which made me even madder.

Eventually, we worked it out; he softened...we prayed. But inside I was still mad, and the thought of traveling for five hours alone with him didn't appeal to me. In fact, by the time we got into the car, I had half a mind to ignore him all the way there and back.

Then it happened. I looked over at him and realized that he needed me to "bounce back." He needed me to forgive him, move on, and restore our relationship.

So a few miles down the road, I reached over, grabbed his hand, and squeezed it three times...I—Love—You. He squeezed back I—Love—You—More.

I'd like to say that that melted my icy heart, but it didn't. It took several miles of talking, teasing, and effort on my behalf before we were...right.

So here's the point: fathering is tough. Sometimes you succeed, but often you don't. That's where "bounce back" comes in. Our children are resilient and are easy forgivers and forgetters, but they need a dad who "bounces back"—who jumps back into the game and hugs after he hollers.

Yet some dads don't bounce back. Some hunker down and refuse to move on. In fact, I know of fathers who have spent years holding on to past failures and offenses, to their own detriment.

So, the next time you blow it, get caught in a battle of the wills, or feel like making someone pay..."bounce back." Like a great prizefighter, you have to say, "I float like a butterfly, sting like a bee, and then "bounce back" for my great fam-i-ly."

You 'da dad!

213

I Don't Do Anything!

2 Corinthians 8:9-24

Hey Dad,

You know, one of the things I've learned out here on the road is that I don't really do all that much compared to my wife. Sure, I man the helm of the Familyman-mobile, keeping it purring like a kitten, and manage to avoid daily disasters. But aside from that, I've come to the conclusion that my wife does all the really important stuff.

It dawned on me early one morning as I was doing a Walmart run armed with a list and toting my youngest daughter, Maggie Rose, as my assistant. "Where do they keep the peanut butter," I asked her, wondering if it was a vegetable, condiment, or sandwich item.

"I don't know," she said sweetly.

After a ten-minute search, I found it. Now all I had to do was find the remaining 20 items—and pick out a birthday card. Man, there were a lot of them to choose from. How does my wife manage to get cards for all of our extended family?

With Maggie Rose riding shotgun, the thought began to churn in my mind that my wife does a whole bunch of stuff that I take for granted. And then I remembered our time at the state park near St. Louis we'd just stayed at.

We'd stopped there to take showers, do laundry, and dump our holding tank. It was dark out by the time I went to take my shower, so I volunteered to fold the last of the six loads of laundry that my wife had done.

In man-like innocence, I opened the dryer door, and out tumbled more shirts, shorts, and underwear than I'd ever seen in my whole life. I assumed she'd jammed the whole five loads into one dryer. But after folding clothes for a while, I realized it was just one load.

I began to ponder just how many loads of monotonous laundry my wife has folded, how many jars of peanut butter she's bought, and how many cards she's picked out. That's when it hit me: I don't do anything! Or at the very least, I've forgotten how much my wife does that goes unthanked.

I need to tell her how much I appreciate all she does, I told myself. I decided to pick out a thank you card to thank my wife for the loads of laundry, tons of groceries, and the hundred other things she does to make our life comfortable.

You know, Dad, I'd just about bet that you've forgotten that your wife does much of the same for you too. So why don't you pick up a card (or make one) and let her know in writing how much you appreciate her?

You 'da dad!

Feeling Groovy

Hey Dad,

Hope all is well for you in the Dad-Universe. I'm telling you…this familyman thing isn't for cowards. Just about everyday I get emails from dads telling me about marriage or kid problems. I know they feel like they're all alone in the dad-struggle, but the truth is that we are all having marriage and kid struggles. Struggles go hand in hand with being a dad.

Why, just yesterday I had to have a long 'talk' with one of my older children. I was dreading it and wished life could be easy…but life isn't easy…especially for dads. So I walked into the room closed the door behind me and dealt with it. But here's the deal: it wasn't as bad as I expected. In fact, afterwards I'm sure we both felt…better. Because when you "take care of business" it feels good.

It happened again this morning when I decided to take a care of a broken window that had threatened to cut one of my kids to ribbons for the last three months. It took all of about 10 minutes to whip off, and afterwards I felt…good. I know my wife is going to be pleased that I finally took care of "business" and that makes me feel good. In fact, I'd even say I'm feeling groovy.

So you want a little tip? Take care of things. If you have a child that needs comforted, confronted, or just listened to, then do it. Maybe there's a spot on the carpet, a piece of trim, a burned out light bulb, or something else that your wife has asked you to take care of. Do it dad, today or tonight.

Not only will your child and wife like it, but you're also going to be feeling groovy for taking care of business. That's the truth!

Hang in there.

You 'da dad!

215

Killing Two Birds with One Tree

2 Corinthians 10:1-18

Hey Dad,

I work hard at making and preserving memories—they help us remember what's important.

In fact, I just came up with a whopper of an idea. Not only does it preserve memories, but it also solves the problem of getting rid of all the junk my wife would like to toss, but I'm still emotionally attached to.

I'm calling it a memory tree. Actually, it's a tree that broke during a summer windstorm, leaving a 10-foot tall trunk behind. So, this past weekend I sawed off the jagged part, had my son Sam (12) carve a big "W" in it, and had my son Ike (8) nail my old favorite sandals to the trunk, plus a few other trinkets.

Voila! Memory tree. I envision a tree covered in old toys, shoes, wooden swords, and other memory-making junk in a decade or so. The kids will bring their own kids back and remember the important stuff as they point out junk on the memory tree and add their own.

Plus, now I don't have to throw it away! That's what I call killing two birds with one tree.

Now, you may not have a tree your wife will let you cover in junk, but maybe there's another way you can preserve memories. It might be a box filled with stuff, a garage wall covered in "treasures," or a 3-ring binder stuffed full of photos and memories.

Whatever you do, your children will come back to it, like the Israelites did with those rocks in the Jordan, point to it, and say, "I remember that…and boy, did my dad love me."

You 'da dad!

Light Bulb

2 Corinthians 11:1-15

July	30

Hey Dad,

The Familyman Factory is in full swing right now getting ready to hit the road Monday morning for our "down south tour." In spite of the busyness, last week we went to see the animated film Despicable Me at a super cheap movie theater ($1.50 per person—YOW!!! With 75 cent Mondays—double YOW!!!). To be honest, I didn't think I would like it, but I just might nominate it for the best Dad Movie of the year.

Not only was Gru a likable villain…but he also becomes a wonderful dad by the end. In fact, I've already stolen one of his memorable lines. He utters it when a good idea pops into his head. His eyes light up and then in his deep Hungarian accent he says, "Light bulb."

When I use it someday, the kids will smile and remember the fun we had watching it together. That made me wonder if you have any great movie one liners that have become a standard line at you house. If you do, share it here.

One last thing before I head out and try to cram the bikes into the trailer: last night I was lying in bed thinking about filling THAT trailer, when I thought about Maggie Rose (6) popping wheelies on her bike. She was so proud of her accomplishment, but what she really wanted was for me to play 4-square with her (which she had asked me to do at least a dozen times yesterday), to which I consistently answered, "I'm too busy."

Lying in bed I thought, if something would happen to her in her sleep, I would regret the day that I wasted with busyness. I thought of a few of my other children who have been asking me to do things, but I have been 'unavailable'. I got that lump in my throat as I was reminded about what matters, and I knew that my daughter would ask me again tomorrow (now today), "Dad, can we play 4-square?"

Light bulb.

You 'da dad!

Like Father, Like Son

Hey, Dad,

This morning started out leisurely…just the three of us lying in bed at 6:20 a.m.…me, my wife, and Abe, our two-year-old human locomotive. I tried to avoid eye contact with him knowing that he would counteract with pinching my nose or sitting on my head.

Most mornings, I hear the pitter patter of little feet and then an unnerving stillness as he stands within a foot of my face.

"Eat! eat!" he announces. Not "Good morning, father; how did you sleep?" Just the sleep shattering, "Eat! eat!"

"Hi, Abe; you're up bright and early," I said cheerfully this morning.

"Eat, eat!"

"Get up in bed with us."

"Eat, eat!"

"I know you want to eat, but it's not time to eat yet."

Moments later, I actually thought he had fallen back asleep, but my wife told me he was quietly lying beside me, imitating me.

I was on my back with my hands folded across my chest so he lay on his back as well. Debbie said he turned his head, studied me, and then folded his hands just like mine. He looked again and then adjusted his position a little more.

He was trying to be just like his dad.

They all are, really. My children want to be like me. Even scarier is the fact that they will be like me. They will like McDonalds, sing loud and obnoxiously, laugh easily, and wear loud Hawaiian shirts. That's fine and dandy, but the ugly truth is that they will also imitate the part of me that I don't like…the part I'd like to pretend doesn't exist. But it does exist, and I'm passing it along to my children as well.

The good news is that it doesn't have to be that way. I can change…they need me to change…I must change. They don't need me to be perfect (it's a good thing, too). They just need me to be real, authentic, trust God, and confess when I've blown it.

You know, dad? Your kids will be like you, too. For good or bad, they imitate you. So if you don't want your children to smoke, then don't smoke. If you want them to talk respectfully to their mother, then treat your wife with gentleness. If you want them to have self-control, then you need to control yourself. If you want them to trust God, then…you need to trust Him, even when life gets kind of scary.

You 'da dad!

Call Me Paranoid

2 Corinthians 12:1-6

Hey Dad,

My children are trying to kill me! Don't tell me to relax...that's the problem. I can't. It's some kind of plot to do away with me through sleep deprivation.

What's the deal with kids wanting to sleep in their parents' bed anyway? I know all about how comforting it is, and some say it's a throwback to the womb thing, but I think it's more than that. I think it is a well-thought-through plan to exhaust and exasperate parents. After all, a tired, bleary-eyed parent is an easy-to-take-advantage-of parent.

Take last night. I'd been asleep for about three hours when I heard a thump and the pitter-patter of little feet running down the hallway. It was Abe (our two-year-old). I knew where he was headed.

He had developed a routine. He ran into our room, climbed over his mother like he was running an obstacle course, and then squirmed his stocky body between us. Seconds later he was snoring and flopping like a fish in a sack. With his leg across my back, I felt like I was sleeping on the ledge of a city building...balanced on the edge of disaster.

"That's all I can stand; I can't stand no more," I hissed. I got up, flipped his lifeless body over my shoulder like a gunnysack, and returned him to his bed.

Tick...tick...tick ...

A while later, I heard the "thump-and-run." He was back.

I gave him two minutes and then took him back to bed.

On my way back to bed, I half excepted to find him lying in my spot. He wasn't but did show up again about an hour later...bless his little heart.

I was too exhausted to care and slipped into a coma, until later, when I was startled to feel his finger in my left nostril.

Like it always does, morning came and brought a new light. I rolled over and saw the perfectly still face of my little boy. He stirred, opened his eyes, and smiled a warm, "I love you" smile.

He had won...and I was tired but glad he was there beside me.

That's what being a dad is all about. We're supposed to be tired, worn out, and under-appreciated. It's a badge of fatherhood and something to be worn with honor.

So...yawn...You 'da dad!

Cool Thoughts from a Hot Dad

Hey Dad,

Ahh…it's finally cooled down a little in northern Indiana. I'm telling you, it's been hot…real hot. Praise the Lord for A/C! But even it has had a hard time keeping our 100-year-old house cool. In fact, last night the kids and I slept downstairs in the cooler part of the house (my wife is hot blooded and didn't think it was that bad).

By the time I hit the hay, the family room floor was filled with snoozing kids, so I bunked down all alone on the living room floor. It was kind of weird sleeping somewhere other than my bedroom. I did a lot more listening and thinking than usual.

Maybe it was due to the fact that it had begun lightning and thundering. I started wondering if the big trees around our house were close enough to smash through my house and which rooms it would take out…or if should I move the kids…or maybe cut down the trees.

I thought about my little kids who are not as little as they used to be…BUT are still littler than they will be one day. I wondered what the house would feel like when they are all grown up and have moved away. Thirty years from now on a hot, summer night, will I sleep down on the living room floor and think about the nights when I used to do that with my kids?

That's the kind of stuff that was bouncing through my head. After I finally fell asleep, a huge BOOM of thunder awakened me, and I heard my son Abe (5) stumbling through the darkness in search of his room.

"Come on, Abe, lie next to me," I said. Five seconds later, he was lying beside me, out like a light. Thirty seconds after Abe had hit the floor, my daughter Katherine (9) was laying beside me as well.

There I was, sandwiched between two of my favorite people in the world and glad to be in their presence…knowing that one day I wouldn't have it anymore.

Dad, why can't I live in those moments? Why can't I treat those I love so much…like I love them so much? Instead, I spend much of my waking hours snapping at them or wishing they would leave me alone so I can get "stuff" done.

"God please forgive me for forgetting what's most important. Let me live in this truth today. And may you, Dad, do the same. Amen."

Just some thoughts on a hot day in Indiana.

You 'da dad!

Go Find Your Children

2 Corinthians 13:1-6

Hey Dad,

Well, we're down to the final two weeks in the pregnancy countdown. My wife embodies the statement, "She looks like she's gonna pop."

It's kind of weird getting all the baby stuff out again. It's like opening up a time capsule. I remember Maggie Rose wearing the little pink sleeper. She felt so frail and tiny in my arms. Now look at her. She's a grown up two-year-old. And the infant car seat….that's like a treasure chest of memories.

I bet I've lugged that thing the equivalent of a couple times around the equator. Buckle it in the van…take it out of the van…put it back in…take it out…in…out. Of course, on at least two occasions, I buckled it in but forgot to take it back out.

So I left a child in the car TWICE. I'm a guy. Sure, one was left out in the church parking lot one evening for about twenty minutes…and there was the time I left one of them in a parking garage, but that was only for 15 minutes at the most. Those things happen. The more kids you have, the easier it is to forget one in the crowd.

Actually, I was reminded about that this past weekend. I needed to be somewhere, and I took Ike (6) along for the ride.

He talked non-stop. We laughed, looked out the windows, told jokes, and I told him how proud I am of him.

And that's when it hit me that maybe Ike has been lost in the crowd of kids and busyness lately. He's the true middle child, although he's number 4 in the lineup. He's the quiet one, the easy one to overlook, and often says, "You aren't listening…I'm talking…Oh, never mind."

The older kids often travel with me alone…but I am rarely alone with Ike.

As I drove that day, I determined that I would not forget ANY of my children (except maybe in a parking lot). I will work harder at spending "alone time" with each of them. I'll take Ike to Lowe's when I need a box of nails, or write a short note telling him how much I love him and place it on his pillow.

Let me ask you, Dad? Do you have a child who you might have overlooked or misplaced? Go find 'em. Do whatever it takes to make them feel #1 in your book.

You 'da dad!

'Da Date

2 Corinthians 13:7-14

Hey Dad,

This is one happy puppy writing you today…because tonight I'm going on a date with my wife. That's right! A real, no-kids, no-interruptions, no-spilled-drinks, no-kids-under-the-table date with my wife. Aaahhh…nothing like a good old-fashioned date to restore the heart and clean out the cobwebs from the ol' libido.

Believe me—we need a date. It's kind of like having your carburetor rebuilt. You just get to the point where you forget what it's like to be in love with your girl. Know what I mean? Truth is, kids (and busyness) have a way of wedging themselves between you and your wife. They don't mean to…at least I don't think they do. But if you aren't careful, you'll find yourself far away from the person you need the most.

Even my wife knows that we're way overdue for a few hours alone. In fact, the other day she sighed and said, "I long for that 'date-y' feeling." I said, "Yeah, so do I."

Now, a little translation is in order. What my bride is saying is, "I want to feel that feeling of excitement and anticipation of being with the guy who cherishes me and treats me tenderly and special." That's me, just in case you're wondering. I confess I don't always make my wife feel that way. More often than not, I treat her like…like…breakfast cereal. You know, same old, same old.

BUT then there's the date. A date won't make everything better, but if I do my job right, I can begin to give her the "date-y" feeling. So here's the plan:

I'll dress up a little, go to her favorite place, open her car door, and tell her how beautiful she is to me. I'll look in her eyes and listen to her…I mean really listen, not just the kind where I look at her but have no idea what she is saying. I'll ask her a few questions about favorite memories to get her thinking about how much she loves me (sometimes she needs little reminders). Afterwards, we'll stroll through one of those womanish stores, hold hands, and laugh. Ba-da-bing! "Date-y" feeling!

How about you Dad? Been on a date lately? Don't tell me you don't do dates…horse feathers! If you're married, you need to have dates! That's just the way it is. So be 'da dad and plan 'da date. Do it!

You 'da dad!

Dad on Duty, Again

Hey Dad,

You know one of the great things about being a dad is that people expect you to repeat yourself. I know my dad told the same jokes, recounted the same old stories, and repeated bits of fatherly wisdom whenever the mood struck him.

I used to make fun of the fact that he repeated himself so often—until I became a dad. Now I do it! And now I know why. It's because those jokes, stories, and bits of fatherly advice bear repeating.

Such is the case with this week's Familyman Weekly. I wrote something similar a couple of years ago, but as I was sitting on the beach in Edisto, South Carolina, yesterday, I thought of its truth again.

The ocean is just so big, powerful, and unforgiving. Let down your guard for a moment, and you can get sucked out to sea or swallowed by Jaws. I've always been a little frightened by its power, and now that I have children—it scares me to death.

It doesn't help when they post signs along the walkway to the beach describing dangerous rip tides that can occur and then warn that there's no lifeguard on duty.

My children splashed in the waves without a care in the world. I, on the other hand, sat in my lawn chair like a coiled spring, scanning the waves, counting the children, and looking out for any potential harm.

Who cares that there are no lifeguards on duty? I thought. This is one dad who's always on duty.

That's when I was reminded again of the similarities between dads and lifeguards. Like lifeguards, our job is to keep an eye out for potential disasters, children who may be about to go under, dangerous rip tides, and vicious sharks who could easily gobble up an unsuspecting child.

The world in which we live is dangerous, and we dads must always be on duty. We must be on the watch for rip tides that can suck our children away—rip tides disguised as bad attitudes, friends, video games, TV programs, magazines, textbooks, and other outside influences.

We don't have the luxury of sitting back and enjoying the view. We must be involved—scanning, anticipating, and praying.

Let our children play and grow up in the safety of knowing that DAD IS ON DUTY!

So even if you've let your guard down, get back in the chair, and stand guard.

You 'da dad and you're on duty!!

Are you REALLY??!!

Romans 1:18-32

Hey Dad,

Just got home after taking a trip to Harvey Cedars Bible Conference Long Island Beach, NJ. Besides my son Ben (17) almost breaking his ankle and a trip to the emergency room, we had a great time enjoying life on the beach...that is, after the kids quit throwing up.

I'm telling you, there's just something refreshing and exhilarating about being where the waves hit the shore. And, boy, oh boy, were the breakers great at LBI! The kids boogie boarded while I stood on lifeguard duty.

On the last day at the beach, the waves were extremely massive and the yellow flags (signifying the safe zone) were replaced by red flags (meaning you could only be out knee deep and no boogie boards).

I was sitting on a towel as some of my littler ones were digging in the sand and my older sons were playing ultimate beach Frisbee when I heard shrill voices call out in delight, "Are you really?!...Are you really???!!!!!"

I looked up to see two pre-teen girls jumping up and down in excitement repeating the phrase almost in disbelief as their dad pulled himself from a comfortable beach chair, pulled off his shirt, and made his way to the surf beside his girls.

For several hours he sat in front of us reading a book, and I assumed he was there by himself. Watching that dad brave the surf with his two girls clinging to his arms in total joy, I was reminded again how much our children want to experience life with us at their side. They want us to spend the night in the tent with them, build the potato canon with them, go bowling with them, go out for dessert with them, walk the beach with them, and stroll the mall...with them. Because Dads make life more fun.

Sure it's easier to drop them off so we can sit in our comfy chairs. I'm betting from that girls phrase that he didn't always involve himself...kind of like me. But as I watched that dad walk towards the sea to the delight of his girls repeating, "Are you really?" I thought...I need to do that more often.

You know what? So do you.

You 'da dad!!!

Do We Have To?

Romans 2:1-16

Hey Dad,

Ever notice that sightseeing is a little like life? Here's what I mean. We've been traveling this great country of ours for the last couple of months. We've seen all kinds of historical sites and beautiful creation, but in all this, I've noticed one constant that is beginning to get on my nerves. My sweet, adorable offspring would sometimes rather go to Walmart than ride to the top of Pikes Peak, spend a few minutes at the Air Force Academy, or visit the boyhood home of President Eisenhower.

The phraseology goes something like this, "Do we have to…?" It's not that I think my children invented the phrase. In fact, I can remember saying the same thing to my parents when they announced that we were going to visit the fort at St. Augustine, Florida. Even last week, we visited the gateway to the Oregon Trail in Leavenworth, Kansas, and I could hear the lingering echoes of children long ago whining, "Do we have to go out West?"

Here's the thing, Dad. When our children ask this question, we are tempted to recant and say," Well, Okay. If you don't want to, I guess we won't." But that's not what dads are supposed to say. When faced with "Do we have to…?", or "I don't wanna," that's when dads need to set their jaw with determination and boldly proclaim, "Yes, you have to, and you're going to like it…and even if you don't like it, you're going to do it."

Somehow in our society, we dads have quit saying, "Yes you hafta." Teenagers give excuses why they don't want to go to great Aunt Ruth's 90th birthday party, and what's worse is—we dads fall for it. It's up to us to do what's right for our children and our family. They may not want to. It may be hard, hot, or inconvenient. But as long as we're the dads of the family, we can say, "YES, YOU HAVE TO!!"

They may complain or huff and pout, but I've learned that after they do what they didn't want to do, they'll be glad that they "had to." And one day they'll even respect you for making them, as I do my father for making me see the fort, take swimming lessons, and visit my grandparents when I'd rather have stayed home.

So Dad, you know those things that you've wanted to do with your family? Don't worry about if it's popular with the troops. Do it! And when they say, "Do we have to?" Answer, "You betcha!"

You 'da dad!

Enter the Twilight Zone

Romans 2:17-29

Hey Dad,

The story I'm about to share with you is weird—I mean Twilight-Zone-kind of weird. In fact, it might be better if you picture me wearing a black suit and tie as I describe it in a Rod Serling voice: "So join me as we enter…The Twilight Zone. Na-na-na-na, na-na-na-na …"

It was a night, like any other night. I was sleeping peacefully when something woke me—maybe it was a child's cry, a dog's bark, or maybe God just wanted to show me something important. Rolling out of bed, I went to the dresser where I keep my glasses and felt around for the familiar frames. Finding them, I put them on, only to discover that I had placed my wife's glasses on by mistake. Everything was blurry at first but, as things came into focus, I became acutely aware that I was seeing life through my wife's eyes—and it was freaky.

Drawn by some will other than my own, I began to walk around the house. I stepped into our garage that we are working on, and instead of seeing a simple project, I saw a huge, hideous beast that needs conquering.

Is that how she sees it? I wondered. But I already knew in my heart that it was.

I looked around the house and saw heaps of endless refuse.

I peered into the pantry and discovered a gaping cavern that cannot be filled.

I ran upstairs and looked into each child's room and saw sleeping monkeys capable of mischief and perpetual messes, who are constantly hungry.

Then a scary thought hit me: How does she see me?

With fear and trepidation (whatever that means), I crept towards a mirror and glanced in. I was aghast. Instead of my usual stud-like image, I saw a six-armed groping "thing" that is only kind when it "wants something."

That's all I could take, so I quickly returned her glasses to the dresser and slipped back into bed.

Since then, I've thought a lot about that night with the glasses and realized (maybe for the first time) that my wife sees things very differently than I do. Things that seem like no big deal to me are overwhelming to her. It used to bother me that she makes such a big deal about them—but that was before I visited the Zone.

The bottom line is…your wife sees very differently than you do. That's why she cries, gets frustrated, or overwhelmed when you wouldn't. So, Dad, learn from my story, or God just might take you to…the Twilight Zone.

You 'da dad!

Example Is the ONLY Thing

Romans 3:1-20

Hey Dad,

We're loading up the Familyman Mobile today for a trip out to Colorado. Lots of miles of empty spaces before we get there...but one thing I can be sure of, my kids will be watching me.

You see this past Sunday, a fellow dad shared some of the mistakes he made as his children were growing up. He shared the heartache of how a few of his children rebelled and became...what he had trained them to become by his own example. His warning rang clear to all of us listening. "If you do not submit to the authority of others, then your children will not submit to your authority," he gently admonished.

Parenting is all about example. As he spoke, I was painfully reminded about an incident that had happened less than two hours before.

We were running a little bit late, and I accidentally turned on a wrong road. When I tried to correct my wrong direction, I saw a large forbidding traffic sign that read, "No Left Turn." Now, unless you're from New Jersey, left turns are like an unalienable right. Besides, there were no other cars around and no one would care...except my son, Benjamin (13).

As I was turning, he said, "Dad, it says no left turn."

Drat! I knew we shouldn't have taught him to read. "I know Ben," I answered, "but..."

I couldn't think of any logical explanation, and I knew that telling him the truth (which was that I just didn't care what the sign said and only cared about getting to church on time) didn't sound very spiritual. So without answering him, I finished the left turn. As I did, a sinking feeling came over me.

Sitting in church listening to the fellow dad reinforced my feeling of guilt.

The truth is I pride myself on being a law abider. I obey the speed limit, return my cart to the cart corral, and don't throw wrappers on the ground. But what I taught my son that morning was that sometimes you can pick and choose which laws you want to obey.

Well, I confessed my sin to my son and asked him to forgive my poor example. Thankfully he did. And since then, I've been thinking about the long drive out West and how much training I'll do by my example...not by my words.

So, Dad, like Albert Schweitzer once said, "Example isn't the main thing; it's the ONLY thing."

Remember...they're always watching.

You 'da dad!

A Storm's a Brewin'

Romans 3:21-31

Hey Dad,

It's a gray, hot, and muggy day today here in Northern Indiana. The weatherman says it might rain, but what concerns me is the dark cloud that is fast approaching. It's the 'back to school' cloud.

It never ceases to amaze me. I've been out of school for a couple of decades, and I still cringe when I see "the cloud." Up until the first of August, we've enjoyed the clear, carefree skies of summer. But now…now the winds have changed, bringing "back-to-school sales" with them.

In fact, with the first week of August, I can start to smell freshly sharpened #2 pencils, stale gym socks, and the cords of school constricting my airway…Okay, so maybe I'm being a little dramatic, but I hope I'm getting my point across.

That's why it's up to us dads to wring the last bit of fun and freedom out of summer. You know all the things you promised the kids, your wife, and yourself that you'd do this summer? Well, make 'em happen before the grim reaper in a school bus shows up at your door.

So, take the family swimming, go to a ballgame, go to the beach, take a trip to an amusement park, stay up late, get up early, have a picnic, watch the stars, catch lightning bugs, go fishing, take a long bike trip, or anything else you can think of to keep the "school clouds" away. They're counting on you. You know why? 'Cause…

…you 'da dad!

My Investment Advice

Romans 4:1-12

Hey Dad,

I'm going to do something I rarely do. I'm going to give sound investment advice. In this time of economic uncertainty, dads are clamoring for safe, secure investments that will pay off in the future. I'm weighing in with the likes of Greenspan and Buffet.

So here's my advice to you: buy cute clothes for your daughter.

Don't smirk. It's true. Just this past week, I made a small investment of 20 bucks and already it's paying dividends.

I was speaking in a town a couple of hours from home and asked Katherine if she'd like to come with her old dad. She accepted the invitation, and we hit the road in the late afternoon. Katherine smiled, giggled, and reached over and caressed my hand somewhere along the way. Oh man, you gotta love that.

We arrived early and stopped at Quiznos for dinner. Afterwards, I told her we were going to run over to Target and pick up a little something for mom (which is my custom when I'm on the road). We found a cute top, and then I looked down at my little girl and said, "Now, let's go pick out something for you."

Her eyes sparkled as we marched over to the girl's section hand-in-hand and picked out a girly outfit. Katherine stepped out of the dressing room beaming and was surprised by how much her normally cheap dad was willing to spend on her and her mom.

"Thanks, Dad, for buying me this outfit," she said sweetly. For the rest of the evening, she loved on me and snuggled deep into my shoulder. And, Dad, that's just the start. Our shopping moment will wear off, but each time she puts on those clothes, she'll be reminded about how much her dad loves her. Next time I see her in them I'll say, "You're wearing the clothes I bought you…you look so pretty."

She'll smile and blush…all for only twenty bucks. Ha! Now let's see Warren Buffet top that financial advice!

Believe me, Dad. It'll work for you too. Pick something out for your daughter the next time you're out together, or pick something up today on your way home from work and place it on her bed for her to find.

Don't have any daughters? It works with wives too.

That's all the sound financial advice that's fit to print.

You 'da dad!

Jerk-o-dad

Romans 4:13-25

Hey Dad,

Know what? We men are jerks. Notice I included myself in the jerk category. I was vividly reminded of our jerkiness earlier this week when I did an hour-long radio interview to discuss "Lies Moms Believe." The interview went nicely, but then we took a couple of calls from the radio audience.

"My husband insists that I keep a spotless house," the caller started. "I have several young children, but he doesn't understand why I can't keep the house immaculate."

Using my best radio voice, I offered some "right" advice. I could hear the emotion in her voice and knew she was on the verge of tears. The interviewer sensed it too and asked the young mom, "So what does your husband say when you talk to him about it?"

"He says his mother used to keep a clean house so why can't I?" I could hear the hurt in her answer. I wanted to smack him...hard.

A few minutes later another mom called in to ask about her husband who didn't seem to want to be intimate with her. Again, her voice was choked with tears. "I just don't understand," she repeated several times.

I tried to offer some more "right" advice.

On the drive home, I had a pit in my stomach. Now, I know I only heard part of the story, but inside I felt ashamed that I was a husband and "related" to them. What made it worse is that I'm probably a lot more like those guys than I'd like to admit.

You know, Dad, we promised our wife that we would honor, protect, and cherish her forever. Yet, like those husbands whose wives called in, we act like jerks, caring more about a clean house than them. We roll our eyes and sigh when they get overwhelmed and tear up, and replace gentle caresses and touches with harshness and indifference. When they need us the most, we let them down, forcing them to call a complete stranger on some radio program in search of hope.

Dad, we have some work to do. You and I both know the areas we need to address. Let's ask God to forgive us for the past and to give us the determination to love our wives when they cry, feel overwhelmed, need us to hold them, need to talk deeply, spend intimate time with them, or discuss things that don't seem very important to us.

Why? Because they need us.

You 'da dad!

Guide to Roadside Emergencies

Hey Dad,

Just got back from speaking in Seattle, WA, and everything went smoothly...unlike our trip the week before to Atlanta. Actually everything went well, if you remove the fact that both a/c's leaked like a sieve, our toilet still doesn't work, and that I noticed a tiny puddle of antifreeze under the motor.

Because of that little puddle, I kept a close eye on my temperature gauge traveling home on THE FATHER ROAD (see below). It all looked fine, until we found ourselves in bumper to bumper traffic just south of Indianapolis, IN. I looked down at my temp gauge, and it was moving up.

A few minutes later, we pulled over on the side of the road to wait for a tow truck. To make a long story short, we had to be towed twice in the next two days and made our way home without our RV. It's fixed now and ready to roll out on the next Familyman Adventure.

My only regret is that during the 'event' I flipped and acted like a non-trusting creep to my family. Man, I wish you had been there to remind me of what is important and what is NOT. I needed you to tell me that God can be trusted, that my family isn't against me, and that everything would be fine.

That's why I decided to write up the following for both of us.

The Familyman's Guide to Roadside Emergencies:

Step ONE – Pray. Before you think about a solution or say a single word of instruction, pray out loud thanking God for what He's about to do in your family.

Step TWO – Set aside your schedule. Say out loud, "We'll get there when we get there."

Step THREE – Remember. This is going to be one of the stories that will be burned into your children's minds forever. They will remember it later and laugh and so will you.

Step FOUR – Don't let 'them' get to you. You're all on the same team. Your wife and children are going to say dumb things like, "Maybe the engine is unplugged." They don't think you're dumb they're just trying to help.

Step FIVE – Smile. You may not feel like it, but do it anyway.

Step SIX – Count your blessings. Consider yourself blessed to be with your family and safely in the palm of God's hand.

I'm just guessing you just might need this postable list sometime in the future.

Don't be a creep...You 'da dad!

I Can Change If I Want To

Romans 6:12-21

Hey Dad,

I don't know about you, but I'm feeling a little depressed and over-whelmed. I don't think it's because of the mountain of stuff that still needs to be done after being on the road for 3½ months, the fact that I still haven't caught the groundhog that's slowly been eating my car, or that we've been running fast and furious for the last 12 days straight.

The real issue is that my wife thinks I'm a creep—not that she said that in so many words, but she might as well have. She actually said that I seem so different from the funny, happy-go-lucky, loving man she married almost two decades ago, and that our marriage has stunk (has stinked? stank? stunked?…you know) for the last few months.

I try to remind her that things have just been hard lately from being on the road for so long, and that we had a baby, and that we're just worn out…but she's not buying it.

What I'd like to do is blow it all off and say, "You're overreacting, experiencing post-something depression, or just going through a hormonal-kind-of-phasey thing." Or even better, I'd like to tell her to buck up. Life changes things and people, and that's just the way it is—so get over it.

But…but…I can't get around the feeling that maybe she's right. Maybe I've taken the easy path and quit trying like I used to. I used to be more patient when she feels overwhelmed, not as easily bothered, and more concerned with the things she is feeling and thinking about.

Man, why can't this marriage thing be easier?! I hate having to work hard to make our marriage good. But I'm 'da husband, right? Man, I hate that phrase—but it's true.

So I guess I will work harder, not because I have to, but because I want to. She's my bride, my best friend, and the love of my life, and she needs her man to woo her once again.

You know what, Dad? Your wife needs you to woo her, too. She needs you to break through any walls that have been built up, scrape away the scum, and pursue her like…you used to. Starting right now.

You 'da husband!

Bug Gut Post-It Note

Romans 6:1-11

| **August** | **15** |

Hey Dad,

Two days ago we were driving along a country road. The sun was just about to drop below the tree line, the air was cool and still, and the kids were quiet. It was a perfect summer evening.

Then something splattered on the windshield leaving a glowing trail of slime about an inch long. It was obviously the unfortunate end of a lightning bug. But looking back, I figure it was some kind of bug-gut post-it note from God.

As soon as I saw the glow, I was reminded that summer is almost over, and I still haven't collected lightning bugs with my kids. Just seconds after the lightning bug collision, I scanned the horizon to see if I had missed lightning bug season altogether. The specks of yellow light told me I wasn't too late.

Sitting behind the wheel, I went though our summer to-do list in my mind. Whoa, we still have a lot to do.

I told the kids we'd play miniature golf this summer, and we still haven't done that. And what about Mount Baldy at the Indiana Dunes, the largest sand dune this side of the Sahara? The kids have talked all summer about climbing her near vertical face, but we haven't accomplished that one yet either.

And the canoe trip! I forgot about the canoe trip promise. I told the boys that we would go canoeing sometime this summer. I can't let them down. Not to mention a few more bike rides, camping in our back yard, looking at the stars, and fixing the tree house.

Summer is going to end soon, leaving me with nothing but bug guts all over the windshield and a pile of regrets.

What about you dad? Do you have some unfinished summer business to take care of? Has God been trying to get your attention with bug-gut post-it notes? The only way we're going to get it done is if we take the lead, make the plans and some sacrifices, and do it.

After all...you 'da dad!

Ghosts From the Past

Romans 6:12-23

Hey Dad,

I've got this weird fixation with PBS documentaries. I like to learn about dinosaurs, the civil war, and biographies of famous people. I like to get a behind-the-scene look at some of the famous and not so famous, names in history.

The common thread in all these people's lives is that they all had fathers. You know what they say, "If your father didn't have children, chances are neither will you."

Anyway, it's amazing how deeply affected these famous people were by their fathers. Some had involved, loving fathers, while others had absentee fathers. Some were raised by alcoholics, some by Baptist preachers, and some by war heroes. The effect on each famous person was profound. What each became was primarily based on the influence or lack of influence of their father.

In fact, I just heard a biography on the radio about a racist murderer who is on death row for the murder of an entire family.

Guess what his dad was like? He was a hate-filled, racist, who treated his children harshly and taught them to hate others who were not like them. The man went to a regular school where they taught love and acceptance and walked around in a society that condemned his father's thinking. But one power was greater than the rest and won out.

Father Power.

That's the irony of father power. It's a two-sided sword for good or bad. That's why alcoholics often grew up in alcoholic homes, children of divorced parents are more likely to get divorced, and workaholic dads beget workaholic sons.

Father Power.

~ excerpt from <u>*Father Power*</u>

God is Your Only Back-up

Hey Dad,

Want to hear something shocking? You can be replaced as the head of your family! Depressing? Not so, when you consider the rest of the story. Dad, you CAN be replaced as a father and a husband but ONLY by God Himself.

It's the truth; the Bible says so. When a father dies, God has made special provision for the hole he leaves in his family and it isn't a handyman to care for the physical needs of the house or an accountant to take care of the finances. It's not even another father-type figure. God, the heavenly Father, alone fills the dad-shaped vacuum.

The Bible says, "That He will be a father to the fatherless." (Psalm 68:5)

So, in your role as father, only God can replace you.

This is not the case in your job. Any shmoe will do. In fact, if you were to die today, someone would take over your job immediately (probably that friend who's been eyeing your position). Don't believe me? Consider this.

The President of the United States holds the most important job in the world. Yet, if he dies, we have a new president within 24 hours. Boom. Just like that. If you think you're the only one who can do what you do, you're wrong. You can be replaced relatively quickly and will be replaced if you disappear.

The job you're enslaved to WILL get done without you. The people you're ministering to at the expense of your family will be ministered to by someone else. The deals that only you can close will happen with or without you.

But if you were to die today, the hole you would leave in your family can only be filled...by God. As far as fathering goes, only God is plan B.

~ excerpt from Father Power

235

I'm a Slow Learner

Hey Dad,

You'd think I'd know a little about loving my wife by now. After all, I travel the country telling men tell men how to love their wives. But 'telling' is altogether different than 'doing'.

Here's what I mean. I don't know how many times I've told husbands, "When you don't care about what's important to your wife she 'hears' that you don't care about her." It's true. I believe it, but when faced with helping my wife choose new fabric for an old couch she wants to reupholster...I blew it! I rolled my eyes, sighed deeply, and looked bored stiff.

It's not that I don't care about fabric swatches...it's just that I don't care very much about fabric swatches.

But I conveyed to my wife that I don't care very much about her.

Now I had to work hard to regroup and prove to my wife that she—and what she cares about—is #1 to me. So, yesterday we drove into the country to see an Amish guy about recovering our couch.

You should have seen all the fabric samples he had...gave me the willies. I confess that in the past I've done the old, "Uh, uh, uh...yeah, that one looks great...love it...good deal...are we done yet? Let's go."

But not this time. This time I looked, compared, and gave thoughtful input, and we chose one...the best one. You know what she said later? "Thanks for taking the time to do that. I really appreciate it." But even if she hadn't said a thing I knew she appreciated it. It's really that simple.

Tonight, I get to try it again because we're going to swing by a scrap-book store...gulp. You know what I'm going to do? I'm going to be interested and give her my opinion on scrapbooky-paper things (if she asks), not because I care about colored paper, but because I care about my wife, and I want her to feel loved and cared about.

Your wife wants the same from you, Dad. She wants to know that what's important to her is important to you because she's important to you. So...if you need to discuss fabric patterns, children's clothes, food preparation, vacation plans, finances, or cellulite in order to let your wife know you care about her...do it!

Prove to your wife that you're not an insensitive bum like me.

You 'da dad!

Kids Are Like Dishwashers

Romans 8:1-15

Hey Dad,

I'm sitting here waiting for the dishwasher repair guy to stop by and take a look at our dishwasher. For the last 3 months, it's been doing a lousy job cleaning dishes. I tried what little I knew to do…like clean the filters, check water openings, and bang on it. It helped a little but not enough.

That's when my wife said, "We've got to do something about this."

I knew she meant hire some guy who charges $150 an hour. I was thinking more along the lines of ignoring the problem and hoping it'd go away. The only problem was I knew that dishwasher problems don't go away on their own. In fact, they usually just get worse.

That's the way it is with kids too. I know I've got a kid issue to deal with. I've been noticing it for a while…a bad attitude, disrespectful behavior, and unkindness to siblings. I'd like to just ignore the problem and hope it goes away, but I know dishwashers (and kids). The problem will get worse if I don't deal with it.

Unfortunately, I can't hire the kid repair guy to come over and give my child the once over. If only it was that easy. Instead, it's going to mean work for me. I'm going to have to spend some extra heart training and retraining time with my child. It will involve spending time in God's word together and dealing with "issues."

Am I looking forward to it? No. I'd rather do fun stuff like go to Dairy Queen or have a family night…but this is what dads must do. We train children so that they grow up to love their wives and train their children.

I won't always be consistent, respond in a godly fashion, or have a good attitude when I have to take my time for repair work. But, I will do it…because if I don't, no one else will, and "the dishes won't get cleaned."

How about you, Dad? Have you noticed that the "dishes" aren't as clean as they once were? Have attitudes gotten stinky? Have your children become disrespectful? Don't ignore it, pass it off as growing pains, or hope that they'll work through it. This is when they need you the most. This is when they need…DAD.

So I'll put on my Maytag repair hat and get down to business. I've got work to do…and so do you.

You 'da dad!

Kill the Beast!

Romans 8:16-25

Hey Dad,

I grew up in the dawn of the video age when Pong was introduced, Atari invented Space Invaders, and Pac-Man could be played in most Pizza Huts. I know the rush of being caught in an asteroid field or being attacked by centipedes. But back then, a video game was brief pleasure; NOW it has become a habitual, invasive pastime.

Just in case you're wondering, we don't own a PlayStation, Nintendo, Game Boy, or an X, Y, or Z Box. Instead, we bought educational "games" for our computer to facilitate learning.

Little did I know then that we had been duped by the old Trojan horse maneuver because, as my children got a little older, the Winnie the Pooh game led to Oregon Trail which then led to Civilization.

"Look how much they're learning," I would say to my wife who was a skeptic.

But as it often does, Civilization led to other "educational" games and our house got quieter...too quiet.

"Where are the kids?" I would often ask my wife.

"Playing the computer," was her usual answer.

"Houston, we have a problem," I said to myself. I had let my guard down, and now the BEAST inhabited my house.

At the same time, I started getting emails from wives who wrote about their video-game addicted husbands who played to the neglect of their families.

That settled it...The BEAST IS MINE! I must make some tough decisions, not just for today but for the benefit of the future dads I'm raising. I must bring the computer under control TODAY so that my children won't hurt their families in the future.

I couldn't just fly off the handle and shout, "That's it...I'm throwing all the computers away." That would just exasperate my children. My plan had to be thought through, reasonable, and enforceable.

Here's what we decided. Our children can play one hour on Monday, Wednesday, and Friday. I bought them each a timer. We aren't buying any new computer games...no matter how educational they are; and there is no debating the subject. And, you know what? They're okay with that.

Dad, if there is a beast alive in your house, don't ignore it, downplay its significance, or think it will take care of itself. If you haven't yet started the video game thing...don't. As I'm learning and continue to see, this beast plays for keeps.

You 'da dad!

Time and Telephone Poles

Romans 8:26-39

Hey Dad,

Over the last several years I've become keenly aware that time is passing. This may not be news to you but to me it has become an ugly revelation. Not that I was unaware of the truth before, but I guess I never really felt it until recently. It all started at an unforgettable pinpoint in time. Until that moment I guess I never took note of the time that had passed me by, but with a recent bone jarring event the realization has pounced upon me, sinking its unreleasing tentacles into my flesh.

It's like a drive along a stretch of Indiana road. Along the side of the road stand those tall slender splinters of wood that have been deposited by Ma Bell carefully strung together with an endless spool of wire. As a kid I'd stare out the window of our blue station wagon with its faded contact-papered-wooden sides as those telephone poles whipped by the window at an incredible speed, but looking out the windshield from the back seat I saw something different, an endless row of telephone poles stretching on forever seemingly standing still. Sometimes when the trip was especially boring I'd attempt to count the seconds between poles but more often than not they passed by faster than I could count—Wilson's have never been known as particularly quick counters actually we're not particularly quick at anything. Those telephone poles marked the distance traveled. They'd speed by the smudged window and then disappear from view almost as quickly as they appeared. Life's like that.

Enjoy today's telephone pole. Get out of the car and hug it tight...because it won't be long before it just becomes a speck in your rearview mirror.

You 'da dad!

Listen to the Old Guys

Romans 9:1-18

Hey Dad,

How are things going, Dad? We have a dilemma at our house: what to name our expected baby. Call me compulsive, but I've always believed that it's important to name your children.

That aside, as I promised last week, I need to ask you a few questions. Rest assured that your wife didn't put me up to this; nor did your mother, or pastor.

I need to ask these questions because the stakes are high. What we do as fathers and husbands affects so many people. It affects not only our children but also their children and their children after them. If we blow it by forgetting our priorities for a couple of decades, we can make a real mess of things.

Old guys know what I'm talking about. They remind me from time to time. Complete strangers walk up to me in McDonalds as I'm herding my children and say things like, "Enjoy them while their young…they grow up so fast."

What they're really saying is, "Hey, dummy, don't get so caught up in work and your stuff that you forget about what's really important…because one day they're going to be gone and you won't get a second chance."

They speak from experience. Some have spent too much time on the road or in the office and warn guys like us, who if we aren't careful, will do the very same thing.

So let me ask you—

Are you spending too much time at work?

Do you travel more than you should?

Do your hobbies take you away from your family?

Don't be too quick to answer. Mull them over in your mind. How would your wife answer the questions for you? What about your kids? They know the truth even if you won't admit it.

A wife once defended her husband who traveled a lot by saying, "I've got big shoulders, Todd. I can take it."

Well, the truth is that she might have been able to "take it," but their kids couldn't, and I did her husband a disservice by not getting in his face.

So, if you're spending too much time away from your family, let me get in your face and say, "Stop it…there's nothing you'll regret more."

Be brave, Dad. If you need to make changes…do it. Your family will love you for it. Guaranteed!

You 'da dad!

Loser Dad

Romans 9:19-33

Hey Dad,

I'm going to have to make this short because this is the day we've been counting down for two months...it's BIG TRASH DAY, a once-a-year occurrence in our small Midwest town. Unfortunately, you can't just pile it out by the road; you have to haul it to the town lot where they have some enormous dumpsters waiting. Oooo..I can hardly wait.

Actually, it's just what the doctor ordered after a dismal last week. Yep, it all started minutes after I sent out last week's familyman talking about something good and mushy regarding fathering. In fact, I bet I had just hit the send button when I heard some commotion coming from upstairs.

Being a good, godly, involved husband and dad, I ran upstairs to find one of my children and my wife duking it out over...nothing. So I jumped in swinging.

"Don't you ever talk to your mother that way," I said losing control quickly. I think both child and wife were shocked by my ferocity, and apparently 'said child' did not agree with my observations or conclusion...and just kept going.

That's when I reached that rare form that is only witnessed on the animal channel when Howler Monkeys are going berserk. In short, I flipped out, blew my top, FREAKED, and lashed into my child with such ugliness that I would be embarrassed for you to witness.

As it always does, the firestorm subsided and I felt like dirt...lower than dirt. I had failed my child, my family, and my God. Usually, within a few minutes I go and apologize, but I was still steaming and allowed a whole day to go by without resolution, all the time feeling like a loser dad.

I wallowed in the fact that I didn't deserve to be a dad or a family leader, and obviously needed to be stripped of my familyman title. But sometime during my miserable day, God whispered in my heart, "You child needs you to keep on...keep trying...to get back in the ring...to ask forgiveness and to embrace him and be restored."

"But, I'm a loser-dad, God," I cried out.

"I know," He said, "but I still love you...and so does your family."

That's when I made it right. Truth is I do blow it. Sometimes I'm mean and insensitive....but they need me and even love me. The other truth is: your family needs and loves you, too.

So, my fellow sometimes-loser-dad...you still 'da dad!

Help, the TV is Calling Me

Romans 10:1-11

Hey Dad,

I had heard about others doing giving up TV and remember piously thinking to myself, "All you have to do is turn it off. After all it's just a TV. It's not like trying to give up something really important like breathing or going to McDonald's." But, here I am typing away on this stupid computer when I'd rather have my feet propped up watching a documentary on the Cattle fish. That's because my TV has been unplugged from its power strip, and from our lives, for the last week. We're going to give it a try for a month. That's all we could take. Some people give their TV's away, or if they're really spiritual, sell them and give the proceeds to buy Bibles for Russia. Not me, we've come too far together, my TV and me.

To be honest, it was because of the kids that we decided to kick the habit. We had noticed that our kids preferred TV over most every other activity of life. Given a choice between playing outside and watching a video, they'd choose the video. Asked about playing inside or watching a video, they'd choose the video. Asked if they would like to go to McDonald's or watch a video, they'd choose a video. That's when we knew things had to change. Instinctively, we knew this wasn't something you could ease into, you just had to...as Jesus put it, "Pluck it out."

We set the removal date and then sat the kids down and told them the news, "We are going to put the TV away for a month." Ben instantly fell apart which came as no shock, but Sam seemed unfazed, which I suspected was a classic case of denial. I, on the other hand, felt in total control¼master of my house. It was exhilarating

The feeling of euphoria lasted well through dinner time, but that night it hit me like a truckload of 52-inch screen televisions.... the TV was gone. The kids were in bed, and I didn't know what to do without my one-eyed friend. Several times that evening, I found myself walking into the room hoping that it had all been a bad dream and that my TV would be in its spot ready to take me away to some educational programming. I was like a junky suffering from withdrawals as I stared at the conspicuously empty spot in the center of our entertainment hutch. It was like a big black hole, and I was being sucked into it.

I used to think it would be easy to kick the TV habit, but it's not. It's hard. It's real hard for a TV guy. But, I must be doing the right thing because the right thing is usually the hardest thing. And like the sailors of old, I'll grit my teeth and stay the course until I hit the open sea. Who knows, if I live through this, maybe one day I'll even give up McDonald's¼¼yeah, right.

~Excerpt from The Bathroom Book of Fathering

Ouch...that hurts!

Romans 10:12-21

Hey Dad,

Here's a little advice from a wife to a dad whose wife is upset with him:

First of all, you men all know exactly how to win a woman's heart – you did it once before. And far too many of you think you're done winning our hearts when we say "I do." Get busy doing the things you did when you were courting her, and you will make your wife feel loved and valuable again. If she has been as cold as ice, I recommend starting very slowly – as though you just met her for the first time.

Sometimes, I withdraw from my husband, too. There have been severe hurts in our marriage, and even though I have forgiven him and it was years ago, the memory is still fresh and painful. Certain attitudes in my husband trigger these painful memories – and leave me feeling like our marriage just isn't worth the struggle anymore. From my husband's perspective, I'm sure it seems random sometimes – or like I'm making a mountain out of a molehill. As far as he's concerned, those past hurts are ancient history – BUT he isn't the one who was injured!

If you were driving and caused an accident that left your wife in a wheel-chair, wouldn't you devote yourself to helping her cope? Sometimes the hurts of marriage cause injuries that need just as much compassion and tenderness.

Ouch that hurt...but just what I (and you) needed to hear.

You 'da dad!

Man, It Felt Good

Romans 11:1-10

Hey Dad,

You know, most of the time, we dads blow it. I know I do. We lose our cool, get all hot and bothered, and…blow it big time. But, yesterday I actually did it right. I responded just like dads are supposed to.

It was one of those days that seemed like a whirlwind of activity…none of it productive. Every time I sat down at my computer, someone interrupted me. My oldest two boys were having a couple friends over, and my daughter Katherine was having a tea party. For a week, Kat had been talking about and reminding me every hour on the hour about her tea party. So, by the middle of the afternoon, I was wound tight.

I had just fired up my computer again, when Katherine stepped through my office door. I could feel my muscles tense.

"Dad, we need some eggs to make the cake in my Easy-Bake Oven," she said sweetly to me since her mom was busy watching all of the other kids. She braced herself for what she expected to be the response.

That's when it came—a fast forward instant replay. Well, I'm not sure what you'd call it, but I saw a few seconds into the future. I saw a father who responded angrily, and a little girl who left feeling very unimportant to her daddy. All that took place in a millisecond, and I changed the future.

"Sure Katherine," I said gently, "I'll go get the eggs."

Her face brightened, her heart was touched, and she thanked me. She ran upstairs, and I got up from my computer knowing I "did good." After all, it would only take five minutes of my time. Man that felt good! Yes!! My daughter needed me, and I came to her rescue.

I wish I had stumbled upon the secret formula to being the world's greatest dad all the time, but the truth is…there is no secret formula. Dads try, fail, get mad, bumble our way through fathering, and…sometimes we succeed. But if there is a secret, here it is: never quit trying. Look into your children's faces and keep at it. Begin again each day, asking God for strength, gentleness, and the grace to be the dad he wants you to be.

Being a dad is tough, but don't give up. Keep asking forgiveness, and start over again and again. Is it worth it? Oh, yeah, it's worth it.

You 'da dad!

Me and My DEAL

Romans 11:11-21

Hey Dad,

Well, it looks like the tide has turned...the clouds have been rolled back...and I'm get'n over my DEAL. The last couple of days have been pretty bleak around here...and I'm not talking about the weather.

I haven't been a very nice familyman lately, and until last night, I didn't know the cause of it, but as I was driving to our church's men's meeting I said to myself in disgust, "What is your DEAL, Todd?"

That's when it hit me...I have a DEAL. I was in a funk that I couldn't shake. I tried all the regular remedies...I prayed, gave myself pep talks, and tried to push through it...with little success. My wife never said it, but I could see the question in her eyes, "What's your DEAL?"

They're nasty critters...DEALs are. In fact, when you have a DEAL, it makes you feel, think, and act nasty. Just ask my family how it's been the last few days, and they'll say I've been snappy, grumpy, and a down-right not-nice-dad.

Here's the deal about DEALs: they sneak up on you when you least expect them. They take seed when you're bothered by something...or someone. Maybe your wife said or did something, the kids are getting to you, or you feel you've been dealt a hand of injustice. A DEAL lays low and simmers, growing with each passing day, until it begins to color all your thoughts, feelings, and emotions.

"They don't appreciate all that you do for them," it whispers in your ear.

"How can she sit there and treat you that way?!"

"How dare they!!!"

"Why don't you show them...make them pay."

It grows until it becomes a full blown DEAL and THEN everyone knows you have a deal and will even say, "What's you're DEAL?"

Here's another deal about DEALs: they're hard to kill...but killed they must be. Even as I drove home last night thinking about my DEAL, I didn't know how to defeat it. Then the thought came to me; "I need to talk to my wife about my DEAL."

Deep in my bowels, I felt the DEAL tremble in fear and I knew the answer was in humbling myself, telling my wife how I felt, and apologizing for allowing the little deal to become a big DEAL.

I did that just an hour or so ago.

You know what? I don't have a DEAL anymore. It was that easy...and hard.

So Dad, not sure if you're dealing with a DEAL in your life, but if you are, DEAL with it. Sit down with your wife, kids, or family and say, "I've felt really bothered lately, and I've let it become a big DEAL; I'm sorry."

My Haunted Aerodyne Bike

Romans 11:22-27

Hey Dad,

This is going to sound weird…but my Aerodyne bike is talking to me. Or at the very least, it's putting thoughts into my head…like some kind of Vulcan mind trick.

Okay, maybe it's just the mindless whir of the gears and fan blade combined with my own creaky joints that causes my mind to wander in all directions. Along with many brilliant ideas, there are haunting visions that visit me as I pedal.

Last night was one of those visitations.

I was pedaling along, when all of a sudden I heard a voice…my voice (Aerodynes are good impersonators) speaking the very same words that I'd spoken last weekend at a family retreat.

"Your children need you to do fun things with them, Dad. They love when you play in the pool with them, wrestle on the floor, or romp out in the snow."

If only I had stopped there…but I didn't.

"Take my children, for example. They love playing the board game Settlers of Catan. In fact, they'd love me to play with them…but I haven't…ever."

Even as I spoke those words, I felt a piercing sensation somewhere through my midsection, but I was on a pontificating roll and didn't have much time to feel the burn…until last night on my haunted Aerodyne.

As the words and scene played out, I thought of the e-mail someone sent me the same day asking about board games to play with their teens…and then my friend Tim's comment about how much he likes to play Settlers with his boys.

"You're right," I said to my Aerodyne, and I'm confessing to you right now: "I need to play the game with my kids."

Now if you've been getting this email very long, then you know I'm not a board game kind of guy. To me, there's a reason they call them BORED games.

But the familyman truth is: Fathering is not about what I like and don't like doing. It's about choosing the best for my family…which just so happens to be best for me, too.

So, Dad, let's hold each other accountable to do the things we know they'd love us to do…but the thought of it chills our bones.

Do it. But if you won't listen to me, then get your own haunted Aerodyne.

You 'da dad!

National Pump Them Up Day

Romans 11:28-36

Hey Dad,

It's a rainy morning as I type to you from a Walmart parking lot in lovely Springfield, Missouri. Things have gone relatively smoothly, if you don't count the tire blowout we had last week…and even that went about as smoothly as it could have.

I know I've said this before, but I'm convinced that I'm the key to the good life at home or on the road. If I lose my cool (and I do), then an RV meltdown soon follows. BUT if I keep focused, remember what's most important, and speak gently, I avoid a Three-Mile Island kind of Familyman disaster.

It's amazing how powerful our words are. A few well-spoken words have the power to pump a child up…and a few harshly spoken words can just as easily deflate those we love.

I used both on my son Ike (he'll be eight tomorrow) this week. He got a pair of Heelys (shoes with wheels) for Christmas and has been practicing with them ever since. Well, this past weekend he had a really smooth floor on which to strut his stuff, and he was trying really hard to look humble.

He whooshed by me, and I said, "Wow, Ike, you're really good on those….Man, I'm amazed at how well you do!" I saw I'd struck pay dirt, for behind his humble expression, he basked in the glory of his father's praise.

If only I could do that all the time. I should say often, "Man, you really were kind just then to your brother….You used such self-control….I'm so blessed to have such a great son as you….You're the best!"

But instead I often find myself being critical, scolding, and harsh. "Why do you always do that? You're acting foolish….You're making this so hard." Instead of basking, I see his eyes reflect hurt and discouragement.

But I have a new day today (a rainy one, mind you, but a new day none-the-less), and as soon as I'm finished typing, I'm going to practice what I preach and head up front and "pump them up."

I'll make it a point all day today to let my children know how blessed I am to be their dad and how awesome I think they are.

Why don't you do the same, Dad? In fact, I proclaim this National Pump 'Em Up Day.

So, spend a couple minutes planning what you might say to each member of your family, and then go home and PUMP THEM UP!

You 'da dad!

Have a Good'un

Romans 12:1-21

Hey Dad,

I'm a little behind today. Just pulled in the driveway from speaking at a family camp in Michigan this week, and now I'm off and running trying to get the RV in shape to take off for another family camp in Pennsylvania.

I'm telling you, Dad, I'm always a little apprehensive about family camp, but it always turns out to be a great family time. One of the added perks is that I get to meet some of the great and normal dads who are a part of Team Familyman which always leaves me encouraged.

As we head into Labor Day weekend, I am remembering my conversation with Familyman, "Charlie horse" Tim out by the volleyball court at camp. It was evening and the sun was low in the sky and everything seemed quiet.

"So what do you want me to get out of this (week of camp)?" he asked.

With a little thought I said, "I just want you to enjoy this fleeting moment of time with your family and to realize this is what's most important in your life."

I thought about that ever since. That's not only what I wanted Tim to get out of this past week, but what I want to realize every day, AND why I write these newsletters. Believe me, I'm not some kind of guy who just needs a creative outlet.

I write these for the same reason I speak at family camps, men's groups, homeschool conventions, and churches...I just want you to enjoy this fleeting moment of time with your family and to realize this is what's most important in your life. That's it.

So, my fellow familyman, make this Labor Day weekend a good'un. Enjoy your children, the break in the normal routine, and your bride. Breathe deeply, hold hands, and draw them up on your lap (if you still can).

Because time's passing quickly and one day all these wonderful days will be gone.

You 'da dad!

Olympic Husbanding!

Hey Dad,

Score one for the big guy! In terms of Olympic husbanding, I won the gold! Well...at least this time. It was simple really. I did a little pre-planning, asked my parents to watch the kids, and then whisked my wife away on the great birthday adventure.

Actually, it wasn't that exciting—just a couple of outlet malls, a downtown hotel, and time alone without children. And here's the best part...we talked about "stuff"...with no interruptions and no distractions. We discussed the coming school year, family goals, and how we can be better parents. I told her how beautiful she was and how lucky I was to have her as my wife.

End result—aahhhhhhhh!!

The great thing about it was that my wife thought I was wonderful. She felt loved, cherished, and special. She even told me that I was the best husband in the world (she doesn't always feel that way—know what I mean?). Had I picked up a birthday card at Walmart and gotten her a blouse, I don't think I would have gotten the same response.

Now don't get me wrong, she would have been thankful...but she wouldn't have felt cherished. So what's the difference between the two?

Effort.

The one takes hardly any, but the other involved calling my parents in advance, packing the kids without her knowledge, making a hotel reservation, spending a chunk of my precious money, and cheerfully walking around an outlet mall when I'd rather do anything but walk around an outlet mall.

Like she said, "I can't believe you did all this just for me."

Dad, that's love! It's going the extra mile; it's sacrificial; it's the way it was meant to be. So, maybe it's time you did a little scheming. Pawn off the kids on someone, book a hotel, and whisk your wife away for a surprise overnight.

Be extravagant. Do what she wants, and then talk about "stuff." She'll feel loved, refreshed, and ready to tackle life again. I would just bet she'll look at you with fresh new eyes, smile, and say, "I can't believe you did all this just for me."

You 'da Olympic gold medalist dad!

Marbles Matter

Romans 14:1-12

September 1

Hey Dad,

I'm not a math guy. I don't do well with fractions, quadratic equations, or pi. I'm okay with counting, but that about does it. But, here I am writing to you about math and fathering...definitely, a Familyman first. In fact, I've been pondering math all week. It all started as I was tooling down the road listening to the radio.

The smooth voice on the other end explained how he was going to place a marble in a jar for every Saturday he had left of his expected life span. Since he was over fifty...it wasn't a lot. Then, he was going to throw away one marble as each Saturday passed to remind him that his time was running out.

I've been thinking about marbles and math ever since. Let's apply this marble principle to fathering. Say we got a big jar and placed a marble in it for every Saturday of our child's growing up years (18 years or 900 marbles).

So if you have an 11-year-old (like I do), you have about 350 marbles left in the jar. You with me? 18 minus 11 equals 7, times 50 equals 350. In the case of my son, Ben, the jar is well over half empty.

Only 350 Saturdays are left to spend with him. That sounds like a lot, but it isn't. And if you have a 15-year-old, you're down to 150 marbles.

The thing about marbles is that you can only use them once. If you waste one by playing with the guys, being away on business, or spending it doing your own thing...it's gone.

Right now, I'm holding a marble in my hand; it's this Saturday's marble. It holds a lot of promise. My kids long for this coming marble...I mean Saturday. They're hoping for a backyard campout...but I might be too tired or the timing might not be good.

That's the thing about marbles. We dads hold them in our hand. We decide what we'll do with them, how we'll use them, and then, when we're done; we reach in the jar and toss them away.

That's why I work so hard to remind you of what's most important, because it all boils down to a jar full of marbles. I've set a jar of marbles on my desk to remind me that marbles matter.

Dad, let me encourage you to do a little math, and count how many marbles you have left with your child. And then make this "marble" a good one.

You 'da dad!

Me, a Workaholic?

Romans 14:13-23

Hey Dad,

I've never considered myself a workaholic. I didn't get all A's, won't be able to retire by the age of 50, or ever be elected to public office. All that to say, I was stunned by what my oldest son said last week when we were preparing for a vacation at my in-laws' lake cottage.

I was telling my wife that I would need to do a little work while we were there when Ben piped up, "You're not going to take your laptop to the lake, are you? It seems like you work all the time now."

I started to say, "Ben, I have to take it along. I have a deadline to meet. Besides, I'll do it while you're asleep. You'll never even know I have it there," But I stopped. The fact was: Ben wanted all of me on vacation. He wanted me to be thinking about our family and all the fun we were going to have, not about work.

The rest of the day, I struggled with this question. I even asked my wife if she thought there was truth to what he felt. When she answered, "Well, it does seem like you do work a lot more in the evenings than you used to," I figured they couldn't both be wrong. The more I thought about it, I knew I was guilty. I was stealing time from them and giving it to work; and I was going to have to make some decisions.

The first one was simple but hard. When we pulled out of the driveway for the lake, we left without my laptop.

The second was just as simple and just as tough. Driving to the lake, I decided to put an end to my nightly computer work. No more checking e-mails, writing notes, or working on projects. My family needed all of me, and I was going to give them all they wanted. It won't be easy. I already feel the pull to pop on and check my e-mail. But a deal's a deal.

How about you, Dad? Are you borrowing time from your family for the sake of your work? Your family may not say it, so let me say it for them. "Dad, we need you and want you—all of you, especially on vacation."

How you pack will be the most reliable response to their plea.

You 'da dad!

251

Me 'da Dad!!

Romans 15:1-13

September 3

Hey Dad,

You know the phrase, "You 'da dad" really packs a punch...and I hate punch. Especially when it's directed at me.

You see, I've noticed some growing tension at the old Wilson house lately. Maybe it's the busy schedule that has worn us down over the last five months. I've observed that I'm snappy, the kids seem a whole lot less angelic than they used to, and my wife is as tight as an over wound watch spring... and that's after a week of vacation!

One specific thing I've noticed is the strain between one of my sons and my wife. They are very much alike and that seems to put them at odds sometimes. She's confided in me that sometimes "he's easy to love but hard to like."

I understand completely because at times I feel that way about one kid or another.

Yesterday, I watched as she showed great restraint to the kid who had gotten under her skin like a bloated chigger. It was then that I heard the annoying phrase, "You 'da Dad!" ringing in my head.

I knew what it meant. It meant that I was responsible to help fix the situation. That's why I close each Familyman Weekly with those words.

"You 'da dad" means that we fathers are responsible, not only for ourselves, but for our entire household. Because whether you like it or not, if there is tension in the camp, it's your responsibility to solve it. If there is a relationship that needs some mending, it's your responsibility to mend it. If your wife is upset with you, it's your job to resolve it.

So, here's what I'm going to do. I'm sending my son and his mother on a date. Just the two of them. They can go out for lunch or dessert, but it will be just them. They'll talk, laugh, and remember once again how much they love and like each other.

Dad, how are things in your house? Do you have a child who is giving you or your wife grief? Is there a situation that is overwhelming your bride? Can you tell it's time for a little family R&R? Are your kids watching too much TV? Is your house plagued by bad attitudes? Are your teenagers suffering from "teen-itis"?

For better or worse, like it or not...you 'da dad!

I Think They're On to Us

Hey Dad,

Greetings from Canadensis, PA. I'm speaking at our second family camp in two weeks. Right now, the kids are off corn shucking and freezing on a 200' water slide. I'm doing sleeping child patrol and enjoying some excellent wi-fi here at Spruce Lake Retreat Center.

Tomorrow we pack up and head home. For those who've been following, I finally got my RV toilet fixed, and it is leak free. Hot pups!!

That's the good news. Now for the bad news...our kids are on to us. That's right, I think they have broken the dad-code (not to be confused with the DaVinci Code).

I was clued into just how bad this is yesterday while I was sitting at the pool-side luau in 60 degree weather when a young girl still in her street clothes asked her father, "Dad, can I change into my swimming suit?"

The dad, in proper dad-form, answered, "I don't think so sweetie...it's pretty cold and I don't want you getting sick."

The girl smiled, turned to walk away, and in the sweetest voice, without a hint of disrespect said, "Oh, you always say that."

Now I don't know if she was talking to her father specifically, was making a broad statement directed to father's across the globe, or was talking to me in particular because the truth is most of us dads 'always say' those kind of things.

It's just part of the dad-code. Instead of saying what we really mean, which is, "No, you can't get in the water because that will mean I'll have to get off my duff and help you in some way and it's just easier to sit her on my duff than to let you have fun," we say, "I don't think so...it's pretty cold, and I don't want you getting sick."

Up until now I didn't know any children knew the truth...but after yesterday, I think the code may have been cracked.

That means they know other things too like: "Not now," means...NEVER. "Maybe later," means...NEVER. In fact, most every answer we dads give means...NEVER. It used to be our little secret, but not anymore; they're on to us.

But here's the deal, instead of re-coding the code, maybe we should do away with the code. Instead of making up excuses of why they shouldn't...maybe we should start saying, "That's a great idea."

So from one code-talker to another, today and for the rest of the weekend, say, "Yes."

You 'da dad!!

One Plastic Container of Memories

Romans 15:22-33

September 5

Hey Dad,

Let me start off by telling you…I am a "collector"…not of valuable coins, antiques, or collectible plates; I just collect stuff. You know, like smooth rocks from Mount Baldy, wooden pegs from an old barn, and the occasional McDonald's happy meal toy.

Now let me tell you a little bit about my wife. She is a "thrower-outer." She isn't impressed by the fact that I still have the trash-bag-type rain ponchos from Niagara Falls wadded up in a corner of my office.

Well, last weekend as we straightened up the basement, the "collector" and the "thrower-outer" collided. Although she was very gentle and willing to allow the "collector" to hold onto his "treasures," I knew it was time to part with some of my hoard.

I decided I would keep only what could fit into a clear plastic container. The rest would go to Goodwill…or be burned.

At one point, my wife looked at me and said sweetly, "Maybe you're not up for this yet."

Actually, I was surprised by how cut and dried it was. I pitched all kinds of stuff and didn't even weep as years of collecting went up in smoke. But, what amazed me was what made its way into the plastic container.

It wasn't the stuff that was valuable or even collectible. In fact, nobody would really even care about it all except me. But, as I held each treasure in my hand, a flood of memories and emotions filled my heart. I thought of vacations long ago, riding in the old van with my brothers and sister, and chasing waves on the beach. A fifth century Ming vase doesn't do that for you.

As I filled the plastic container, I knew that one day my kids would come to the same point in their lives. They'll fill their containers with souvenirs from time spent as a family: a root beer bottle from the time we met their cousins in Kansas, a wooden sword we made together in the garage, and rain ponchos from Niagara Falls (I knew there was a reason I was keeping those).

That's the important stuff, Dad. It's not about giving them shiny new stuff or the best that money can buy. It's about time spent with you that matters most. Keep the wrapper from the ice cream cone that you shared together…and they'll remember that time forever.

Have a great marble…I mean Saturday!

You 'da dad!

Every Dad Needs a Boot Box

Romans 16:1-7

Hey Dad,

Just coming off my wife's birthday celebration, and I've been thinking about birthdays—and our roles in them. Actually, I started chewing on the thought after my weekly breakfast with my friend, who just happens to be an old guy (it's amazing what you can learn from old guys). Anyway, I showed up at his house at the usual time and sat down at their breakfast table for some light chitchat when his wife reminded him, "Don't forget you have to fill the boot box."

"What's the boot box?" I asked.

Together, they told me that for the last 50 years, Mr. G (the father) has filled the boot box with birthday stuff like that child's favorite soda pop, Archie Comics, M&Ms, and a card. I was especially intrigued when Mrs. G got up and retrieved the old boot box from the garage and held it in her hand.

"You mean you've done that for 50 years?" I asked, somewhat amazed by the feat.

"Yeah, about that," he said nonchalantly.

"The kids and grandkids love it," Mrs. G added. "They know that the other presents are from Mom and Dad, but the boot box is from DAD."

Well, ever since that conversation, I've been thinking about the boot box wrapped in newspaper comics and how much love and interest this old dad conveys to his children and grandchildren through a few predictable items in a 50-year-old shoebox.

It's not so much that the kids love getting a present wrapped in a foot-wear container, but they like knowing that their dad (and grandpa) loves them so much that he takes the time to do the boot box thing every year.

Sadly, most of us dads have delegated the birthday/Christmas gift buying to our wives. After all, dads are busy doing important stuff. Often the event comes and the children joke about how Dad probably doesn't even know what the gift is that is said to be from him. Or maybe dad isn't there at all because he's busy reading the newspaper or watching the game or doing some important stuff.

But not Mr. G's kids. When they see that old boot box, they know—or if they ever doubted, are reminded again—of how important they are to their dad.

I'll tell you what, Dad. That makes me want to go out and buy a pair of boots. And it should you too.

You 'da dad!

The Perfect Gift

Romans 16:8-16

Hey Dad,

I've just given my son one of the greatest gifts, the gift of believing in him and allowing him to pursue his dream even if it doesn't look like the kind of dream I would have picked for him. Some of my sons' dreams aren't necessarily bad or wrong, but my practical father-side of my brain wonders if it will be the best way to provide for his future family. But I know now, that it doesn't matter. It's not just about the best way to provide for a family, it's about dreaming and doing what God has placed in his heart. He'll take care of the providing.

My oldest son has always been a gadget guy. As a little boy, he filled his pockets with little wrenches, pocket knives, and gizmos. We'd walk through a store and he would eye the small do-dads that clicked, blinked, and spun around.

As he got older, he fell in love with technology, laptops, iPods, and cell phones. We were at a Best Buy recently and the employee that he was questioning asked, "How old are you, and why aren't you working here?"

I know he would love that. He knows more about gigabytes and terabytes than anyone I know. He listens to podcasts about the newest phones and future technologies. But here's the deal, I want more for him. I want to push him into something bigger, something respectable where you don't have to wear a bright blue shirt with a yellow logo emblazoned on it.

We've mentioned other IT options but nothing seems to captivate his passion like a phone that can be played like a trombone. He likes gadgets!!

A couple of days ago, as I was driving down some country road, I had a vision of my son as an adult wearing a blue shirt with a yellow logo. He was talking to someone about a cool phone and he was smiling, his heart filled with joy at doing what he loved to do.

I thought then, "That's what he needs to do."

As soon as I thought that, I could almost hear God say, "Just because he starts there doesn't mean I'll have him finish there."

That was comforting...but as I thought more about it I decided that even if he finishes there that's okay because that's what he dreams about.

What a great gift to give your child...the gift of believing, of placing your blessing on his dream. That's what everyone wants but few receive. But not my children and not yours; we're going to let them dream.

You 'da dad!

Excerpt from Dream Big

Our Submarine Adventure

Romans 16:17-27

Hey Dad,

Sorry I missed you last week, but it was just one of those weeks. Everything decided to break—my car, my van, the spring on my garage door, and my DSL modem. Ahhh, the life of a dad. You gotta love it.

Anyway, the week wasn't all bad. In fact, I got to experience the best part of being a father when we surprised my son Ben with a special 13th birthday adventure. Actually, we had been planning for some time to do something special to help usher him into manhood. I wanted it to be big and memorable, something he would remember forever.

Unbeknownst to him, we made arrangements to spend the night on an actual WWII submarine in Muskegon, Michigan, along with 24 dads and sons from our church. They gave us the run of the sub, and it was awesome.

We walked to the beach, toured the sub, watched fireworks across the water, and slept on bunks in the sub. But that wasn't all.

At midnight, we gathered on deck for an "ushering into manhood" ceremony. I presented Ben with a Bible and a honking big sword (just like King Peter's in Narnia). It was neat as the sons shared special Bible verses and the dads challenged my son and prayed blessings upon him.

Ben is still basking in the glow of our incredible adventure.

Before you think I'm some kind of super dad, I should admit that the idea wasn't mine. In fact, I stole it about three years ago from a dad in Michigan. That's the great thing about being a dad. We don't get extra points for originality. Why reinvent the wheel? If you hear a good idea…steal it, copy it, and make it your own. Your kids don't care.

I also learned something out there on the sub. My son will indeed remember the submarine adventure forever, but it probably won't be what I had planned for him to remember (i.e., the big ceremony). What he will remember is that his dad loved him so much that he went all out just for him.

That's what our children and wife really want to know…that we'd spend it all, give it all, and do it all—JUST FOR THEM.

So, dad, why don't you do a little scheming? Maybe you have a significant birthday, anniversary, or occasion for which you can go all out…FOR THEM.

You 'da dad!

Overwhelmed but Still Swimming

Acts 1:1-11

Hey Dad,

Just got back from a speaking trip in Seattle with my son, Ben (15). While there, I learned that true Washingtonians pronounce Spokane—Spokan. Blows to bits all that stuff about "E'" on the end of a word making the vowel long, and makes me question all the other stuff Mrs. Mayfield taught me back in the third grade.

Anyway, I'm feeling a little overwhelmed in the dad department. It's more than just having so many things to fix, projects to complete, and mountainous messes that my children create seemingly out of nowhere.

The real thing that's got me feeling down is the fact that fathering takes more effort, determination, and stamina than an Olympian needs to get the gold.

First, there's Maggie (4) and Cal (2) who are going through a "just make me obey" stage. At least a couple times per day, I have to take them to the bathroom to take care of business. Just a few minutes ago in fact, I had one of those "business meetings" with Cal, who doesn't want to take no for an answer.

Then there's Abe (7) and Ike (9), who need me to watch them or "come here" every-other minute. Katherine (11) needs special understanding, as she's going through some kind of woman metamorphosis. She's a bundle of raw emotion, and the slightest cross word brings torrents of tears with the often-used remark, "You're always mad at me."

Sam (13) is easy. He rarely needs attention or maintenance, which makes me think he needs attention and maintenance.

Ben (15) is bored and wants me to run to Walmart to buy some airsoft gun replacement parts. He also mentioned this morning that he'd like to do a little research on the computer but that I'm never willing to help him (we won't let him do it unsupervised).

About the only easy one is Jed (6 months). Besides the drooling and dirty diapers, he's pretty much low maintenance (for me anyway). Stick him in his bouncer, and he's good to go.

All that to say, I'm overwhelmed. So what's a dad to do?

I guess I just keep swimming (to quote a blue fish).

Dad, I know the demand is relentless. I know you get discouraged, overwhelmed, and are tempted to turn up the volume on the TV to drown it all out. Let me encourage you (and myself) with that same blue-fish advice— just keep swimming.

You 'da dad!

Play It Again, Dad

Acts 1:12-26

Hey Dad,

Florida has Disney World, Ohio has King's Island, California has Disneyland, and Indiana has…Indiana Beach. And just as Mickey Mouse is the spokesperson…ur rodent, for Disney World, a big crow is the spokesbird for Indiana Beach. He's smiley and dressed in a striped shirt and reminds folks that "there's more than corn in Indiana."

Actually, I'm not sure Indiana Beach should even be mentioned in the same sentence as Disney World (although Disney does not have a place where about 10,000 carp gather to be fed), but still, my kids think it's fun and every few years when we spend a few days at my in-laws' lake cottage, we spend an evening strolling the quaint, little amusement park on the lake.

We were there about a week ago, just for an evening. It was cool, and the smell of corn dogs, sun tan lotion, and…carp filled the air. It's kind of like a permanent state fair midway. The rides are cheesy and the music blaring, but after visiting for so many years, it feels nostalgic and comfortable.

We don't actually ride anything except a few kiddy rides, because although it's not in the same league as Disney, they charge about the same. So we mostly walk around, watch the ski show, and eat an elephant ear.

I don't know when it was exactly, but at one point we walked over to the kiddy land where half a dozen ancient carnival rides spin around and make honking sounds as little kids wave to their parents.

As I watched my youngest kids, Caleb, Maggie, and Jed, on the carousel, waving each time they passed by me, the thought hit me, "I have to do it ALL again." My oldest kids may be beyond little kiddy rides but my younger children are just the age that I need to allow them the pure joy of sitting in a little car, pulling the bell string, and honking the horn.

And it's more than that. I have to do backyard campouts with little ones who've never done that, take them down to the creek to catch crawdads, have pillow fights, take them to the Statue of Liberty, ride the elevator to the top of the Empire State Building, and feed the carp at Indian Beach.

All the stuff I thought I had done…I need to do again for the ones who've never experienced it…because I'm 'da dad.

So my fellow familyman, if you've got more than one child (that's not a twin), in the words of Humphrey Bogart, you need to play it again, Dad.

You 'da dad!

Plug 'dem Holes!

Hey Dad,

Hot dog! The Familyman Mobile 2 is sold—sold at a ridiculously low price, but sold nonetheless. A lump rose in my throat as fellow Familyman Kris R. pulled out of our driveway in it.

Okay, enough reminiscing. Dad, I need to get serious for a few minutes.

This past week, a dad over at the Familyman Forum shared that his 14-year-old son came clean about a year-long pornography stint. What got to me is that the dad told about all the precautions he had taken to make sure it could never happen…but it did.

He's not alone. I've heard several recent stories of boys struggling with internet sludge. They're from good families, and yet, somehow—through some hole, they've gotten hold of it…and now it has gotten hold of them.

One dad shared how his son would sneak onto the internet on the family computer while they were asleep. Another dad's son discovered it at a friend's house. Kind of made me think about all the images that I was exposed to as a kid and the "safe places" where I found them.

In fact, it's amazing how many boys start down the crud path by looking at the educational National Geographic, Christian sex books that are left on family bookshelves, inappropriate TV, or grown up videos that are kept out of reach.

That's because, if the crud is in your house, your kids will find it. If we leave the internet unguarded, it will get our boys. Husband-and-wife books will fall into less mature hands, and scary things will happen at innocent sleepovers. That's just the way "crud" works.

Oh, I know, I can't control everything; but it's not going to happen in my house because I mistakenly assumed it was safe. I'm going to turn off the computers at night, add password protection, check the history, make sure older boys don't have too much alone time, and talk to them about temptation, and what to do when they're faced with it.

Now let me talk to you, Dad. What do you view on the internet? If you're looking at crud…your children will find it too. If you have some bad magazines stuffed under a mattress, your children will find them. You've got to stop— not only for yourself and your marriage, but also for your children's sake—because if you do crud, your children will do crud.

You can plug 'dem holes! You have to!!

You 'da dad!

Rainy Days and Fridays

Acts 2:14-36

Hey Dad,

Well, it looks like another day of rain. For having had such a dry summer, it sure has rained bucketloads in the last week. Today's rain seems even rainier because we were planning to take the kids up to Michigan City to the Indiana Dunes.

It's a great place. The kids run up and down the gigantic sand hills, dig big pits in the sand, and swim. That is—it's a great place when it's sunny. We canceled the day because of the rain.

The kids were disappointed, but they're okay now.

Actually, I don't mind all that much because now I can get some stuff done—and I like getting stuff done. But there's something about a soggy, wet day that makes you feel tired and unmotivated—like you should get a blanket, sit on the couch, and read a good book or watch a sappy video.

That gives me an idea. I know what we can do. Tonight, we'll have a family night—a rainy, just-lie-around-eating-popcorn-while-watching-a-video-or-playing-a-board-game kind of family night. No hype, no bells or whistles, just the Wilson family forced inside due to the rain, enjoying the shelter, the quiet, and each other.

We need it, too. It seems like in the heat of the summer, we've been busily running every which way. And it's almost like God has sent these rainy days to help us slow down.

Ahhh—sounds good.

So, Dad, if it's raining where you live today, maybe you need to call for a Family Night. Order pizza, get a big box of popcorn, play a game or watch a family video, bring down your pillows and blankets, and enjoy your family.

If it's not raining where you live, pretend it is and have a Family night anyway.

You 'da dad!

A Horn-Honking Dad

Acts 2:37-47

Hey Dad,

Whew! I'm bushed. After searching and praying for a larger Familyman Mobile (FM3), we finally purchased one off eBay, and I had to make a quick down trip down to Florida to pick it up and drive it home.

I'm not complaining, because it was a great feeling sitting behind the wheel of our big rig. This new RV (14 years old) is a diesel pusher, 8 feet longer, runs great, and looks great, thanks to a new paint job. But the coolest thing is the air horn.

FM2 had a dinky little horn, but FM3 has a big, honkin' air horn. I'm talking a train/tanker-ship kind of horn. It's awesome! When I was driving down the highway all by myself, I just let her wail! Man, this is going to be a great RV.

When I got home, however, my wife almost burst into tears. She didn't appreciate all the bells and whistles—or the horn. All she could see was the crummy, rough, old, and worn interior. She's such a…woman. But now, two days later, she's caught the RV makeover vision, and we've torn up the inside and are on our way to creating our home on wheels.

But I'm really writing to remind you again about the influence you have in your children's lives, and I'm not talking about all the stuff you try to influence them in. It's not the sit-down kind of lessons they'll learn. It's the very fabric of who you are that is the real influence.

I was reminded of that myself as I came tooling up I-75 just north of Orlando. It was about 7 o'clock at night when my phone rang. It was my son Ben (14).

"Hey Dad," he began without any other greeting, "what time is it?"

After a slight hesitation, we both blurted out, "My FAVORITE time to drive."

He knows me. He knows that's what I always say when I'm behind the wheel of our RV as the sun hangs low in the sky and the air is cooler. A thousand miles separated us, but he knew that's what I was feeling right then. In thirty years, when he's a dad and I'm old, he'll be driving down the road as the sun sinks and think, "This is Dad's favorite time to drive." He'll think about me, our RVing days, and our life on the road.

You know that thought may not seem like much, but it's huge. Our influence is huge. Your influence is huge. Just be there, Dad. Don't worry about whether you're doing enough teaching or training—just be there, modeling what you want them to live.

You 'da dad!

The Family Code

Hey Dad,

A while back a dad posed the question "Do you have a family code of conduct?" several; dads offered their suggestions. Here is my favorite:

1. Obey all rules (Andy Griffith fans will know this one)
2. No Writing on the walls (another reference to a Barney-ism)
3. No fighting, hitting, kicking, pinching, shoving, biting, or spitting.
4. No running
5. No jumping on the furniture
6. Take turns
7. Share
8. No screaming...Use inside voices
9. No T.V. or videos on the Sunday
10. Help with household chores
11. Do not interrupt each other
12. Take care of your body: eat well, exercise, get enough sleep, and keep clean
13. Speak and act towards each other with love and respect.
14. Obey parents
15. Be slow to speak, slow to become angry, quick to listen, and quick to forgive.
16. Above all, we will remember to honor and love God with all of our hearts.

These are posted prominently. When broken the offender is referred to the rule they broke and disciplined.

Not bad ...and I bet you could come up with a few of your own.

You 'da dad!

She Told Me to Tell You

Acts 3:11-26

September 15

Hey Dad,

just got back from speaking at Spruce Lake Camp in Pennsylvania and then had to be in Chicago to speak shortly after that. My beloved bride thought it would be a great time to kill two birds with one stone so we all went and tackled IKEA the same day. Now, we're bushed and running on fumes.

While we were in Pennsylvania, I told the group a story about a dad who travels too much and whose child asked him to "please come home." Afterwards, I walked out of the building with a couple, and as soon as we hit the outdoors, the wife took off unannounced and walked right into the woods.

"I guess she's going on a hike," the husband said with a look of surprise.

Later, the wife came up to me and apologized for "running off." Being a man, which means I am almost never offended by anything, I assured her I didn't think anything of it. Then she explained her "need for a hike."

"After you told that story about the traveling dad...I just lost it." I expected her to tell me that her husband is a workaholic and that he is gone all the time, but that's not what she said. "My dad traveled and was gone A LOT," she said through teary eyes. "Forty years later, I still feel that impact."

She paused, and for a moment I saw a little girl who desperately needed her daddy. Then she added, "Tell that to all those dads you speak to."

And so I am. Because one day, even if it's forty years later, your son or daughter will still feel the impact of your absence. That's the power you have in their lives. That's Father Power.

You 'da dad!

Sir Todd, the Dragon Slayer

Acts 4:1-11

Forsooth, Dad,

You know there are times in every man's life when he stumbles into greatness. That was my lot this past week. I wasn't looking for any accolades or parades, but my wife had just about had it with some pesky mice who were leaving their telltale signs underneath the kitchen sink, and I was beginning to tire of her comments.

So, I set out some traps (remember Killer?) and the next morning…bingo! Then I disposed of the body, cleaned out under the sink, and resumed normal life at the Wilson household. Little did I know what awaited me.

A few hours later, my wife walked over to me, smiled warmly, and said, "Thanks for slaying a dragon for me."

She couldn't see it, but my chest puffed out, and I felt as though the queen had laid her cold blade across my shoulder and knighted me Sir Todd, The Dragon Slayer. I'm telling you, I've set out mousetraps every night since because I like being my wife's dragon slayer.

In fact, I've been looking for other dragons to slay, and there are plenty of them around here. The truth is dragons are those things that are too big, too messy, too heavy, too far out of reach, and just way too huge for my wife to accomplish.

A dragon might be a stuck window that needs opening, a piece of furniture that she'd like moved, a room that she'd like painted, a burned out bulb in a hard-to-reach spot that is bugging her, or a gross mess that needs to be cleaned up.

Sometimes we dads overlook a dragon. It doesn't feel urgent that it be slain, so we ignore it and hope it goes away. But with each passing day, the dragon grows in the sight of our wives until they either try to kill it themselves or nag us into doing it.

But the dragon is only truly slain when a willing knight (that's you) takes it upon himself to vanquish the foe to save the damsel in distress.

So, my fellow knight, today is the day of reckoning! A day when dragons quake and fall! A day for glory and for honor! Strap on your armor, grab your paintbrush, your tools, or your mousetrap…and do battle with the dragon.

I knight you Sir Dad, the Dragon Slayer!

You 'da dad!

Take It From a Bum

Acts 4:12-22

September 17

Hey Dad,

Don't you just love it when someone points out to you that you're a bum? That's what my wife did the other day. Okay, in all fairness to my wife, she didn't actually say that, imply that, or even hint at that, but that's how I took her simple comment.

We were lying in bed talking about kids, home, and stuff when she blindsided me by mentioning, "You know Ben (14) would love it if you did something fun with him that he likes to do."

That was it. She didn't say it with any animosity or criticism. She didn't even raise her eyebrows or smirk. She just gently laid the truth on the table.

"Yeah, I should do that," I said in agreement, but inside, I felt the conviction and realization grow that I was...a bum.

A bum takes the easy way out. He lays back and does what he likes to do, when he likes to do it. That's what I've done. Oh sure, I try to show my children how much I love them, but it's usually on my terms. I work on my projects until I'm tired and then say, "Let's do this" because it sounds fun and easy to me.

But when they say, "Hey Dad, can we do this_____?" I run it through my bum grid—sounds hard...it will be messy...I'll get mosquito bites...I'm busy...I don't like to do that—and then I answer, "Not right now; maybe later."

So I've been thinking about my wife's comment lately. My son (actually all my children) would love it if I spent some time doing what they like to do when they'd like to do it. Really, all children love it when Dad steps out of his world and into their world.

My wife is 100 percent right. Ben would love it if I did something fun with him. You know your son or daughter would love it too if you would do the same—not what you think sounds fun, but what sounds fun to them. Tonight or this weekend would be the perfect time.

So from one bum to another...

You 'da dad!

Dear Dads

Acts 4:23-31 **September** 18

Hey Dad,

Here's a letter from a fellow dad...one that we should pay special attention to.

"Guys, I am a dad of 7, well 6 now. I took my 20 year old to Air Force Basic training today—WOW! I haven't had a flood of emotion like that since they were all born. We have the 20(b), 14(g), 12(b), 7(g), 5(g), 4(b), 2(g) and I love them all, as I am sure we all do. I felt regret, more than anything else as I drove away today. I can remember being mad at the failures to perform his schoolwork, mad at the failure to do the chores, mad at all the times he let me down—now I am mad at me for spending so much time being mad. I had to write something to help heal my failures at recognizing his failure so much—Dad's please hold them close while they are with you—I wish I had some time back to do over again."

Makes things a little clearer, doesn't it?

You 'da dad!

Parallel Universe

Hey Dad,

Hope things are good in your neck of the woods. Our 'neck' is cold and snowy. And, to tell you the truth, I've been struggling lately.

Call me paranoid, but I think I've stumbled onto some kind of time-continuum-quantum-something-or-other that affects the world our children and we dads live in. I've discovered we don't live in the SAME WORLD.

For example: after the kids are in bed, sometimes my wife and I like to sit by the fire and watch a video. Inevitably, right when we get to the best part, the DVD freezes. We get it out, rub it down, and skip and complain through the damaged scene.

But that rarely happens to my youngest children. They watch certain DVDs over and over and they look as though they've tied them to their feet and run around our gravel driveway, and yet Bob the Builder never freezes!

Next example: batteries. I bet we change the batteries in the remote every 45 minutes, but my children have these really obnoxious toys that will not die. "Hi, let's say our ABC's" one demonic toy calls to me every time I walk by it. If you ask me, it's just plain spooky.

The same is true with computers. I have forbidden the kids to breathe on my main computer, and yet it gets slower and slower and continually locks up. But not their 9-year-old computer. They jam plastic plates into the CD ROM, hit the power button in mid program, and treat it like dirt...but the thing still purrs like a kitten.

And sometimes I'll give one of my children a clear instruction to do a task or chore, then come back an hour later and find that it looks exactly the same as before. Bothered that my command was ignored, I bark, "Son, I told you to straighten up the mud-room."

Without looking up, he'll respond in an angelic voice, "I did."

Or take for example, when we do something "fun." They'll argue and complain, and I'll yell and scold. We'll get home and as I tuck them into bed, they'll say, "Thanks for taking us, Dad. That was so much fun!!"

I'm telling you, it's a parallel universe or something.

I'm not even sure what the point of this email is except to tell you to take a deep breath and enjoy the world you live in. Keep doing what you're doing, stay in the game, don't try to make sense of it, and get a good couple's video tonight to enjoy with your wife (we watched Miss Potter last night...thumbs up).

But be prepared, it's gonna freeze.

You 'da dad!

The Love of My Life

Hey Dad,

Two days ago, my wife accused me of having a love affair with my email. Now, she didn't say that in as many words...she really said, "You care more about checking your email than you do about how I feel.

That's ridiculous...I mean...I love my wife. She's my best friend and partner in life. My email is, well, just a way of reaching dads all across the country.

It's true that I do enjoy turning on my computer, the adrenaline rush as it boots up, and the tingles that race up my spine as the machines talk back and forth in their electronic grunts and squeals. Oh, and whose heart doesn't quicken at the melodic 'ding' announcing that I have mail in my mailbox?

But a love affair with my email? No way!!!

OK, so maybe checking it a dozen times a day is a little overboard...and...I guess I do think about email even when my wife is pouring out her guts about how she feels drained and overwhelmed.

Truth is, I feel my email calling to me even as I type.

You know what?

She's right. I am having an affair with email.

I've been pouring my thoughts, time, and emotions into a stupid machine until my wife feels like I care more about email than I do her. That's an affair. We men are prone to having affairs with our jobs, golf, cars, finances, hobbies, lawns, or friends.

We've made our wives feel like they're number #2 on our love list.

So what are we gonna do? We need to be drastic...like cutting out (or way back) those things that steal our affections from our wives. I know what I need to do...now, I just need to do it. In fact, I'm fighting the urge to check my email right now. Earlier, I walked by the machine and had to look away just so I wouldn't hit the 'check mail' button. It's killing me, but I'm 'da dad.

What about you, dad? Would your wife say she's #1 in your life? If not, make it so.

You 'da dad!

269

The Day the Egg Stood Still

Hey Dad,

Just heard on the radio that today is the autumnal equinox (the first day of fall). Not important enough to throw a party, but it is one of two days that you can stand an egg on end. After I'm through writing this, I may go up and test it out with the kids because it's important for dads to do that kind of stuff.

It's funny…we dads have trouble remembering what's important.

A couple of days ago I had an appointment with one of the most influential Christian leaders in the country. To meet with him, my wife and I had to fly out of state for a quick overnight (not a bad perk).

Abe (age 4) and Ike (age 6) were pretty weepy the day before we left because we were going to be "gone." Actually it was a little annoying after a while, and I found myself comforting less and snapping more.

"We'll only be gone for ONE night…you'll have fun with Grandma…it's not that long…STOP IT!" I responded.

It didn't work and the tears came in waves during the day and into the night. The final straw came at 2 a.m. Ike stumbled into our room crying, and I escorted him back to his room and lay next to his bed until he drifted off.

An hour later, our bedroom door opened and the light from the bathroom spilled in. It was Ike—again.

I expected more tears but none came. Instead a little voice whispered, "I love you, Dad."

"I love you, Ike," I answered using great self-control for 3 a.m.

"I love you more," he added and then closed the door.

The next day on the airplane I was rehearsing the meeting I was about to have with the Big Guy. I was excited, nervous, and pumped about the importance of this meeting…then I heard a small, gentle voice that said, "I love you more." It was Ike, and I replayed the nighttime exchange over in my head.

I realized then that what had taken place in the middle of the night was infinitely more significant and important than what was going to take place later in the day. It always has been and always will be, whether I remember it or not.

The truth is, Dad, the most important matters of your day today have little to do with the work you do, the people you'd like to impress, and your lifetime achievement plan. What matters are the boys and girls who call you "Daddy."

Don't forget that…ever.

You 'da dad!

The Rest of the Story

Hey Dad,

Today, I'm going to tell you "the rest of the story" to demonstrate the great power we dads have over the lives of the people we love.

You may not remember, but six months ago I wrote that my precious and sweet, little daughter, Katherine, had become less than…precious and sweet. My little Tinkerbell needed a Tinkerbell-oscopy.

My diagnosis was that I was the cause of her downhill transformation. I had treated her harshly and insensitively, but I was determined to change that.

I have.

I know this might sound too good to be true, but I have my Tinkerbell back BECAUSE I am treating her like my Tinkerbell once again. I stroke her back when she cries, hold her on my lap, kiss her cheeks tenderly, and when she needs correction and discipline, I do so with a gentle, loving voice (most of the time).

EUREKA! It's working. She's begun responding to my gentleness by writing me notes and coming to my office to tell me that she loves me. She climbs up on my lap, wraps her arms around my neck, and buries her head in my chest.

You should have seen her this past Sunday. She asked to sit on my lap, and I agreed. As the pastor spoke, I held her tightly and whispered in her ear how much I love her. Katherine snuggled, kissed my neck about a hundred times, and stroked the back of my neck until I felt a little embarrassed by her outpouring of love.

Did I tell her to stop? NO WAY!

So here's the point, Dad. Do you know why she's gone from stand-offish to Miss Public Display of Affection?

Father power!!

That's the power we have over our children. Now don't get me wrong; I'm not done with Katherine. I still have to keep at it, because I can change her back just like that.

Dad, you have that power. You can take your child who is insecure and turn him around. You can take a cold, indifferent wife and help her to love again. You can do it…because you have the POWER.

It's never too late. Start today. Believe me; it's worth the hard work. And, it IS hard work. You'll have to give when you don't feel like giving, forgive when you've been wronged, and speak softly when you feel like yelling.

You can do it 'cuz you' da dad!

They're Not Dumb, Just Normal

Acts 5:33-42

Hey Dad,

I used to be under the impression that my children are brilliant…loaded to the brim with brainpower. Now I'm starting to wonder if they have enough power in the tank to get out of the driveway.

Lately I've caught myself saying things that a father just shouldn't have to say. These are actual statements that have come out of my mouth in the past 3 weeks:

"Why did you cut slits in the screen door with your pocket knife?"

"Abe, don't rinse out your toothbrush in the toilet!"

"Don't shoot holes in the siding of the house with your BB gun!!"

"Who drilled holes in the wagon??"

"Ike, don't lick the bricks!!"

To add insult to injury, when I question the perpetrator, they look at me with that "what?" look. Take the BB gun incident for example …

"Did you shoot these holes in the house siding?" I asked.

"Yeeesssss," he answered softly.

"Did you KNOW you were putting HOLES in the siding of OUR HOUSE?"

He looked at me like I was the one who was having trouble comprehending all this, "Yeeessss."

I searched my brain trying to come up with some kind of "Mr. Brady" explanation of why people shouldn't shoot holes into houses. My brilliant response? "Well, don't do it again!"

I walked away mumbling to myself, "What is he, dumb or something?"

I know he won't shoot any more holes into the siding…he'll think of something else instead…like shooting holes in the side of the van, pounding nails into the kitchen counter, or scratching his name into the wood of his bunk bed. Oh yeah, he already did that one.

Then I discovered something this weekend as I was talking with my brother-in -law. His kids do the same things. In fact, he said that one of his kids recently drilled a bunch of holes into his dry-walled garage.

Then it dawned on me: my kids aren't stupid…they're just normal, red-blooded, curious, adventure-seeking, information-gathering kids.

And so are yours. They WILL break things, drill holes, dent cars, burn stuff, and lick bricks, and then they'll look at you like…"What?"

I don't know if this will help, but remember: they're not dumb, they're just normal. So Dad, keep training, keep encouraging, keep hugging, and keep laughing.

You 'da dad!

To Boldly Go

Acts 6:1-15

Hey Dad,

I'm bound for the promised land...my wife and I are going to leave the kids for a whole day and night and stay in a hotel...without THEM.

We'll have dinner without distractions. No one getting out of their seat, spilling drinks, or hurting one another. Instead, my wife and I will look into each other's eyes, hold hands, and talk uninterrupted.

That's the good news. The bad news is that I have three days of wandering in the wilderness before I get there.

Translation: my wife is going to a women's retreat this weekend, leaving the kids with me for a whole weekend...alone...by myself...no help...adrift on the ocean of fatherhood.

Apparently you haven't grasped the seriousness of what I just said. I'm being left alone with five kids. I have to cook the meals, teach a day of homeschooling, keep them out of the emergency room, AND entertain them.

You see, they expect me to do something special. They anticipate surprises, special privileges, and junk food with Dad in charge. Greater dads than me have been found in the fetal position crying like a baby after such weekends. I have to be strong because kids can sense fear.

Right now, I don't feel up for the task. Hopefully by Friday morning I'll be ready, because whether I like it or not—they will be.

I want it to be a special time, not only for my wife to recharge her batteries, but for us. You know, a little dad/kid time. It'll be exhausting, and I'm afraid it may get ugly—my wife likes it when it does, so I can get a taste of what her life is like—and so does your wife.

Well, anyway, I'll let you know how it turns out.

You 'da dad!

They're Playing Our Song

Hey Dad,

Last night I finished up (well, almost) a house project that I started seven years ago, and yesterday the kids got a thumbs up at their doctor check-up...although Abe (4) is still talking about the "turn your head and cough" part.

On top of that, Debbie and I were able to get away for an overnight to West Palm Beach, Florida, last weekend, as we had the privilege of speaking to a great group of moms and dads.

While we were there, I discovered the secret of keeping love in your marriage (okay, one of the secrets)—you gotta have a song. You know...one of those songs that when you hear it, you say to your wife, "They're playing our song."

I discovered ours this past weekend.

It was at an outdoor plaza after dinner. A saxophone playing, one-man band named Billy Bones entertained the crowd that had gathered to enjoy the night breeze, the lighted palm trees, and his music. Just as we were about to leave, the tempo changed, and he began playing Nat King Cole's, "Unforgettable." I looked into the eyes of my beautiful wife and said, "Let's dance."

A little background on my wife...she doesn't like attention and feels uncomfortable dancing at all, let alone in public (maybe it's her Baptist upbringing)...especially when no one else is dancing.

"You're kidding," she said, but her eyes sparkled.

"No one knows us here," I said. "Come on."

It took a little doing, but a few seconds later I had her in my arms dancing as Mr. Bones crooned, "Unforgettable...that's what you are...unforgettable ..." My wife and I were in love.

It was right then that I thought, "This is OUR song! Every time I hear this, I'll remember this moment and look at my wife and say, "They're playing OUR song." The years will pass, and we'll get old and decrepit, but when we hear OUR song, we'll remember that night under the stars when Billy Bones reminded us how much we love each other.

So Dad, if you and your wife don't have a song, get one. If you used to have one, hunt down the CD, tape, or record (remember those?) and play it after the kids are in bed. Then take her up in your arms, look her in the eyes, and...remember.

You 'da dad!

The Third Law of Family Dynamics

Hey Dad,

Greetings from the repair bay at Felt's Truck and RV Repair in Bowling Green, KY. Yep, one of the great things about RVing is all the wonderful repair facilities you get to visit. Yesterday, we were on our way home from a week of speaking and recreating. The sky was blue, the RV was running great, and the horse had seen the barn.

All was well until I looked down at my temperature gauge and saw that it was super high. At first I thought it had to be a faulty gauge; it was fine just minutes before. But knowing that one should never ignore a gauge, I pulled over and shut it down.

A while later, a tow truck and an extra truck (to pull our trailer and haul our family) was on its way.

I expected the worse and was pleased as punch and praising God when they diagnosed that it was just a cracked hydraulic hose to a radiator fan. I was sure I had ruined my motor.

So now they're working, while we're waiting, and hopefully we'll be back on the road soon.

I'm feeling a little frazzled and can't make a smooth transition into something witty or insightful. So let me just get right to what I was going to write about before all of the above happened, and that's 'everything's better when everybody does it' (sounds like a Blue Bonnet butter commercial).

My son Ike (10) told me that last week. I think it was a normal night and we wanted something to do as a family. We couldn't think of anything creative so we got a movie that we had all watched several times.

Normally, after popping the DVD in, my wife and I will go do something productive, but for some reason we didn't and just sat watching the scenes we all knew and laughed at the lines we always laugh at.

It was a good night, but Ike was the one who showed me why. A few minutes later we were upstairs and he said to me, "It was fun watching a movie." He smiled and I smiled back and then he added, "It's funny how everything's better when everyone in our family is doing it."

"You're right," I said, and I have been thinking about that since. Family is better when everyone does it and funner when everyone in the family participates. It's like The Third Law of Family Dynamics.

It's the same for your family. Things are better when you do it ALL together. And although you can't always do it together, I bet you could plan something this weekend that everyone can do.

And you know what? The Third Law of Family Dynamics is true even when you're sitting in an RV repair shop...I think.

You 'da dad!

275

OH, to be Like IKE

Hey Dad,

Greetings from a parking lot in Tulsa, OK. I've spoken here for the last two days, and today we drive to Oklahoma City to speak for another couple of days. So far, everything has run great…although my kitchen sink is dripping every time I turn the water pump on, which is like the Chinese water torture for a guy.

Yesterday, the kids turned on the rotating spot light and ran down the chassis battery leaving me dead on the water. Fortunately, I was able to turn on the generator, and plug in my battery charger…and now we're back up and running.

About the only bit of sightseeing we've been able to do was a quick stop at Purina Farms. I'm guessing if you were a dog lover it might have seemed like paradise…but to non-dog lovers who don't like drizzly cold rain, it won't make our best-of-the-road list.

Everyone complained about the weather and the 'boring' exhibits, and asked about every ten seconds, "Whose idea was this anyway? Everyone complained, that is, except Ike (who just turned 11 on Tuesday). God gave Ike the gift of seeing everything as awesome.

"That was an awesome dog show," he said of the 6 minute dog show in the drizzle.

"Wow, look at this!" he said as he swung with exuberance form a mock hay mow rope that was the whole length of three feet long.

"You're the best dad in the whole world," he added later.

"This was my best birthday ever!" he said as we were opening his presents between speaking events in a parking lot.

It's that way all the time…he loves it all. It's all the best…most awesome everything!!! Man, I wish we all could be like that. I wish we could all say, "Wow, this is the best Walmart parking lot we've ever stayed in or…boy, this was the best day we've ever had driving all day long. I just bet if I responded like that, my family would follow suit. Because as some famous person once said, "As the dad goes…so goes the family.

So Dad, whatever your plans are for the weekend and however the weather turns out, say throughout the day, "Man, this is a great day together as a family."

You 'da dad!

A Manly Man

Hey Dad,

We've been fed a lie that says: For a man to be a man, he needs to do "manly" things and act according to his "natural" tendencies. Really, what is being said is that we have to do what WE want to do to be truly masculine. That line of thought is based on selfishness, not selflessness. It is a worldly philosophy not a Biblical one.

If you were to follow that line of logic then one could easily say, "Since men are drawn to sensual images, then it can't be wrong to 'look' at them because that's how God created man to be. God certainly wouldn't create someone with a particular bent and then expect him to deny it or even call it sin. In fact, maybe it would be better to nurture the desire."

Now I know that I just pushed my point a little far, but the same line of thinking is put forth in the idea that men get their self worth from their job. That may be true, but that doesn't make it right to be a work-a-holic, nor does it mean that we should live in such a way as to gratify that desire.

Can a man turn the other cheek, communicate with his wife, offer to do the dishes, and still be a man? Yes! In fact, that's the kind of man God wants us to be. Yes, some have feminized men, BUT working to be a good listener, servant, and communicator, isn't feminine, it's "living with your wife in an understanding way." It's manly, manliness!!

Let me set the record straight that I'm no wimp. I own all kinds of power tools, spit, played football in high school, and go days without shaving, BUT that isn't what makes me a manly-dad. I'm a manly-dad because I deny myself and serve others. I set aside my "natural" tendencies and sweep the kitchen, change diapers, give baths, talk with my wife about fabric colors, and try to be interested when my children describe their latest LEGO creation.

Now I fail a good chunk of the time (just did about 10 minutes ago), but I never give up. I apologize (another "unnatural" thing to do) and try again.

That's what a real man is…a biblical, selfless, go-ahead-and-punch-me-in-the-face-cuz-I-can-take-it kind of man. That's what God has asked of us.

Defend your family, rescue your damsel, and don't forget to take out the trash.

You 'da dad!

Bye Bye Struggle

Acts 7:41-53

Hey Dad,

It's been a busy week around here trying to finish up a few house projects that I started a couple years ago. You know they never go like you expect. I ripped off the old siding to find some rot and then my son Ben (17) dropped the ladder through the family room window. All par for the dad-course. But now, the rot has been replaced, the window is in the glass shop, and we're just about done.

Today, I've been feeling a little sloggy. It comes with the territory of working from home. I know some dads think I'm lucky to be home all day long, but sometimes there are drawbacks…like struggling with what's important and what isn't and the feeling that I'm wasting my time with stupid, little things when I should be doing the BIG, IMPORTANT things.

For example: this morning I cleaned out our Familyman shop when I should have been doing important stuff. I wiped a bottom or two when I should have been doing world changing things. I had to deal with bad attitudes in kids and an orange juice spill when I should have been doing Familyman things!!!

In fact, I was starting to rebel against my situation when my daughter Maggie (6) came to me screaming, like her hand had been amputated below the elbow.

"What's wrong, princess?" I asked, assuming it wasn't that bad.

She continued crying and pointing to her finger. "It's bleeding, right there," she said as she pointed to a microscopic prick of blood.

I coddled her hand, gently blowing magical father powers across the injury. A few minutes later she was healed only to return holding a "Busy Town Book."

"Dada, can you read me this book?" she asked sweetly.

I sighed, looked at the title knowing there were like 100,000 tiny words in the book, and agreed to read three chapters. She was delighted and sat in my arms (and a couple other children joined in) as we read about Lowly and Huckle and the rest of the bunch. As I read, the 'struggle' flitted away, and I knew that what I was doing at that moment…was the important, world changing stuff.

My fellow dad, if you're feeling a similar struggle, let me say loud and clear that all the family stuff that is robbing your potential…is THE important, world changing stuff. Don't ever forget that. Or at least don't forget it for long.

You 'da dad!

Shot Out of the Sky

Acts 7:54-60

Hey Dad,

Well, it's a sad day in "I'm a pretty good dad-Land" when you learn that the thing you 'don't do'…you do.

Actually, my wife has accused me for quite some time (read—our whole married life) of not always listening like I should. She's had the nerve to say on more than a few occasions that I don't let her share what she's feeling, that I barge in and tell her why she shouldn't be feeling what she's feeling, why she's mistaken in her feelings, or why I'm right about the situation and she's wrong.

Up until recently, I thought she was overreacting and wrong in her assessment and that I was actually a very understanding husband (after all—I am the Familyman) and quite the listener.

Then, my daughter Katherine (13) shot me out of the air like a slow duck on the first day of duck hunting season. I was on the porch with my shot gun-toting daughter, frustrated by the fact that her mother didn't think I listened to her.

I was mid-sentence when Katherine pointed the gun towards me and said, "You don't listen to her, Dad. You don't let her tell you what she's feeling."

Shocked, I quickly responded, "But I let her tell me what she's feeling, and I don't understand why she says …"

She intercepted me politely and said, "You're doing it to me, now." KERPOW!

I dropped to the ground like a rock.

There was nothing I could say. Cause the truth is: if two people tell you the same thing about yourself…it's probably true.

I've got a long longgggggg way to go, but I've been working on it. So here's the take away for you. You're not going to like this, but…if your wife and one of your children say you don't listen…you don't.

If more than one of them says you're grumpy all the time…you are.

if more than one of them says you work too much…you do.

If more than one of them accuses you of being gone too much, being selfish, or being a couch potato who watches too much TV or plays too many video games…you are.

Whether we like it or not, if two or more are saying the same thing about us…IT'S TRUE and it's time to face up to it and change.

I know we can do it. Because…

You 'da dad!

Forever 'da Dad

Acts 8:1-8

Hey Dad,

Things are pretty calm around here...except that vermin are overrunning our house. I've caught enough mice to make a mouse-skin coat, and pesky fruit flies are driving me nuts (one just flew by my monitor as I type this!). In fact, if you have some kind of potently lethal remedy to get rid of them, I'd love to hear it.

This week we've been putting on the final touches to a Christmas board game that will be available in November. The purpose of the game is to give dads a tool that will help them create loads of great family memories. Because you know what? Your kids will forget many details, people, and events in their lifetime...but they'll never forget you and the time you spent with them.

Just a few weeks ago, I was at my parents' house and noticed a shoebox of ancient photos sitting around. Curious, I asked my mother why they were out.

"I took them up to my mother," she said. "I thought she'd enjoy looking through them." My 90-year-old grandmother (her mother) has been in a nursing home for the last several years and her mind is failing.

"Did she recognize the people in the pictures?" I asked.

My mom told me that she didn't recognize her own children's pictures or even her husband's...but she still recognized her father's photos. She even talks more about her father who passed away 40 years ago than she does about her husband of 60 years.

That's amazing, but it shouldn't surprise me. For 10 years, I went to a local nursing home once a week and saw the same thing happen. Confused, elderly people talked lovingly about their fathers as though they were still alive.

That's FATHER POWER, Dad! It's the life-long imprint you make on your children.

So, let this thought blow your mind. Eighty years from now, your children may be sitting in a wheelchair parked along a hallway in a nursing home...thinking about you and the times spent with you. Your child may not be thinking about his/her spouse or children but may very well be thinking of YOU.

Kind of puts things in a different perspective, doesn't it?

So, Dad, snuggle up to each of your children tonight and give them the memory of a dad who loved them more than anything.

Forever 'da dad!

A Gift to Dads

Acts 8:9-24

Hey Dad,

Finally, a little fall weather has arrived in Northern Indiana. It's been balmy around here lately and has felt more like late July than October. I'm convinced that fall is one of God's greatest gifts to dads.

There is nothing better than cool, crisp nights of campfires, s'mores, and snuggling. My sons, Ike (8) and Abe (6), have been begging me to have a campfire, but I've been putting them off by saying, "It's too hot for a campfire."

But no more. In fact, I'm thinking that this Friday or Saturday night would be the perfect time for a little marshmallow roasting. About the only drawback is that it's pretty much a big pain.

In my head I picture laughing, roasting, and singing. In reality, it's gooey hands, potential 3rd degree burns, and flaming sticks being swung around like light sabers. I'm sure I'll do more yelling than singing—but you know what? It's worth it.

I know that there is no better feeling than to sit around a warm fire with the people you love the most. In fact, if I were only given 24 hours to live, I would spend at least a couple of those hours around the campfire with my family.

So, Dad, let me encourage you to enjoy some of that good, God-given fall weather with your family this weekend. Make a campfire, go pick apples, drink apple cider, or make s'mores.

If you live where it's perpetually warm, be creative and have your own fall night. Go get some fallish leaves and apple cider from Walmart and have a campfire anyway. If you don't have a fire pit, pick up a metal or ceramic one from Lowe's (they're probably on sale).

It will be sticky, messy, and inconvenient—but I guarantee it will be good.

Well, I've got to go. My darling children just spilled—oh, about 10,000 air-soft BB's on the kitchen floor. Big mess, cool sound.

You 'da dad!

Being a Dad Is Like Childbirth

Hey Dad,

Ever notice that being a dad and birthing a child are a lot alike? I was reminded of how this is so on my birthday this past week. The plan was to leave mid-morning, eat at a favorite restaurant, and do some shopping. It sounded like the perfect way to spend a beautiful autumn birthday.

And it was perfect...in my head. Then we pulled out of the driveway, and reality struck. Perhaps it was the combination of tiredness, crowded stores, and six energetic kids, but the stress began to build. "Don't touch that!" I snapped. "Abe get off the floor...don't touch your sister again...where's Ike?...Don't bang on the glass. It makes the Chinchillas nervous...Where's Ike?...I don't know why Mom's taking so long...Yes, we'll be going home soon, REAL SOON...Where's Ike?"

By the end of the afternoon, I was beat. The happy birthday boy had been replaced by a grizzly bear. I was silent on the way home, too tired to move my mouth.

Now here's where the childbirth thing comes in.

After everyone was tucked in, I plopped on the bed next to my wife.

I felt exhausted and emotionally spent. But then a familiar, warm, fuzzy feeling climbed up on the bed and burrowed itself into my heart, and I was glad to be a dad.

"I had so much fun today!" I said cheerfully as my wife looked at me perplexed.

It's like my wife's delivery experiences. For 9 months, she excitedly anticipates the birth of a child. During delivery, she vows never to do it again. And then, ten seconds after the baby is born, she radiates with happiness, forgetting how hard it was, knowing it was worth it.

That's fathering! Sure it's hard, but the hardness is quickly forgotten, leaving only wonderful memories and feelings of love and gratitude in its place.

So, if you've been putting off that family vacation because it sounds too hard with the kids, or you dread the holidays because it's exhausting, or you've put off a dozen other things that the children have been begging you to do because you know it will be difficult—put it off no longer.

Believe me, Dad, it will be hard...but it will be worth it! It always is, and you, like a mother who has just given birth, will bask in the joy and privilege of spending time with your family. Ahhh...God is good to dads.

You 'da dad!

Bumper Sticker Dad

Acts 9:1-19

Hey Dad,

We had to brave Chicago traffic last week. Not only was it congested and slow, but it also seemed as if every road we turned on was under construction.

While we were creeping through Chicago, a bumper sticker not only caught my eye, but also struck a nerve in the deep dad-recesses of my mind. The bumper sticker was just three words on a plain background, but it spoke volumes.

Deer Hunter's Widow

At first I wasn't quite sure what it meant, but then I realized that a longer version might read, "My husband is gone so much during deer hunting season that it feels like I'm all alone in our marriage."

I'm sure the person bought or received it as a joke, but I felt myself getting mad as I stared at the tail end of that car. In fact, I had half a mind to follow the car to its home and chew out the guy for abandoning his family in favor of sitting out in the woods with a bunch of buddies to plug some animal.

As the car pulled away, I began thinking of similar bumper stickers that might have a market.

Golfer's Widow

Businessman's Widow

Pastor's Widow

Football Fan's Widow

Internet User's Widow

TV Watcher's Widow

Traveling Salesman's Widow

Truth is many wives feel alone in their marriages, their families, and their lives. They got married thinking they were going to travel life's highway together hand in hand with their men and what they got were men who were so busy doing their lives that they didn't have much time for them. It might be one of the reasons why Facebook is so popular among the female folk. We've let them down.

Truth is: deer hunting is fun. Golfing and watching football are too. Ministry, business, and our jobs are important. But none of it matters as much as the promise we made to our wives to love, honor, and cherish them.

So let me ask you a question: What kind of bumper sticker would be on your wife's car?

You 'da dad!

The Battle of a Lifetime

Acts 9:20-31

Hey Dad,

There are many famous battles in the history books: The Battle of the Alamo, Bull Run, and Gettysburg. A lesser known struggle is the Battle of the Thermostat.

It usually begins when the furnace is kicked on for the first time. There are basically two sides: hers and MINE. She likes to be comfortable and I like to be…cheap.

The first shot was fired yesterday. I was lying in bed when I smelled the faint odor of burning dust. It smelled familiar…comforting. Then I realized what it was—the furnace. Something inside me snapped. It was only the middle of September!

After all we live in Northern Indiana, not Iceland. I mean, what's a little chill in the air? The furnace shouldn't be turned on until the first of November…at the earliest!

I slipped downstairs and planned to secretly turn off the furnace when my wife wasn't looking…but somehow I opened my mouth and said in a rather annoyed tone, "Does it bother you that we've gone from air conditioning to heat in two days?"

Apparently it didn't, but it did bother her that I cared more about saving a few bucks than I cared about her. What made it worse was that it bothered me too. In my heart I know that Debbie is worth more than the $13 that I would save by being stingy, but somehow when the furnace kicked on, my brain kicked off.

That was yesterday. Today I surrendered. I laid my weapons down and will not say another thing about the thermostat, the cost, or the insane timing of turning it on so blasted early. From now on I will care more about the comfort of my wife than the size of my heating bill.

So, what battles rage in your house? Is it the battle of the thermostat, the battle of eating out, the battle of arriving late, or the battle of high expectations? Whatever the battle, your strategy should be the same.

Surrender.

Prove to your wife that she is more important than high prices, inconveniences, and yourself.

You 'da dad!

Change Back

Acts 9:32-43

Hey Dad,

My son Abe (6) recently told me that there are only 79 days 'til Christmas. That means it's time to start thinking about what to get your wife for Christmas and to start planning all the fun that the month of December has to offer dads and their families.

For a lot of dads that's hard—because we aren't fun anymore. Oh, we used to be fun, but something happens throughout the course of marriage and we often quit trying.

My wife and I see examples of this all the time. Why is it that when we see a middle-aged man and woman holding hands, laughing, and stealing kisses, we assume they're probably not married? We glance at their left ringfingers—nothing. Yet, when we see a couple barely speaking across a table, we assume that they're married, and they usually are.

Even the other day, I made a food run, and as I stood in line a young couple stood off to the side holding arms. I tried not to stare, but they seemed so engrossed in each other. He was listening to her, smiling, and she was laughing at what he said. They looked really happy.

Not married, I thought to myself. Let's see what happens after they walk down the aisle. I wanted to say to the young lady, "Don't be fooled. He may seem fun now, but he'll change—believe me. I used to be way more long-suffering, patient, loving—fun! But I changed. We all change!"

I had half a mind to go over and poke the guy in the chest and say, "Don't ever change! Keep laughing, holding hands, smiling, and being fun."

But I didn't. Instead I poked myself in the chest and said, "Don't change, Todd. Your wife needs you to laugh more, forgive more, smile more, and be more fun. Hold hands more often, cuddle on the couch, listen to her thoughts, fears, and concerns more…Change back!"

Let me do a little Christmas poking in your chest, Dad, and say, "Change back!" If it sounds impossible, then take baby steps. Make it a point to smile more. Hug everyone in your family—twice. Ask your wife, "What sounds fun to do this Christmas as a family?" Then hold your wife's hand and listen and talk. Before you go to bed tonight, pray and ask God to make you fun again, like before you were married.

You 'da husband!

'Da Plan

Acts 10:1-23

Hey Dad,

Today I'm going to share with you my plan to prepare my children to meet God one day (which is a dad's main objective).

I've kind of let things slide around here over the summer. There were lots of lame reasons, but now it's time to get back to business.

So here's my plan and advice for 'making sure your children are with you in heaven:

As the old adage says, "If at first you blow it, try, try again—and again—and again." That's the secret of fathering. No matter what—KEEP TRYING. Forget the past failures, don't whine and make excuses…just try again.

Next comes…'DA PLAN (not to be confused with Fantasy Island's 'Da Plane). My wife and I brainstormed and came up with a list of areas we wanted to work on and focus on in our family. For you, it might just mean resurrecting an old plan that has gone by the wayside. But you need 'da plan.

Once you have 'da plan, you need to be the enforcer. Your wife might carry out some of the plan, but the buck stops with you. Be warned! If you're going to pull off 'da plan, it's going to cut into YOUR time and affect YOUR schedule. You'll have to view it as one of your top priorities.

For example: If you want to start family devotions—again, then you're going to have to sacrifice some of your time to be there (family devotions isn't family devotions if the dad is not there).

Your plan (like mine) may include a prolonged bedtime, instead of the rush-it-through to gettt'r done kind. I'm going to spend time reading The Bible in Pictures to my little kids and working thru the Bible along with a Scripture memory program with my big kids.

Sounds like a lot of work and makes me tired just thinking about it (I really do like a short bedtime ritual). But that's OK. I'm 'da dad, and I want my children with me in heaven!!! They won't know and trust God unless I show them how to do that. And that takes time—my time. It also takes my example, even more importantly, because more is caught than taught.

The same goes with your children. They need us to get them ready to meet God. So what are you waiting for? Start tonight with 'da plan!

You 'da dad!

286

Hard But Not That Hard

Acts 10:24-33

Hey Dad,

The skies are clear, the temperature warm, God healed my RV brake lights, and I was reminded that being a good dad or husband is hard BUT not THAT hard.

It can be done. I can respond like I'm supposed to, I can be gentle when I don't feel like it, I can be involved when I'd rather not be, and I can do the right thing just because it is the right thing. I just have to DAD UP.

I've been having a little issue with one of my female children. Every time I asked her to do anything it was like unleashing a dam of emotion and "Why do I have to always-ESE?" It was getting on my nerves, and I found myself being unkind and loud with my daughter.

It wasn't like I made some kind of covenant to be more fatherly from that moment on, I just DADDED UP and thought, my daughter needs me to love her...even if she isn't being very lovable. So I made a conscious effort to ask her about her things, brag on her about her things, tell her she looks pretty and that her hair looks nice, and stroke her back and give her lots of hugs and kisses.

And she responded with kindness and gentleness.

I was walking downstairs after a sweet encounter with her when the thought hit me, "That wasn't so hard." I didn't have to do anything difficult, cut off a limb, or donate an organ...I just had to DAD UP and do what dads are supposed to do. The thing is I don't usually do that. Even right now as I type this, I can think of a couple of my children whom I need to spend a little extra time with to let them know how much I love them...and then there's my wife who could use a little heart listening to. Man it sounds hard.

But that's the LIE. It may sound hard...but it's not that hard. I just need to DAD UP...and so do you.

So Dad, let me encourage you to ask your wife what she's feeling, sit on the edge of your son's bed and talk about, sports, iPhones...or whatever, or look into you daughter's eyes and say, "You look beautiful today." It's not that hard. You just need to...

...DAD UP.

You 'da dad!

287

The Will of...Todd

Acts 10:34-48

Hey Dad,

Sometimes I hate being "The Familyman"...especially when my wife uses it against me.

You see, four months ago, I loudly proclaimed that we were going on a Wilson family vacation to Florida. After all, I was going to be speaking down south and Florida wasn't that much farther.

Now, I feel like I'm rushing around trying to meet a bunch of deadlines...and I could really use that week to work instead. "Besides," I told my wife, "we probably shouldn't spend the money...and it is out of our way."

For several days, my wife and I went back and forth discussing the pros and cons, and all the while, I became more convinced that we should abort. I reasoned that maybe we could go in the spring...or better yet, we could plan for the next November.

That's when she reminded me that I'm the Familyman.

"You know," she said, "I guess I feel a little disappointed in your decision. It's not a very "Familyman" kind of answer. The "Familyman" would say, "Vacations are more important than getting 'stuff' done, and sometimes money is just an excuse." And then she added, "We don't want to communicate to the kids that 'work' is more important than family."

Ouch! That hurt...I mean really hurt, because I knew she was right. Family is way more important than getting work done and being a tightwad. I want my children to KNOW that family is more important than schedules, deadlines, and bank accounts. I can't just say it; I have to prove it to them by living it.

That's right! I was blind, but now I see! So I announced yesterday (again) that we're going to Florida!

She didn't say it, but I could hear her think, "That's my Familyman."

Dad, I almost listened to the practical side of my brain instead of the dad side—which is usually the right side.

How about you dad? Have you been listening to the dad side of your brain lately? Or has the practical side gotten in the way? It's time to throw some cold water on your face, puff out your chest, and make decisions that teach your children about what's most important. So cancel a business trip, don't work late tonight...or...go to Florida.

You 'da dad!

Get Out Your Mucklucks!

Acts 11:1-18

Hey Dad,

It's cold outside. Yesterday, they were predicting the possibility of snow. Yow! Luckily, it didn't snow, because if it had, I would have had to scramble to get ready for the celebration. What? Don't you celebrate the first snowfall of the year? You're kidding me, right?

About four years ago, I heard a gal on the radio tell how she gave each of her kids a new book on the first snowfall of the year. I was hooked right then and there.

So now I pick up a little something for each of the kids that has to do with snow. It might be a snowflake ornament from Walmart, a fun new winter hat, or a cheap saucer sled. This year things are kind of tight, so I stopped by the Dollar General to see what I could find. I didn't buy anything (hoping I still have a few more weeks), but I saw all kinds of things like Chapstick, gloves, pj's, and slippers—plus they're cheap!

When it actually does snow, we'll drink hot chocolate, and I'll give them their small gifts and a small card or bookmark that I'll print off of my computer reminding them of the first snowfall of 2003 and that I love them.

Now, I know what some of you are thinking. "Give me a break, Todd. Do we have to make everything a big deal?"

Answer: No, you don't have to. But why not give it a try? I'll probably spend less than 30 minutes investing in the big day, but the dividends are staggering. Because what we end up celebrating, is not the first snow...but the importance of family, and my commitment to them. Ker-ching!

It doesn't have to be the first snow, either (which for those of you in Michigan could have been in early July). It might be your child's first lost tooth, the birthday of your dog, or, if you live in the south, the first tropical hurricane of the season.

Take the lead, go the extra mile, and your family will know you're committed to them by your actions, not just by your words.

So pick an occasion and make it a good 'un!

You 'da dad!

Girls Is Girls

Hey Dad,

Picture me atop a crooked blue stool with an umbrella in my hand and an elongated red and white striped top hat perched on my head. Now let's begin...

Big girls, small girls, Old girls, tall girls

Small girls like to play with dolls, Big girls like to shop at malls.

Sometime girls just cry and cry, Sometimes girls just buy and buy.

All girls own a bunch of shoes, browns and blacks and lots of blues.

Some are snappy and some are quiet, Some can't decide and some just buy it.

One day they're glad and the next day they're sad, And sometimes they are very, very mad.

Why are they glad and sad and mad? I know I should know 'Cause I'm 'da dad. (Applause)

Okay, here's my point. Girls is girls. They may wear diapers, have braces on their teeth, or live in a retirement home...but girls is girls. They think, feel, and respond differently than boys...BUT they think, feel, and respond the same as all other females.

This week, I've been conducting an experiment. I've worked hard at being tender and adoring to my daughter Katherine (9). When she talks, I look her in the eyes and listen intently. When she gets hurt, I comfort her with tender touches until her crying stops.

The bebop music on the stereo caught my attention, and without thinking, I took Katherine by the hands and danced her around the kitchen table, swinging and twirling to the music.

Her eyes twinkled, and she blushed at my outpouring of love. Instead of pulling away, she held on and giggled with pleasure. I finished by giving her a big hug and then went back to my task, but inside I was reminded that my little girl needs her daddy to show his love...not just say it.

I decided to work hard at being kind, gentle, and comforting...and Katherine has responded lovingly to me because of my efforts. And it does take effort, not because it's hard...but because I'm a boy and not a girl.

Now here's the deal. My wife would love for me to treat her the same as I have worked at treating my daughter. And so would your wife, your daughters, or the old ladies down at the nursing home.

You know why?

Girls IS girls.

So, Dad, take the Seven-Day Challenge! Treat the girls in your life like girls want to be treated. Talk softly, listen intently, touch lovingly, smile often, and maybe even buy them a little token of your affection.

R and R

Hey Dad,

You know when you're a dad R&R just doesn't measure up to Rest and Relaxation. So, I asked a bunch of Familymen to define R&R for dads. Here's what they came up with:

Retrospect & Regret
Retired & Regular
Rolaids & Resuscitation
Regroup & Refocus
Rant & Rave
Recover & Restart
Reorient & Restore
Remind & Reward
Recoil & Reload
Rinse & Repeat
Reevaluate & Recommit
Recognize & Repent
Reassess & Retaliate
Rock & Roll!
Rowdiness and Rejuvenation
Roughing up and wRestling down
Rest and Renewal
Recess and Recreation
Retreat and Restoration
Rollicking and Reward

So Dad, pick your favorite or make up one of your own and then do a little of that tonight!

You 'da dad!

291

Throw Yourself Through a Window

Hey Dad,

I had some website problems and was up late trying to work it out. Although exhausted by the web dilemma, my brain couldn't fall asleep. One of the things I pondered was a conversation that I had with a fellow dad who is recovering from a moral failure.

He told me that prior to his actual "failure," he confided in a couple of fellow dads about his struggles. To their shame, they failed to follow-up with their friend. I'm sure they had their reasons…we—I mean they—always do.

Never for a moment did my friend blame them for his failure…but he felt let down. Had they gotten in his face and put him in a headlock, maybe things would have turned out differently.

It reminds me of a story about a man who happened to be driving by his buddy's house late one night and noticed a flame flickering in an upstairs window.

Alarmed, he pulled into the driveway and pounded on the door to wake up his friend…but no one answered. Knowing that time was of the essence, the man got a good running start and hurled himself through the large plate glass window near the front door.

Cut and bleeding, he struggled up the stairs and kicked open his friend's bedroom door only to find his friend and wife embracing in bed with a lit candle near the window.

Sadly…the story is made up, but the point is that this is the kind of friend I want to be…one that would pick embarrassment and possible error in order to save his friend from possible death.

That's the kind of person my friend needed…we all need…and we all need to be.

Dad, can I encourage you to be that kind of friend to your fellow dad? Maybe you need to confront a dad about some suspicions you've had, ask some tough questions—or throw yourself through his plate glass window.

Think how sad the story would have been if the man had ignored the signs and the flickering light had been a blazing fire. The man would have had to assume some of the guilt as he looked over the charred remains of his buddy and was forced to admit, "You know, I wondered if it was serious."

Until tomorrow…you 'da dad!

Gooder than Anything

Hey Dad,

I don't mind telling you that being a dad is hard. In fact, I'd liken it to peddling up Pike's Peak. There's a lot to enjoy along the way, but if you stop peddling for even a moment, you're doomed for a world of hurt.

And if fathering wasn't hard enough, there's also husbanding, which is something akin to trying to juggle pudding. It might be fun to watch, but it sure ain't easy—and can get mighty messy.

"Familyman-ing" is so—daily. You wake up and it's there. Walk in the front door after work and it's there. It never rests. And just when you think everything is okay, everything turns to not okay.

And you know what? All of us dads are in the same boat. I was reminded of that as I was talking to my friend OBB (I scrambled the letters to protect his identity). He shared how he "felt" as though he had been pretty much a failure in the Familyman department lately.

I know he thought that I have it all together—I am the Familyman, after all—but I set him straight by telling him he was looking at the biggest loser-dad of all. I think he was shocked but enjoyed hearing that I also struggle with teenagers with bad attitudes, with instilling godliness into my children, and with spending vital time on stuff that doesn't matter squat.

The truth is, we are all in the same dad boat together. This Familyman gig is hard. Anyone who tells you otherwise is either a bold-faced liar, a delusional lunatic, or—not a dad!

But here's the deal: it may be hard—but it is good. How good? To quote a couple of my boys, it's "Gooder than anything."

Don't forget that. Write it out, and post it on your computer, dashboard, or bathroom mirror. And keep at it; don't give up or throw in the towel, and never ever think you're alone in the struggle.

I know it's hard, but it's gooder and besides…

You 'da dad!

Get 'R Done!

Hey Dad,

It's a chilly morning here in Northern, Indiana. Just the way Hoosiers like it. The tractors are in the field, the leaves are just beginning to change, sweatshirts are out of storage, and the apple cider is flowing. Ahhh—there's nothing better than autumn in Indiana.

There's just something about fall that feels "familyish." Fathers pile up leaves and kids jump in them, marshmallows are roasted over campfires, and tractors pull giggling children on hayrides.

Maybe it's the change in temperature or the fact that it gets darker earlier that drives families inside to light candles and snuggle under blankets. Whatever it is, autumn is one of God's greatest gifts to dads and their families.

But it goes fast.

A couple of weekends and it's gone.

So, Dad, if you're planning to have a campfire, get it done. If you're planning to pick pumpkins at a pumpkin patch, get it done. If you see your children raking leaves into a pile, show them how a pro does it. If your wife wants to go to a fall festival, go. If you're thinking it would be fun to take a hike in a park, do it.

Autumn is here, but it won't last long.

Get 'R done!

You 'da DOG

Hey Dad,

We're almost home. We left sunny, green Florida behind and are now in gray, leafless Indiana. Ahhh, God's country. Along the way, we passed through the peanut capital of the world, cotton fields, and learned that Georgians call shopping carts "buggies."

While we've been gone, a little dilemma has arisen that calls for the family watch dog to bare his teeth, stand his ground, and growl. I am that dog. It's my job as 'da dad, to guard what comes into our house (or RV) and into my children's minds and hearts—which isn't always real popular.

The issue in question is the latest Disney/Pixar adventure. Since we hardly ever go to movies, the kids and I have been anticipating its release in hopes that it would be one we could go see.

But as the family watchdog, I never assume that everything that hits the market is suitable for my children. And, after a little investigating on a reliable website, we found out that this film might not be the best for children. The kids were bummed and frustrated. After all, millions of kids are going to see the movie.

I carefully explained how it is our job as parents to guard what goes into their hearts whether they like it or not and that I would reassess after I viewed the movie. I confess that I was a little bummed, too. After Finding Nemo, I assumed their next one would be fun too.

Now maybe you're saying to yourself, "What's the big deal? It can't be that bad."

My answer to that is, "It is a big deal, and it might not be THAT bad, but it might not be appropriate for my children. And, yes, it is a big pain, and people WILL think we've gone overboard, or are backward and prudish.

But you know what? Guard dogs don't care what others say. It's my responsibility, and I'm going to do it.

It's your job too, Dad. Whether your kids like it or not, your job is to protect their hearts. So do it. It's your job to sift through all the stuff that can go into your kids' heads. That includes books, magazines, videos, music, activities, friends, and everything else that you can think of. And here's a hint. If everyone else is doing it, beware.

So give me a growl and stand your ground.

You 'da watchdog!

295

Leaf Jumpers

Acts 13:44-52

Hey Dad,

Northern Indiana is gorgeous. The weather is warm, the sky is blue, and the trees are bursting into color. I love this time of year-the crisp temperatures, the smell of burning leaves, hayrides, and campfires.

The only problem with the season is that it is way too short. Whereas summer and winter stretch on for months, autumn sprints past. One day the leaves start to change, and the next thing you know the trees are bare and…it's CHRISTMAS!

For dads, the season is even shorter. I mean, summer was great. If I forgot to catch lightning bugs with my kids in June, I still had July AND August. There were four glorious months to procrastinate. Not so with fall.

There are leaf forts to make, pumpkins to pick, and bulbs to plant. It all has to happen in the next few weeks. If for some reason I'm feeling exceptionally lazy or put out, I'll miss my chance.

Even this morning, I noticed more leaves on the ground. It's only a matter of time before the kids ask to make a jumping pile. Boy, you should have seen the leaf forts and piles I used to make as a kid. What am I saying? You made them too. We dads need to pass on those trade secrets to the next generation of leaf jumpers.

Three weeks max. That's it! If we don't do it now, we won't get another chance this year…who knows, we may not get another chance—ever.

I know my kids have been asking about getting some pumpkins. Like any father worth his salt, I've put them off with the pat answer, "We'll do that soon." Well, you know what? Soon isn't good enough.

I need to get off my derrière, load the kids in the van, and head over to the local pumpkin patch. I need to pop for a couple glasses of apple cider or caramel apples. I need to get out the rakes and help the kids make the biggest, whoppin' leaf pile in Northern Indiana. I need to stuff scratchy leaves down their shirts and let them do the same to me. I need to walk with them through crunchy leaves and sit around a campfire singing songs.

I need to do all those things…YOU need to do all those things…and we've only got a few weeks to do it.

So…on your marks, get set, GO!

You 'da dad!

I Love Being on Team Dad

Acts 14:1-28 (sorry, this is a long one) | **October** 18

Hey Dad,

I love being a dad. I'm not talking about loving everything that comes with fathering at this moment, but more the love of being part of the group of human beings who call themselves DADS.

I see them wherever I travel. Recently, at the airport, I saw a dad saying goodbye to his twenty-something son. I could tell he was trying hard to hold it all together. I watched as the father looked on as his boy walked down the long hallway to catch his plane. His eyes were wet, and I could feel his emotion as he stood there.

I wanted to get his attention and say, "You 'da dad," but I was afraid of interrupting the moment.

Just this last weekend as I was driving in northern Michigan I spotted two cars alongside the highway. It was obvious that someone was having trouble and had called for help. When I got close, I saw a teenage boy standing beside the car as his dad lifted the hood of his car.

My heart swelled, and if I'd had a few more seconds, I would have rolled down my window and shouted, "YOU 'DA DAD!!" Looking in my rearview mirror, I knew the dad already knew that. He was doing what he was created to do—be a father.

All that to say, I love being a part of Team Dad. Everyday I'm encouraged by dads just like you who are doing the best they can to love their families and train their children. But we need each other, and that's why I do what I do.

But truth is, I can't do this job all by myself. There are bunches of dads who need your encouragement and insights as they face situations that you may have already faced yourself. That's why we've just added a brand spankin' new Familyman Forum* to our website: so you can share your thoughts...or ask questions, seek advice, or just be reminded that you're not alone in fathering.

So, Dad, thanks for being part of the team—you make me proud. Hey, and if you ever find yourself fixing your son's car along the highway, you just may hear a loud voice holler, "YOU 'DA DAD!!"

You 'da dad!

Finding ET

Acts 15:1-12

Hey Todd,

"The other night, I was on the computer researching something, I don't remember what. My 6 year old came down before bed looking for his "E.T." (what he calls his blanket who actually according to him has a personality and is alive, he can't sleep without him). He saw I was on the computer and said "Dad, can you help me find E.T.?" I'm not sure why, but I emphatically said "Sure!" and started looking with him.

Later on that night, my wife said while she was tucking him in, he mentioned to him who initially when he came down to ask me to help him find his "E.T." that he thought I was going to choose the computer over his son, but instead I chose him. "Whew!" That was a close one. He is only 6 and can already conceptualize where I spend my time and where I prioritize things. Thanks for the reminder."

~ Kirby

Ike and the Pirate Tooth

Acts 15:13-35

Hey Dad,

My son, Ike (6), lost his pirate tooth. About four years ago, Ike bashed his mouth on the fireplace, and one of his upper front teeth was damaged and turned black. What made it worse was the way he smiles for photographs. He does this weird smile where he curls back his upper lip making him look like a big, blond-headed rodent, exposing his dead tooth. It was so obvious that I tried to distract him when he looked at pictures of himself.

Then, one day he pointed to a picture of himself and the black tooth and said, "Neat, you can see my pirate tooth." After that, he and I proudly referred to his tooth as the pirate tooth. That was...sniff, sniff...until last week when he lost it. The tooth sits on my dresser in a plastic baggy. I'm going to frame it along with a picture of Ike smiling his rodent smile and put it above my dresser.

Every time I see the tooth in the bag, I feel a lump rise in my throat. I project myself 40 years into the future standing beside my dresser looking at a faded picture of Ike and his pirate tooth. I'll miss that little rodent smile and energetic boy with his pirate tooth.

Then, I'll remember how Katherine used to sit in the chair in our bedroom and read out loud to herself, how Abe would traipse around in his skin-tight Superman underwear, and how Sam would wag his tongue and make this really loud, goofy noise. I'll wish then that I could go back and experience one of those times again...but I won't be able to.

We dads get one shot at enjoying today. That's it. In 24 hours, today will be gone...forever. So that explains my urgency in last week's email and why I write so passionately. I know that what we have today can be taken away from us just like that (snap).

So Dad, wring every ounce of today out of...today, like water from a towel. Don't waste it on TV, working late, or something that won't matter. Spend it on...THEM.

You 'da dad!

I'm a Criminal

Hey Dad,

Hope you've had a better week than I have. First, there was the news of Michael Jackson's death and then…I can barely say it, there was my run-in with the law.

I was on a routine pizza run when a police car flashed its lights and pulled me over. In my mind I ran down the checklist and knew I hadn't broken any laws and was a little shocked when the officer said, "Your license plate tags have expired."

We're usually on top of those things and later found out it was because of our personalized UDADAD plate. With my registration and driver's license in hand, the policeman went back to his car and returned a few minutes later and said, "Can you step out of your car; I'm going to have to impound your vehicle?"

"You're kidding me?" I said nicely as I stepped from the car.

"No sir. And could you face the car and put your hands on top of your head?"

"You're kidding me?!" I sputtered again.

"I don't know you or what you might have in your pockets," he answered.

"Well, do it fast because someone might see me!" I squealed.

Fifteen minutes later, my car was loaded on a tow truck and I stood holding three pizzas and a gallon of milk waiting for my wife…humiliated beyond all reason.

Just thought you'd like to know, in case you don't like associating with criminal types.

That incident, combined with Michael Jackson's death has thrown me for a loop. It isn't so much that I was a MJ fan as much as it is a sad ending to such a sad life. It was also a reminder that what really matters most is not what happens in this life but the next. MJ feared death and yet he could not avoid it. In fact, all his fame and fortune doesn't matter squat now.

I mean, we can have camp outs, catch lightning bugs, celebrate kid's day, and have tea parties and pillow fights, but if we do not prepare our sons and daughters to stand before God, we will have let them down and doomed them and us to an eternity of regrets.

Dad, it's not your wife's job, the church's job, or your pastor's job…it's YOUR job. That's why I plan to spend more time than usual talking to my family about the Bible, God, Sin, and how Jesus came to make a way for us to enjoy all this good family stuff FOREVER.

So Dad, do what's eternally important…and make sure your license plate hasn't expired.

You 'da dad!

I'm Sick, So This is Short

Hey Dad,

I'm sick, so this is going to be short. In fact, I'm going to forgo my usual witty remarks and just say, "You guys bless me." I was over at the Familyman Forum when I read this post from "sjvnync" (I'm guessing that's not his real name). It spoke to my heart, and since I'm sick, it's an easy way to fill space.

"Guys, I am a dad of 7, well 6 now. I took my 20-year-old to Air Force Basic training today—Wow! I haven't had a flood of emotion like that since they were all born. We have the 20(b), 14(g), 12(b), 7(g), 5(g), 4(b), 2(g) and I love them all, as I am sure you all do.

"I felt regret, more than anything else, as I drove away today. I can remember being mad at the failures to perform his schoolwork, mad at the failure to do his chores, mad at all the times he let me down—now I am mad at me for spending so much time being mad.

"I had to write something to help heal my failures of recognizing his failure so much. Dads, please hold them close while they are with you. I wish I had some time back to 'do over' again."

Thanks, sjvnync; I needed that. I'm guessing (although my head is a little cloudy right now) that a bunch of other dads need it as well.

I gotta go blow my nose. Love those kids of yours, Dad.

You 'da dad!

One of Those Not Days

Hey Dad,

We didn't choose the Familyman motto just because it had a good ring; we chose it because it's the truth: "I'm a pretty good dad—except when I'm not."

Yesterday was one of those not days for me. It started out good. We had a somewhat meaningful family devotion time, the kids got started on their chores, and I jumped onto the computer to take care of some Familyman details. It looked to be a good day of fathering.

As I typed away, I heard a rather heated exchanged between two of my children. I didn't pay much attention until I heard my wife's voice, a seemingly disrespectful comment, and then a loudly closed door.

Boom!—I was on the move. Actually, if I hadn't blown it, I think it would have ended with an explanation and some fatherly instruction.

Instead, I pushed open my son's bedroom door, and my son, who was on the other side of the door, pushed back, thinking I was his upset brother. The combined forces slammed my glasses into my eye, causing a fair amount of pain—and at the same time detonating a nuclear warhead, causing a combination of Sergeant Carter and Attila the Hun to appear in my place.

I hollered until my son was in tears. But that didn't stop me; I yelled, ranted, and lectured up a storm.

If it wasn't for the broken look on my son's face, I might still be hollering. But the look in his eyes showed me I had blown it big time and the storm in my heart blew out.

"I'm so sorry," I apologized, "You didn't deserve that."

I hugged him tight and asked his forgiveness. And you know what? He forgave me.

"Do you know how much I love you?" I asked, excepting him to say, "No, I don't."

But instead he said, "Yes."

"Do you know how much I like you?" I asked, assured that he would say, "Not much."

"Yes, I know," he said softly.

We hugged some more, and this morning during family devotions I apologized to the entire family for my lousy "dad-ing."

And once again—life is good. And the truth remains: I'm a pretty good dad—except when I'm not.

So dad, maybe you, too, had a not day yesterday or the day before. Let me encourage you to make it right today. They need you to, and you'll be glad you did. After all...

You 'da dad!

302

Feeling Popeye-ish

Acts 16:22-30

Hey Dad,

There are times in a dad's life when he feels somewhat Popeye-ish. You know the routine: Popeye is getting thumped by Bluto, when suddenly he announces to everyone watching, "That's all I can stands, I can't stands no more." He pulls a tin can of spinach from his shirt, the music plays, he swallows the contents, and wham-o…Bluto's on the run.

Like I said at first, I'm feeling a little Popeye-ish. I've reached my limit, I've hit the wall, I'm in the vise-like hold of Bluto—all because my kids are driving me nuts. I was outside two nights ago working around the house and could hear their sweet, angelic voices screaming at each other like deranged killers.

They had made even larger messes out of my big construction mess, and when asked to clean up, I could smell their stinkin' attitudes from across the yard.

"That's all I can stands, I can't stands no more," the Popeye within me announced.

Yesterday morning we had a short family meeting after devotions, and their mom and I told them what was expected from them. It helped a little, but by evening I felt like I was snappier than ever at my little Blutos.

The truth is there are no special spinach powers for dads. Yes, we must rely on and rest in God's enablement. There is no silver bullet, no magic pill, no one bit of advice to swallow and make our muscles bulge and attitudes cease. It's like life. You fall and get back up. You fail and ask forgiveness. You give instructions, re-tell, and then tell again as though they never heard them. You just keep on keeping on.

That said, I think it's time for a little extra something. In fact, I was thinking about writing up a standard for Wilsonliving when I saw over at the Familyman Forum that the question had already been asked about writing a code of conduct.

Yes, we have the Bible which is sufficient, but I was thinking along the lines of 10 things written in blood that every family member knows…I mean really knows. It might be along the lines of how we talk to each other, how we honor each other, or how we obey when asked to do something.

I just know something's got to change.

But I need your help. I'd love to hear your thoughts about a Family Code of Conduct. Maybe you've implemented something similar at your house, have some good ideas, or just feel like me…"That's all I can stands, I can't stands no more.".

From one Popeye to another…

You 'da dad!

303

Praying Tyrants

Acts 16:31-40

Hey Dad,

I was talking to a fellow Familyman from Florida (I like the sound of that) last week, and I could hear the tiredness in his voice. Because of past conversations I asked him, "You being a tyrant?"

Without hesitating, he answered, "Yeah, man."

"Me too," I said. Maybe it is all the busyness and having kids who could care less about how busy I am and who need so much attention. Without thinking I said, "How about I pray for you and you pray for me?"

He said he would, and I have been praying for him since then that he won't be a tyrant, that he will live with his wife in an understanding way, and that he'll love his family.

That's when I started thinking that maybe it's really that simple. Maybe it doesn't have to be through accountability groups and partners (who often just lie to one another). Maybe it's just about two tyrant dads who pray for one another faithfully. Cause don't you just suppose that if I pray (and I mean regularly) and ask God to help my fellow dad not to respond a certain way that God will honor that prayer and help him not to respond a certain way? I do.

So my fellow tyrant dad, can I encourage you to find another dad and say, "How about I pray for you and you pray for me?" And then do it. You know that just might change the world...or at least help a few dads not to be tyrants.

You 'da dad!

The Nicest Dad

Hey Dad,

    I love this kind of letter…and I thought you would to.

Todd,

    I wanted to tell you what happened to me last Friday night. My wife was off with her girlfriends to a movie, and I had kid watching duty. My oldest was over at a friend's house and our youngest was already asleep in the crib.

    My middle 3 children had been begging me for 10 days to carve the pumpkins for Halloween, and I had been putting it off…I am a football coach so the fall is a busy time for me…but even though I wasn't too fired up about carving pumpkins, I relented and we open those 3 beauties up….scooped out the goo, I did my best Michelangelo work on carving the faces, and then we put the candles inside; turned out the lights and lit them up. The kids were fired up and very happy with their creations….we then took them outside and put them on the front step to scare Mom when she came home.

    Then we hit the tub and went downstairs to watch a Little House on the Prairie episode. After the show I put the 3 kids to bed.

    As I was leaving my son's room after prayers and story-time…he grabbed me…gave me a hug and said "DAD, this is the nicest you have ever been!"

    It just reminded me how important carving those pumpkins was to my son. I almost missed it.

    ~ RK, Pella, IA

    Is being a good dad really that easy? Is that all it really takes? A little effort and time? The answer is……..yes.

    Go be an awesome dad!

You 'da dad!

On Guard

Acts 17:10-15

Hey Dad,

Ever notice that you can't coast as a father?

Even this past week, a friend forwarded me a link that identifies convicted child molesters in any town.

Oh great, I thought, now I have to be on guard even in our sleepy little town.

I get tired of being on guard. I'd like to assume that the world is a safe place for my children. But the truth is…the world is not safe. And if we're not careful, our homes can be just as dangerous.

Think I'm overreacting?

I recently talked with a godly father whose good son has been involved in internet pornography for several years…on their computer. He assumed his son was safe…he wasn't.

Yesterday, I heard a report on the radio that kids are using their cell phones to text-message inappropriate content to their friends about things that we dads would never allow our sons and daughters to do.

I don't even need to mention video games, DVDs, and television. There is a lot of crummy mainstream entertainment that will sweep our children away if we assume that it's safe just because everyone else is watching it or playing it.

Even books can be unsafe. We came across some great history books that my son Ben would love to digest, only to find out there is some offensive content.

Now I could take the easy route and say, "Oh, who cares…how bad can it be?" and let him read away. Or I could say, "No, you can't read that." The first response would put him in a potentially dangerous place; the second might exasperate my history-loving son.

The third route would be to take the time to check it out and do some selective editing or read it out loud with him. That's hard! But that's my job…because I'm 'da dad.

Let me challenge you, Dad, to take a good look around your house and judge how "safe" it is. Then, take the route less traveled…and do what you have to do to make sure your kids are safe. They may not like it—or you—for putting your foot down on cell phone usage, playing certain video/computer games, controlling internet access, or spending time with friends, but one day they will thank you for guarding them.

On Guard!

It's All About Follow-through

Hey Dad,

Boy, it's been busy around here as we scramble to get a few exciting Familyman projects finished up in time for Christmas. During these busy times, it's real easy to drop the ball in the Familyman department.

In fact, my wife pinned me to the wall the other night. It started out as one of those times when she was pouring out her guts to me. To be honest, I just listened, knowing that it had nothing to do with me. Then she said, "I feel like sometimes you say something just to appease me, but then you don't ever follow up on it. It makes me feel like you don't really care about what I think is important."

I felt like a deer caught in the headlights. I just stared at her knowing I had done that on numerous occasions. I always have good intentions. She shares an idea, it sounds like a good idea, and then I say something like, "Yeah, we should do that. How about we start tomorrow...or next week?" Then in the busyness of "me" and "mine," I get sidetracked and forget.

Even as she poured out her guts, I knew I had no excuses and apologized for not following through. "You're right," I said, "I do do that, and I'm sorry."

I got an A+ in apology, but I still haven't followed through. The more I think about it, one of the key ingredients in good fathering and husbanding is follow-through.

I say, "Sure Honey, I'll read that chapter you want me to look at," and then months go by, and I still haven't picked up the book.

I say, "Yeah, let's talk to the kids about that." Still haven't.

I get a D- in follow-through, because in husbanding and fathering good intentions don't matter diddly. It's all about follow-through.

So, my fellow Dad, take a good look at some of the things you may have said "Yes" to but haven't followed through with yet. You may have to apologize, but you certainly need to follow through.

You 'da dad!

Motor Oil vs. Charades

Acts 17:22-34

Hey Dad,

If I were given the choice of drinking motor oil or playing charades, I'd choose the motor oil. With that little insight, let me say that I played charades with my children the other night. It was Ike's idea (age 4).

I didn't want to. Boy, did I not want to, but I put my "wants" aside and said, "Sure Ike, let's play charades."

He loudly proclaimed to everyone that we were going to play and then we did. They laughed, I laughed, and we had a good time.

Now take today. Outside, there is an 8-to-10-inch blanket of pure, untouched snow. Instead of admiring its beauty, all I can think of is that the kids are going to ask me to play in it with them. I'll have to leave the comfy confines of our house, shed my sweatpants, and suit up for toe-numbing snow play. I know that they love it when I go out and tromp around the back yard with them, build snow forts, and have a snowball fight, but to me it sounds about as good as playing charades…in the snow.

Here's my point: fathering never gets easier—ever.

I don't like playing games anymore this year than I did last year. I'd still rather sit inside on a snowy day while the kids go out and play by themselves. When they want to linger and talk in bed, I still want to rush through the routine and get on with my life.

I wish I could say now that every time they ask me to do something, I cheerfully answer, "sure!" but that's not the case. Fathering is a definite act of the will to do what's best. My natural bent is to do what's easiest…and that's not good fathering.

AND it will never get easy. It will never come naturally. I will always have to choose to do what's right.

Bummer.

Enough about me.

How about you? Have your kids been asking you to go sledding, build a snowman, go to the mall, read a book, work a puzzle, build a model, or one of a million other things that kids love to do with their dads? Of course, it's not easy…it may not even sound fun. But you 'da dad! So bite the bullet and do it.

Well, gotta go suit up. We're headed outside for some cold, snow-down-your-boots, family fun!

You 'da dad!

They're Getting to Me!

Acts 18:1-22

Hey Dad,

Being a dad is just plain freaky. Those kids of ours bring great joy and at the same time take us to the point of...freaking.

Right now, I'm supposed to be watching napping kids while my wife and other kids are at a Bible study. Easy job, right? Only problem is they ain't napping. I went up a few minutes ago to find my son Cal (4) grappling with his brother Jed (2). Jed was covered in purple marker streaks that he tastefully applied to most of his exposed skin. Cal insisted that he was not to blame, and in fact, was trying to prevent Jed from doing so...yeah, right.

Cal was already on probation for having 'freaked' at the dentist earlier today. Luckily, I wasn't on hand to witness it, but my wife said it took 3 hygienists to hold him down while filling a cavity (how embarrassing).

But then there's also the joy part which is a close relative to the freaky part. After 'dealing' with my two napping kids, I went in the basement to put spray paint away. Something in the corner of the room caught my eye. It was a little pop-up tent. My son Ike (11) had mentioned something about building a laboratory to me that morning, but I was a little distracted at the time.

Hmm...I growled, expecting to find every tool I owned ferreted away inside. Instead, I found little strings hanging from the ceiling, batteries, books, and half finished projects. It really was a little laboratory and it made me smile. That boy is going to do something special, I thought. Already this morning, he has designed and built a rifle-looking bottle rocket launcher out of a junk night stand that I had thrown away.

As I type, my daughter Kat (13) is taking cake decorating lessons from a girl who comes to our house once a week. She's so excited...but I know she'll create a humongous mess right along with her masterpiece.

That's the way it is with fathering. It's a journey of contrasts. Joy and anger. Masterpieces and master messes. Warmth and frustration. Being under-appreciated and overflowing with gratitude. Looking forward to the freedom of having them all grown up and wondering what we'll ever do without them.

The thing I love best about being a dad is...just a minute, someone's calling me. What? Again!!???

I gotta go (sigh). Jed's out of bed.

You 'da dad!

Feeling Groovy

Acts 18:23-28

October **31**

Hey Dad,

Hope all is well for you in the Dad-Universe. I'm telling you...this familyman thing isn't for cowards. Just about everyday I get emails from dads telling me about marriage or kid problems. I know they feel like they're all alone in the dad-struggle, but the truth is that we are all having marriage and kid struggles. Struggles go hand in hand with being a dad.

Why, just yesterday I had to have a long 'talk' with one of my older children. I was dreading it and wished life could be easy...but life isn't easy...especially for dads. So I walked into the room closed the door behind me and dealt with it. But here's the deal: it wasn't as bad as I expected. In fact, afterwards I'm sure we both felt...better. Because when you "take care of business" it feels good.

It happened again this morning when I decided to take a care of a broken window that had threatened to cut one of my kids to ribbons for the last three months. It took all of about 10 minutes to whip off, and afterwards I felt...good. I know my wife is going to be pleased that I finally took care of "business" and that makes me feel good. In fact, I'd even say I'm feeling groovy.

So you want a little tip? Take care of things. If you have a child that needs comforted, confronted, or just listened to, then do it. Maybe there's a spot on the carpet, a piece of trim, a burned out light bulb, or something else that your wife has asked you to take care of. Do it dad, today or tonight.

Not only will your child and wife like it, but you're also going to be feeling groovy for taking care of business. That's the truth!

Hang in there.

You 'da dad!

Mouse Hunter #1

Acts 19:1-10

Hey Dad,

I have to tell you I'm feeling very manly right now. Not only have I beaten back most of the dreaded fruit flies, but today we caught two mice in one mousetrap. That's right two in one! Of course we got 'em with our trusty, blood-stained Ol' Killer. I've got other mousetraps, but I've tweaked the catch on Ol' Killer so that if a mouse so much as breathes on it—SNAP! I pity the mouse that stumbles upon it.

If only the rest of life were so easy.

Outside of fruit flies and mice, the Wilson household has been in turmoil the last couple of days. If you homeschool, then you know it's because school just started back up, and well, my wife is already overwhelmed.

But look, up in the sky—faster than a speeding fruit fly, stronger than a strong-willed child, able to catch two mice with one trap!—it's me, the Familyman. The truth is I have the power to make or break the atmosphere in our home.

Yesterday, I got off to a shaky start. When my wife needed me to understand, I tried—for about two minutes, and then I told her it was her job and she needed to buck up.

I know, I know, not the right thing to say. If I had been a mouse, she would have thrown me on Ol' Killer right then and there. I tried to salvage it, but the more we talked, the madder I got and the uglier it got.

But after that shaky start, I finished victoriously. It wasn't easy. I had to ask forgiveness and sit and listen (when I'd rather be getting stuff done). And then do it all again and again.

In fact it took most of the day, evening, and night...but we won. Did you read that? We won.

And we won because I flexed my Familyman muscle and made it happen. I didn't give up (although I felt like it), I didn't let my pride or schedule get in the way (as I have in the past), and I took it to the end...the painful end. But we won!

I'm telling you, that's better than vanquishing fruit flies and killing two mice with one trap.

Shaky starts don't matter; it's all about finishing. So, Dad, if your family is in turmoil or if your wife is upset with you, do whatever it takes for as long as it takes; fall and get up, but finish it. Believe me, everybody wins.

You 'da dad!

Take an E-Vacation

Acts 19:11-20

Hey Dad,

Here's a tip I picked up from an automatic message bounce back that I got several weeks ago after I sent out the Familyman Weekly. Actually, I get a bunch of bounce backs whenever one of you goes on vacation or is out of the office. The messages usually go something like this: "I'll be out of the office through next Thursday…if you need to get a hold of me…" You know the ones.

Not that I'm so bored that I read all the bounce backs to keep track of whose on vacation, but somehow God wanted me to see this one sent by one of you. All it said was, "I'm on an electronic vacation and can't be reached until____."

As I read it I thought, "Light bulb." That's a great idea. A vacation from cell phones, texting, Facebook, and email.

So Dad, can I encourage you to take a little break from electronics? After all, your family doesn't want you constantly glancing at your phone to see who buzzed or left a text. They want you to be there with them…ALL of you…no sharing.

You 'da dad!

Mr. Wonderful, the Talking Doll

Acts 19:21-41

Hey Dad,

I stumbled upon something quite disturbing the other day when my family and I road-tripped to the mall. Along the way, we stopped at a mega kitchen store, and that's when I saw HIM.

At the end of the checkout line, there was a box filled with about three dozen little men on key chains. Above it was a sign that read, MR. WONDERFUL.

What kind of insane nonsense is this? I thought. I picked up a smiling little man with a big head and squeezed his hand.

"Have I told you lately how beautiful you are!" he said with a smile. I squeezed his hand again.

"The ball game isn't really that important. I'd rather spend time with you." I squeezed again.

"I seem to be lost. I think I'll pull over and ask directions."

That was it! I tossed Mr. Wonderful back into the box with disgust. I turned away, only to come face to face with another display five feet away of giant Mr. Wonderfuls.

What is this? A plan to make the whole husband population look bad? Someone is going to make a lot of money with these guys, I thought, knowing that every wife longs to hear words like those.

Standing in the mega kitchen store, looking at his used-car-salesman smile, I decided that I hated Mr. Wonderful.

Then the thought hit me: could it really be that simple? Is it possible to make my wife feel loved with my words? I mean Mr. Wonderful only says twelve phrases. He doesn't change the oil, earn six figures, or take out the garbage. All he does is say nice things.

Then another thought hit me: I can do that. I can tell my wife how wonderful she is. I can offer to do what she wants to do. I can even stop and…stop and…ask dir…directions.

Then a final thought hit me: I CAN BE MR. WONDERFUL! You know what? So can you. It might take a little work, but we can do it!

Start tonight. When you get home, wrap your arms around your wife, smile, and say, "I'm the luckiest guy in the world to have you for my wife. I love you."

Then take out the garbage. Let's see Mr. Wonderful do that!

You 'da dad!

313

My Autumn Death Fixation

Acts 20:1-12

Hey Dad,

I've been thinking a lot about dying lately. Not morbid-like—but I feel sobered by how quickly kids grow up, young people get old, and old people die. Maybe it's autumn that brings on the feelings of change and barrenness. It might be because I've been reading a current copy of Reminisce Magazine.

The pages are filled with photos and fond memories of the past. There are stories of young families and old cars, Halloween costumes made from curtains, and Grandma's applesauce cake. The faces look young and alive. Now, most of them are wrinkled or dead.

Even in my own house, I'm surrounded with photos of my children dressed in faces and ages that I can barely remember. "Was Ben really that young...Maggie looks just like Jed when she was a baby...I forgot we did that."

It won't be all that long before my very chaotic and messy home will be quiet and clean, and all the fun things we take for granted will be over.

My son Sam (13) reminded me of one of those things a week or two ago. It was Sunday night, and we were headed over to a family's house for dinner. Everyone was looking forward to the evening, so I was a little taken aback by Sam's comment as we passed in the kitchen.

"Hey Dad," Sam initiated, "the only bad thing about going over to their house tonight is that we can't go to Chico's House of Italian Dining [name changed to hide its identity]."

Now I should explain that we go to "Chico's" just about every Sunday night. It's our family place. We sit around a large table and talk about the fun we've had or are going to have, issues that need to be addressed, and laugh and tease. It's a great place.

In fact, I told my wife a few years ago that I when I'm old and the kids are all grown with families of their own, I hope that every once in awhile we can go back to "our place," sit around the table, and laugh like old times. It gives me a lump in my throat even as I think about it—"Drat you, autumn!"

So all that to say, enjoy your family today, this weekend, and this season, Dad, because one day your house will be too quiet and they will be gone.

I need to go get some Kleenex.

You 'da dad!

Play Ball!

Acts 20:13-27

Hey Dad,

Well, it happened. I knew it would, but still I'm still taken by surprise when our first throw up of the season occurs. It's kind of like the first pitch of the baseball season, the first kickoff of football season, or the first blasted deer of buck season.

I have to admit I had a little trouble identifying the familiar sound of a child upchucking. My first thought was, "Oh, no!" My wife didn't move, and I quickly remembered it's not her job. She takes care of schooling, finances, cooking, cleaning, and shopping; I take care of body fluids.

As quickly as I could muster, I ran into the dark hallway and met the perpetrator heading for the bathroom. It was Maggie (3), who is not as experienced or as "accurate" as her older brothers and sister. This would not be pretty…and it wasn't. Her arms were wet with…you know. Her bed was soaked, and she left little landmines for me to find with my bare feet all over the floor of her room and along the path to the bathroom.

The worst part was the smell. We had eaten breadsticks for a Sunday evening snack/dinner and the smell of garlic butter permeated everything. All that said, it was terrible. She threw up at least eight times during the night. I made a little bed for her on the bathroom floor, and I slept next to her so she wouldn't be alone.

The next morning she woke up as perky as ever, and I was doomed to roam the earth as the living dead. She didn't thank me for cleaning up her mess, didn't appreciate the lack of sleep I got on her account, or the sacrifice I made to make sure she wasn't left alone. Nothing—nada.

But you know what? That's okay. That's what we dads do. We sacrifice, go without, and get thrown up on to boot. It's our job—so bring it on.

So Dad, consider this the first pitch of the throw up season. There will be plenty of action in the coming flu months, so get warmed up and PLAY BALL!

You 'da dad!

Face Your Fear and Saddle Up

Acts 20:28-38

Hey Dad,

After having speaking engagements just about every day for the last two weeks, we stopped for a little R&R (whatever that means for a dad) at Ft. Wilderness Campground in Disney World. After spending only one day in the park, I had half a mind to keep score of how many kids I saw crying or parents losing it (myself included).

You know somehow we dads have fallen under the delusion that for something to be GOOD, it has to be FUN. In fact, I was talking to a fellow dad at the pool who was just about fed up with the whole vacation scene. "They're just so hard," he said referring to his kids.

"Tell me about it," I said in agreement. "But it's the only thing that really matters."

He nodded in agreement and a little while later, we parted ways.

I know dads who would rather not go on vacation and avoid other activities…because it's just too hard with kids. They stay in the safe shallows of their comfort zone and miss the best. They choose EASY and miss the GOOD. What I want to say to them, you, and me is "Face your fear and saddle up anyway."

Sure it's a hard road, but it's worth it, so saddle up anyway. Plan the vacation, have another kid, do a family night, go out for ice cream, go bowling, roller skating, or take them hunting. They may cry, make it hard, and you might even lose 'it'…but it is still GOOD.

Well, I gotta go do some fun stuff. You can be sure that it will be hard…but GOOD.

You 'da dad!

Stuck in the Muck

Acts 21:1-14

Hey Dad,

Today looks to be a good day. The sun is shining, the air is crisp…and my wife is smiling at me again.

I'm telling you it's been pretty bleak around here lately. We were stuck in the marriage muck. I hate that place but not enough to make the effort to get us out of it…because it wasn't my fault!

You see it all started when my wife felt like I cared more about myself than I cared about her. Sure, I had made a few promises…which totally slipped my mind. I was busy…and it wasn't like I was goofing off…I just didn't have time. I said I was sorry.

Isn't that enough? Oh, no. She wants me to FEEL sorry and talk about it with her.

We did talk about it. I said I was sorry.

That's when we slipped into the muck. She wanted to talk more about the details, motives, feelings…and I didn't. So, I hunkered down and thought, If she wants to stay in the muck, FINE. I've tried…but I'm not trying anymore.

The only problem with that is that I was miserable (and so was she). There were moments when I'd soften and think, Okay, I'll try some witty conversation, flash her one of my debonair smiles, and coax her out of the muck. But she didn't want witty conversation and silly smiles…she wanted to talk about the details, motives, and feelings.

NO! I refused. I was not going back there…besides, I didn't do anything wrong. So, the days dragged on, and even though I loathed the muck, I couldn't bring myself to start the process…the long, painful process.

Then God spoke. "Hey Dummy, have you had enough of the swamp yet? It's time to get off your keister and get your marriage back on solid ground."

"Yeah, but I didn't do anything," I answered. "I tried…and she won't…uh…um…okay."

So, last night we talked about the details, motives, and feelings—finally. We weren't completely out of the swamp by the time we went to bed, but this morning my wife rolled over, and I held her…ahh. Solid ground.

Here's the deal, Dad. You may have been in the marriage muck for the last month, year, or decade. Like it or not, it's up to you to start the process. Your wife wants to talk about "it" and re-talk about "it." But, I'm telling you— the solid ground is a lot better than the muck.

You 'da dad!

Take That About THAT!

Hey Dad,

I know this is no shocker to you...but women think funny—not funny, "Ha ha," but funny like, "That's the weirdest thing I've ever heard!"

Take my wife and me for example: her idea of being on time means arriving right on the dot, while I believe you show up at least 30 minutes early.

She thinks the kids need to have baths and showers regularly to be clean...I think once a week IS regular. She thinks you need a bunch of shoes to go with different outfits...I think shoes come in three types: brown, black, and tennis.

I say I'm sorry, but she wants to know why I'm sorry, what I'm sorry about, and how I could have responded differently so I wouldn't have to be sorry. We also have different views on climate control. She turns the temperature knob back and forth on the van constantly adjusting it. I just deal with whatever temperature it happens to be.

She throws out a whole bag of chips because they spilled on the floor...I just scoop them back in, and we're good to go. She thinks that if someone buys you a gift, then it is proper to reciprocate; I think it's more blessed to GET than give.

I bring this up because this past week my wife and I had one of THOSE talks where I finally saw how strangely she really does think. Actually, the talk was about...um...you know...um...uh...come on, you know...THAT.

I was bothered that her thoughts on...THAT weren't like mine. I mean my ideas on THAT are along the lines of "Wa, Wa, Wa." Her ideas on THAT are along the lines of "Ho hum," especially during the exhaustion that comes with a baby.

In fact, she said she feels as close to me when we watch an instructional DVD together about parenting as when we...you know.

In my mind I thought, You're kidding me, right? How can "that" make you feel as close to me as THAT?

But as I thought about what she said, I realized that she really does think differently than I do because God created her different from me. And you know what? I need her differences, AND I need to be understanding of her differences, enjoy them, and love her for them...and so do you.

So, maybe you need to turn up the thermostat for your wife, put your clothes in the hamper instead of on the floor, wait patiently as she talks through another option to a decision, or spend some time doing whatever it is that helps her feel close to you instead of...THAT.

You 'da dad!

Snowsuit Demon

Acts 21:27-40

Hey Dad,

Augggggg. It's awful!!! Sure, I knew it was coming...but..but..but...I didn't think it would come so soon. What? I am trying to calm down...but the terror!! The nightmare has begun!!!!

You wonder what am I talking about? Are you out of your mind?

I'm talking about snowsuit season of course and the mountain of snowsuits, boots, hats, mittens, slush, and hassle that comes with it. Aggggg!!!!

Yesterday, we had our first "official" snow of the season. It was enchanting as the snow floated down covering the ground. It was beautiful, and excitement permeated our house as we doled out 'first snow' gifts and later proceeded to Long John Silver's for our annual first snow meal.

I should have seen it coming, but this morning as I was sitting in the bathroom...er...you know, I heard that familiar swishing nylon sound like the wheezing breath of a demon.

Knock, knock..."Hey Dad, look at me," Maggie Rose (6) said on the other side of the bathroom door.

Without thinking, I cracked the door open to the sheer horror of seeing my daughter in a pick and purple snowsuit and boots.

"AAAAAGGGGGGGG!!!!" I wanted to shout, thinking of the perpetual messes and hassle that the snowsuit heralds. I didn't say that; instead I said, "Maggie, there's not enough snow out there for snowsuits, you can probably just wear your coat." Then I shut the door to...finish.

So I came to my computer to vent, when my little girl reappeared decked to the snowsuit hilt and asked me to push on her gloves, which I did with great force, jarring her body with each thrust. I think she was taken back by the gusto I used because I could see the delight in her snow-frolicking eyes vanish only to be replaced by hurt and tears.

You see, Dad, the horror is not in messes, hassle, or snowsuits...it's in me. That's why I'm writing, so it won't be in you when you see that child of yours show up in a snowsuit, wetsuit, or desert suit. Sigh. Why do I do that?

I've got to go repair some damage...that I caused. You know why?

Because I'm 'da dad.

That Was Yesterday

Acts 22:1-11

Hey Dad,

Yesterday was a hard day. It wasn't because it was Election Day or my birthday—but I sure was a lousy dad.

All week I had been looking forward to the day because we were going to spend it doing fun, family stuff. The plan was a good one: we would get up, vote on our way out of town, eat at Logan's Roadhouse, do some pre-Christmas shopping, and have pizza at home while we watched a family video.

In my mind, I pictured a happy family led by a happy dad. But something went wrong on the way to "happy family day." Maybe I had set the bar too high…but by the time we got home, I was tired, worn out, and could hear the faint hiss of a fuse burning toward a pile of dynamite. The explosion came as the kids were loading their plates with pizza and arguing about their seating positions.

"You sat there last time."

"I did not."

"Did TOO."

"Did NOT!"

Something snapped in me, and I started hollering and saying things like, "I just wanted this to be a fun day for all of us…but you're all so selfish…you ruined a great day."

They looked at me hurt, and a couple of them started crying softly because they had wanted it to be a good day—for me.

You know, I hate the way I act sometimes. Before I sat down to eat, I asked each child to forgive me, but I felt as though I had just crushed my wife and children.

But here's the amazing part…they still loved me. My daughter Katherine lay down beside me on the floor and stroked my side…it felt so good and yet it reinforced the fact that I had let them down. At bedtime, I did my best to smooth things over and apologize again…but I knew they deserved better.

That was yesterday…God gave me another chance today. He won't always do that. One day, way too soon, I'll have used my last chance for good.

I don't have any plan for today. There won't be any special lunch or great video…but I'll just show them that I love them—and LIKE them.

So, Dad, don't know how you did in the dad department yesterday…but I know how you can do today.

You 'da dad!

320

The Best and Worst of Times

Acts 22:12-30

November 11

Hey Dad,

I'm writing to you from sunny Florida. We've camped at Ft. Wilderness, been to Disney World, eaten at the Rain Forest Café, and swam up a storm. And Ike (our 5-year-old) swallowed a stainless steel marble (I have the steel marble now—cool!).

The thing about vacation is that it would be a lot easier if you went alone. Don't get me wrong; we've had a great time as a family…but vacations also bring out the worst in dads.

I was reminded about the universality of this truth as I sat in Pecos Bill's Restaurant waiting for Debbie to return with a tray full of expensive, fast food. As I waited, I observed people.

I was struck by how all the parents around me were barking at their children for a variety of reasons. I'd like to piously say that I was not among them, but I think I had three of my children crying at the time. Way to go, "Familyman."

Fortunately, children are resilient, and they bounced back quickly after I apologized…but a couple of hours later…grumpy dad was back. Why are we dads like that? We pray, we try, but still, we seem to botch it more than we succeed.

If you're like me, sometimes you feel like you're not the dad your kids' deserve or the man your wife needs.

Well, let me set the record straight. You are EXACTLY what your wife and children need. God knew that when he made you their father and husband. The truth is, good dads aren't perfect. They blow it and do things they hate doing…but good dads never throw in the towel. They apologize a lot and keep at it.

It looks like we're headed to the beach today. Man, it's going to be fun. We'll gather shells, dig in the sand, and run down the beach. That said, I'm almost positive that things will get a little ugly at some point too. I mean, you can't mix sun, sand, six kids, and an RV and expect anything less.

But we're going anyway.

So get in there, Dad. Keep at it. Apologize if you need to (and you probably do), get back on the horse, and never take the easy route.

You 'da dad!

Coordinating Underwear Theory

Acts 23:1-11

Hey Dad,

Have you ever noticed that women think differently than men? Of course you have. What I didn't know is that apparently some women match their underwear with the blouse they're wearing. Not long ago, I noticed that…uh…a certain woman I'm married to was getting dressed and her celery green shirt and…uh…her "underclothes" matched.

"Hey, Babe," I said casually, "You match."

Without turning, she said matter-of-factly, "I know."

"Are you kidding me? You mean you actually pick out…uh…undergarments to match the shirt you're wearing?"

"Yep, sometimes."

I must have been laughing about my discovery as I walked out of our bedroom because my daughter asked me why I was laughing. "Did you know mom tries to coordinate her underwear and shirt?" I asked, expecting her to laugh as well…but she didn't.

She looked at me strangely and said, "So do I."

I was stunned. It was obviously a girl thing because I've never even thought about matching my underwear to anything. I can't even fathom why I would.

A few days later, my wife and I were in the airport and this rather large woman bent over in front of me showing the whole world her undergarments. I turned my head away quickly, but not before I noticed that her understuff matched her bright pink shirt exactly. "It must be universal," I thought.

Since then, I've been thinking about the "coordinating underwear theory" (or CUT) and have transferred it to other areas of different thinking between husbands and wives…particularly between my wife and me. Maybe some of the conflicts that arise over the temperature of our house, our priority lists, and the reason she gets overwhelmed more easily than I do is because we just think differently.

But here's the kicker: God wants me to understand those differences and adjust my way of living accordingly. So, if she likes the thermostat set higher (even with escalating fuel prices), I can show my wife I love her by setting the thermostat higher. If she thinks our relationship stinks, and I think otherwise, I prove my love to her by talking to her about our relationship. I love my wife by making her priorities my priorities.

Why? Because of the "coordinating underwear theory." So show your wife how much you love her today by adjusting your "normal" thinking. You know what you need to do.

Oh yeah, and ask her about the "CUT".

You 'da dad!

Battle With Myself

Acts 23:12-22

Hey Dad,

Last night I did battle with myself. It was intense. My wife was meeting a friend, and it was my job to feed the kids. I did that, and then the battle started. I was clearing the table, when I saw a large, sticky spot encrusted with food and dirt under my youngest son's chair.

"You ought to mop the floor for your wife," a voice said. I looked around to see if my wife had said it. She hadn't. I was alone, and the voice had come from within my own head. So I answered myself.

"I fed the kids and did the dishes…isn't that enough?"

Myself responded, "Yeah, but wouldn't it be nice if you mopped the floor so your wife won't have to?"

"Apparently you didn't hear me, because I said I fed the kids and did the dish …"

"I heard you, but you need to mop the floor too." By this time the voice was shouting.

It didn't help that yesterday the pastor mentioned that the same voice told him to clean up the kitchen the night before for his wife. He confessed that he had failed. Now here I was, faced with the same decision. It should have been an easy one. After all, it wouldn't take more than 15 minutes. But then again, I was pretty tired and I fed the kids and did the dish …

And then in a moment of Herculean strength, I forced myself to get the mop, and I mopped the floor. The really weird thing is that I hear the voice often. It encourages me to clean up my own messes, bathe the kids, and (here's a big one) hang up my clothes instead of leaving them in a heap on the floor. Sometimes I ignore the voice and lose the battle; other times I win. And although my wife may not fall on her knees and worship the ground I walk on for doing those little things, I can almost hear God say, "Well done, Dad."

You know, Dad, now that I've mentioned it, you'll start hearing the voice too. Even tonight, it'll ask you to give of your time and energy. The battle will be fierce, but I know you can do it! Your wife may not thank you, but that doesn't matter, because…

…You 'da dad!

323

White House or Your House

Acts 23:23-35

Hey Dad,

Tuesday was a gray, drizzly day in northern Indiana, but I made the two-minute drive to the Milford Fire Department to vote. For months, all shapes and sizes of candidates who had been promising a brighter future hade bombarded us.

Commentators tried to predict the outcome…but it turned out to be a squeaker. If you're the theological type, you're quick to point out that God appoints kings and presidents, and that He will put the man he wants in the White House. All the same, there seemed to be uneasiness about the day, and the question kept whispering in my ear, "What if 'he' is elected president?"

Then I cleared my head and came back to this important truth: What happens in my house and your house is more important than what happens in the White House. Mind boggling, I know, but true.

Our influence on our children and wife is a million times greater than whoever gets to put his pencil sharpener on the oval office desk.

Don't believe me Dad? Let me ask you this: which president was most influential in your life as a child? Carter, Nixon, JFK, Reagan? How did he affect your choices, your moral character, and well-being?

Now let me ask this: how did your dad influence your life? Kerpow! Your dad hugely influenced who you are, for better or worse. If you didn't have a dad, then you were affected by his absence.

It's still the same today. Your influence over your children…and your children's children and their children's children is vastly greater than the future president's influence upon them. And your influence on a few children can change the unknown course of the world.

Why?

Father Power!

Now I don't know if that should make you feel good or scared spitless (maybe both), but regardless, that's the whole truth and nothing but the truth.

So Dad, pray for the winner of this year's election, but remember that what's most important today is what happens in your house—not the White House.

You 'da good dad!

I Died This Week

Hey Dad,

Maybe you didn't hear about it, but I was killed this past week. I was on my way to speak in Los Angeles when American Airlines flight 2405 went down somewhere over the Rocky Mountains.

There was a nice little write-up in the local paper. A short paragraph listed my accomplishments, funeral arrangements, a reminder to purchase your You 'da Dad daily calendars in time for Christmas (gotta like that), and then closed with: "Mr. Wilson is survived by his wife Debbie, and his children Ben, Sam, Katherine, Ike, Abe, and Maggie Rose. They were expecting their seventh child in April."

I know you're not supposed to be sad in heaven, but I feel a lump in my throat and pit in my stomach because I left so much unsaid and undone. All the promises I made to my family are never going to happen now, and all the little things I rushed through or took for granted, haunt me.

I promised Ike and Abe that I'd sleep in their room with them sometime...but now it's too late. I wish so badly that I hadn't rushed through those bedtime rituals with the little boys. I was always in a hurry to get it over with so I could have some time to myself.

Ben and Sam are becoming young men. They need my direction and guidance to prepare them for the time when they will be fathers themselves. I knew I should have spent more time with them, but I never felt like I had the time. "Not tonight boys...maybe tomorrow night," I said too many times.

Now there aren't any tomorrow nights.

Oh, and my sweet girls. I've been a little grouchy with Katherine and Maggie lately. I've brushed off their needs for extra daddy time. Man, I wish I could hug them tight and tell them I'm sorry and that I love them...but it's too late because I'm dead.

The good news is...I didn't really die this week (you probably guessed that already). I just imagined that I did as I got bumped about in a little airplane over St. Louis on Tuesday. Actually, it was good for me to look at my life from the other side. It's a good idea for you too, Dad. It helps us focus on what matters and what doesn't.

So why don't you spend a few minutes tonight, on the way home, or right now...and imagine you're dead. Then, make the most of your "living" time.

Rest in Peace.

You 'da dad!

Use Your Gifts

Acts 25:1-22

Hey Dad,

You probably don't know this, because the liberal news media didn't cover it, but I was recently given a 'major award' for being the "WORLD'S BEST ENCOURAGER." It was given to me by my good friend and familyman Coach Rick. Now I don't know what criteria he used or how he knew there isn't a better encourager, say...in Sweden, but I got the award and that makes it official (see photo).

I was flattered by the trophy and was feeling pretty good about my 'encouragement abilities', even imagining myself flitting about speaking words to uplift discouraged dads and down-in-the-dumps husbands. Then my rose-colored bubble popped as I wondered if my own family would give me the same award.

You see, Dad, the truth is that I AM an encourager, but I don't always use my gift of encouragement on my family. Instead, I point out their failures, remind them of how they let me down, and mumble hurtful things under my breath just loud enough to make sure they hear it. But I'm going to use the trophy as a reminder to me to use my gift of encouragement on my family...and I will (except when I don't).

Here's the deal, Dad; you have gifts as well. You use them at work every day. You have skills in relating to others, solving problems, managing resources, and being nice...but do you use those same skills at home? Sometimes we check them at the door when we walk in from work. Those talents and gifts were given to you by God to build up your family. SO USE THEM at home.

You 'da dad!

We Get No Respect!

Hey Dad,

Dads get no respect. I know this doesn't come as a shocker to you...you're a dad. We work hard to provide a good life for our children, keep them well clothed, provide a warm shelter, and prepare them for adulthood. In response, they cough in your face.

Take this morning. I was sleeping away when I became keenly aware that our youngest was hacking in my face about every six seconds. It was a deep, chesty cough, and I wondered how many days it would be before I got it. Not that it mattered to him. I was his dad...that's all.

It wasn't like I was bothered by his behavior. It's pretty much par for the course for "daddom." His brothers and sister do the same. I've been coughed on, thrown up on, pooped on, and even had my hair used as Kleenex.

I guess I should be flattered by the comfortable relationship that I enjoy with my children, but sometimes I just feel plain USED.

Maybe that's why some dads have opted out of fathering for a more gratifying "profession." After all, at work you're appreciated. You do a good job, work hard, and someone rewards you with a pay raise, a pat on the back, or a gold sticker, AND no one ever coughs in your face or wipes his nose on your hair.

That's why we dads need each other. I was reminded about the power of encouragement when I met with a fellow dad at his office last week.

As we talked, another dad passed by, and the dad I was talking to looked him in the eye and said, "You 'da dad."

Now he might have just been saying that because that's how I close my weekly emails, but there was something encouraging in his voice.

I thought, Wouldn't it be great if dads all across America encouraged each other with, "You 'da dad!" It might counteract the tiredness, the non-appreciation, and the urge to jump ship.

It begins with you and me. Try it for a day with the dads who cross your path.

I'll start ...

You 'da dad!

327

Why Can't She Be Like an RV?

Hey Dad,

Well, we're making progress on the Familyman-mobile III. Last weekend, Merle, the Amish carpet-laying guy, spent a day-and-a-half laying the floor coverings. So far, we've torn out tons of stuff, re-wallpapered, installed the triple bunk bed, replaced or painted the cabinet hardware, pulled up and replaced the flooring, and painted the shower stall trim.

To top it off, even the clear, acrylic door handle on the outside of the coach now glows. Oooh! That's right, my son Ben (14) removed the handle and found that an itty-bitty bulb had burned out. We jumped in the car, ran to NAPA, replaced the bulb, and ba-da-bing, it worked. Just the way I like it: quick, easy fix!

If only my wife were as easy to fix as an RV. It's been a hard week on the home front. It could be because my wife is pregnant and getting larger by the day, making it harder for her to breathe and move. Her energy level is almost non-existent. That could be the reason for her gloominess—or it could be because she's married to me, and often I don't spend as much time caring for her as I do my RV (ouch!).

Have I mentioned how easy RVs are to fix? I mean, you take something apart, fix it, and then it works for another 5 to 10 years. Wives aren't like that. They need you to talk to them. And by talking I don't mean, "So how are things…I see…Well, hope things work out…I'm going out to work on the RV now."

Oh, no. Wives need real talk: the I-need-you-to-listen-and-empathize kind of talk.

Not to toot my own horn, but I can be that kind of husband for one night. But if the next day brings the same gloominess, I want to say, "Didn't I fix you last night? Didn't we talk about that? Didn't I empathize—kind of?"

Henry Higgins of My Fair Lady had it so right when he said, "Why can't a woman be more like an RV?" (or something close to that). But the truth is—they're not. They don't need fixed; they need understanding. They don't always need solutions; sometimes they just need to know that we care. They don't need a husband who tries once and then moves on; they need a man who will sit and talk night after night if that's what it takes.

Is that easy? No way. But I can do it…and so can you.

So, Dad, maybe your wife needs you to sit down beside her tonight and say, "So tell me what you are feeling", and you need to be ready to listen.

You 'da dad!

You Sunk My Battleship

Acts 26:15-32

Hey Dad,

I'll be the first to admit—I don't like board games. I was raised in the '70s. We did TV. TV was easy. We turned it on, plopped down on a bright orange-and-green couch, and watched our favorite people…the Bradys, the Flintstones, and of course, Mr. Rogers and Captain Kangaroo. It was wonderful.

Board games involve setting up pieces, strategy, and THINKING. There are no comforting laugh tracks or singing puppets…just your own family members sitting around a square piece of cardboard moving plastic houses and metal thimbles.

Don't get me wrong. Now that I'm a father, I think playing games as a family is 50 times better than sitting around watching TV…but it still doesn't sound fun. The first thing I hear when someone says "board game" is "bored game."

But yesterday, my son Ben (age 10) asked if we could have a championship board game night tonight. He's got it all figured out. We'll each play a different board game and have some kind of elimination contest until there is only one winner left standing.

You should have seen the look on his face when he asked. He was so excited. Unlike his old dad, he is not a TV kid (he doesn't even know who the Flintstones are). To him, playing a game is about the best family time he can imagine. We roll the dice, move the pieces, and laugh (no sound track this time).

How could I say no? So…tonight we're having a championship board-game match. He's pumped…I'm dreading it.

BUT, I know that once we get started, it won't be as bad as I anticipate. In fact, deep down (really, really deep down), I know that we're going to have a great night tonight. Maybe I'll even print a ribbon off my computer for the champion. Whoever wins will stick it on his bulletin board as a reminder of the fun we had…which will assure future board game championship matches…and my kids will grow up enjoying board games with their own families—not watching some other Hollywood family.

You know what? I would just about bet the farm that your kids would love to have a board game night at your house too.

Besides, misery loves company.
Keep your dice on the board.

You 'da dad!

I Don't Get It

Acts 27:1-13

Hey Dad,

I just don't get it! Sometimes I think I do. I'm just about to grab the brass ring of understanding my wife when BAM, it vanishes, and I blow it big time.

You'd think after years of being married to the same woman that I'd have it down by now, but I don't. Take the other night. My wife was feeling overwhelmed by the future and the upcoming school year. She was uptight and irritable.

Trying to be the husband that I tell others to be, I asked her to spill her guts and told her I'd listen to her.

"You can't handle what I'm feeling," she said. "You'll just want to give solution and won't try to understand what I'm feeling."

"That's not true," I answered. "I'll let you talk." In my head I saw her talking, crying, and resting her head on my big, strong shoulder. After all, I'm her man!

The look in my eye was convincing, and she began to talk.

You guessed it. Before she had finished her third sentence, I interrupted. "That's not true...see, if you would only do this ..."

She stared at me, and I knew I had blown it again. I was close, but I just couldn't keep my mouth shut! Yes, there are times when she needs and wants my input, but then there are times when she just needs my understanding.

I've begun to notice a pattern. She shares, I get defensive, talk too much, and then next thing I know, I'm sitting alone wondering where I got the "jerk" part of my DNA. Maybe I could blame it on Adam...but that doesn't make me feel any better.

The only solution is for me to suck it up, apologize to my wife, and try again. I know she'll be a little gun shy next time, but that's what being a husband is all about. It's proving to your wife and children that you're in it for the long haul.

It's failing, trying, failing some more, and trying some more.

Is it worth all the effort?

You bet.

Is it the same for you and your marriage?

Yep.

You 'da dad!

A Tip from Mr. Destructo

Hey Dad,

Well, I made it. I survived the weekend with no wife. It was tiring, but overall it went well. We ate pizza in the family room, cooked hotdogs over a campfire, and even had a burping match.

The only mishaps that occurred were with Abe, our two-year-old, who, by the way, is a great belcher for his age. He swiped candy from the upper kitchen cabinets, spilled red pop all over the floor, and when I went to check on him during his nap, he had five of his older brother's pocketknives in his bed.

You know, if he was a comic book character, he'd be named Mr. Destructo.

Just a half hour ago, I found him at the top of the steps holding our expensive camera in one hand and a bag of grated cheese in the other. I'm not sure what he planned to do with the combination, but as soon as he saw me, one hand went to protect his back end.

The funny thing is the "Mr. Destructo" taught me a valuable lesson last night. I was in another room when I heard him run up to his mom who was typing on the computer.

"Mom...Mom...Mom," he repeated.

"What do you want, Abe?" she asked as she worked.

"Mom...Mom...Mom."

No kidding, this went back and forth for at least a minute. What struck me was that although Debbie was listening, he knew she wasn't really listening because she wasn't looking at him and was still typing. He wanted eye contact.

That's really the secret of listening—whether you're listening to your wife talk or one of your kids. I've tried to fake it. Matter of fact, I just did it ten minutes ago as my oldest son was describing in great detail some complex trampoline maneuver.

"Yeah, neat, Ben...cool...keep at it...uhh...yep."

How pathetic. I feel ashamed when I think of how excited he was to tell me and how the only thing I wanted was for him to stop talking.

How about you, dad? How are you doing in the listening department?

You 'da dad!

Thunderstorm Thanksgiving

Acts 27:31-44

Hey Dad,

Just wanted to drop you a quick line before Thanksgiving weekend arrives. The temperature has dropped here in Northern Indiana making it feel a little more Thanksgiving-ish. It certainly didn't feel like that yesterday.

Yesterday felt more like a warm, spring day. In fact, we had thunderstorms. Last night as I was turning off lights and locking doors I was surprised by the flash of lightning and boom of thunder that rattled the old windows in our house. Two seconds later, I heard the pitter patter of little feet running down the hallway.

With my youngest sons Cal (4) and Jed (2) in my arms, I walked them back to their dark room, promising to lie between their beds on the floor for awhile. And there I lay, using a teddy bear as my pillow, wondering if the floor always felt that hard and calculating how long before I could creep back to MY bed unnoticed.

Actually, I was feeling a little perturbed by the whole situation until I felt the odd sensation swoosh over me that one day I would miss doing this. Then I prayed, "Thank you God for thunderstorms and for little boys who need their dad."

On that uncomfortable floor, I spent time thanking Him for so many things that I tend to take for granted. Maybe it's ironic that it happened this week of Thanksgiving…but I should do it more often. It's just that things get so busy and crazy that I forget. But then God graciously sends a thunderstorm and two frightened little boys to remind me of what's important.

So Dad, you may not have a thunderstorm tonight, but tonight spend a few minutes lying on the floor of a child's bedroom in the dark…thanking God for the great privilege of being a dad.

Happy Thanksgiving…you 'da dad!

Show Up and Stay in the Game

Hey Dad,

Just wanted to wish you a Happy Thanksgiving as you enjoy one of the best weekends of the whole year. I also want to get you thinking right for the next few days.

Thanksgiving Day

The temptation is to kick back and relax and let your wife do everything. Fight the urge, and think 'helpful' thoughts. Help tidy up the house if you have company coming over. Get the little kids dressed, ask to run any last minute errands your wife may have, or keep the kids busy while your wife putters along.

Even when the ball is on the 3-yard line and the game is in triple overtime, don't forget that above all...YOU 'da Dad!!!

Black Friday

This is the day the horses are let out of the starting gate for Christmas. Insist that your wife gets some fun Christmas shopping in and then meet her for lunch at a fun family restaurant. I know the lines will be killer long...but who cares?! There's nothing better than enjoying the hustle and bustle with your family.

The afternoon is also a great time to play a little touch football, put up a few Christmas lights, do a little deer hunting, or watch a holiday movie or DVD. The important thing is to avoid 'real work' at all costs.

Red and Green Saturday

I don't know about your family, but my family will be going to harvest the Wilson family Christmas tree on Saturday...our annual after Thanksgiving tradition. We have high hopes but usually end up mad at each other. This year is going to be different. I'm going to can my agenda and concentrate on family fun, not the task at hand.

That night, we'll get out the family heirlooms and decorate the tree, enjoy its splendor, and watch an old Christmas television classic.

I'm telling you, Dad, this is the best weekend of the year, and all you and I need to do...is show up and stay in the game.

Happy Thanksgiving!

We Gather Together

Hey Dad,

I've been feeling pretty thankful—not just for the usual stuff of having a job, good health, and a roof over our heads, although I'm deeply grateful for all that stuff.

I've just been feeling especially thankful for all the chaos, commotion, and pandemonium of my house—that is, when it's not driving me insane. I'm not sure what's come over me, except that I was lying in bed the other night and a wave of "I'm running out of time" swept over me.

I've always been aware that my children aren't going to be around my house forever, but that night, as I lay there, it hit me that it's going to be a whole lot sooner than that. My sons, Ben (15) and Sam (13), probably won't be around in 5 to 10 years. That's it. I have shoes older than that. I can barely imagine coming downstairs in the morning and not see them sitting at the table or on the couch reading their latest book. A few more years beyond that and Katherine won't be making crafts and messes in her room. A few years after that, Abe and Ike won't be leaving my tools scattered around the garage anymore. I could go on, but I won't. Instead, I'm going to be thankful for:

-unrelenting messes

-constant chaos

-clutter galore

-fighting and bickering

-bad attitudes

-noise

I almost wrote "unending" hard work, but one day it will end, and I will miss it. I already do, just thinking about it. So, my fellow Dad, can I encourage you to take three minutes and give thanks to God for all the stuff that annoys you now and will all too soon be over.

By the way, I'm thankful to be your friend.

You 'da dad!

Christmas Starting Gate

1 Chronicles 16:8-36

Hey Dad,

The kids just ran down to my office to announce that it's snowing. That makes it official—the first snowfall of the season. Perfect timing. Here we are arriving at the Christmas starting gate, and God is gracious enough to send a little snow. It always feels like Christmas starts right at the end of the Macy's Day Parade. You do watch the parade, don't you? I'm not referring to one of the imitation Thanksgiving parades that take place in Hawaii or California. I'm talking about the New York original.

Talk about great father/kid time. The kids love the marching bands, floats, and gigantic balloons (mute the commercials, of course). We'll wrestle on the floor and eat donuts or pecan rolls. Afterwards, we'll go over the river and through the woods to...the Wilson Thanksgiving.

The day after, we'll go to the mall and drink in the Christmas sights and sounds as we are crushed by the masses of people. Then—oh boy, I can hardly wait—on the weekend, we'll go cut down our Christmas tree.

You want a great piece of advice, Dad? Take your family to cut down a real live Christmas tree this year. If you have an artificial tree, give it the year off and get a real one. You can bet it will be a whole bunch uglier, but you'll make a ton of memories going to get it.

Gotta go! There's first snowfall "stuff" to do.

You 'da dad!

It's All About Tools

Psalm 8:1-9

Hey Dad,

The way I see it, tools are important to dads. Now, I'm not talking about drills, wrenches, and hammers. I'm talking about the tools that make fathering easier.

For example: pillow fights. I'd forgotten how powerful a tool it is in the old dad tool shed until the other night. I was dog-tired and felt about as energetic as a slug. We had just eaten dinner when my son Ike, who has seemingly limitless energy said, "Hey, Dad can we have a pillow fight tonight? We haven't had one in a really long time."

Everything in my body, soul, mind—and all the other parts—wanted to say, "Not tonight, Buddy." But I knew I had already used up my entire "Not tonight, Buddy's" for the next couple of years. "Sure," I said flatly.

Twenty minutes later all the kids were whapping the daylights out of each other and me. It was a great time. I'm telling you, dad, it's about the tools. I didn't have to do anything except pick up a pillow and whap! The good times followed and the fun took care of itself. I love those easy-to-use tools that help me be a good dad—and the easier the better.

That's why I like the Thanksgiving jar that I tried last year. All I did was stick a jar along with a pencil and some scraps of paper on the table and gave the instruction, "Write down things you're thankful for." It worked and for a whole week we all thought about the things for which we are thankful.

It's really the reason behind our Family Advent nights, too. One night a week for the four weeks leading up to Christmas, we gather in the family room, do an easy craft, read a Christmas story and a portion of the Bible, and then eat a fun snack and drink sparkling grape juice.

My kids think they're the best nights of the entire year and look forward to them about as much as opening presents on Christmas morning. That's because the tools sure help, Dad.

In fact, that's the reason we've placed a Family Advent Guide on our website and offer ready-to-make advent crafts, Christmas books, and the You 'da Dad Daily Calendar. I want you to have the tools you need to help you be a great dad. And they're all certified as easy.

You 'da dad!

"I a Good Boy?"

Hey Dad,

It's amazing how much my son, Abraham (3), has taught me.

The most recent lesson came this past week. It wasn't particularly funny or spectacular, but he bared his three-year-old soul and revealed to me a deep need of his and every child…including yours.

Let me set the stage: Abe was in trouble, and I started yelling. I wasn't screaming-yelling, but it was obvious from the tone of my voice that I was mad. After the yelling part (which was wrong of me), I got control, disciplined him, and then explained how he had disobeyed and acted foolishly.

As I was wrapping things up, he whimpered softly, "I a good boy, Dad?"

I knew from the tone in his voice that our relationship felt shaky to him.

"You sure are a good boy, Abe. You're a great boy," I affirmed. Then I hugged him and kissed him, and he ran off to play. The thing that troubles me is, he's asked that a lot lately…"I a good boy, Dad?"

It usually comes after I've disciplined him or he's gotten in trouble. It's his way of saying, "We're okay? Right, Dad? You still like me, don't you?"

The more I think about it, the more I am convinced that every child wants to hear from his dad, "You're good."

I know it works on me. The old guy I have breakfast with each week often tells me, "You're a good boy." Now I wouldn't tell him this, but I like that. And when my wife threw her arms around my neck last week and told me that she thinks I'm great…I really liked that!

That's because everyone needs to hear the words, "I think you're good." Your kids and your wife need to hear from your mouth, "You're a good boy (or girl)." They especially need to hear it when they're not acting good…because it's not based on their behavior; it's based on our loving them no matter what.

I've been putting this into practice, not only with Abe, but also with my other children. When I say goodnight, I also add, "I think you're a great kid." As they play, I come up behind them, rub their head, and say, "You're a good boy." They don't say anything back, but I know it's important for them to hear.

So, Dad, tell your children, and your wife, today or tonight, "You're a good boy (girl)."

You 'da good dad!

337

What the Doctor Ordered

Psalm 100:1-5

Hey Dad,

It's another blah day here in northern Indiana. It must be all that global warming that's making it so cold. I keep thinking that the sun's gotta shine and it's gotta get warmer one of these days, but it's just rainy and cold every day.

I think it's starting to affect my mood. I feel cold, gloomy, and Eeyorish inside. It doesn't help that every time I turn on the radio some expert is telling me that the economy will get worse, we're running out of fuel, the climate is changing, terrorists WILL get us, and pandemics are around every corner.

I'm telling you, the media is more poisonous to the average father than a truckload of rattlesnakes. The sludge they peddle causes us to doubt and worry and sucks the joy right out of our homes. Instead, we should trust God to meet our needs and enjoy our families today because that's all we got. Because if anything is running out, it's time.

My prescription for a media-antivenom is…a campfire. We had one the other night. We had some scrap wood to burn so after it burned down we cooked hot dogs, roasted marshmallows, and made s'mores. It didn't take all that much time, but something about the fire's warmth and smell slows us all down and highlights the joy of family.

A video night will do the same thing. Enjoy a fun family video (a double feature) or board game, apple cider, and popcorn. Better yet, make or order pizza, get some vanilla ice cream and toppings, fill the family room with pillows and blankets, put on your pjs, start a fire in the fireplace, and bask in the glow of God's goodness.

Because that's what it's all about…enjoying all that God has given you…today.

You are blessed, Dad, and nothing the media can dish out can ever take that away…just don't miss it by worrying about the future.

You 'da dad!

Mr. Wing-it and Mrs. Detail

Isaiah 9:1-7

Hey Dad,

We're all a little disappointed right at the moment. We were anticipating our (very late) first snow of the season and all the fun connected with the first snow this morning. The weatherman assured us that we were going to have some white stuff but...zippo!

Other than that, there's not a lot to report. Everything feels kind of quiet on the home front. We had our first advent night last night, and I don't think I had to spank anyone, which is always one mark of a good family night.

To be perfectly honest, I'm feeling a little blah. Don't know exactly why. Usually I'm on top of my Christmas game this time of the year. But right now I feel...blah. It might be that a few of our kids just can't seem to lick this 'ick' that we've all had. They keep coughing and hacking. Or it could be that I have some Christmas gifts to make and don't feel much like starting them.

But, I think the real root of the problem is that my wife and I are not 'right,' nothing major, just that in the Christmas busyness it's easy for us to 'miss' each other. She's my detail girl who is so wonderful when it involves electricity, eating, paying bills, Christmas gifts, and just about everything else that I take for granted.

The only problem is that...she is my detail girl. Sitting across from her, I can see the wheels in her head turning as she makes lists of Christmas gifts to buy for everyone, Christmas cards that need to be sent, and projects that need to be completed.

I'm Mr. Wing-it who would put all the stress off until Christmas Eve and then like a mad man do all my shopping at CVS or the corner gas station.

That's how we miss each other. I'm thinking fun all day; she's thinking details. Sometimes I like that...sometimes I'm bothered by it...and I act like it. I pout and treat her like she's a stick in the Christmas mud instead of talking things through to help her.

The truth is Mrs. Detail needs her Mr. Wing-it to be Mr. Understanding.

You know, Dad, you might be a Mr. Wing-it OR a Mr. Detail, but at Christmas time, like the rest of the time, you need to be Mr. Understanding.

You 'da dad!

Sometimes It's Hard to Like Them

Hey Dad,

I have a confession to make—I'm having trouble liking my daughter. Don't get me wrong. I love her more than anything—I'm just having trouble liking her right now, and I'm feeling pretty bad about that.

Oh, I want to like her all right. It used to be so easy. I'd walk down to the family room in the morning and sit down beside her and say, "Morning, Sunshine. How'd you sleep last night?"

Even if she didn't answer, she would snuggle up in my arms and hug me tight. Now I come down in the morning, sit beside her and say in the same gentle voice, "Morning, Sunshine. How'd you sleep last night?"

Instead of snuggling, she looks like she might cry and blurts out, "Why are you always teasing me? Can't you just stop!?!"

To be honest, I'm not one of the easily hurt dads who say, "Fine—see if I'm ever nice to you again!" I keep trying. I use my most gentle voice, try to understand, hold her in my arms, and hug her firmly. And she responds. She tells me she loves me, apologizes for the way she's acted, and then—accuses me of making her do everything!!

I know it's a hormonal woman thing and that she is overwhelmed with the changes of life—but she is getting a little hard to like right now. But I know she wants me to hang in there and not give up on her. She wants me to love her, even when she's hard to like. She wants me to keep hugging, even though she pulls away. She wants me to keep saying, "I love you," even when she isn't very loveable. She wants me to hold her hand as we walk to the mailbox, put my arm around her when we stand in the yard, or hold her on my lap when we talk about the day.

I guess that's what dads do. We love our children (or wife) even when…we don't like them very much. We don't just say we love them—we prove it by our actions. Now I know, Dad, that you may have a really hard-to-like child. Maybe he/she has made some poor choices, told you to bug off, thumbed her nose in your face, or told you that she hates you.

It may be tempting to say, "Fine. I quit." But let me encourage you to…keep loving. I know it's not easy—but being a dad never is.

You 'da dad!

Be Vewy, Vewy Quiet

John 1:1-14

Hey Dad,

All is well at the Wilson house. We put up the Christmas tree, decorated the house, cleaned up the mess, and even turned our flagpole into the world's largest Christmas tree …well, Milford's largest.

Tonight, we're having our first advent night. We started the tradition a few years ago to help us focus on the birth of Christ. We'll light some candles, read the Bible, sing a few songs, do a craft, have a fun snack, and read a Christmas story. The kids love advent nights and say they're their favorite part of the season.

Now it's time to turn my attention to even bigger matters …picking out a Christmas gift for my wife. The problem is, I'm just not satisfied with some lame gift card. Sure, it's an okay gift, and she'd use it, but I want to pick out something that will show her how much I love her, need her, and appreciate her.

I feel like Elmer Fudd stalking the perfect gift, "Be vewy, vewy quiet; I'm hunting wabbits."

Here's my plan:

I'll spend a few minutes thinking and brainstorming. 1) What gift have I gotten her in the past that scored big time? …Mental note—stay away from anything that comes in a 3-pack. 2) What kinds of gifts does she like to buy others? Often, what our wives buy others is what they'd like themselves. 3) If nothing comes up in the brainstorming, call her sister or friend and ask them to do a little covert Christmas gift probing.

I know it sounds like a lot of work and effort for one little gift. But believe me, your wife can tell how much time you spent picking out her gift. When you present her with a coupon for a gift of her choice, a gift card, or simply say, "Honey, I didn't have time" …it communicates that you don't care about her. But when you've made something special, had something engraved with a loving message, or gone to great lengths to get that something special, it sings, "I think you're worth it!!"

Now, before you even say, "My wife and I decided not to exchange gifts this year," hear my answer: "So! That's a promise you'll just have to break." It doesn't have to be expensive …just extravagant.

Enough said. Strap on your Elmer Fudd hat and get hunting! No excuses!

You 'da dad! [Elmer]

Ebenezer Dad

Matthew 1:18-25

Hey Dad,

I'm not sure why, but for some reason, I feel drawn to the story of Ebenezer Scrooge. I like the idea of a man who is given the gift of seeing the past, present, and future and changes his lifestyle to avoid what awaits him if he does not.

I'm even thinking about writing and directing my own version (starring either myself or Robin Williams). Ebenezer would be a typical dad who has gotten too busy over the years until he is neglecting the important things of life for things that don't matter squat.

The Ghost of Christmas Past would show him the good old days of being newly married, the birth of their first child, and the joy of buying their first fixer-upper house.

Then, The Ghost of Christmas Present would show him his family sitting around eating dinner or playing a game, wishing that their dad were with them instead of away on a business trip or working late at the office.

With the Ghost of Christmas Yet-to-Come, Scrooge sees himself sitting all alone. His wife, after years of being ignored, has been pushed away and into the arms of another man, his children have moved away and feel little emotion or commitment to their father who had so little time for them.

Scrooge finds out that these are shadows of things that might be if the course he is on is not altered. Now, here's where my version differs from the original. Scrooge awakens, feels bad for a little while and vows to make changes. But it doesn't last, and he continues business as usual.

Maybe it wouldn't be the cheeriest Christmas movie on the market, but it would be a realistic one.

So, I ask you, Dad,—and myself—the following questions: If we were shown where our present lifestyle is leading, would we change? If we knew that our harsh tones and critical attitudes would push our children away from us, would we stop? If we knew that our business travel and long working hours would eventually distance our wife and children from us, would we stop?

Chew on that for a day or so.

We can sponge the writing from the stone...but we may have to make some changes. In fact, I know we will. So, why don't you pick up a copy of A Christmas Carol at your video store, pop some popcorn, watch it as a family, and learn the lesson of our good friend, Mr. Scrooge.

You 'da dad!

Don't Wait

Luke 1:1-4

Hey Dad,

My family is as sick as a dog. Everyone is hacking, feverish, and slumping around. My wife has been hit the hardest, and I've already learned that I'm not very sensitive to HER father's little pumpkin. It doesn't help that I don't feel very hunky dory either but that shouldn't matter 'cuz I'm 'da dad (I hate that I ever invented that phrase).

Anyway, it's been a weird week. Usually, I'm starting to feel the Christmas tingle by now, but I'm not feeling very 'tinglish.' I'm excited about the new Christmas Carol movie starring Jim Carey though. As A Christmas Carol connoisseur, I'm always on the lookout for a new version.

Plus, it gives me another vehicle in which to be a good dad. That's the thing about the month of December; it's like a 'freebie' for fathers. It just doesn't get any easier for us; all we have to do is show up and we get an A+.

Take the movie A Christmas Carol or all the various Christmas Carol movies. All I have to do is watch it with my kids and they feel good, not about the movie, but about ME. They feel loved because I showed up, made a tiny bit of effort, and made sure they ate popcorn.

About the only thing standing in the way of success is me. Sometimes, like right now, I just don't feel like making ANY effort. I make promises to myself of 'maybe later.' But you know what? Sometimes 'later' is too late. I was reminded of that the other day.

I was talking to a dad who spends a lot of time with his grandchildren. Tragically, his six-year-old granddaughter died during heart surgery about 6 months ago. I hadn't seen him in a while and somehow we ended up talking about Disney World.

He shared how he had taken them all to Disney about three months before her death. "We had a great time," he said with a smile. But there were tears deep in his eyes and his lips were fidgety. "I had wanted to do it for several years...I wish I wouldn't have waited."

I could tell his thoughts were of a little girl enjoying the Magic Kingdom and then he said again, "I wish I wouldn't have waited."

So my fellow dad, listen to his words and, "Don't wait." Be there for every Christmas video they watch. Make popcorn every time. Help decorate the tree, string lights on the front porch, do advent nights this year, and plan to do that one thing you've wanted to do for several years now.

DON'T WAIT!!!! And make sure you use some hand sanitizer after reading this email.

You da dad!

343

I've Created a Monster

Luke 1:5-25

Hey Dad,

I feel a little like Dr. Frankenstein who, while trying to make the world a better place, created a monster. At least I haven't been sewing body parts together in hopes of creating a golfing buddy.

I just love Christmas and, like the Ghost of Christmas Present, I drink deeply from the milk of human kindness—and would love to know where he got that really cool wreath hat. My family loves the whole ball of wax—the smells, sounds, sights, and feelings that go along with the greatest month of fathering.

The only problem is that…I've created a Christmas monster. My kids are driving me nuts with Christmas-mania.

"Can we decorate tonight?"

"Can we decorate our rooms?"

"Can we decorate something?"

"When do we get our tree?"

My son Ike (9) is the family Christmas Crier. Every morning within three minutes of waking up, Ike walks up to me and announces, "Only 'X' days 'til Christmas, Dad." He then reminds me at least a couple more times before the sun goes down.

I've tried to put the brakes on and slow them down, but they're barreling down the Christmas highway of life and can't be stopped…and have made snowflakes, paper chains, and anything else that will pass as a decoration.

About the only things that keep me from my putting my foot down and shouting, "Would you give it a break!!" are the twinkles in their eyes and excitement in their voices as they rattle off all their plans for the coming month.

I'm telling you, Dr. Frankenstein would have been hard-pressed to destroy the monster if it had been wearing the contagious grin of an 8-year-old boy or the pixie-like expression of a 4-year-old little girl. Dr. Frankenstein wouldn't have killed the monster; instead, he would have helped him decorate his room.

So here's my plan: We're going to decorate early this year, and I'm gong to enjoy it—whether I like it or not. When they ask, "Can we ___?" I'm going to smile and answer, "Sure."

Dad, maybe the Christmas monster has invaded your house already too (it took over Walmart before Halloween). Instead of fighting it, embrace the monster. Pick up some twinkle lights or candy canes and watch your children's eyes sparkle.

You 'da dad!

Real Men Do Christmas!

Luke 1:26-38

Hey Dad,

Whew, I'm tired. Christmas will do that to a dad…if you let it…and you should. Since Thanksgiving, we've cut down and decorated the Christmas tree, done a little inside and outside seasonal enhancement, and had our first Family Advent Night.

It's been a good couple of days—not perfect—but good. It rarely goes smoothly. Usually, my wife and I are hardly talking by the time we've selected a Christmas tree. She likes nicely shaped trees, and I like "ruggedly handsome" ones, and it's hard to come to an agreement. This year we picked out the best tree ever…and it was only 12 bucks!!

Even the decorating went pretty good by Wilson standards. No heirloom ornaments were shattered, Abe didn't pull the tree over, I didn't have to spank anyone, and the lights worked. What more could I ask for?

Trying 3 for 3, we had our first Family Advent last night. Thanks to my wife's planning and a bottle of sparkling grape juice, it went off without a hitch…I'm beginning to wonder if this isn't the calm before the Christmas storm.

The kids love it all. They love to turn the house lights off and sit in the glow of the Christmas tree. They love lighting another candle on our advent wreath and hearing me read a portion of the Bible and then one of my Christmas stories like Captain Chaos and the Manger Blaster or Cootie McKay's Nativity. They like snuggling on the couch or the big bear chair and watching "The Grinch."

I guess what they like most about the season is the time we spend as a family. They just like doing things…together. Most of the year we're too busy, but Christmas gives us the opportunity to do more stuff together.

Sadly, most of us dads miss out on all the Christmas fun because we get busy with "work" and delegate the Christmas activities to our tired, overworked wives. But when we do, we miss out—and so does our family.

How about you, Dad? Put your work away, dress up in your best Christmas plaid, and get involved. Go pick out the tree as a family, plan an advent night, watch an old Christmas video, pop popcorn, go shopping, sip sparkling grape juice, and enjoy the birthday celebration.

And never forget…
…REAL MEN DO CHRISTMAS!

You 'da dad!

No More Mr. Stop-That

Luke 1:39-56

Hey Dad,

We're in the Christmas countdown.

Last night we had another advent night and then slept in the family room underneath the Christmas tree—a Wilson tradition. That's when I was visited by the Ghost of Christmas Past. I know, it sounds hard to believe. But it happened…kind of.

Somewhere around midnight, I found myself staring into the faces of our sleeping children, thinking about how much they have grown and how one day soon they will be lying around their own Christmas trees with their children. That's when I was visited.

Maybe it was the soft glow of Christmas lights, the quiet stillness, or the sound of their breathing that set the stage for what happened next. But right then I heard the unmistakable voice of the Ghost of Christmas Past…or the garlic toast that I had for dinner.

All it said was, "You've kind of been a creep to your children, you know?"

Ouch.

I thought about it for a minute but knew the voice was right. I had been a creep the last few days. I didn't mean to be…it just kind of happens at Christmas.

Things start out fun, but then the kids get excited and start bouncing off the walls, making messes, and getting hurt, and I become Mr. Stop-That.

You know, "Don't do that Sam…Settle down Ike…Ben, quit acting so goofy…" We dads do it a lot, mostly without realizing it.

After the ghost vanished, I decided to take a Christmas break from holding the reigns so tightly. For the next few days, I'm going to let the kids make more messes, act excited, bounce off the walls and each other, stay up later than usual, possibly break a few ornaments, and enjoy the weeks before Christmas.

I'm going to care less about my little plans and vision of what I think an advent night should look like and let them determine what it becomes. In short, we're just going to enjoy each other and Christmas.

How about you Dad? Do you find yourself being Mr. Stop-That? It's not too late to change. These last days before Christmas, put away your expectations and enjoy your family.

You 'da dad!

Because...That's Why

Hey Dad,

Every year the temptation arises to daydream about wonderful Christmas family times, like decorating the family Christmas tree. In my head, I picture us hanging all the cherished ornaments, laughing as we talk about the events and memories surrounding each one. In my mind, we're all in fuzzy bathrobes and fleece slippers while Christmas music wafts through the pine-scented air and a fire blazes as I sip my steaming coffee...even though I don't drink coffee.

The only problem is—my mind's picture IS NOTHING LIKE REAL LIFE! This last weekend, I spent most of my time blowing fuses, replacing burned out lightbulbs, fixing the leaky Christmas tree stand, and trying to tame the herd of "howler monkeys" who broke heirloom ornaments as quickly as they were pulled from the box.

You'd think I'd have learned by now...but every year the same thing happens. Even tonight, I'm already seeing that picture-perfect family all aglow in Christmas tree lights as we read portions of the Bible...in fuzzy robes...with a cup of coffee in my hand (what is it with coffee?).

Guess what? I'm pretty sure that those same "howler monkeys" will show up tonight. They won't be impressed with my deep spiritual Christmas teaching, they'll spill their sparkling grape juice, and they'll probably argue over who gets to light the Advent candle.

A lesser dad would say, "So why bother with all that Christmas stuff? Why go to all the effort, when they'll just ruin it?"

My answer: "Because."

Huh?

Because. Because—they won't remember the chaos; instead, they'll remember fondly the great feeling of family as we prepared for His "coming." Because—they love sitting around and asking each other which ornament is their favorite. Because—they learn from their dad that family and family times are more important than effort, chaos, and blown fuses (mine as well as the tree's).

BECAUSE—I'm da Dad and THAT'S WHAT DADS DO!

So, I'll try not to get my hopes up for tonight's Advent night...and maybe things will go smoothly...NOT! But we'll do it anyway, and the kids will love it. So, Dad, let me encourage you to go for it. Take the family to cut down a Christmas tree, have an Advent night, or string popcorn with your kids—just like in the good old days.

Why?

Because.

You 'da dad!

Tackling the Big Ugly

Hey Dad,

I don't mean to alarm you, but there are only 17 days 'til Christmas. How about surprising your holiday sweetheart with a pre-Christmas gift?

I heard that moan.

Here's what I'm thinking: why don't you get your shining armor getup on and tackle that big, ugly, half-finished project that has been sitting around your house for the last several weeks?

For about a week, my wife had been looking at a big wreath and ladder propped against the front of our house. Most of the lights were burned out, and I'd been meaning to string new lights on the wreath and get it back in its yuletide position. In fact, I had the new lights for almost a week...but it sure looked cold outside...and I thought maybe I'd do it on the weekend...and so it sat.

BUT...a few days ago when my wife was out of the house, I decided, Enough of this. I'm going to do the wreath...even if it takes all day. Know what? It didn't take all day; it only took about 20 minutes. In fact, I felt so good after beating "the big ugly" that I tackled another little job, which I knocked out in fifteen minutes.

It was so easy, and for the rest of the day I basked in the glory of knowing that I had beaten "the big ugly."

Here's the only problem: when one "big ugly" is defeated, it's replaced with other big uglies, like the half-dark Christmas tree in our living room, the banister rail that one of the kids knocked out, and the garage that needs to be cleaned...again.

I know my wife would feel cared for and cared about if I tackled these projects...and so would your wife.

So, Dad, let me encourage you to give a pre-Christmas gift to your wife. Finish that little job that she's given up hope will ever be finished, discuss the things she's been wanting to talk about but you've been avoiding, or clean that disgusting place that she can't reach.

I promise it will be a lot easier than you think. And you will show your wife once again that you're her "Big Ugly"-defeating-knight-in-shining-armor.

You 'da dad!

The Lesson of the Frozen Keister

Hey Dad,

Tonight we're going to sleep around the Christmas tree as a family. Truthfully, it sounds exhausting. The thought has crossed my mind to let a few of the older kids sleep under the tree by themselves, while my wife and I sleep in our nice, comfortable bed. But I've pretty much buried that idea, especially after the other night.

It was a bitterly cold evening, and there were four inches of snow on the ground. The kids had played outside several times during the day. They'd bundle up, romp in the snow for thirty minutes, and then come in and dump all their snow gear in a pile...only to ask an hour later, "Can we go outside and play in the snow?"

That was all well and good, but as we ate dinner, it all took a dreadful turn for the worse. It was dark outside, and I could tell the kids were going to ask to go back out in the snow—again.

"What's the harm?" I thought to myself. "If they want to freeze their keisters off, so be it."

Then the conversation turned and included my keister.

Without looking up, Ben (11) said, "You know what my favorite part of playing in the snow is?"

A chill ran down my spine, and then he answered exactly what I feared.

"I love it when Dad and Mom come out and play too."

The next thing I heard was my own voice say, "I'll go out and play in the snow with you." Fifteen minutes later, I was outside freezing my keister off right beside my children. They were having a great time throwing snowballs at me and loved it when I shoved them down in the snow and tromped around the yard with them.

OK, here's the lesson of the frozen keister. Your children like you. They like it when you stop doing what you're doing and play in the snow with them. They love it when you leave your lawn chair and get in the pool with them. They love it when you stop doing whatever you're doing and involve yourself in their fun...because it's just more fun when dad (and/or mom) is involved. I'm sure it's some kind of biblical truth.

Dad, you'll get plenty of opportunities in the next week to be involved with your children. They'll ask you to make cookies, play games, go shopping, wrap presents, and sleep under the Christmas tree.

Do it just because they like you and because...

...You 'da dad!

Christmas Checkpoint Charlie

Matthew 26:1-13

Hey Dad,

Do you realize there are only 15 days 'til Christmas?! That means the Familyman-mobile is on the Christmas runway headed straight towards December the 25th. Let's run through the pre-flight check list:

• I'm assuming you already have your Christmas tree and have strung any lights you're going to string.

• How ya coming on your wife's Christmas gift? Since this might be your last Christmas, make sure you get her something that conveys your great love and appreciation (a top quality blender doesn't do that). Stymied by the whole process? Then stop by Brighton.com and pick out something shiny.

• This weekend is the perfect time to sleep around the Christmas tree. I know we're planning to do it on Friday night. We'll get pizza, watch a family favorite Christmas video, have ice cream sundaes, and fall asleep to gentle, Christmas lullabies sung by Nat King Cole.

• Ooo—I almost forgot, I need to call Salvation Army to do a little bell ringing at the local Walmart. The kids won't admit it—but they like it.

• During this economically turbulent time maybe you could bless another family who is struggling. Have the kids pick out a few gifts, take up a family collection, or buy gift cards to Walmart or a favorite family restaurant.

• Plan to help your wife wrap gifts. I know one dad who has a gift-wrapping party with his wife. They have fun snacks, stay up late, and wrap like crazy. Not only is it good husband/wife time, but it allows you to be your wife's knight-in-shining-giftwrap.

• Help your wife crank out those dreaded Christmas cards. Think assembly line—she writes notes; you address and stamp.

• Plan a date night between now and Christmas Eve to take your wife out. Believe me, you both need it.

• Talk with your wife about your Christmas plans and schedule. Remember a couple that plans together—uh—jams together (it's the only thing I could come up with that rhymes).

• One more thing: take the family to a synchronized light/music display. We discovered one in the town next door and went last year—wow. This year, we're going to go again, and maybe we'll enjoy some hot chocolate afterwards. Or better yet, you could find a live nativity or Christmas pageant to attend.

I know this sounds like a lot, Dad, but don't feel like you need to do it all. The important thing is to spend the next __ days enjoying your family, loving your wife, and preparing for God's greatest gift.

Prepared for take-off... 'cuz you 'da dad!

The Old Lady in the Wheelchair

Matthew 26:14-19

Hey Dad,

Hope you're making the most of 'the most wonderful time of the year'. The weeks leading up to Christmas are some of the most powerful memory making days of the entire year, memories that last forever. In fact, that is what I have been pondering the last few days. It all started with a vision.

The other night I was standing at the kitchen sink minding my own business when the scene around me changed from my own house to a brightly lit hallway filled with old people in wheelchairs. It was obvious from the smell, sounds, and sterile feeling that it was a nursing home.

On the walls and around doorways were Christmas decorations and soft Christmas music was playing, although I was pretty sure that most of the people in the hallway were unaware of the season and their surroundings. They were old and placed there either because they needed special assistance or because no one else could care for them.

I didn't recognize any of the people, but for some reason my eye was drawn to one specific wheelchair along the wall. In it sat a little old lady slouched over. Her hair was unkempt and she had food dribbled down the front of her shirt, but interestingly enough the corners of her mouth curled up in a faint smile.

As I looked at her face, I realized it was my daughter Maggie Rose and somehow I knew she was thinking about...me. The music and decorations reminded her of her father who had been gone for forty years. She was thinking about decorating the house, sleeping under the Christmas tree, and having her back stroked by her papa.

She couldn't remember her own children anymore or where she lived, but she still remembered...me. Even as I type this, my eyes are filled with tears and I feel overwhelmed by the love I feel for my family. I don't always show them...but I love them so much, and I know they'll remember that even when they remember little else.

Most likely Dad, YOU will be one of your children's last memories. When they have forgotten everything else...they will remember you. Make these next couple of weeks good ones. Don't waste your time on projects, work, or stuff that doesn't matter. Your family is what matters.

I'm a blubbering mess and you 'da dad!

It's Beginning to Look a Lot Like...

Matthew 26:20-25

Hey Dad,

How's your Christmas journey going? Have you ever noticed how kids always want to involve us in their fun? They want us to play the board game, watch the Christmas video, decorate the tree, and other inconvenient stuff with them. I guess some things are just more fun with Dad involved.

I was reminded of this the other day as we were driving along a snowy stretch of Indiana road. It was the kind of winter day I like—cold and blustery. It was really our first good snow of the season, and I was basking in the holiday feeling of crunching snow, bitterly cold, clean air, and the thought of a hot, chocolaty-warm house.

The kids were enchanted (you gotta like that word) by the swirling snow, and I knew they were hoping it would never stop...EVER!

That's when Ike's loud, squeaky voice came like a slick patch of ice, slamming my winter thoughts into a cold snow bank. "Hey, maybe when we get home, DAD can have a snow fight with us!"

Warm fuzzies, gone. "Why does this have to involve me?" I thought disgustedly. Fortunately, they forgot about the snow fight, and I was off the hook. Score one for Dad. But even as I record my victory...I feel like I lost.

It could have been fun. They would have laughed and loved it. I would have been miserably cold, probably injured, and gotten angry...but I would have loved it as well. But it never happened...because I didn't make it happen.

Even now, my two youngest boys are playing out in the snow on our little hill. I just checked on them and watched Abe (4) tumble upside down and Ike (6) slide backwards on a snowboard. You know, I should go out there and play with them for a few minutes. Yeah, I should...I mean it...they'd like it...I'd like it...yeah, I should do that...maybe later...no, now...yeah, I should.

While I argue with myself, let me ask you a question, Dad, "What should you be doing with your children tonight?" You might play out in the snow (if you have snow), go surfing (if you have surf), take them to do their Christmas shopping, or watch their favorite Christmas video with them. It might be as simple and as messy as making hot chocolate and talking about your favorite Christmas traditions. Whatever it is that you know you should do...don't argue, just do it.

You'll be glad you did.

You 'da dad!

Reindeer Feathers

December 13

Hey Dad,

We had an advent night planned for last night, but I had to pull myself out of the game. I was afraid I might go berserk. It was just one of those days. Instead, we watched The Muppet Christmas Carol, ate popcorn, and sucked on dynamite-stick-sized candy canes. The advent night is rescheduled for tonight.

I'm writing to remind you that there are only 12 days 'til Christmas. Translation…you have less than two weeks left to get your wife a gift.

Okay, here's the deal, Dad. This is one of those window opportunities to show your wife how much you love her. Don't muff it.

What? You say you don't get your wife a present?

Reindeer feathers!

Christmas is a time for giving gifts. Husbands give gifts to wives. That's just the way it is.

Now there are several types of gifts, but for our purposes we'll divide them into two groups:

—The kind that say, "I love you."

—The kind that don't.

For example, a silver ring engraved with the word "Forever" says, "I love you." A Crock-Pot doesn't. Now don't try to convince me that your wife is the practical type and would rather have a new iron than a piece of jewelry 'cause I'm not buying it.

There isn't a woman alive who wouldn't feel loved, cherished, and delighted to unwrap a small token of love from her man. It'll take some doing and you'll have to spend a little money, but your wife is worth it.

Oh, Oh…I almost forgot. If you do stockings for the kids, you need to do one for your wife. Fill it with all kinds of stuff from warm socks, Chap Stick, and her favorite candy to…a lacy little something.

Dad, I'm not kidding about this. I overheard one wife last year talking to a bunch of ladies about the ring her husband bought her for Christmas. She beamed and said, "I always wanted to be one of those women who could say, 'My husband bought this ring for me.' Now I can!"

He scored. Big time.

So can you.

You 'da dad!

0 for 2

Matthew 26:36-46

Hey Dad,

Last night was the first time this month that we played To Bethlehem, and the kids had a blast—and so did we. I know this sounds like a commercial, but if you haven't gotten your own To Bethlehem game, you are missing out.

Last week was not great, however. In fact, if Christmas were like football, I'd say I fumbled on my 20 yard line.

As planned, I announced that we were sleeping around the tree on Friday night. I was so looking forward to the look of awe in their eyes and the fun we were going to have as we stuffed ourselves with popcorn and giggled ourselves to sleep.

That's how it was supposed to happen, but then I fumbled the ball. They complained about things and teased each other incessantly. I tried to corral, calm, and disarm them but nothing worked—until I blew!

"Auggggg," I growled, "Can't you just make this easy? I wanted this to be fun for you. I planned a great night. Do you have to ruin everything?"

They stared at me, knowing they had pushed the old man too far. They tried to be extra good, but now I was bound and determined to make everyone miserable. Oh, I walked through the motions but made it clear—quite clear—that they had ruined the night.

Fortunately, kids bounce back quickly, and the next day, when I announced that we were going to the big city to do some Christmas shopping and eat dinner out, they were all hunky dory. Unfortunately, I didn't bounce back as quickly, and by the end of that night, I was 2 for 2 in ruining special nights.

Here's the amazing part: my kids still had fun.

In fact, as I tucked them into bed that night, several apologized, and my son Ike (8) thanked me for taking them. "It was a fun day," he reminisced.

I had half a mind to check and see if he had a temperature. There's no way it could have been fun …. but the truth is that for them—it was fun.

You know, Dad, our kids have impaired memories. They won't remember all the frustrations and hardships, but they will remember a dad who made the effort—even if he acted like a creep some of the time. Go figure!

So, Dad, get plenty of sleep, lower your expectations, and make the effort. You might blow it somewhere along the way, but take heart; they won't remember that as much as they'll remember special family times and how much you tried.

You 'da dad!

Doing Something Big...REAL BIG

Hey Dad,

Today, I need to call The Salvation Army to reserve a bell-ringing spot at a nearby Walmart. Tonight, we'll watch the holiday classic, The Muppets' Christmas Carol—whew doggie! Being a dad doesn't get any better than this.

Although...I do need to confess that the other night I wavered a little on the "life importance scale." If it weren't for the fact that God set me straight, I could have started down the slippery path of stupidity.

Just a little background—I'm a storyteller. I love a well-told story wrapped around the truth. My imagination is big, and I like creative communication. So with that in mind, let me set the stage. It was a perfect Christmassy night. The tree lights were glowing, the fire was burning—and everyone was in bed but me. Man, it was quiet. I popped in a Christmas video and watched as a very green Jim Carrey's heart grew three sizes that day.

With a cast of hundreds, a budget of millions, and computer graphics galore, and added to that, incredible music and a heart-warming conclusion, I found myself in imagination heaven. To top it off, millions of people have viewed it. That's when I got disorientated and began to slip down the success-driven path of stupidity. In fact, I even lifted up a spontaneous, passionate prayer, "God, can I do something BIG like that—to impact the world?"

God must have anticipated my question, because before the words were completely out of my mouth, he whispered, "You already are—they're sleeping in their beds right now."

I knew he was right. He always is, and later as I lay in bed, I thanked him for reminding me, because I need reminding. All of us dads need reminding. The success-pull is so great. We really think that if we were just given the opportunity to do something big, we could change the world—forgetting that fathering is the BIG, world-changing thing.

So, Dad, if you've found yourself daydreaming about doing something BIG, let me point you back home and whisper, "You already are."

You 'da dad!

Do Some Christmas!

Matthew 26:57-68

Hey Dad,

Right now it looks like a Christmas card outside with some old fashion, big flake, SNOW. I hope this doesn't come as a shocker, but Christmas is gaining on us mighty quickly.

I don't know about you, but I still have a bunch to do before the big day. First of all, I'm way behind the ball on my wife's Christmas present. I know we said we weren't going to do anything for each other this year because of our over-the-garage-add-on...but forget that.

How can a husband NOT give the person he loves the most, a token of his affection? Besides, we mentioned the idea in front of our kids, and they were aghast that we would even consider that. As my son Cal (3) said the other day, "Christmas is about presents." And he's right.

From the first gift that was wrapped in swaddling clothes and laid in a manger, it's been about giving. That's why we do it and why I'm going back on my promise and getting something for my wife...and so should you no matter what flimsy reason you may have for not doing it—and being broke doesn't count. You just have to be more creative.

This year, I'm making gifts for a couple of my kids because I know that dad-made gifts become cherished heirlooms, AND because I said, "I can make that," as I was looking at the expensive magazine model.

Not only do I have gifts to buy and make, but I need to call the Salvation Army to sign up the Wilson Bell ringers for some red-kettle action. If you've never rung a bell at Christmas time, it's a must do.

I also have a stack of Christmas classics that we need to watch, including a couple from the list of Christmas movies you mentioned last week (I can't believe I've never even heard of Emmet Otter's Jug Band Christmas).

Well, I've gotta go Dad, because "I'm busy, busy, busy," to quote a line from a Christmas classic."

So, don't get caught watching the Christmas paint dry. Get out there and 'do some Christmas.' Spend a few minutes (if you haven't yet) thinking about what you can get your wife for Christmas, stop at Blockbuster and get a Christmas video and a box of candy canes, and give the Salvation Army a jingle.

You 'da dad!

...Hacking All the Way

Hey Dad,

I can't believe that Christmas is only eight days away. I feel a little like we're in the final kick, cramming all the fun we can into the season.

It doesn't help that I've had a hacking cough for the last several days. It's the kind of cough that comes in fits, leaving you worn out and achy...and this is not the time of year to be worn out and achy. I still have advent nights to plan, presents to wrap, a treasure box to make for Ike, and special family Christmas outings to lead...not to mention all of the normal workload.

Right now, I'd rather take a nap.

At least we've already got in our "sleeping under the Christmas tree" tradition. It's been an annual thing at our house. We gather our blankets and pillows and scatter them out on the floor around the tree and fall asleep in the glow of Christmas tree lights.

The kids loved it, but I felt stiff and achy the next morning. That's when the coughing kicked in. In fact, the next two nights I slept downstairs on the couch just so my coughing wouldn't keep my pregnant wife up all night and possibly infect her with the "hack."

However, the bone-jarring hacking made it tough to sleep, and I found myself staring at a darkened Christmas tree and listening to a silent house instead.

It was an eerie silence...the kind that would be perfect for a visit by the ghost of Jacob Marley. No ghost came, but during the silence in-between hacks, I thought about missed opportunities with my family, children who are growing up faster than I like, and a pregnant wife who needs some special TLC.

In the darkness, I decided that I would spend the remaining days 'till Christmas sittin' around and talking more, working less, and listening more intently...as I hack my head off.

So, Dad, make the most of the eight days until Christmas. Gather the family around the Christmas tree. Dim the lights, talk, and soak up the wonderful feeling of family like a dry Christmas tree soaks up water in its pan.

You 'da...hack, hack, hackkkk...dad!

357

It's Almost Christmas!

Matthew 27:1-10

Hey Dad,

I can't believe it. Only a few more days until Christmas. I'm not sure who's more excited—the kids or me. They're excited to open presents...I'm excited to see the looks on their faces as they experience just how much we love them. Oh, I know you can't buy your kids' love...but each of the gifts that sit under the tree is a demonstration of how much someone means to us.

After all, we've planned, brainstormed, paid hard-earned cash, and lovingly wrapped each one in hopes that the receiver will know how much they mean to us.

I love seeing the growing pile of brightly wrapped packages under the tree. But for the last four years, a strange sadness and urgency creeps into my heart at the same time.

It first happened four Christmas eves ago. It was snowing out, making it perfect for a candlelight service. We dressed the kids in their Christmassy best, bundled up, and drove the eight slippery miles to church.

We turned the radio on hoping for some Christmas music, but instead a news reporter announced that the roads were bad and that there had been an accident, leaving three people dead. After a few more items of news, the music I had been hoping for began to play.

But I couldn't even hear it because I was still thinking about the accident and the three people who were killed.

Driving along, I imagined the families who had just begun their Christmas festivities when suddenly, a phone rang and they heard the news that someone they love had been killed. Coats were grabbed, radios left playing, Christmas trees still lit, as crying people scrambled to their cars.

That's when I thought about the unopened Christmas presents underneath the tree, lovingly bought and wrapped but never to be opened. Who knows whether they were returned, stored in a basement, or left wrapped and preserved as a reminder of those special people.

Since that Christmas Eve, I've though about those unopened packages often, and I think about icy roads, sudden illnesses, and freak accidents. I don't know what next year holds for my family...or even tomorrow, for that matter.

All I have is today. I must cherish it and the time we get to spend as a family.

So Dad, with that morbid Christmas thought, I wish you a very blessed Christmas with YOUR family. Lavish them with your time. Speak words that need to be heard, and take a good long look at the presents under your tree and think about those still unopened gifts around someone else's tree.

You 'da dad!

The Christmas Dilemma

Matthew 27:11-26

Hey Dad,

It's the week before Christmas and to my children's delight, it looks like we'll have a white Christmas this year. My kids are running on high-octane tinsel. They're about ready to drive me nuts as they wake up each morning and debate over how many more days there are 'til Christmas. I guess one of the great dilemmas in child-dom is whether you count the current day during the Christmas countdown.

I mean every morning they go 'round and 'round.

"It's only seven more days 'til Christmas!"

"Uh, uh—it's six."

"No it's not, it's seven!"

"Six."

"Seven."

And on it goes. Anyway, no matter how you count it, it's close. Now don't panic. There's still plenty of time to get in a night under the tree, watch a special Christmas video like "A Christmas Carol," read the birth account of Jesus (Luke 2:1-20), or even buy your wife a token of your affection (read: not a toaster).

Let me encourage you to leave work early this week, take a day or two off if you can, and plan to do a lot of nothing except enjoy God's best—your family.

Let me also say how much being your friend means to me. I count it a great privilege to be on the Familyman Team with you. And just knowing that you're going through what I'm going through is encouraging to me.

So, Dad, have a wonderful Christmas with your family.

'Twas Five Days Before Christmas

Matthew 27:27-32

Hey Dad,

'Twas five days before Christmas, and the house was a disaster. We tried to keep up, but the kids were just faster. The tree was dried up, and the lights were burned out. If it got any worse, I was going to shout.

With my wife in her pj's, and I in my shorts, We had fallen asleep with grumbles and snorts. The children were tangled in covers and sheets While Legos and dress-up lay in great heaps.

When all of sudden, I heard a loud gurgle I rolled out of bed as quick as a turtle. I walked down the hallway and into his room And I knew what was happening in spite of the gloom.

The stench in the room arose from his bed. He was covered in vomit from toe to his head. He heaved once or twice with cries in between; In all of my life, this was as bad as I'd seen.

I pulled off his clothes as chunks fell on the floor They tickled my feet and splattered the door. I patted his back and said I love you; He smiled but once and then started to spew.

Like lightning I grabbed a small pail by his bed; His neck was all sweaty and his face was all red. He coughed and sputtered until the last drop, Then the last little chunk fell with a plop.

My wife who stood in the hall with a bag Wanted to help but started to gag. I shooed her away with a jerk of my head. I was doing my job; she had nothing to dread.

In no time at all, I had mopped up the spew And tucked him in bed with the bucket in view. He smiled a tired smile, and I felt so in love, Like the very first Christmas he was a gift from above.

As I lay in my bed with the stench on my knees, I was thankful to God for times just like these. I was doing what fathers were created to do, And I love being a dad…in spite of the spew.

May you find great joy this Christmas in being a husband and father.

You 'da dad!

The Last Christmas

Matthew 27:33-44

Hey Dad,

I'm not sure what your feelings are about Christmas, but what if I were to tell you—this is your LAST Christmas?

Let me tell you a story.

Just about every Tuesday morning I have breakfast with an old guy at McDonald's. For years now, we walk in and he greets all the other old guys who are gathered in the old guy section solving world problems. We order and then take our favorite seat near the kids' playland.

As we talk, you can hear the hum of old guys and the occasional bigger-than-life laugh of Terry, a local cop, who has been adopted into the old guy crowd. I'm telling you, his laugh fills the restaurant and is infectious. Well, about two years ago Terry had a bout with cancer. Usually, before he left McD's, he'd walk over to our table and share how God takes good care of him and how he just takes one day at a time.

The good news was, that after some heavy-duty chemo treatment, the cancer disappeared. I can vividly remember the smile on his face as he stood beside us with the good news.

Then it came back. This last time, the chemo was hard on him. I knew he was not feeling well, not because he looked any different, but because his laugh was gone. Last Tuesday, he sat quietly with the old guys.

As he left, he smiled and nodded in our direction and walked to his van. Now, only a few days later, he's in heaven—pain-free and laughing as only he can laugh. But I'll tell you, he left a big hole in his family and at McDonald's. Here's the thing that I can't shake. What if an angel had appeared to him a year ago and said, "Terry, this is your last Christmas—make it a good one"? As I think about it, this may be my—last Christmas. Next year, I may not get to sleep under the Christmas tree with my children, buy a gift that shows my wife how much I love her, or point out the twinkling lights as we travel the snowy Indiana roads.

It's really an awesome thought to think, "This might be my last Christmas." But it's a thought I think I should think—and so should you.

Dad, I know this is a busy time of year, the economy has tanked, and you have a lot on your mind. But allow me to put on my angel costume and whisper in your ear, "This might be your last Christmas—make it a good one."

You 'da dad!

Tis the Season to be Messy

Matthew 27:45-56

December 22

Hey Dad,

The kids are bummed that there isn't any snow on the ground. In fact, my sons Abe (8) and Ike (10) are hauling buckets of water from our old cast iron tub out to a barn ramp to see if they can freeze a sledding hill.

My daughter Katherine (12) is busily preparing for a Christmas tea-party she's having with some friends later today, and I just finished cleaning up the humongous mess that I helped create when I was trying to be Martha Stewart the last two nights.

It all started when I noticed that the usual tray of iced sugar cookies had yet to appear. Thinking it would be 'fun' to have the kids cut festive shapes from cookie dough AND thinking I would be some kind of Christmas hero to my wife for not involving her, I made the announcement, "We're going to make sugar cookies tonight."

That was two nights and at least one mess ago. Piece of cake right? NOT.

It wasn't long before I had dough glued to the table, flour clouds floating around the kitchen and kids who were sticking cookie dough where it should not be stuck. Of course this was all accompanied by me yelling at them.

"Get the cookie cutters out of your mouth!"

"Don't lick the dough."

"Don't rub your hands on your shirt."

"Isn't this fun?!!!"

We got through MAKING the cookies, and last night I decided to have the kids ICE the cookies for our advent night.

We got through that seemingly unscathed, but this morning I had to spend a chunk of the early morning chiseling out hardened, left-over icing from bowls, the table, and counter.

But now we have a heaping plate of iced sugar cookies that the kids will probably empty by lunch today, and I'll be lucky if I get the sorry-looking, headless reindeer that Maggie (5) iced.

And that my fellow Dad is about as good as it gets. I'm glad I have someone like you to remind me of that, because sometimes I think, "What's the use? They don't care...it won't be easy...it will make a huge mess...and it won't be fun."

Most of those things are true. It will be a huge mess, and it may not be fun (like I think fun should be), but they DO care. They care tons. And that's why I do it...and why you should too.

So put on your apron, snow suit, swimming suit, or roller skates and do it for them.

You 'da dad!

Christmas Cards of Gloom

Matthew 27:57-66

Hey Dad,

Well, here it is two days 'til Christmas, and instead of my normal excitement, I'm a little on the gloomy side. It might be because we had an Advent night last night, and I almost ruined it. I'd like to say that my kids almost ruined it...but they were just being kid-like. I let it get to me...and, well, you know how it goes.

I think the real reason for my gloomy feeling is...Christmas cards. It's not that they're less cheery than in past years...it's just that sometimes they announce changes that I don't like.

It seems that every year we hear the news that another friend or family acquaintance is no longer married. Sometimes they come right out and say something like, "Steve and I were divorced this past year...it's been hard, but I'm doing okay...." At other times, it takes a little reading between the lines to sense that something has happened.

Yesterday, it was as simple as an odd return address label in the upper left-hand corner of the envelope and the absence of the spouse's name in the signature.

Oh no, not them!! I knew there were some struggles, but how could they end it? They used to be such a fun couple that did stuff together and really enjoyed each other.

I know it didn't happen overnight...it never does, but they have so much to stay married for. They have children, grandchildren, and great memories...not to mention a testimony to the rest of the world. Now I don't know all their circumstances, but I guess they thought that things would be better for everyone if they went their separate ways.

I wonder if they realize how their breakup affects so many other people? That's the thing about your marriage and mine; it's not just about two people, it's about whole communities of people...maybe even the whole world.

That one little Christmas card has me thinking about all the other "couples" I know that aren't couples anymore, and it makes me gloomy and sad to see so many marriages around me ending.

So, Dad, let me plead with you...don't let that happen to your marriage. Fight for your woman. If you have some mending to do, then do it, whatever it takes. No excuses. Ask forgiveness, prove your commitment, and then take your punches until your face is bruised and bloody...and then take them again.

We're all counting on you.

You 'da dad!

363

Merry Christmas Memories!

Matthew 28:1-15

Hey Dad,

It's the day before Christmas. My kids can hardly stand the excitement. They know it's all about the birth of Christ, and remind one another about that fact, but it's awfully hard not to be excited about the gifts that will be opened. It's to be expected and probably the way it should be...because Christmas really is about gifts. It's about the gifts of hope and love, and the greatest gift of all: a Son who saved the world.

Still, I feel a little thoughtful this morning as the kids prance around...probably because we got the news a few days ago that a friend of the family died. What made it especially sobering is that he was a dad and left behind a wife and three college-age children.

I'm not sad for him...he's gonna have his first Christmas in heaven. It's thinking of his family that sobers me. His kids and wife of two decades will open presents around the tree without him. Dads leave huge holes when they're gone. Holes that will be felt...until they join him one day.

So dad, enjoy your family today and tomorrow. Give them your full attention, assemble the toys, give your opinion when they try on their new clothes, play their new games...and tell them over and over how much you love them.

Because...you never know what next Christmas holds for you.
Merry Christmas.

You 'da dad!

And to All a Good Night

Matthew 28:16-20

Hey Dad,

Well, it's here! I just want to take a few minutes to wish you and your family a very Merry Christmas and to tell you how much I appreciate our friendship. Everyday I hear from dads all over the world who face the same situations and challenges that I face.

I hope you realize what an incredible fraternity of dads we belong to—"the father frat." You encourage me by your prayers, questions, and comments. For all of that, and for you, I am so thankful.

Now, just a little Christmas coaching before I shut down the Familyman Plant for a couple of weeks: slow down and enjoy Christmas. Indulge your children with your undivided attention.

Enjoy this precious time you have with your wife and children because the truth is, it may be your last Christmas together. Just imagine what Christmas would be like next year without your oldest child…your youngest…or your wife. Don't squander the time this year or take lightly the great gift God has given you.

So, until next year, have a wonderful Christmas and never forget…

You 'da dad!

A Christmas Eve from Hell

Hey Dad,

I'm telling you, next year is going to be a great year. I mean it can only get better after our Christmas Eve from hell. I'm not sure exactly how it all started, but shortly before we left for church, I blew my cool and went into a nuclear tirade, yelling at anyone who walked into my line of fire. Oh, I was in rare form and had several of my family members in tears.

At the top of my lungs I roared, "We're NOT going to churchhhh!"

Man, I wish you had been here to slug me, put me in a headlock, or slap me around.

Fortunately, my wife gently insisted that we go—and I was glad she did. God was gracious, softened my heart, and allowed me an undeserved second chance. He's good to dads that way.

BUT…that was last year. It's the new year, and things are looking good—not just for me but for you as well.

In case you don't know, I'm not a big New Year's resolution kind of dad, but I do see January 1st as a time for fresh starts. In fact, I'm not so sure that the successful-fathering race isn't all about starting…over and over again.

So many dads get frustrated in fathering because they think they have to be perfectly consistent all the time—and they're not. They hear a motivational speaker, or read a good book on child rearing, weight loss, or financial planning, and try to implement the strategies for success, only to let it go by the wayside after day four. Feelings of failure, defeat, or "what's the use" soon follow.

Well, I'm here to tell you, it's going to be a great year! Who cares that you failed in the past or might fail again in four days…start again! Have personal or family devotions become ancient history? Start again! Have you added more pounds than you'd like to admit? Start again! Do you feel like your children are out-of-control beasts? Start again! Do you feel a hundred miles from your wife? Start again! Have you slipped back into working too many hours? START AGAIN!!

I gotta go now and jump on the exercise bike…I'm starting again!

You 'da dad!

Hallelujah! I am NOT Stupid

Revelation 19:1-10 **December 27**

Hey Dad,

Hope you had a great Christmas season with your family. To be honest, I'm kind of glad to be back in a routine. We did a lot of running back and forth during the week of Christmas.

Actually, we were about to leave my parents' house on Christmas Adam (the day before Christmas EVE—get it), when I was pleased to find out that my parents don't think I'm stupid.

They didn't say it in so many words, but that's how I took their comments, and it felt good to this 44-year-old kid.

All that day the weatherman had predicted freezing ice, and by the time we were ready to leave, the sidewalks were "slippery-er than a hog's gut."

My brothers insisted that we'd have to stay, but after testing the main roads, I was sure we could make it safely home. So I loaded up the van, all the time expecting my mom and dad to say, "Todd, you can't drive all the way home—you should stay here another night—you'd be stupid for attempting this."

BUT THEY DIDN'T.

In fact, my dad stood beside me and encouraged me in my decision, and my mom said, "You're smart enough to do what's best."

I'm telling you, Dad, I was shocked by how good it felt that my parent's didn't think I was stupid because I'm not too sure they always believe that. Like all good parents, they sometimes say comments like, "You really need to be careful—don't drive too fast—don't forget to tell Aunt Martha, thank you."

I know parents mean well, but when they tell us the obvious, it feels like they think we're STUPID.

But my parents didn't—not on that night.

I thought about the power of the words they DIDN'T say as I inched my way home and thought how often as a parent I show my kids that I think they're stupid.

I know I do it because they respond with phrases like, "I know, Dad— Yes, I did that, Dad—You don't have to tell me that again, Dad."

So here's one of my New Year's resolutions: By my carefully placed silence, I will show my children that I think they're smart. I'm going to hold my tongue and my 'obvious instructions.'

You know, I bet your wife and children would love to know that you think they're smart too. So when you're tempted to say things like, "Don't forget to wear a coat—put that away when you're finished—don't get hurt," don't.

You 'da smart dad!

367

Soooo Worth It

Revelation 19:11-21

December 28

Hey Dad,

It's amazing how often the phrase "It was worth it" is used. I hear it on TV, the radio, and by fellow dads. Usually the first "it" means "the result" and the second "it" means "the effort." This letter from one Atlanta dad brings the phrase into living color.

Todd,

I was busy with work as usual, as the snow was coming down in Atlanta. As you might expect, we don't see much of that white stuff here.

Our neighbors and their three girls happened to stop by to see if my son wanted to go sledding. Todd, given how little snow we get in Atlanta, this could be the one time that my six year-old got to go sledding.

I want to let you know, I put work aside long enough to pull my son down a hill in a sled 6-7 times (until his hair was wet from the snow—he is on the autism spectrum and does not wear hats—and it was time to get back inside and dry him off)

Man…..was it soooooooooo worth it, Todd. Seeing him smile and laugh as his daddy went "VROOOOOOM" while pulling the sled down a small hill. This was one of my best days!

~ Doug

You know, Dad, as far as family goes, the result is always worth the effort/sacrifice. I bet you could do something even tonight that would be "worth it."

You 'da dad!

You're That Hero!

Hey Dad,

It's another gray, snow-covered day here in Northern Indiana. One of the drawforwards (opposite of drawbacks) of winter is that it gives us some great movie nights. We've watched a bunch of old movies like Mr. Smith Goes to Washington, Harvey, The Incredible Mr. Limpet, Calamity Jane, and last night we watched The Adventures of Robin Hood starring the dashing Arrow Flynn.

There's something heroic about a smiling guy in tights who out-foxes all of Prince John's schemes and armies. In a way, I envision myself in his place battling insurmountable odds to save the lovely Maid Mario…Debbie (my wife). In stark contrast to his joyous manliness, she's fragile and dainty. She needs her hero…like my wife needs…me.

But somehow it's easier on old Technicolor movies than it is in real life.

Then I got a letter yesterday….from a wife who drove the point…DEEPER.

Todd,

…I feel as if everything is on my shoulders. I deal with (kids) ALL DAY LONG. I have been sacrificing for 16 years now and I am burnt out. I think it is so important for husbands to hear...KEEP PURSUING YOUR WIFE. Keep fanning the flames. Keep speaking words of appreciation and encouragement. Keep wooing her. KEEP HER HEART. It is not an easy task but it is so necessary. I have talked to too many stay at home moms, and I know that we all feel the same way. As soon as our husbands leave the door, we are an open target for the enemies of our soul. We are bombarded with thoughts that we know are from the enemy, yet we do not know how to control or stop them.. I feel as if I am dying inside and so alone. If this goes on too long I am not sure what I would do in order to climb out of this downward spiral…

You know what she needs, Dad? No, not a tranquilizer!!! She needs a HERO. YOUR wife needs a hero…MY wife needs a hero. But, we don't have time to be heroes because we're busy with our own things. Heroes have to sacrifice their lives for damsels. The sad truth is that sooner or later heroes become…husbands.

But not today. Maybe you need to do a little heroing today or tonight, Dad. After all…

You 'dat hero!!

Teasers Never Win

Revelation 22:1-7

Hey Dad,

Well, I wouldn't have called it a blizzard of historic proportion…but it was OK. I know my children were hoping to have to crawl from our upper story windows because of the depth of the snow.

Of course they wanted to go out and brave the elements and begged me to go out as well. After thirty minutes of suiting up, we got out and started piling the snow for an igloo. We got a pretty good pile…but the wind forced us in before we scooped out the inside. Actually, the kids are suiting up right now to go finish the job.

Really, blizzards are special gifts to families because there's nothing better than snuggling inside to beat the cold. Just don't ruin it by working on your laptop. Ugggh.

Besides that, I've been working lately on teasing less…because I'm a teaser…and sometimes teasers can go too far. Sometimes I go too far. I think it's funny, but it's not. I think that it will make the mood less tense thereby causing the tension to simply blow away…and it doesn't. In fact, oftentimes it makes everything worse.

Case in point: About two weeks ago my daughter Katherine (13) and I were 'discussing' something. Trying to lighten the mood I started teasing. Instead of smiles it brought tears….lots of them. She went to bed sobbing, and I walked away knowing I 'teased too much.'

Ten minutes later I walked into her dark room and apologized for being a teaser, and I meant it. I asked her to forgive me and she did with a clinging hug and gentle kiss. She needed her dad at that moment…not a teaser.

Since then I've been trying not to tease as much. Oh, I still like to make them laugh…but I know there are times with daughters, sons, and wives…where teasing makes things worse.

Dad, I don't know if you're a teaser or not…but if you are, you're only making things worse. Like the old adage goes, "Teasers never win."

I gotta go check on the igloo.

You 'da dad!

First Tip – Roller Skate

Revelation 22:8-21

Hey Dad,

Hope you had a great Christmas/New Year with your family. All our plans crashed due to sickness at the Wilson camp, starting the day before Christmas and going all the way through...TODAY! Did I mention that we took my son Jed (2) to the emergency room on Christmas Eve? But, thank God, the CAT scan showed no brain/skull injuries...just a mild concussion and neck sprain.

We don't even know exactly what happened. I ran to the store to get some sickness provisions, like Sprite and popsicles, and when I got home my wife was cradling him in her arms trying to determine how hurt he was. No one saw what happened, but apparently...he fell hard. He's doing fine now...but it's amazing how fast your plans can change.

"That's what being a dad is all about, Charlie Brown." I think Linus said that.

Anyway, I'm a little slow out of the starting gate this year but wanted to offer my first familyman advice of the New Year — go roller skating, and make sure you skate.

To be honest, I hate roller skating and gulped when my sick wife suggested that I take the kids to Christian Family Skate Night. We try to fit it in about one time a year, and I guess she thought it was time. The kids jumped right on the idea so we piled into the van and rented enough skates for a small army. I didn't get skates because of my sore and broken ankles from a car wreck that happened almost 20 years ago. The kids all asked if I was going to, but I stated, "Sorry guys, but my ankles are just too sore." But I wasn't sorry. In fact, I was glad for the excuse.

It wasn't until the night was almost over that I was sorry, not for having sore ankles, but for allowing the excuse to rob me of the experience of skating around holding my daughter's hand.

It was toward the very end when my daughter Katherine (13) said something like, "You would have skated if Mom had come...because you would have wanted to skate around with her." As she said the words, I remembered the sweet look on Kat's face the last time I had skated around and around holding hands with her, like we were in love...because we were.

So, Dad, first tip for new year—go roller skating and hold hands with your kids. The perfect recipe for the beginning of a great year of fathering.

You 'da dad!

About Familyman Ministries

Familyman Ministries' mission is to remind dads about what's most important. They produce books, seminars, audios, and products to help dads be the men, husbands, and fathers they were created to be.

If you would like to learn more about Familyman Ministries or have Todd speak to your group, go to **www.familymanweb.com**.